Reading Adoption

Reading Adoption

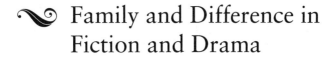 Family and Difference in
Fiction and Drama

Marianne Novy

The University of Michigan Press

Ann Arbor

First paperback edition 2007
Copyright © by the University of Michigan 2005
All rights reserved
Published in the United States of America by
The University of Michigan Press
Manufactured in the United States of America
⊚ Printed on acid-free paper

2010   2009   2008   2007   5   4   3   2

A CIP catalog record for this book is available from the British Library.

Library of Congress Cataloging-in-Publication Data

Novy, Marianne, 1945–
    Reading adoption : family and difference in fiction and drama /
Marianne Novy.
        p.   cm.
    Includes bibliographical references and index.
    ISBN 0-472-11507-3 (cloth : alk. paper)   1. English literature—
History and criticism.   2. Adoption in literature.   3. American
literature—History and criticism.   4. Oedipus (Greek mythology) in
literature.   5. Family in literature.   I. Title.
    PR408.A36N688   2005
    809'.933556—dc22   2005003517

ISBN 978-0-472-11507-5 (cloth : alk. paper)
ISBN-13: 978-0-472-03264-8 (pbk. : alk. paper)
ISBN-10: 0-472-03264-x (pbk. : alk. paper)

Illustration: two plants, growing close to each other, grafted together by
inarching. From *Le Jardin Fruitier* by Louis Noisette, 1839. Courtesy of
Hunt Institute for Botanical Documentation, Carnegie Mellon University,
Pittsburgh, Pennsylvania.

For my daughter, Liz Carrier

and in honor and memory of her three grandmothers

> *Dorothy Kern, mother by adoption*
> *Louise Carrier, mother by birth and adoption*
> *Geraldine Govier, mother by birth*

Acknowledgments

It took the equivalent of a village for me to write this book.

First, it took a social movement—the open-records movement and its founding mothers, Betty Jean Lifton, Jean Paton, and Florence Fisher, who were helpful to me personally as well as through their writings, and in Jean's case through the resources of her collection of books about adoptees and orphans.

It took other people personally involved in adoption, and especially in adoption and literature, with whom I talked about my experience. I'll begin with the adoptees and near-adoptees: long ago, Jim Simmonds, Suzanne Polen, Pat Hinchey, Anne Steytler, and Jean Vincent; near the beginning of this project, Penny Partridge, Amy Cheney, Katie Lee Crane, and especially Margot Backus, Jill Deans, and, more recently Emily Hipchen, who have been active in the Alliance for the Study of Adoption, Identity, and Kinship. Judith Modell, Barbara Melosh, and, especially, Carol Singley, longtime cochair with me of the Alliance, bring the professional and personal together in studying adoption as adoptive parents, and they too have been helpful to me for years.

I needed audiences to try out my ideas, and I thank the audiences and organizers at a number of conferences: the American Adoption Congress; the University of Richmond conference "Shedding Light on Secrecy and Openness in Adoption"; the Pennsylvania Adoption Forum Conference; the Three Rivers Adoption Council Annual Meeting; Seen and Heard, a conference on early modern childhood; the conference of the Association for Research on Mothering; the International Shakespeare Congress; the Shakespeare Association of America; the American Anthropological Association; the International Conference for the Study of Narrative Literature; the Kansas State Cultural Studies Symposium on Family, Kinship, and Cultural Studies; conferences at the University of Pittsburgh on Theater, Drama, and History and on Children, Literature, and Culture; and the University of Auckland Women's Studies Program. I would also like to thank the students in my classes on adoption literature.

In chapter 5 of this book I expand on my essay "Adoption in *Silas Marner* and *Daniel Deronda*," previously published by the University of Michigan Press in my anthology *Imagining Adoption: Essays on Litera-*

ture and Culture, and I use a few sentences from my introduction to that book in the first chapter of this one. A portion of chapter 3 was published in 2000 as "Multiple Parenting in *Pericles,*" in the anthology *Pericles: Critical Essays,* edited by David Skeele, and is reproduced with additions by permission of Routledge/Taylor & Francis Books, Inc. A larger portion was published in 2002 in the anthology *Domestic Arrangements in Early Modern England,* edited by Kari Boyd McBride, and is reprinted with additions by permission of Duquesne University Press. I am grateful for permission to reprint.

I also thank the many people who helped by reading and commenting on my work in progress. Kathryn Flannery, Molly Shanley, Carol Singley, and Emily Hipchen read the entire manuscript carefully. Others who commented thoughtfully on more than one chapter, or an especially difficult one, are Nancy Glazener, Barbara Melosh, Margot Backus, Barbara Katz Rothman, Lynne Dickson Bruckner, Meredith Skura, and my classicist colleagues, Nicholas Jones and Mae Smethurst. Rachel Brownstein and Suzanne Juhasz answered my request for advice on personal writing with regard to an early version of my Eliot chapter though I had never had any previous contact with them. I am also grateful for readings by B. J. Lifton, Tess O'Toole, Heather Dubrow, Rebecca Bushnell, Nancy Henry, Susan Harris Smith, Anita Mallinger, Sarah Beckwith, Iris Young, Michael Witmore, Peggy Knapp, Kellie Robertson, John Twyning, Susan Andrade, Jean Ferguson Carr, Magali Michael, David Moldstad, and Jonathan Arac. And I would also like to thank my editor, LeAnn Fields, for many kinds of help with this project.

For contributions to the appendix, I thank Bill Gage, from whose online bibliography most of the entries were drawn, and also Jill Deans, Paris De Soto, Susan Ito, Marah Gubar, and Carol Singley, whose reading lists I used, and the many other people who sent in proposals in answer to my calls for papers in the newsletter of the Modern Language Association since 1993. I am also grateful for the texts of two plays sent to me on e-mail before publication—Carol Schaefer's *Sacred Virgin* and Lauren Weedman's *Homecoming*—and to Pam Hasegawa for her listserv.

Finally, I would like to thank Kathy Coulter-Wein, with whom I talked about this project in recent therapy, and Morton Aronson, the therapist with whom I discussed my search for my birth parents while it was in progress in the 1970s. And I am especially grateful for the love of my husband and my daughter—David and Liz Carrier—and my two mothers—Dorothy Kern, who accepted my search, and Geraldine Govier, who accepted me when I found her.

Contents

One ❧ Reading from an Adopted Position

> Until we can understand the assumptions
> in which we are drenched we cannot know
> ourselves.
>
> —*Adrienne Rich*

How do we get our ideas about what adoption means? Whether we grew up in an adoptive family, adopted children ourselves, relinquished them for adoption, know people who did any of these things, or not, we live in a world in which adoption is represented in film, theater, literature, television, and other media. People not personally involved with adoption may form their main impressions from these sources, unless they have friends who discuss adoption openly. Even people who are personally involved may find themselves interpreting their own experiences in terms of adoption plots well known in their culture. Those plots loomed heavily over me as I grew up in the 1950s and later, an adoptee not supposed to discuss adoption, and knowing no one who spoke of it.

In her recent book *But Enough about Me,* Nancy Miller discusses the interplay of identification and disidentification she feels when she reads memoirs.[1] This book grows out of a similar interplay I feel when reading literature dealing with adoption.

Most of the adoptees in canonical literature, fairy tales, and folklore, find their identity in meeting their birth parents. In the story of Oedipus, for example, a man discovers that he was born to a different set of parents than the ones he knows. He has unwittingly killed the man who begot him and married the woman who gave birth to him. After this discovery the parents who raised him no longer matter. Shakespeare's play *Winter's Tale* is less famous and has a happier ending, but it also shows the adoptee leaving the adoptive family behind after meeting birth parents. These plays have rarely been discussed in terms of adoption, but how much did the cultural knowledge of their plots, and similar ones, contribute to the fear of many adoptive parents that their family won't survive contact between adoptee and birth family, and indirectly to the laws sealing adoptees' birth records? Or, in the case of *The Winter's Tale,* encourage the dreams of adoptees that meeting their birth family will tell them who they are?

Once I identified with these plots. For years I believed that my adoption had barred me from the people who would understand me most. Now I both identify and disidentify. In fact, finding my birth mother made me appreciate my adoptive mother more and see what I learned from her, though I also find my relationship with my birth mother valuable. And though my birth father is probably a happier and more successful man than my adoptive father was, and though he looks like me, I negotiate my life knowing that he has closed the door to a meeting or relationship.

According to the language used in folklore, most popular speech, and most literature up until recent times, I have now found my real mother and been rejected by my real father. But that is not what it feels like. I need to use different language, and so does our culture. This is why terms like *birth mother* and *birth father* have been invented.

Being adopted is a passive situation. Looking for birth parents, by contrast, is a choice. And so is deciding not to look, when it is indeed a decision and not the default result of sealed records and family discomfort. But what the adoptee finds out about them, or experiences, if lucky enough, in meeting with them, provides another situation of choice, though not a unilateral choice in a vacuum. How much, and in what way, can the adoptee identify with them? How much will they become an active part of the adoptee's life? How does knowing them affect how the adoptee sees or relates to the adoptive family? Where does the search belong in the adoptee's narrative of her (or his, but many more searchers are female) life story? By juxtaposing my story with the literary narratives, I want to emphasize the roles of narrative and choice in self-construction, and also to suggest something of the great range in the possibilities for adoption plots.

This is a book I wish I could have read when I was younger, and a book I wish my literature teachers in high school, college, and even graduate school could have referred to when teaching literature dealing with adoption. It is, for one thing, a book through which I hope to mitigate for other people the aloneness that some still find a part of living in an adoption plot (whichever role in it they play), the aloneness that I felt in my childhood because it was such an unmentionable topic. "Other people won't understand," said my mother when she told me, at age five, that she and my father had adopted me. I was given up so that I could be better taken care of, I was chosen, but I shouldn't tell others. Our family was different from others in how it was formed, and I was different from other people, and if I wasn't allowed to talk about them, these couldn't really be good kinds of difference. I hardly ever broke that rule before I was twenty, and for years after that I still thought of revealing I was adopted as a special gesture of intimacy, like taking off my clothes in someone's presence.

Adoption practices have changed in many ways since my childhood, but there are still many people uncomfortable about the adoption in their life story. One kind of evidence of this discomfort on the part of some adoptive parents is the fear of adoptees' contact with birth parents, which contributes to the practice of sealing records. In this book I hope to diminish this fear by analyzing some of the literature that has transmitted it. I think this book can, in many other ways, help adoptees, adoptive parents, and birth parents to understand their lives. I also want to present literary examples as equipment for thinking about adoptive family construction and adoptee identity in a way that could be useful to people considering any kind of family construction or identity.

An analogy may be useful. Since the 1960s, feminist critics have pointed out that many literary plots identified women's destiny as either marriage or death, that many fairy tales encouraged little girls to look forward mainly to a happy ending with Prince Charming. These plots were part of a cultural pressure that channeled most female expectations into a single track. However, some writers began to turn aside from these plots as other possibilities opened up for women. While factors such as economics were undoubtedly influential as well, writers both influenced, and were influenced by, different female behavior. At the same time, other feminist criticism looked back at the literature of the past to find moments of possibility among its confining narratives for women.

In this book I discuss adoption literature in an analogous spirit. Using adoption as a lens, I see patterns previously unnoticed. I point to adoption plots that have been the dominant cultural influence, but also to elements in literary works that complicate them. I point to works that deliberately rewrite such traditional plots, indicating possibilities for new life stories. And I occasionally tell how my own life influences my reaction to literature, sensitizing me to the fictionality of certain plot elements, such as the search that ends with finding true identity in one's birth family.

Truth and Fiction, Reality and Pretense

This book is about how adoption has been treated fictionally, in novels and plays. But it is also about the contrast between, on the one hand, considering adoption itself as a fiction in the sense of pretense, or constructing it as something that should imitate the traditional biological family as closely as possible in appearance, in the so-called "as-if" family, and, on the other hand, considering it as a different but valid way of constructing a parent-child relationship.

Truth and fiction, reality and pretense—these oppositions are impossible to escape in considering the literary and historical treatment of adoption. Not only does literature sometimes use the term *real parents,* but also adoption has repeatedly been called a fiction of parenthood. The classic use of this term in analyzing adoption is in Henry J. S. Maine's *Ancient Law* (1861). This book is distinctive for the view that "without the Fiction of Adoption which permits the family tie to be artificially created, it is difficult to understand how society would ever have escaped from its swaddling clothes and taken its first steps toward civilization."[2] In the late twentieth century, the anthropologist Judith Modell quotes Maine as an example of how established is the psychologically somewhat self-contradictory view that adoption is a fiction, the biological family is the reality, and the two should be regarded as legally and socially identical: "'We must try to regard the fiction of adoption as so closely simulating the reality of kinship that neither law nor opinion makes the slightest difference between a real and an adoptive connection.' No one doubted, then or now, that the 'real connection' was the genealogical connection."[3]

Adoption plots often move toward an end that defines what is to be considered the true family of the central character. The longer literary tradition is behind the idea that adoption is a fiction and the biological family is real, as in the Oedipus story and *Winter's Tale.* But in novels such as George Eliot's *Silas Marner,* Charles Dickens's *Oliver Twist,*

Lucy Montgomery's *Anne of Green Gables,* and Barbara Kingsolver's *The Bean Trees,* the ending is the confirmation of adoptive parenthood. *Silas Marner* and *The Bean Trees* make very explicit points of defining parenthood by behavior rather than by biology. The move toward acceptance of nontraditional parenthood in these novels parallels the argument made by many anthropologists today that, rather than distinguishing fictive from authentic kinship, we should say that all kinds of kinship are fictive, because all institutions are constructed by social agreement.[4] But *Silas Marner* and *The Bean Trees* present the redefinition of parenthood as not a conclusion arrived at by retheorized scholarship but as an emotional victory for characters marginalized in their societies.

In my childhood, during the postwar baby boom and era of assimilation of the 1950s, the association of adoption with pretense was at its height. A friend of my mother's wore a series of differently sized pillows when she was in the process of adopting a baby, so that everyone would think she was pregnant.[5] This was the exaggeration of the "as-if" model, which dictated that adoptive parents should be a heterosexual couple of the right age to conceive the children they adopt, with some physical similarity to them. I was adopted according to this model. Still, I would never consider my mother just a pretend mother.

In the homes of most adoptive families and their friends, it is obvious that adoptive parenthood is real to anyone who uses that word. However, many people still call birth parents "real parents." For part of our society, parenthood has been redefined to focus on behavior rather than on biology; part cling to an older definition, and others would say that the redefinition should be expanded to include the possibility that a child can have more than two parents. The United States today is divided in its understanding of motherhood, fatherhood, parenthood, and corresponding issues of family, kinship, and identity.

Custody Battles and Adoption Plots

That division was particularly evident in 1993, when a two-year-old girl known as both Jessica DeBoer and Anna Schmidt was the center of a custody battle between the DeBoers, who had raised her and wanted to adopt her, and the Schmidts, her genetic parents, to whom she has now been returned. In this case, Jessica/Anna's birth father, Dan Schmidt, had not been informed of his parentage, and so was not given a choice about her relinquishment for adoption. After her birth mother, Cara, told him the child was his, and they got married, the Schmidts sued the DeBoers for custody. In the extensive media coverage, which involved both a *Newsweek* cover story and a long article in the *New Yorker,* many writers reflected not just on this case but on other adoptions that the authors experienced or observed.[6] It was in this year, not just because of this case but partly because of the public interest it revealed, that I decided to try to bring into this conversation the literary history of adoption, as I read it in relation to my own life.

Jessica/Anna's contested parenthood resembles in some ways the situation at the heart of novels by George Eliot and Barbara Kingsolver that I will discuss later in this book. Both emphasis on parental behavior and emphasis on heredity have a long history, and have changed their forms at times during that history.[7] Janet Beizer has argued that today the increased emphasis on genealogy in the United States (the second most popular hobby and the second most searched-for subject on the web) is a reaction to the increase in adoptive and other nontraditional families.[8] Each view of parenthood has left its trace in literature dealing with adoption, which then reinforces that view and its social, political, and psychological effects.

Adoption has figured importantly in literature for a number of reasons. Adoption plots—like contested custody cases—dramatize cultural tensions about definitions of family and the importance of heredity. Representing adoption is a way of thinking about the family, exploring what a family is, that is at the same time a way of thinking about the self, exploring distance from the family. As Freud discussed in his theory of the family romance, for most people—nonadopted people—the fantasy of discovering that they were adopted and can be reunited with a different family elsewhere is a way of dealing with negative feelings about their parents.[9] So is the fantasy that they are orphans who are happily adopted by someone else. And so is the fantasy that they are outsiders who belong in no family at all. Adoption narratives can also help consider family issues from a parent's perspective. I have a daughter (by birth and nurture) who is very different from me. Liz is a risk-taking athlete, and I am a physically cautious scholar. I barely glanced at the sports pages before she was in them. In a novel that focuses on an adoptive mother's difficulties in dealing with a child from a different culture, I see a reflection of my life with my teenager.

European and American culture has typically used three mythic stories to imagine adoption: the disastrous adoption and search for birth parents, as in *Oedipus,* the happy reunion, as in *Winter's Tale,* and the happy adoption, as in *Silas Marner.*[10] These stories are myths, even though they conflict, because they act as paradigms to shape feelings, thoughts, language, and even laws about adoption, and to reflect deep cultural beliefs about family. In the two versions of the search story, the birth parents are clearly the "real parents." In the happy adoption story, the birth parents may exist in memory, but no matter how important this memory is, as in *Oliver Twist,* it does not constitute a living complication to the reconstructed family.[11] What all three have in common is the assumption that a child has, in effect, only one set of parents. To many readers, this will still seem like an inevitable axiom. But for others it is not so obvious. These narratives provide conflicting interpretations of the DeBoer/Schmidt story, my own story, and other stories of adoption. For Jessica/Anna, for me, and for many others, all three narratives are inadequate.[12]

Although these are the dominant paradigms through which our culture has tried to imagine adoption, much literature complicates them considerably, as this book will show. Even the works I mention have more dimensions to their analyses of adoption. Some texts follow these dominant plots; others, however, look at them obliquely, examine their cost, follow their characters after their supposed end, or play off against readers' expectations, explicitly dramatizing deviation from them. One of the purposes of the book, indeed, is to emphasize how much variety is possible in imagining adoption, even though many of the same conflicts recur in different contexts.

Orphanhood in literature has been discussed much more than adoption in literature.[13] Many people associate adoption with orphans—and indeed Jean Paton, the first U.S. author to write about searching as an adoptee activist, named her organization and her book *Orphan Voyage.*[14] But there is a significant difference between the conditions of adoption and orphanhood, and adoption today is usually not the adoption of orphans. Though adoptees have often been told that their parents are dead, typically they do have other parents alive in addition to the adoptive parents. The law of most states in the United States, however, tries to make the birth parents not legally dead but nonexistent in relation to the child by erasing their names from the birth certificate once the adoption is final, and then preventing even the adult adoptee from learning about them.[15] The extreme denial of the birth parents' existence here sometimes represents an attempt to fend off one of the myths of adoption—to make it impossible to find out that this child has the curse of illegitimacy. However, today it may be even more significant as an attempt to keep in place the family boundaries established by the adoption process: to assure that the adoptive family doesn't lose a child, and that the birth parents don't experience the return of one that doesn't fit into their current families.

But as the DeBoer/Schmidt case shows, law and popular culture are internally divided on the issue of which are the rightful parents, and this division, which parallels contradictions surrounding other recent reproductive and familial trends, emphasizes reasons to question cultural definitions of parenthood. Is parenthood defined by genetics? By gestation and childbirth? By the work of child care? By fighting to have, keep, or reclaim a child? By not fighting if it might hurt the child, as in the judgment of Solomon? By the child's best interest as defined by a court? By the meaning those involved give to their biological link or child care? By the child's preference? According to any of these definitions but the first two, a child may have two "real" mothers and two "real" fathers, or if adopted by a gay couple, three mothers and one father or the reverse.[16]

The public conflict over Jessica/Anna, who was born before the Schmidts were married, was possible partly because of the decline of the mythic curse of illegitimacy. Partly because of the decreasing stigma of birth out of wedlock, and partly for other reasons traced by Rickie Solinger in *Wake Up Little Susie,* there is now somewhat less popular foreboding about the character of a child so born, whether raised out of wedlock or adopted.[17] But the Schmidt/DeBoer conflict also dramatizes the failure of the two happy-ending myths. Jessica/Anna was not an orphan whose adoption provided a family-less child with a home. On the other hand, she did not immediately recognize her birth parents by an instinct of blood and happily join them without protest.

The case of Jessica/Anna drew so much attention because it focused so many key problems in current adoption policy. It was a kind of Rorschach test in which many people with very different kinds of experiences of adoption nevertheless identified with the contested child or one set of parents, and used the conflict as a jumping off point to write about their lives in newspaper columns and letters to the editor. It was a stark example of a situation where a plausible argument can be made for each set of parents to have custody, depending, on one side, on genetics and the mother's experience of pregnancy, childbirth, and loss, and, on the other side, on the child's experience of care in infancy. It exemplifies the economic imbalance that typifies adoption in our society and many others: most often birth parents have more economic difficulties than parents seeking to adopt; therefore, if the best interest of the child is seen in terms of economics, adoptive parents will usually have an advantage. It evokes the typical association of the birth mother with illicit sexuality: for Cara and Dan Schmidt to seek custody, they had to make public Cara's sexual history to explain why she put another man's name on the original birth certificate, an act that prevented asking Dan about custody at the time. It raises the question of how much time ought to be given the birth mother to make decisions about giving up custody after birth, since the speed with which Cara was pressured on this was part of her case against the DeBoers.

The one belief the Schmidts and the DeBoers seem to have held in common was that parenthood involves absolute rights of possession over a child and that a child, therefore, cannot possibly have more than one set of parents. This is a belief that they share with the legal system of most of the United States. It is the belief of many other Western countries—but it is not the belief of all cultures, and not all cultures maintain it in the same degree at all times. Even countries as similar to the United States as Canada, the United Kingdom, New Zealand, and Australia allow adoptees, at least in adulthood, to see their original birth certificates. This position is still consistent with the belief that the adoptee while a child belongs only to the adoptive parents but nevertheless needs information about birth parents. The most radical position, practiced in Polynesia and Micronesia—that parental nurture does not entail exclusive ownership—is now being developed by a few adoptive parents, scholars, and theorists such as Janet Beizer, Judith Modell, Drucilla Cornell, and Mary Lyndon Shanley, and occasional courts and individuals that award or work out shared parenting. Barbara Kingsolver's *Pigs in Heaven*, we shall see toward the conclusion of this book, ends with this model. Many more families than these now have a less radical kind of open adoption in which it is clear that the adoptive parents have authority over the child, but one or more birth parents have a place in the extended family in a position comparable to that of aunt or uncle. I will return to discussion of open adoptions and their implications for kinship later in this introduction.

Parentage

Unlike Jessica/Anna, I met my birth mother as an adult through my own choice. My adoptive mother had saved the papers with my original name on them, and when reunion stories were beginning to appear in newspapers and I was, in my late twenties, finally talking about the issue, she gave me the papers. This enabled me to get my original birth certificate and write a cautious, guarded letter to my birth mother asking about her parents. I sent it to the address listed on the birth certificate. A neighbor forwarded the letter to her current address, and she wrote back, "You must be my daughter. I'd like to hear from you." She couldn't travel and was unsure about where we could meet (what other people would she have to tell?), but after six months of correspondence and occasional phone calls, I took two planes and visited Geraldine at her home.

Meeting her was a happy event. She is a kind person and a loving one, and brave enough to tell her family, her minister, and some friends about me—no small matter in her setting. However, I was struck more by our differences than by our similarities. After giving me up for adoption, she had married and had seven sons. The demands of raising them had left her little energy, apparently, for any interests outside of fundamentalist religion. To count our interest in religion as a similarity I would have had to elide the difference between her conservative evangelical Church of God and my liberal ecumenical-minded Catholicism. (At a meeting of the American Adoption Congress, someone tried to persuade me that having strong views about religion and politics—though on opposite sides—is having something in common. It doesn't feel that way.) She is fair and I am dark. You could see a similarity in the way our hair falls if it happens to be cut the same length. The space between her front teeth is the way mine used to be, and, alas, we both have a tendency to depression and are not good at housekeeping. What sort of interests did she have before life wore her out? She did win an art contest, she told me, but that has little resonance with any of my talents. Meeting her was important to me, but it did not really tell me who I am.

Meeting Geraldine gave me a new appreciation of my adoptive mother and of the advantages that she had and could give me partly because of her temperament. Twelve years older, Dorothy had much more energy. She could take a three-hour bus ride to visit me, while Geraldine was tired walking around the block. Neither one had gone to college immediately after high school: Dorothy was the daughter of a printer and Geraldine was the daughter of an accountant, so Dorothy's class wasn't higher than Geraldine's to start with, but she had worked before and during the Depression of the 1930s to put her brothers and my adoptive father through college, and then put him through medical school. When I was older, she gave music lessons in the neighborhood, got a high school equivalency diploma, and began evening college (a very unusual thing for a woman of her age to do at that time). She survived and outlasted an increasingly difficult marriage, lived on her own for more than ten years, mostly teaching kindergarten in a Catholic school and continuing those college courses, and was, when I met Geraldine, preparing to marry again. She had passed on to me her desire for education, her active religion, some of her interest in music, and a general (if often naive) enthusiasm for high and middle-brow culture. We both sometimes thought my graduate school education put me in a world different from hers, but once I met Geraldine, it seemed that Dorothy and I were really in the same world after all, by contrast with the world of small-town fundamentalism.

But Dorothy was not without her biases. She had told me about my English, German, and Norwegian nationality, as we then called it, not telling me that was just on one side. It was only when I was out of graduate school, teaching at the University of Pittsburgh, and with a psychiatrist talking about adoption for almost the first time, that she mentioned, seemingly accidentally, my biological father's Jewishness. I had gone through grade school, high school, and college in schools where the students and faculty were virtually all Catholic, and there were no Jews in any of our neighborhoods in Cleveland's West Side suburbs. But in graduate school I had made Jewish friends for the first time, and by the time I was teaching in Pittsburgh my mother had met some of them. This may have contributed to the emergence of her memory about my ancestry.

My birth father's name—I'll call him Murray, though that's not it— was on my birth certificate. When they met, he in his late teens and Geraldine a naive twenty-six, they were both in the service, in Virginia. After her time in an unwed mothers' home and his in a POW camp in Germany, they went back to their previous neighborhoods half a continent apart. A few months after I met Geraldine, Murray answered the second letter I wrote him seeking contact. What he sent was not a letter but a newspaper article about himself (how I learned about the POW camp), complete with photo. At least in terms of coloring and height, I look more like him. We have the same dark hair and eyes and dark circles under our eyes, and maybe even similar scrawly handwriting, assuming he addressed the envelope. He was then (1978) running for a political office, portraying the incumbent as soft on crime. I imagined he feared an Ibsenesque scenario in which an opponent (or perhaps I myself!) would discover and expose my relation to him, and did not proceed further. He lost anyway. According to the newspaper, he had had a certain amount of success as a lawyer, helped start a community center, and was active in the Free Soviet Jewry movement. He had three children, then teenagers, and a wife who for a long time had been in partnership with him as a lawyer.

I tried a few more letters, with no response. Many years later, after I sent one very guarded letter about doing research, not mentioning my relation to him at all, he called back, but hung up when he realized who I was. Once when I happened to be in his city, I found his name on the building directory, though he had retired. I went up to his floor and knocked on the door to borrow the rest room key. A dark-haired young man—my brother?—seemed to be packing things up.

Should I have tried harder to meet Murray? This man who, the article suggested, would probably agree with me on little socially and politically and didn't want contact? Someone could say once again, "You both care about politics and religion." Cold comfort. More relevant, though, may be memories of my dear uncle Dan, a man sometimes seemingly obsessed with the need to punish criminals, but also a charmer who got me interested in opera and poetry and the Greek classics at a young age. But Murray wouldn't have been a charmer to me.

I have inherited his appearance, more than anyone else's (some people have thought me Jewish, though others have thought me Italian), and one could argue that his legal career and my career as a literary critic and teacher involve similar interests in language and argument. The newspaper article credits him with knowing Russian, French, Spanish, and Yiddish. I was thought to be good at learning languages as a child, though I haven't kept it up much, and I could see my linguistic ability as inherited—but who knows if the newspaper isn't exaggerating his skill, anyway? He does sound more successful at life than Frank, my adoptive father, who was president of Kiwanis in our Cleveland suburb when I was seven, but then had a serious heart attack, cut back his medical practice, and became the distant, depressive man I remember. I thought of Murray sometimes when my daughter worked on her high school mock trial team, but not enough to send him another letter sure to be unanswered. I have, however, looked for mentions of him on the World Wide Web, and there are some recent enough to assure me that he is probably still alive.

Many autobiographies by adoptees, like some fictional works I shall discuss, present the discovery of biological parents as the key to the adoptee's identity. Indeed, such autobiographies were important in developing the adoptee rights movement, and short versions of such stories and similar rhetoric fill the newsletters of many search and support groups.[18] The meeting with my birth mother, and the information about my birth father, were important to me, but did not tell me who I am. Thus, while I advocate open records and the right to search, in this book I critically analyze myths in fictional treatments of search and discovery. I want, for example, to point out erasures of adoptive parents, and fantasies of mirroring between adoptee and birth parents. Yes, I know that adoptees often find birth parents who look more like them than my birth mother looks like me, but even that is still not the absolute mirroring that some literature imagines. Yet on a listserv I recently found an offer to adoptees to reconstruct their unknown mother's face from a picture of the adoptee.[19]

But I also want to point out fantasies of ideal harmony between adoptive parent and child, and erasure of birth parents. I want to explore the variety of ways that literature constructs the adoptee's identity, the dominant elements in each work as well as submerged ones, hints at across-the-grain possibilities. And I want to suggest that adoptees' experiences differ so much among themselves that there are some not yet represented in literature at all.

Ethnicity and Religion

Many adoptees who lack information about their birth parents feel the lack of knowledge about their ethnicity as an important aspect of their deprivation. Sociologists developed the concept of ethnicity as a way of getting away from biology and race, but in discussions of ethnicity by adoptees (and other people as well) assumptions about biological transmission frequently emerge. Barbara Katz Rothman points out that a standard definition of "ethnic group" is "a group with a common cultural tradition and a sense of identity which exists as a subgroup of a larger society," but also that "to the extent that ethnicity leads people to marry and to procreate more within than outside of ethnic groups, it lives on in the body."[20] Unless child and family are matched with remarkable precision, the ethnicity that lives on the adoptee's body may be very different from that which predominates in the subgroup in which they grow up, though in America today fewer and fewer people live in subgroups characterized by ethnicity.

I had some information about my birth parents' ethnicity early in my life, and I now know much of the rest of that story. My mother's withholding of my birth father's Jewishness from me is one of the silences in my childhood and young adulthood that I regret, though I have no idea how I would have dealt with the information at that time. Several other adoptee narratives I have read (and other autobiographies as well) tell similar stories; these silences are effects of our culture's deeply rooted anti-Semitism, analogous to silences about black ancestry.[21] It was important that I finally found out the truth, and yet this truth did not provide a simple message of how or whether, given this ancestry, I should redefine myself. I will discuss this problem further in my George Eliot chapter when dealing with *Daniel Deronda,* her novel about a character in a somewhat analogous situation.

I grew up the only child in a family that was mixed ethnically, religiously, and in appearance—my mother was fair and my father was dark; my mother was Irish, English, and German and my father was Czech. My mother was Catholic, but her mother was Protestant; my father was a nonpracticing Protestant, but his mother had been Catholic long ago. I was conceived by parents who were also ethnically and religiously mixed—also a fair mother and a dark father. My placement was probably an example of the matching between adoptee and adoptive parents that was prized in adoptions in the 1940s. Frank's partner in his medical practice took care of the Florence Crittenton Home in Cleveland (one of a national network for unwed mothers) and helped with the placement, perhaps expecting that whichever biological parent I looked like, there would be some resemblance to one of my adoptive parents. It may also be relevant that adoption matches were ordinarily made by religion, and someone from a mixed couple, or a mixed couple trying to adopt, might fall through the cracks if they were not grouped together. Or maybe I was just the first girl to come along at the right time—my father's partner had considered adopting me himself, and, with two girls already in his family, chose a boy instead.

But in spite of his willingness to adopt me, Frank was at least mildly anti-Semitic. I remember a group conversation when I was quite young in which this nonreligious man, said, apparently out of nowhere, "I don't understand why the Jews didn't accept Christ." I imagine my mother stopping him from going further. Long after his death, his partner's daughter gave me a thank-you letter my father had written him when I was a baby, in which he joked that, because he had adopted me, he must be kosher, and remarked on my intelligence. Were it not for the "kosher" remark, I might think how lovely for my father to be seeing me as intelligent from the beginning. But since intelligence is part of the classic ambivalent anti-Semitic image of Jews, I wonder how complicated it was for him later when it was clear that I was doing very well indeed in school.

Mostly, ethnicity didn't seem very important in my childhood family. After all, in the 1950s and early 1960s the melting pot was really supposed to melt. A girl I met on a summer job in high school tried me out in a game in which you pick three words to identify yourself. What I said was "Marianne Novy, American, Catholic." (She said that most people she asked began, "I'm a girl.") My father, whose parents had emigrated from Czechoslovakia together long before, did not belong to any group based on being Czech, and had no Czech friends, to my knowledge. (Did he have friends of any kind?) Our one Czech neighbor was someone my mother, not my father, had known as a child. My mother's mother was German; Dorothy told me that her father emphasized being Irish (though he was, she thought, half English), but she didn't explain behavior by "nationality" nearly as much as she said, for example, "Boys will be boys." (As I look back, I realize that her two closest friends were German and Irish-German, but it is probably more relevant that they were both adoptive mothers, one of orphaned nephews and one after giving birth twice.) If I was asked about my nationality I said, "Czechoslovakian, from Bohemia, English, Irish, German," that is, if anybody let me say all of that without going on to the next person in line. However, I had very little sense of particular traditions associated with any of these groups, except for St. Patrick's Day, celebrated enthusiastically and nonexclusively at my Catholic grade and high schools and college.

I both did and did not believe that the combination of my parents' nationalities I have just listed was mine. On one hand, I thought of Frank and Dorothy as my parents, not as my adoptive parents, and so in some way I thought of their nationalities as mine. On the other hand, I did not then have the concept of cultural transmission. My adoption was supposed to be a secret; my mother told me I was English, German, and Norwegian, and that was supposed to be a secret as well. So claiming the nationalities of my adoptive parents was part of the act of covering up the differences in our family, and I do mean act. (I remember telling someone that I was supposed to look like my father and act like my mother: I meant that "supposed to" in a more literal way than the hearer probably thought.)

As far as I can tell, my only parent with a strong ethnic identification—considering Jewishness here as an ethnicity (I don't know what country his ancestors were from; later I will consider Judaism as a religion)—is the one I have never met, who does not want to meet me.

Perhaps this is the consequence of the opposition between adoption (especially as it was practiced in the 1940s and 1950s) and the predominant popular construction of ethnic consciousness, which does emphasize "blood" and heredity rather than cultural transmission. Presumably it was partly because of his valuation of Jewish heredity that Murray did not want to marry Geraldine in the first place, thereby making it difficult for her to keep me (though it was probably even more because he never really cared much for her), and it is partly because of his valuation of Jewish heredity—transmitted according to Orthodox law through the mother—that he now feels little connection with me, the daughter of a gentile. On the other hand, it was partly because of my adoptive parents' comparative lack of ethnic identification that they could adopt a child whose heredity was different from their own.

Although I value multiculturalism as an ideal, I am ambivalent about ethnicity and uncomfortable with folk associations between ethnicity and personal characteristics transmitted by genetics. Perhaps it's partly because of my realization that what I learned further about my ethnicity didn't really tell me much about myself, though it did tell me more about my history. When I was asked to fill out my daughter's nationality on a form for one summer camp, I wrote, with a sense of irony, "European-American." The space on the form was not big enough to list all the ethnicities that might be relevant; furthermore, we had just returned from visiting Germany, the Czech Republic, and Austria (the home of my husband's grandmother). The ethnic subgroups in both my biological and adoptive families are all white; my adoptive parents' comparative lack of ethnic identification could be reframed as white ethnic identity in opposition to the racial other. But identity as white simply because not black or Asian is not the kind of identity I want.

If ethnic identification was limited in importance in my adoptive family, religious identification was very important. I was raised in Dorothy's Catholic religion, which was always much more attractive to me than Frank's position of being a nonpracticing Protestant—she was a warm, generous, lively person, he was solitary and irritable, and the nuns at school liked me. I went to a Catholic college during the opening up of the Second Vatican Council, and my religion evolved into an ecumenical left-wing Catholicism with a concern for social justice. About the time I began working on this project, my parish was dissolved for lack of membership and my admired pastor was exiled, or so it seemed, to a rural church in the hinterlands, and after a year of exploring others, I began to participate regularly in an Episcopal parish nearby.

My birth mother's Church of God has little appeal to me. Judaism—the term to use now considering it as a religion—has more. If my birth father had acted differently, if my best Jewish friend were not a Unitarian, it might have been a more important issue in redefining my identity, fighting more actively with the Christianity that feels so much a part of me. Upon reading Adrienne Rich's essay "Split at the Root," about her experience of reclaiming a Jewish identity in midlife, I was startled to discover that only her father was Jewish.[22] But he was her father in a much fuller sense than Murray is mine. Reclaiming her Jewishness gave her connections with her family in a way it could not for me. For her it replaced a Christianity that was merely a social form. Not so for me. Like many in the nonevangelical tradition, I am not comfortable talking or writing about my religious beliefs, but for all my secular behavior, my Christianity links universal human dignity, inclusion, forgiveness, reconciliation, and hope, which are my ideals, with the message of Christ, and I feel passionate about this linkage. I know that many people find something similar in Judaism and others in other religions and in humanism, and I also know that the institutional Christian churches have often gone against this message. Fortunately, at this point in history, I can affirm that the religious tradition of Christianity is more than prejudice, and also both find common cause with and explore the differences of other traditions.

By "blood" I am as Jewish as Adrienne Rich. But now I use "blood" only with quotation marks, visible or invisible, when referring to genetic ties. I found it revelatory to learn that the usage comes from an ancient (false) tradition that semen is refined blood.[23] "Blood" in the sense of biological kinship is a fiction—especially when applied to fathers, since the tie of pregnancy is a more literal tie of blood. I hold on to this information from the history of science as if it explains why the language of blood and ancestral identity doesn't work for me the way it works for many adoptees who have found their heredity.

Today, many adoption agencies and activist groups emphasize ethnicity, and urge telling all adopted children about the ethnicity of their birth parents. In cases where children's ethnicity is visibly non-European, many adoptive families join together and find authorities on the relevant culture so that their children, inevitably identified as foreign, can develop a sense of group membership as, for example, Korean. These practices are, of course, unlike the usual processes by which culture is transmitted. But what else can the adopted parents do to give content to ethnicity, other than rely on stereotypes?[24] In *Ethnic Options*, Mary Waters quotes an interview subject, Susan Badovich, who after adopting a son she says is Irish, Austrian, and English, decides to celebrate St. Patrick's day and asks a friend who goes to Europe to bring him back "a pair of lederhosen, these little Austrian pants, for the Austrian part of him, and I hope to instill in him some pride in his ethnic background."[25] To me, lederhosen seem an inadequate basis for such pride, yet according to Waters's book, most Americans who identify strongly with some ethnicity have little content to their identification except a few such symbols. Indeed, Badovich reports that her husband, who grew up with a Baptist mother, identifies himself as a Russian Jew and has a mezuzah on their door and thinks his Jewish and her Catholic traditions are similar. Maybe this idiosyncratic use of symbols is easier in San Jose, where they live, than in Pittsburgh, where there are many people for whom Judaism has a more definite, if contested, content. Presumably the less content one's sense of ethnicity has, the fewer stereotypes one has to deal with, which might be good except that one still has to deal with other people's stereotypes; a better alternative would be a knowledge of some of the complex history of each tradition involved.

The Badovich interview is the only place where Waters mentions adoption. However, her book is suggestive for an adoptee because she emphasizes that ethnic identification is a matter of choice, although she notes "the common view among Americans . . . that ethnicity is primordial, a personal, inherited characteristic like hair color." (Indeed, one of her reviewers, Alan Wolfe, has argued that "ethnicity with freedom of choice is no longer ethnicity.")[26] Like many sociologists, she critiques the biologically based view of ethnicity, but admits that it involves "the *belief* on the part of people that they are descended from a common ancestor" (17). Studying answers to questions about ethnic identification on the census and in interviews, she analyzes some of the factors involved when people with a multiethnic heredity decide which one or two of their ethnicities they will claim (this is not necessarily determined by which one or two involve the largest number of their ancestors). She argues that the white Catholic suburbanites she studied in the late 1980s have an almost contentless "symbolic ethnicity" that "makes you both special and simultaneously part of a community. It is something that comes to you involuntarily through heredity, and at the same time it is a personal choice. And it allows you to express your individuality in a way that does not make you stand out as in any way different from all kinds of other people" (150).

Even though Waters emphasizes the idea of choice in ethnicity, her language reveals that ethnicity works differently for adoptees. Those who know they are adopted cannot have "the belief that they are descended from a common ancestor" with their adoptive parents, unless they were adopted by relatives or placed with a family of similar ethnicity, so an "institution" such as ethnicity that is, in the United States today, perceived as centered on the family does not provide a common bond in their childhood home, unless their parents make exceptional efforts of imaginative sympathy. The adoptee does not have an ethnicity that comes involuntarily through heredity. What heredity she has, she may have had to struggle hard to learn, or else her parents have had to struggle to find its symbols for her. What comes involuntarily to her may be the habits and customs her adoptive family has because of their culture, and if she claims this culture as an adult, identifying with an ethnicity that is not biologically hers, it may be even more of a conscious decision than the choices of Waters's interviewees.

Waters observes that most people are between the ages of seventeen and thirty when they choose which of their ethnic identifications to maintain, and she acknowledges that surveys sometimes force people to name fewer heredities than they actually have. I think she does not give sufficient attention to the possible choice of maintaining multiple ethnicities. She does, however, note that a complex genealogy may be one reason for simplifying ethnicity to "American." As one respondent said, "I would just have to say 'American,' because otherwise it would just go on forever" (48).

Adoption and American Optimism

While Waters provides material for deconstructing the myth of heredity as identity, the frequent simplification of ethnicity to "American" among her respondents also elucidates some elements in the myth of adoptive family as identity. The idea developed in the founding of the United States that membership in the nation was a matter of citizenship rather than "blood" would seem to predispose Americans in favor of adoption. Many countries in Europe have a long tradition of emphasizing a national "bloodline," and the late-twentieth-century emergence of nationalism has involved the dissolution of a number of other countries—Yugoslavia, Czechoslovakia—into the component parts of their most obvious ethnic mix. The fact that France and Germany, for example, each included heterogeneous ethnic and cultural groups has not been part of the French or German national mythology in the way that diversity has been in the United States, though in this time of global migrations both European countries are struggling with it. By contrast, our motto "E Pluribus Unum" (out of many, one), originally referring to the many states made one nation, has been for a long time reinterpreted to refer to ethnic multiplicity. With the same emphasis, Herman Melville wrote, "You can not spill a drop of American blood, without spilling the blood of the whole world."[27] Adoption has, of course, been practiced in many other countries—revolutionary France, significantly, promoted it strongly as a matter of equalizing its society—but that kind of adoption did not last long in the French code of laws. Adoption was possible in nineteenth-century France under much more restrictive rules. It was long after the nineteenth-century formalization of adoption law in the United States that adoption became institutionalized in most of Europe.[28]

Adoption has sometimes been practiced primarily as a way of controlling how one's money is transferred into the next generation, or of getting an unpaid household servant, but for more than a century it has been associated with a very American interest in social reform. It has long been part of U.S. mythology that we do not give up on problems; instead, we try to do better. This optimism—closely related to Enlightenment ideals—has influenced the American institutionalization of adoption.[29] Gradually, in a process documented by Rickie Solinger and Barbara Melosh, a belief spread that out-of-wedlock birth, though a disgrace at the time, need not mark mother or child for life—so long as the mother in question was white.[30] Especially as the profession of social work expanded, experts emphasized children's need for a nurturing environment, and reassured potential parents that "good homes" were more significant than "bad blood."

Adoption is also highly compatible with the U.S. belief in choice and freedom. According to the dominant paradigm in the mid–twentieth century, adoption would permit an unmarried mother to make a new start in life, while allowing a married couple to have a child they wanted. For the adopters, it could seem like an affirmation of their membership in a larger human community; it could also affirm their ability to surmount fertility problems, and emphasize that parenthood is a matter of conscious work rather than of biologically based instinct.

But the choice and freedom involved with adoption have their limits. Many advocates of reform in adoption law have criticized the Enlightenment optimism of American midcentury adoption as a quick-fix solution that neglects feelings, particularly those of the birth mother. Since white single women were pressured to have their children adopted and black single women were expected to keep theirs, adoption practices have often used "women's bodies and their reproductive capacity . . . to promote political agendas hostile to female autonomy and racial equality."[31]

Furthermore, the image of adoption as an act of unlimited freedom for the adoptive parents who bestow a new identity on the child breaks down in practice as well. Choosing a child in adoption is usually choosing under rather severe constraints, accepting or rejecting one, for example, with the chance of having another limited choice months later. Adoptive parents, like parents of all kinds, must confront the limits of their children's malleability. A nurturing environment can help children grow, but it cannot necessarily make them grow along a particular, specific line of development you plan for them. Ellen Goodman has even suggested that adoptive parents are likely to recognize that their children are different from them from the start and so have, in this respect, an advantage over other parents who must learn it as their children grow up.[32]

The adoptive relation reproduces the quintessentially American issue of communicating culture across "bloodlines": if immigrants have often been referred to as America's adopted children, their teachers and their government deal with issues of accepting difference that are related to those that face adoptive parents (though the situation is even more complicated for the parents of children internationally adopted). Optimism about both adoption and Americanization can be based on a belief in the universal similarity of human nature, and in its infinite malleability, but it need not be. The attempt to define America as a culture of pluralism and diversity, in Henry Louis Gates's phrase "a conversation among different voices," parallels the attempts by many transcultural adopters today to learn from and celebrate the culture of their child's birth parents, some of the recent experiments in open adoption, and the more ordinary openness of adoptive parents such as those Goodman describes.[33]

I shared many of Dorothy's values, and she accepted my differences from her to a large extent, but not always enough for me. I remember a particularly painful scene of screaming at her (in my twenties!) that I couldn't be the person she wanted me to be. I did credit to her in many ways, and I know she appreciated me, but I was never the good decorator and neat housekeeper she was. Nor, on the other hand, did she and Frank provide as much of a two-parent family as Geraldine hoped—nor did I bring them together as Dorothy probably hoped. Frank's emotional health was declining during the years I was growing up. They fought more and more, and separated during my return home after my freshman year of college. Frank died a year later. Dorothy, however, survived admirably for twenty-five more years.

My adoptive family exemplifies how social workers can make mistakes about stability. Yet for all the problems I had growing up, I feel that I benefited from being adopted rather than being raised by Geraldine, given her temperament and the environment in which she lived. I feel this, of course, because of the influence my adoptive environment has had on me.[34]

Both the myth of the adoptive family as identity and the myth of heredity as identity, though better than the myth of disaster, are inadequate not only to the Jessica/Anna story but also to my own life as an adoptee, and to much interesting literature by and about adoptees. I believe they are also inadequate to the lives of many others.

Yet they are powerful myths in our culture. As an adoptee, no matter how much I stress the importance of environment and the possible benefits of adoption, I must deal in some way with the issue of heredity, especially since I live in a time when the language of hereditary identity is used so often. On the other hand, no matter how much I stress the problematic aspects of adoption, often it does present the best possible solution for a child. The possibility of finding a nurturing family not determined by biology is an important affirmation of human freedom, educability, and ability to love across boundaries. However limited the accomplishment of these goals may be in practice, they are better ideals than ethnic purity. While the U.S. practice of adopting children from other countries may have problematic tendencies toward cultural imperialism, the prejudice that has existed in countries such as Italy, Romania, and Korea against adopting children of their own culture—especially if they are racially mixed or illegitimate—is hardly superior.[35] The summer of the DeBoer/Schmidt case was also the first summer of war between ethnic groups in the former Yugoslavia. A country that had officially emphasized peaceful multiculturalism split violently under the influence of ethnic nationalism. Emphasis on genetic ties does not, of course, always lead to civil war, but it can. Given the power of belief in heredity, twenty-first-century culture desperately needs some belief in bonds that cross "bloodlines."

Adoptees and Community

At the beginning of her influential search autobiography, *Twice Born*, Betty Jean Lifton wrote, "The adopted child can never grow up. Who has ever heard of an *adopted adult*?"[36] Jean Paton, in her pioneering work, wrote not of "adopted children" but of "adopted people" and "the adopted."[37] Katrina Maxton-Grahame called her search autobiography *An Adopted Woman*.[38] But when the term *adoptee* became widely used, a self-identification cutting across age and many other categories became easier to formulate.[39] A group consciousness began to develop.

As a child, and through college, graduate school, and my first job, I had no other friends I knew to be adopted. (I didn't even know that one of my father's sisters had adopted rather than given birth to my cousin June.) But when I was almost thirty, people were beginning to open up about adoption. I answered a personal ad in the *National Catholic Reporter* from a woman in New York State who wanted to discuss being a feminist adoptee, and corresponded with her for years. I discovered that a local female friend was adopted and a male friend had been raised by foster parents; I met Betty Jean Lifton after she spoke at my university, wrote to Florence Fisher and Jean Paton, and joined with other local adoptees to form Pittsburgh Adoption Lifeline, a search support group. Such groups were forming all over the country. Adoptees previously largely invisible to one another have begun to develop a community. However, this is not an easy task. Unlike many minority groups, neither adoptees nor adoptive parents necessarily grow up among, raise children with, or wish to socialize with others in their category. But the experience of searching, or of trying to open records legally, or of dealing with a blended family provides more of the basis on which a community can grow.

Sometimes I think that, because of the laws of secrecy it is trying to combat, the adoption reform community's public voice has emphasized too much the importance of heredity. However, like many adoptees, including many in the American Adoption Congress, I feel strongly the importance of environment as well as heredity. Many of us emphasize positive feelings about our continuing bond with adoptive parents. As adoption becomes more visible, I as an adoptee find myself feeling an affinity with adopters as well as with other adoptees. I have an impulse to celebrate nurturing that crosses over heredities, even while recognizing its difficulties. But I also celebrate my own birth mother's ability to welcome me, crossing over environmental obstacles, and I want birth mothers, and potential birth mothers, to receive fair treatment. I want a community in which members of the adoption triangle can speak to one another and also provide perspectives and resources to others considering adoption. As part of establishing this community I want to examine a range of literature that tells stories about adoption, including its relation to the cultural myths I have described and its attempts to suggest new myths and new plots.

Adoption and Feminist Criticism

I come to this project not only as an adoptee but also as a woman and a feminist reader, influenced, in several ways, by feminist criticism, and hoping that the experiences of feminist criticism will be useful for readers interested in adoption. First, I want to write about literature in something of the spirit of pioneering feminist critics such as Mary Ellmann, Kate Millett, and Simone de Beauvoir—that is, I want to analyze the relation of literary works to cultural myths and social history that obviously still affect people's lives. I assume that people often respond to the world partly with attitudes they have unconsciously drawn from literature they have read, and that analyzing the assumptions governing that literature—or offering other ways of reading it—may help them consider different possibilities for seeing themselves and others. Just as feminist critics recognize different aspects of literature by reading with special attention to gender, and with a critical attitude about myths of gender, I have been seeing different aspects of literature by reading with special attention to adoption, and with a critical attitude about myths about adoption. And since some of these myths about adoption are myths about birth mothers and adoptive mothers, these ways of reading sometimes overlap.

But my book will of course have the mark of its own time, and its approach will be influenced by later feminist critics as well as those early ones. I have learned from many feminists who include their personal voice in their scholarship and criticism, such as the historian Carolyn Steadman, whose *Landscape for a Good Woman* exemplifies the possibility of writing about the mismatch between one's life and cultural myths, the contributors to the Greene and Kahn anthology *Changing Subjects,* about the interplay of the personal with one's scholarly and critical development, and the novel critics Rachel Brownstein and Suzanne Juhasz, who wrote about their experience of reading.[40] There will be much more in this book about readers' responses and possible reader and viewer identification than in most works of criticism today—though this has continued to be one strand of writing in feminist criticism. But writing as an adoptee is inevitably different from writing as a woman or a feminist in some ways.

Feminist criticism has affinities with a feminist movement that critiques many different aspects of its society, with a broad consensus on many necessary changes (for example, ending employment and other economic discrimination against women, ending rape and sexual harassment), even if in disagreement about strategies. It has much convincing evidence of oppression against women that can plausibly (though not inevitably) be related to cultural myths of idealization and degradation. Adoptees are a much smaller and much less visible group than women; it is impossible to make a reliable estimate of our numbers, or to test any claims that we are discriminated against in any way beyond the denial of our genetic records. Arguments that adoption—or a certain system of closed adoption—is psychologically damaging rely largely on some autobiographies, case histories of adoptees who are not necessarily representative, selective use of psychological research, and a cultural belief in the importance of heredity. Arguments that adoption, or a certain system of adoption, is beneficial, made in particular by the National Council for Adoption, the main group supporting closed records, also rely largely on autobiographies, case histories, selective use of psychological research, and a cultural belief in the beneficence of adoptive parents.[41] Psychological research in this area is especially problematic partly because one's assumptions determine who would be the relevant comparison class—those raised in biological families in the same environment as the adopted subjects, or those raised in circumstances close to those the adopted subjects' birth mothers would be able to provide.

Some adoptees and adoption reform activists have made their belief in inevitable psychological damage due to closed adoption the basis for their politics. Others, and I count myself among them, would say that even if only part of identity is based on heredity, and even if many adoptees are not psychologically damaged by closed adoption, at least all adult adoptees who wish should have the right to open records.[42] Perhaps women's history provides another useful parallel here. Can we compare the women who, in presuffrage days, never wanted to vote, to adoptees who don't miss the information that they can't have? Adoptees claim a great variety of different experiences. Besides those who stress heredity, some emphasize their relation to their adoptive parents, others the mix; still others find both sets of parents irrelevant. I would not claim that those in any of these categories are in denial. The voices of the angry and the victimized are important testimony, but to read as an adoptee, it is not necessary to read as a victim.

Yet, if not necessarily victimized, adoptees and adoptive families are still marginal in our society's understanding of family structure, in spite of all the ways that contemporary families have changed. Adoptive mothers are still writing in to women's magazines complaining about the attribution of maternal love to blood. Attacks on the possibility of gay marriage—ignoring many other people besides adoptive parents— frequently say that procreation is essential to marriage. But it has been argued by many writers, especially those associated with the philosophical position called standpoint theory, that people in marginal positions have a special opportunity for insight into their society. This doesn't lead to a simple conclusion. From this point of view, it might be said, for example, that adoptees have a better chance to see that parenthood is actually more about love than about biology, as the literature of adoption indeed shows; or, as I have argued already, that all parents have to deal with their children's difference from them; or, alternatively, that adoptees have more of a chance to see the predominance of commodification in our society (the conclusion to which Albee's *American Dream* points), or the extent to which it still considers genetic ties important; or that, living in border-crossing positions, adoptees have a better chance to get beyond our society's dichotomies.[43] Thus considering the thematics of adoption in a literary work, we (not necessarily only adoptees) can understand more deeply how it presents parent-child relations, or nurturing across difference, or the social stress on genetics, or commodification, or border crossing.

In addition to the insight that adoption literature may provide in dealing with issues beyond adoption, I am interested, as I said earlier, in what its study can do to help people feel less alone in their involvement with adoption. Many adoptees and birth parents don't have such a sense of aloneness, but it may be a vulnerability that happier ones can identify with—just as women without breast cancer or sexual harassment can feel solidarity in working against these threats. Adoptees usually grow up looking more different from their parents than do other children, and they grow up in a family in a way made, from the beginning, differently from the norm. If their family tries to hide this, that secret is another difference. I think I grew up feeling those differences to be basic, and then struggling to find similarities, which seemed like an effort. I want more of the next generation of adoptees to feel less alone, and more of the next generation of adoptive families to be comfortable talking about adoption, and I think writing about adoption in literature can contribute to this goal. I hope that adoptive parents can learn something from literature about the special challenges of their situation, and I hope that if they, adoptees, and birth parents understand something of the way literature has fantasized about them, they may be able to break the hold of some of those fantasies. And in addition I hope that readers who are not personally involved with adoption can find here insight that will help them be more self-critical about such fantasies, in the same way that seeing women as a group with a history that is partly a literary history enables us to be aware when literature produces fantasy images of women. Just as feminist criticism can help young women see through Prince Charming, Sleeping Beauty, and Cinderella stories, and help them be aware of when such fantasies are limiting their life choices, I hope that analysis in this book may help point out, for example, the fantasy nature of plots in which adoptees find their true identities and home in finding their lost birth parents. Indeed, the romance plot that ends in a reunited birth family and the romance plot that ends in marriage are structurally similar. The language of "sacredness" that Judith Modell finds in some adoptees' descriptions of their reunion might remind us of language used in the literary tradition of romantic love.[44] Now that more adoptees have met their birth parents and shared the changes in their relationship over time, books about these relationships sometimes use a metaphor from marriage to hint at the transience of emotional peaks; they refer to happy times shortly after a reunion as a "honeymoon phase." In life partnerships and in post-reunion relationships, we all need to negotiate cultural traditions if we are to build human rather than fantasy relationships. Somewhat as knowing women's history can be helpful to parents of girls, knowing adoption history and literature should make adoptive parents more aware of the struggle sometimes necessary to meet the psychological needs of their children.

And if teachers in grade school, high school, and college can teach literature with more sensitivity to literary adoptees' situation, their students living in variant family structures may have more tools for thinking about their own lives. My book discusses many frequently taught works, from the long canonical *Oedipus* to Barbara Kingsolver's *Bean*

Trees, which has quickly made its way into the high school curriculum as well as many readers' hearts. If more teachers who taught either of these books made a point of locating the silences in their treatment of adoption, the alternative plots theoretically possible (Kingsolver has made this easy by also writing *Pigs in Heaven*), more people in our culture might get over the idea that it is a threat to the adoptive family if adoptees meet, or even know something about, their birth parents. The next chapter will conclude with pedagogical suggestions; I hope that readers who are teachers will extend pedagogical thinking to the other chapters as well.

The adoption scholar David Kirk has differentiated adoptive families according to whether they acknowledge or deny differences from biological families; yet Kirk has been criticized for emphasizing these differences too much, and he has acknowledged that there are times when the adoptees' differences are less relevant.[45] This problem of emphasis is similar to that confronted when feminist theorists argue about whether to emphasize women's equality with men or differences from men. I find some persuasive arguments on both sides, and perhaps most persuasive the views of writers as different as Nancy Cott, Joan Scott, and Jane Gallop that theory and tactics can best emphasize both at different times and in different contexts.[46] Analogously, adoptees are like others. We can, for example, have feelings about members of our adoptive families that are as strong as those in biological families, and stronger than in some. We can also have curiosity about our ancestors as strong as those in biological families, and stronger than in some. Also, like other people, we don't wish to be defined entirely in terms of our families and childhood situation. But in our experience of double parenthood, usually with one set of parents unknown for most of our lives, we are different from others.[47] Sometimes this experience is an important, conscious issue in our lives, and sometimes it is not. My argument here is parallel to Denise Riley's argument that one's identity as a woman is conscious and important in some situations and not in others.[48] Adoptees can well argue that in order to have an equality of rights with others, including such a simple thing as knowledge of our medical history, we need some laws particularly aimed at remedying our (in large part socially constructed) disadvantages, just as women have made analogous arguments.

In most of the literary criticism that I have done up to this point, I have written with my identity as a woman quite salient. But in reading or moviegoing, which aspect of my identity dominates may be quite unstable; there are passages of Joyce, for example, that I read less as a woman than as someone raised Catholic (and to add to the specificity, a liberal rather than a conservative Catholic), and similarly in this book I read Albee's *The American Dream* less as a woman than as an adoptee, though the extent to which Albee identifies the adoptive *mother* as the more active cause of problems in the adoption he portrays is worth considering. I read one plot of *Daniel Deronda* primarily as a woman and the other plot primarily as an adoptee. Yet the particular way I read as an adoptee cannot be disentangled from my being a woman; most of the leaders in the adoption search movement and the greater proportion of the adoptees who have, like me, found part of a birth family are women.[49] Since many parents are more interested in adopting girls than boys—presumably seeing girls as more malleable or affectionate—it is even possible that more adoptees are women.[50] A woman has had to think about what she would do if unintentionally pregnant, and so she may find it easier to identify with her birth mother on that basis. Furthermore, an interest in family relationships is culturally marked for women; though a woman can turn to an exclusively nonfamily world of work, politics, culture, or hobbies, she is less likely to do so than a man.[51] Thus, an adopted woman's relation to her adopted and her birth relatives may well keep confronting her throughout her life.

Thus, while this book will be an experiment in reading as an adoptee, it will be feminist criticism as well. One of the important elements of early feminist myth analysis on which "adoption criticism" can draw is the recognition that our culture contains a contradictory set of beliefs, and that idealization is as much of a myth as degradation. Experienced in analyzing how some literature splits women between the exalted and degraded, we can observe how some literature about adoption exalts the adoptive mother and degrades the birth mother, and how other literature does the opposite; we can see how the two mothers of the "adoption triangle" make it particularly tempting for representations of adoption to exemplify this cultural split of views about women. We can also question to what extent such polarization occurs in cultural representations of adoptees and of adoptive and genetic fathers.

Scholars such as Marianne Hirsch have argued that feminist criticism so far has been too much from the daughter's perspective, and not enough from the mother's perspective.[52] But neither has enough attention been paid to the standpoint of the adopted daughter, the adoptive mother, the birth mother, or the men in similar positions. Perhaps the situation of the literary adoptee, in whose life nurture and biology identify different parents, is a particularly interesting location to explore in relation to conflicting views about biology within the feminist movement and within feminist criticism. From some feminist viewpoints it is important to demystify biological maternity, lest women be confined to it; from others it is important to celebrate it. Feminist comments on surrogate motherhood are split. But adoption is a different issue. Sara Ruddick is one of the few who has explicitly noted that her concept of mothering is not biologically based and thus includes adoptive mothers.[53] Most of the arguments about the relation of mothering to biology have been made without regard to the specifics of the adoption triangle and how it is presented in literature. But looking at adoption in literature has implications with regard to many other nontraditional families beyond adoptive ones.

Kinship

In our society today, traditional genetic kinship is not enough to meet the needs of an increasing number of children, and the desires of an increasing number of adults. Not only adoptive families, and foster families but also stepfamilies, blended families, and families made by new reproductive technologies deal with the question of how you construct kinship bonds without genetic bonds. The history of adoption should provide some cautionary notes for the development of new reproductive technologies, including cloning. The vexed status of secrecy in adoption should provide warning that a kinship bond may be threatened rather than preserved by hiding from the child the truth about how that bond was initiated. Otherwise, constructing kinship without genetic bonds has much in common with constructing kinship *with* genetic bonds—for no matter how much a mother and child are genetically similar, they are still two different people—as my daughter, who looks like me more than anyone else I have ever seen in the flesh, constantly shows me.

We are used to the idea that mothering is a continuous activity of nurturance. Sara Ruddick, developing the concept of "maternal work," goes so far as to say, "All mothers are 'adoptive.'"[54] The relationship of a parent and child who have always been together, the relationship of a reunited birth parent and child, and the relationship of an adoptive parent and child—all of these are in some sense constructed relationships— are built up out of many small interactions. In her book *Kinship with Strangers,* Judith Modell argues that openness in adoption is forming the basis for a new American system, "in which the significance of *work* in kinship will increase" and "genealogy is only one way of construct- ing parenthood."55 In this system, the idea that a child can have two mothers, or even more, may become much more accepted. No matter how important genetic makeup is, everyone needs nurture, and many different sources of nurture can be encouraged and valued. From this point of view, the reality of adoptive parenthood comes not just from the social or legal agreement to consider someone a parent—the sense in which, as I pointed out earlier, all kinship can be considered con- structed—but even more importantly, from construction by individual work. The adoptive mother in Jackie Kay's *The Adoption Papers* says, "She's my child, I have told her stories / wept at her losses, laughed at her pleasures / she is mine."56

But where does the adoptee fit in a world where—even as nurturing is scarcer—genetics is increasingly researched by scientists with an aim to discovering its predictive qualities? Perhaps this is not so far from the past world of "blood" and "race" that several of the works I shall dis- cuss show us. But unlike some critics who discuss such works, I shall call attention to these concepts and not take them for granted. Today's adoptees may reject the way some previous literature—including litera- ture they love—would position them; it may well be revelatory to them to see the fictions about them envisioned in that literature, and the assumptions they involve. Like Adrienne Rich, in a different but not unrelated context, I am pursuing "Re-vision—the act of looking back, of seeing with fresh eyes, of entering an old text from a new critical direction," because "Until we can understand the assumptions in which we are drenched we cannot know ourselves."57

The Range of This Book

One of the many ways in which this book is unusual among studies of literature today is that it does not confine itself to adoption in the liter- ature of one country or to a limited time period. Instead, I deliberately move here from ancient Greek literature to Shakespeare to nineteenth-century British literature to late-twentieth-century America.[58] I focus to a large extent on works in which the issue of defining parenthood, family, and the adoptee's identity is important, and not much on writings in which the adoptee is pathological or antisocial, or the adoptive or birth parents are monsters (apart from *The American Dream*). My selection is partly made to allow me to use my own reactions as case studies of how adoptees respond to literature, combining them with scholarship on books that I have lived with for a long time. Since high school I have been interested in classical Greece. Shakespeare was also an early love; I wrote my dissertation on the recognition scenes in his comedies and my first book on gender in his plays, and continue to teach them. George Eliot's relation to Shakespeare was the center of my second book, and my connection with *Daniel Deronda* is especially personal, as I shall discuss. As an adoptee coming of age in the 1960s, I had a special feeling for Albee's putting modern American adoption on stage for what seemed to me like the first time.

But the writings I discuss in these chapters have been widely read and formed many people's attitudes, not just mine. Many of them—*Oedipus, Winter's Tale, Silas Marner, The Bean Trees*—are taught in colleges and high schools, usually without much critical attention to their treatment of adoption. And yet, if we consider that treatment, these works can be seen as part of a tradition—the literature of adoption—that spans centuries and genres. Authors of many of the later works knew the earlier ones and sometimes refer to their attitudes critically by writing stories that end differently. George Eliot knew Shakespeare and Sophocles well.[59] Albee knew Sophocles too. An early review that he liked enough to include at the end of his preface to *The American Dream*, speaks of his play's "horrible aspects, which reach directly back to the butchery and perversion of the Greek theater . . . Sophoclean dismemberment."[60] Barbara Kingsolver knew George Eliot, and even mentions *Silas Marner* in a throwaway line in *The Bean Trees*.

Thus, my second chapter discusses a text long influential about adoption, and the way it has been used and responded to, Sophocles' play *Oedipus*. This play emphatically defines genetic parenthood as the only real parenthood, and associates adoption with denial. Oedipus has been used as a model by pioneers of the adoption search movement, but I argue that doing so is problematic.

My third chapter discusses three aspects of adoption in relation to

Shakespeare. His plays emphasize the birth family in the happy reunions of *Pericles, Cymbeline,* and *The Winter's Tale.* The representation of foster parents in these and other plays begins to suggest a different definition for parenthood, and the treatment of bastardy is closely related to adoption since its stigma has been one of the chief reasons given for closing adoption records.

My fourth chapter discusses the way in which a number of British novels of the eighteenth and nineteenth centuries—by Fielding, Burney, Austen, Brontë, and Dickens—portray the importance of both heredity and the influence of adoptive parents. It shows how these novels use adoption plots for psychological and social exploration: to dramatize struggles against stigma, to show class differences, and to emphasize the unexpected connections of widely separated characters. In these three chapters, adoptive parenthood becomes progressively more important, and this move could be associated with an increased emphasis on psychology and sentiment in literature and culture.

My fifth chapter focuses specifically on three novels by George Eliot that, unlike those discussed in the previous chapter, suggest that the adoptee faces a choice between two different ways of life, associated with two different sets of parents. It shows that in *Silas Marner* and *Felix Holt* Eliot goes further than any of the earlier novelists to suggest that parenthood is defined by nurturant behavior and not by genetics, and that, in her last novel, *Daniel Deronda,* genetics turns out to be more important, though not exclusively. It explores the reasons for this change and finds that both criticism of English society and the increasing influence of the ideology of race affect the celebration of hereditary Jewishness in this novel.

The sixth chapter discusses adoption in drama from Edward Albee's *American Dream* on. It will show some influence of the adoptee search movement on the theater: whereas *The American Dream* presents adopting parents as controlling figures who commodify their child and leave him powerless, *Evelyn and the Polka King, Redwood Curtain, Mask Dance,* and *Homecoming* use adoptees' searches for parentage to explore American culture, history, and, to varying degrees, adoptees' consciousness. It will also compare three recent plays that focus on different kinds of parents' struggles over an infant: Jane Anderson's *The Baby Dance,* Kristine Thatcher's *Emma's Child,* and Albee's *The Play about the Baby.*

The seventh chapter considers the representations of cross-cultural adoption in two novels by Barbara Kingsolver. In *The Bean Trees* (1988), Taylor's adoption of the abused Cherokee child she calls Turtle is seen as an unproblematic good for Turtle as well as part of Taylor's creation of a happy nontraditional family with Turtle and Taylor's friend Lou Ann and Lou Ann's son. In *Pigs in Heaven* (1993), however, the illegality of the adoption, anti-Indian prejudice, Turtle's Cherokee relatives, and her hereditary lactose intolerance must be reckoned with.[61] These novels change position on the environment/heredity balance much as do Eliot's.

The afterword briefly discusses four recent novels that portray adult adoptees as parents and would-be parents—Toni Morrison's *Jazz,* Chang-Rae Lee's *A Gesture Life,* Margaret Laurence's *The Diviners,* and Oscar Hijuelos's *Mr. Ives's Christmas*—showing that dealing with adoption is a lifelong experience in each of these books set in multicultural and multiracial America. I will then turn to my current relationship with my birth and adoptive families and discuss how becoming a mother myself has affected my understanding of adoption.

More of the nineteenth- and twentieth-century works I discuss take the influence and commitment of adoptive parents seriously, even though some are set in a country where adoption was not formalized by law. Unlike the works of Sophocles and Shakespeare, Eliot's novels, the twentieth-century search plays, and the recent novels of the Afterword present adoptees as having a choice in defining their identity. This anticipates (in Eliot's case) or correlates with the late twentieth-century development of a community of adoptees, including many interested in finding out about their heredity.

There are two simple views that public discourse about adoption falls into too easily. One is the view that only adoptive relationships matter; the other is the view that only birth relationships matter. Some people have articulated a third viewpoint, that both can matter but probably in different ways, that it depends on the circumstances, that adoptees can have a choice about how to negotiate their identity and their relationships. But this approach still is not as widespread as it should be. I hope that this book, by analyzing places in literature where simplifications are found and places where they are transcended, will show more people how the world looks with that third view.

I am the daughter of Dorothy and Frank, of Geraldine and Murray, in four different ways. I am different from each of them, and I am marked by all of them, in ways I know and in ways I will never know.

We adoptees are hybrids with heritages full of questions. But our position has, as well as a personal history, a cultural one—how adoption has been envisioned in the past—and in this book I attempt to claim, explore, and analyze some of that history. However different my readers' experiences have been, I hope that they will find my exploration a precedent for their own coming to terms with assumptions in which our culture has been drenched.

Two ∾ *Oedipus:* The Shamed Searcher-Hero and the Definition of Parenthood

Two leaders of the movement for adoptees' access to their records have made Oedipus a key figure in their books. Jean Paton begins the introduction to *Orphan Voyage* with these words: "In Greece, about twenty-four hundred years ago, there was written the first adoption life history."[1] She goes on to summarize the events of *Oedipus the King* and *Oedipus at Colonus* as the "chance discovery of adoptive status, the reaction, first search, interval of maturation, second search, denouement, exile, and ultimately . . . return and completion." In *Twice Born: Memoirs of An Adopted Daughter* Betty Jean Lifton takes her first epigraph from *Oedipus,* Teiresias's question, "Do you know who your parents are?"[2] Very early in the book she calls Oedipus her "fellow adoptee," and she refers to him on many pages.[3] In addition to these activists, H. J. Sants, a psychiatrist, quotes Oedipus in developing his concept of genealogical bewilderment among adoptees, which would become influential when publicized by Lifton and others: "I ask to be no other man than that I am, and I will know who I am."[4]

Reactions to *Oedipus* can be stunning examples of how positioning affects reading. Classical scholars are unlikely to refer to Oedipus as adopted, because ancient Greece had a different kind of adoption, which usually was a legal affiliation of a younger and older adult. But he was raised by different parents than those to whom he was born and, like the modern adoptee in a closed-record adoption, was kept in ignorance of his ancestry. Sophocles' play *Oedipus* begins late in the story. An oracle had predicted that Oedipus would kill his father and marry his mother, and as an infant he was abandoned by his birth parents, Laius and Jocasta, the rulers of Thebes, because of this curse. He was taken by a shepherd, and raised by the previously childless king and queen of Corinth, Polybus and Merope. Told by a drunken stranger that he was "an invented, fabricated, fictitious son for [his] father," Oedipus went to the oracle, which gave him the same prediction given to Laius and Jocasta, but did not tell him who his parents were.⁵ So he left Corinth to avoid fulfilling the oracle's prediction. When he arrived in Thebes, he became king and married the queen, Jocasta. Years later, when Sophocles' play begins, the city is devastated by a plague. Oedipus vows to find the cause of the plague and discovers that the man he killed at a crossroads on the way to Thebes was Laius, and that the woman he married was his mother. Thus his unintended incest is the cause of the plague. Jocasta kills herself, and Oedipus blinds himself and goes into exile.

Critics have often discussed *Oedipus* in relation to themes apparently unconnected with double parenthood. These themes may be abstract and apparently unfamilial, such as the conflict between fate and free will. Alternatively, Bernard Knox's influential book *Oedipus at Thebes: Sophocles' Tragic Hero and His Time* discusses the play in terms of the relation between human pride in achievement and religious belief, and relates Oedipus's imperious character to the quality of the Athenian city-state for which the play was first performed.⁶ When family issues enter the interpretation, the specifics of Oedipus's family life are still usually absent. The interpretation of the Oedipus story known to most people beyond classicists today is Freud's reading of it as an allegory for a widespread unconscious human desire, originating in childhood. In *The Interpretation of Dreams,* he writes, "It is the fate of all of us, perhaps, to direct our first sexual impulse towards our mother and our first hatred and our first murderous wish against our father. . . . King Oedipus . . . merely shows us the fulfilment of our own childhood wishes."⁷ Furthermore, he likens the play's action, "the process of revealing, with cunning delays and ever-mounting excitement," to his own kind of searching, "the work of a psychoanalysis."⁸

But what if we take seriously the fact that Oedipus was raised by a set of parents to whom he was not born? What, then, would the play have to do with our cultural mythology about adoption? What might it have to do with beliefs about what adoptees should know about birth parents and about what will happen if they meet?

When I was in college, and still keeping the secret of my adoption from everyone, I wrote—but never published or showed anyone—a tacitly autobiographical essay about loneliness, which discussed why lonely people might identify with Oedipus.⁹ I give three reasons. He "discovers his apparent heritage is not his true one," he "has something to hide, something which cuts him off from other people" (according to most readings of the play, of course, Oedipus did not consciously hide his secret, which was secret from himself as well—here my identification with him led me astray), and he is a "great but misunder-stood" tragic hero (I use some irony about this line of identification). For the adoptee's shame, isolation, and heroism, *Oedipus* is the key text in the literary canon of my education; but these themes depend to a large extent on how his double "heritage" is constructed, a question rel-evant to all representations of adoption.

What does parenthood mean? Is it a matter of begetting and birth, so that adoptive parenthood is always just a pretense? Or is it nurturing behavior? If so, adoptive parenthood can be just as much parenthood as any other kind. The plot of *Oedipus* is based on the assumption that parenthood is a matter of genetics, which determines identity. The play presents searching for biological family as dangerous. But it is also heroic. I shall return to Oedipus's combination of pollution and hero-ism in relation to the adoptee later.

Most of those who have written about *Oedipus* over the years have taken for granted the assumption that identity and parenthood are based on birth connection. Critics almost always refer to Laius and Jocasta as Oedipus's father and mother, without regard to the fact that they both wanted him killed as an infant, or that Jocasta spent only three days with the baby before giving him to the shepherd to expose. One critic, John Gould, does begin by referring to "Oedipus's adoptive father, Polybus" and the discovery that he was not "Oedipus's natural father."[10] But by the end of the essay, Gould has committed himself: "He *is* Laios's son (not Polybus's)."[11] And this, of course, is the way Oedipus, too, speaks of his parentage at the end.

Anagnorisis, recognition or discovery, is one of the key elements in tragedy, according to Aristotle, and *Oedipus* is the tragedy that he thinks has the best kind of recognition. While later plays and many crit-ics consider a more abstract recognition tragic—for example, the hero recognizes that he is only human and has been too proud—for Aristotle the most important kind was recognition of persons of the kind that leads to reversal. According to Gerald Else, still one of the most influen-tial translators, it is, in Oedipus's case, a shift into "the objective state of being *philoi,* 'dear ones' by virtue of blood ties."[12] Discovering that he was born to Laius and Jocasta literally changes his identity, and thus changes his condition from happiness to misery.[13]

There is a logic in associating with tragedy rather than comedy a plot in which heredity is both defining and dangerous. Both tragic plots and genetic ancestry are irrevocable. Parents by "blood" can be replaced in their capacity as nurturers, but not in their identity as parents by "blood."[14] Furthermore, *Oedipus,* even more than many other tragedies, emphasizes the force of destiny and of curses and connects them with heredity too.

But one recent critic, Pietro Pucci, sees something different in the play. He suggests that its "central question is, What is a father?"[15] Pucci points out that the prediction that the oracle makes to Oedipus is not exactly that he is fated to kill his father, but, as Grene and Lattimore accurately translate, that he was "doomed / to be the murderer of the father that begot me" (ll. 794–95).[16] He thinks that the oracle cryptically suggests that Oedipus had many different kinds of fathers.

Is this simply Pucci's deconstructive ingenuity, or was another definition of fatherhood possible in Sophocles' time? And, if so, does it make any difference to how we interpret *Oedipus?*

There were indeed circumstances in which "father" in Greek culture meant something other than "begetter." Law formalized adoption by men so that they could plan their inheritance, preserve the *oikos* (usually defined roughly as household) and have someone to remember them in burial and tomb cult rituals. At least one orator assumed that this relationship also involved an emotional bond with the adopter: "for childless men the only escape from loneliness and the only consolation in life was to be able to adopt whomever they liked."[17] Adoption was usually of adult males but sometimes of women or, with the agreement of their birth fathers, of children. Most of these adoptions, but not all, were of relatives in the extended family.[18] They were frequent enough that Sarah Pomeroy makes a point of saying that the *oikos* "refers to people related by blood, marriage, and adoption."[19] With this kind of adoption, the bonds were clearly more limited and inferior to those of the immediate biological family. Adopted sons could not make a will; they were easier to repudiate than biological sons.[20] Their loyalty was thought to be dubious,[21] and the adoption never broke the bond with the birth mother.[22] Officially it did divide the adopted son from the birth father, but this legal rule was "felt to be contrary to natural feeling and [was] often circumvented."[23]

But along with this legally formalized kind of adoption there was another, more secret, kind that involved infants. Precisely because it was intended to be secret, remedying infertility or perhaps the birth of a child of the "wrong" sex, this kind of adoption is impossible to document from historical records. But it frequently appears in the literature of ancient Greece. When *Oedipus* was written, there already were many legends in which the hero was raised by foster parents and discovers his ancestry later in his life, happily.[24] This may have been a plot pattern developed in part from the custom of sending noble children to extended family members to raise.[25]

But to investigate the historical possibilities of secret infant adoption, we must turn to the complicated issue of infant exposure. This clearly was practiced in ancient Greece. We don't know how often it happened; the frequency was surely less than in its literature and in the frequent literary fantasy that wives might fake a pregnancy or switch children with someone else and thus introduce another's child into the household.[26] As Nancy Demand writes, "At birth the guardian (kyrios) of a newborn infant, who was usually the father in the case of a child born to a citizen woman, had the right to decide whether to accept it into the *oikos* and raise it, or to expose it, but not to kill it outright. . . . A person taking in an exposed child could rear it as either free or slave, but the act of exposure did not break the legal tie between the child and its kyrios, and the child might later be reclaimed if it could be identified."[27] The exposure might occur because the child was thought to have originated in adultery, because it was a girl, or had a deformity; it might be a response to the family's economic difficulties, perhaps combined with one or more of the other circumstances.[28] Some believe that many exposed children were found and raised; others equate exposure with infanticide. In *The Kindness of Strangers,* John Boswell summarizes the arguments on this last point with regard to classical Greece, and devotes most of his book to similar issues in Rome and the Middle Ages, warning readers from the very beginning how difficult infant abandonment and informal adoption are to document from historical records.[29] Since this kind of adoption was done secretly, not legally, it does not show up in the history of laws; such adopted children were not known to be adopted and could therefore enjoy the rights they would have had if born to their parents—unless the secret was found out.

While this informal kind of adoption is close to the kind recently most common in the United States, because it takes place in infancy and leaves the adoptee and adoptive parents in the dark about who the birth parents are, in ancient Greek society it seems to have been sharply distinguished from legal adoption. Two different Greek words, coming from words meaning "making" with different connotations, were used for the two processes. The informally adopted child is termed *plastos,* which is translated as "invented, fabricated, suppositious."[30] This is the accusation that the drunkard made against Oedipus. To refer to legal adoption, however, the Greeks used the words *poeisis* or *eispoeisis,* coming from a verb meaning "to make" without negative connotations, used for all crafts and the origin of our word *poetry.*[31] The etymological connection between making and writing and adoption is also found in Latin-derived English in the similar link between *fictive,* as in fictive kin (for example, women called "aunt" by their close friends' children), and *fiction.* Yet this word family can include some of the negative connotations of *plastos,* for example if someone's claim to a child were referred to as fictitious.

Thus in ancient Greek culture there was a respected kind of fatherhood not defined by genetics—though this redefinition of parenthood apparently did not extend to mothers—and there was also a condition of "fabricated" parent-child relationship, which involved pretense (sometimes a wife's deception of an innocent husband as well as the rest of the society). There were doubts about how strong the bond was even in the case of the respected adoptive fatherhood, because genetic kinship was valued so highly; nevertheless nongenetic kinship was imaginable.

The term Aristotle used for the relationship discovered in a tragic recognition—*philoi*—could be used of bonds that were not genetic. According to Humphreys, "The term *philos* overrides the distinctions we make between love, family, and friendship."[32] Furthermore, the parent-child relation was not just a matter of biology: "the idea that children were expected to repay their parents for rearing them, with care in old age, is quite common in Greek texts."[33] Perhaps the fact that being born into a family did not in itself entitle a child to being raised by that family—exposure sometimes took place even when no doubt about the child's heredity was expressed—might have encouraged at least some people to conceptualize the idea that nurture rather than birth makes kinship.

So while the idea that adoptive relationships are constructed in a sense suggesting fabrication was dominant in ancient Greek society, parental relationships known to be legally constructed, involving nurturing rather than heredity, were imaginable. And similarly in *Oedipus* itself the association of parenthood with nurturing is still present, even if not the dominant theme. In the very line in which Oedipus speaks of the drunkard's accusation that he was *plastos,* "an invented, fabricated, supposititious son," he adds the phrase, "for my father."³⁴ The idea that Polybus is his father proves to be hard for Oedipus to give up. He goes to the oracle to find out who his father is, and when the oracle predicts the murder, he leaves his former uncertainty and assumes Polybus is the one he must avoid. Later, when the messenger tells Oedipus about Polybus's death, he speculates, "perhaps he died of longing for me / and thus I am his murderer" (ll. 969–70). When he hears that "Polybus was no kin to you in blood" (l. 1017), he wonders, "Did he love so much what he took from another's hand?" (l. 1023). This is the play's most positive—or only?—picture of Oedipus receiving parental love.³⁵

Strangely, Oedipus says little about Merope. He doesn't speak of her love for him as a child, nor of her reaction to Polybus's death, nor of her offering a haven for him when he leaves Thebes. She is present in his mind only as another possible temptation to violate taboo—if he went back to Corinth, even though Polybus is dead, he might somehow still fulfill the prophecy by marrying her. The old shepherd also fails to mention her—it is Polybus to whom he remembers giving the child Oedipus now is. Perhaps the reason for this neglect of Merope is a combination of the general male domination of Greek culture and the fact that legal adoption, basically an agreement between men, did not break the tie with the birth mother, so that the Greeks were less likely to think of loving adoptive mothers than of loving adoptive fathers.

But what if we do raise the question of what motherhood is in this play? One effect of the inattention to Merope is to make Jocasta's role even more important. Many critics see her attitude toward Oedipus as maternal. She enters the play trying to stop the conflict between him and Creon, and she often takes what seems to be a protective attitude toward Oedipus—which is of course also a way of protecting herself. But at the climax of the play we learn (while she is offstage killing herself) that it was she who gave the infant Oedipus away to the herdsman to kill it, to avoid the murder of Laius predicted by the prophecy. Oedipus's final attitude toward her seems to be anger; the messenger says that Oedipus burst in on her with a sword and found her dead. But his gesture of blinding himself with the brooches from her robe is also an acknowledgment of their inextricable tie.

What difference does it make if we speak of Oedipus as unknowingly committing incest with his birth mother, instead of his mother, now that consciousness of the different situation of adoptees has developed this term? It emphasizes that the incest comes from what we might call Oedipus's cosmic bad luck as opposed to his guilt—and as we shall see in discussing *Oedipus at Colonus,* the concept that lack of knowledge makes a difference was thinkable at the time. On a rational level, incest is wrong because it violates a trust in a close family relationship. But Oedipus and Jocasta did not have a close family relationship when he arrived in Thebes. It was Merope with whom he had a mother-son relationship. Oedipus and Jocasta have done wrong not at the rational level but at the irrational level of taboo. Similarly, killing the father who raised you seems worse than ordinary murder—cross-culturally, I would expect—because it involves betrayal and ingratitude. Unknowingly killing the father who begot you but then wanted you dead involves no ingratitude. It is a kind of nemesis on Laius, as well as a sign of the danger of Oedipus's temper. Nevertheless, Sophocles' original audience is not the only culture to find this a specially horrible fate. It is as if, in killing Laius, Oedipus was killing part of himself. Regardless of whether he acted in self-defense, this act makes the world seem terrible.[36]

The plot is full of ironies that work somewhat differently depending on how we define parenthood. When Oedipus, concerned enough about the question of his heredity to consult the oracle, assumes (without thinking that he might find his parents elsewhere) that the way to avoid the oracle's prophecy is to leave Polybus and Merope, we can see this as denial; he doesn't want to admit the bad news the drunkard has given him. On the other hand, we can see this as a sign of his great attachment to the only parents he knows, which paradoxically requires that he leave them. But most often the irony involves strong suggestions of Laius and Jocasta's parentage before Oedipus knows of it. Some critics have even hypothesized that Oedipus might have considered that Laius and Jocasta might have been his parents but decided to ignore that possibility.[37]

There was already a tradition of presenting reunions between family members in tragedy. About thirty years before, Aeschylus's prize-winning *Libation Bearers* had shown the recognition between Orestes and Electra, and that scene would have been familiar to Sophocles' audience (just a few years later, Euripides rewrote it critically in his *Electra*). The conventional belief was that unknown relatives would be of like mind even before meeting each other.[38] *Oedipus* may allude to that convention ironically when we hear of the similar rage of Laius and Oedipus at being challenged at the crossroads. Furthermore, Jocasta even makes a retrospective comment on their similar forms. All this irony continually impresses on the audience how blind—whether willfully or not—Oedipus is.

The image of Oedipus as a blind seeker is so similar to Freud's reading of the play, and so closely linked to the issues of Oedipus's shame and heroism, that I need to pause on Freud's approach before I consider the relation of Oedipus's shame and outcast status to the adoptee. The most remarkable thing about Freud's interpretation of the play and the myth in this context is that he foregrounds Oedipus's violence and sexual desire, and does not consider how Oedipus's relationship with his birth parents is different because he is adopted, but rather makes it an allegory of everyone's unconscious relationship with the parents they have always known, and the way it shapes their other relationships. (A Freudian, on the other hand, would consider it remarkable to foreground Oedipus's adoption rather than his crimes.) While adoptees focus on the fact that Oedipus does not know his genetic parents and in the course of the play finds out who they are, Freud focuses on the fact that he does not know that his murderous and lustful deeds were directed against his parents and in the course of the play finds out that they were. Both the adoptee reader and Freud are interested in Oedipus as a searcher. Betty Jean Lifton identifies with Oedipus not only as a searcher but also as someone in denial: "Perhaps Oedipus and I both knew through that middle knowledge one has when one knows and does not know at the same time. At first to survive, we do not know, then to survive, we know."[39] For Freud the denial and search of the play are allegories for denial and search for one's own desires. The adoptee searches outwardly, but the search has inward implications as well.

Many adoptees have feared finding out bad things about their biological parents, and this has been a reason that some social workers and parents have advised them not to search—but for an adoptee one of the real terrors of finding out anything bad about biological parents is the questions it raises about one's own possible behavior. That Oedipus himself has committed the crime he discovers dramatizes this fear.

On the other hand, Oedipus contains a kind of consolation for the adoptee. Here is the search, no matter how badly it turns out, considered heroic. Here is a play famous for thousands of years, and a quest like ours is at the center.

But Oedipus believes he was evil even before he committed this act:

and it is in saying this that he mentions his adoptive family for the first and only time since the revelation.

> O Polybus and Corinth and the house,
> the old house that I used to call my father's—
> what fairness you were nurse to, and what foulness
> festered beneath!
>
> (ll. 1394–97)

Something mysterious has been wrong with him all his life, then, connected with his birth: "Now I am found to be a sinner and a son of sinners" (ll. 1397–98).[40] His birth parents were sinners, perhaps, because they knew the oracle predicted a son would murder his father and went on to conceive him anyway, but that reference to their sin resonates with the transgressive sex outside of marriage that was my origin and that of most other adoptive children today.

Lifton focuses on the quest element in the Oedipus plot, rather than the tragic. But she is also interested in the social stigma in Oedipus's story. Oedipus discovered that he had violated taboos; she discovered that contrary to her adoptive mother's insistence, she was born out of wedlock. She parallels the curse of unwed motherhood with the curse foretold to Laius and Jocasta. "When I was born society prophesied that I would bring disgrace to my mother, kill her reputation, destroy her chances for a good bourgeois life. (It didn't raise an eyebrow for my father.) And so a kindly shepherdess who worked in an adoption agency put me out in the marketplace."[41] Lifton distances herself from this comparison by the joke about the shepherdess. In today's world, her comparison may seem like a trivialization to some, but if illegitimacy were not a stigma at least for the mother, would there be such resistance to opening adoption records? Jocasta is, in a sense, the extreme case of the figure invoked by the lobbyists for closed adoption records—the birth mother whose life is destroyed, not in this case by the return of her adopted-away adult child, but by his discovery and making public of their relation.

Oedipus envisions himself as an outsider even before he knows that he must be an outcast. For example, like many adoptees in life and literature, he develops his own fantasies about who his mother might be, and they take him far from his current position; at one moment she is a third-generation servant, at another, the goddess Chance. Analyzing the point where he thinks of the months as his brothers, Gould says that now his image of himself "is as a being from another world of discourse than the now familiar political world of Thebes or of Corinth." Gould concludes that Oedipus "is an alien; he does not belong and his not belonging is figured in the contradictions of his human relationships."[42] This resonates with the image of the adoptee as outside the ordinary ties of human nature, which appears in a number of other literary and mythic works, as well as with my college reading of the play quoted earlier.[43] But in this play, as Gould notes, it is the fact that he has those ordinary ties, and does not know with whom they connect him, that makes him an outsider.

Adoptee status is, in some ways, the most invisible minority status. There are no telltale gestures, skin colors, or identifiably shaped features that in themselves reveal a person is adopted, although in a family group physical contrasts between parents and child usually identify transracial adoptees. The lack of an original birth certificate, or of knowledge of genetic relatives, is an invisible deprivation—and to some adoptees it means little. The discovery, as an adult, of your illegitimacy before adoption, brings social shame if it means that your birth mother or father won't acknowledge you, or won't acknowledge you to others, but this, it would seem, is far from the outcast state that Oedipus experiences.

Yet many lawyers and lobbyists today are committed to keeping adoption records and information about birth parents unavailable to adoptees. In most states of the United States (unlike the situation in many other countries), adoptees lack rights other people take for granted. The more our society puts emphasis on heredity and ethnicity, the more this lack is noticeable. Why is this information thought to be so dangerous? Oedipus's discovery of incest made apparent one kind of confused family structure; perhaps adoptees' discovery of their genetic parents is dangerous partly because it makes apparent other kinds of confused family structures. We, as a society, still tend to believe that a person has only one set of parents; it's confusing to imagine that there might be two sets, in spite of the increasing frequency of stepfamilies. Furthermore, identifying genetic and birth parents reveals that many people who now appear to be respectable citizens have what is considered sexual misbehavior or parental inadequacy in their past. This may confuse their moral authority in their family and community, if known. And on the other hand many adoptive parents are afraid that their relationship with their children will be damaged if possibly competing parents are identified. So the issue with which this chapter began, what parenthood is, returns.

Lifton, Paton, and I all took Oedipus's situation as a metaphor for our own, partly because both the taboo against the adoptee's raising questions about heredity and the stigma of illegitimacy were so great at the time. Oedipus—an adoptee, and a cultural hero looking for truth no matter how disastrous the outcome—was almost an inevitable model for search activists with literary interests. In order to violate so strong a taboo, they (I was not yet a search activist) needed a strong language of entitlement. To define your parentage as your identity, as Oedipus does in the Watling translation, saying "I will know who I am," is powerful in our culture. Though using different translations, Paton says that Oedipus is asking, "Who am I?" (*Orphan Voyage*, 16). Lifton refers to his journey and hers as "the call to self" (*Twice Born*, 5). Paton and especially Lifton wrote when identity language was becoming increasingly influential, and the use of this language by them and others in the adoptee rights movement has helped to shift our culture's attitude about adoptees' heredity.[44]

Much of the language of the search movement is drenched, to use Adrienne Rich's term, in the assumption that finding your birth parents is finding your identity: "who you are," or perhaps, with more qualifications, "the missing piece." Typical interpretations of *Oedipus* show how deeply rooted that assumption is; the practice of raising adoptees without telling them about their birth parents, which seems like a contradiction to this assumption, can also support it to the extent that it is based on the view that information about birth parents must be kept secret to prevent adoptees from identifying with them more than with their adoptive parents.

But at this point there are many adoptees who, like me, would testify that they did not find their identity when they found their birth parents. Glad as they were for the information, in many cases they were left with more questions to answer, and often realized that their identification with their adoptive parents remained and that their appreciation of them increased. The equation of identity with genetics found in *Oedipus* is not the inevitable way to imagine identity, but an ideology present in various societies in differing degrees. Even people who undertake the search having accepted this ideology may alter it in the light of their own experience. For example, Lifton and Paton revise the Oedipus story in their use of it. Lifton puts a visit to her elderly adoptive mother near the end of her book, a few pages after she has stated that "the adoptive parents are the *real* parents in the most meaningful way."[45] Paton, whose adoptive parents are dead, tries to straighten out her birth certificate, receives one that is made out as if she had been born to her adoptive parents, and, in spite of her strong belief in heredity, is "satisfied to recognize the social family" she has known.[46] And finally she takes her identification with Oedipus to the sequel, *Oedipus at Colonus,* in which the former exile has a blessing for the city, using as the epigraph to her epilogue his line, "The words these lips will utter, shall be full of sight."[47]

In this play, Sophocles, in his last years, returned to Oedipus, imagining him in *his* last years. Oedipus, having lived for many years in exile, with the support of his daughter Antigone, returns to the place, close to Athens, where an oracle had predicted he would die. Thebes considers him still a dangerous source of pollution, but Athens, in the person of its king Theseus, welcomes him. In this play, unlike the first, Oedipus maintains his innocence:

> If then I came into the world—as I did come—
> In wretchedness, and met my father in fight,
> And knocked him down, not knowing that I killed him
> Nor whom I killed—again, how could you find
> Guilt in that unmeditated act?[48]

Oedipus and Theseus are convinced, at the end, that his special destiny brings favor to the place where he is buried; his mysterious disappearance at his death, as if taken away by the gods, seems to mark his vindication. Thus he argues in favor of discrimination in the way that acts against relatives are judged, saying that those done in ignorance should be considered differently. He also treats his own children differently according to their behavior toward him. Polyneices, his younger son, asks for help in overthrowing his brother, and Oedipus refuses, since both sons refused to help him, and curses them. Froma Zeitlin sees both of these positions as weakening the claims of blood ties. She argues that for Oedipus "the genos [family] . . . is first of all an ongoing relation among its members of shared reciprocities and obligations, so that entitlement to its privileges depends upon actions each individual knowingly and voluntarily undertakes. Oidipous [a transcription of Oedipus's name in Greek, in place of the more familiar Latinized spelling] therefore reserves his love for the daughters who have tended him in spite of the social conventions that would keep them stay safely at home and repudiates his sons who have intentionally behaved contrary to family rules in refusing the nurture they owe to their father."[49] However, in this play Oedipus never mentions Polybus or Merope, or argues that Jocasta and Laius have lost their title to be his parents by their behavior in his infancy.

Earlier in this chapter I mentioned that Greek culture did have an institution of legal adoption that took nongenetic parenthood seriously. Let me contrast with the *Oedipus* plays, which don't validate adoptive parenting, one by Euripides, which does. Indeed, here adoption seems to be the play's happy ending. In *Ion,* written probably just a few years before *Oedipus at Colonus,* the title character was born to Creusa and begotten by the god Apollo. Creusa abandoned him at the temple of Delphi, and he was raised there by the prophetess. When the play begins, Creusa and her husband Xuthus are childless; Apollo mystifyingly tells King Xuthus, who goes to the oracle to pray for children, that Ion is his son; Xuthus remembers a festival where, in his carousing, he might have begotten a child. Creusa meets Ion and hears his story of being abandoned and raised at the temple, but does not recognize him. Encouraged by the chorus (her serving women), she takes up the suggestion of her father's tutor that he should kill the boy, out of resentment that he lived and her child died. The gods prevent it, but Creusa is implicated. When she takes refuge in the temple, Ion tries to kill her, but the prophetess saves her and produces the basket in which Ion was abandoned, which identifies Creusa and Ion to each other as mother and son. Athena appears at the end to predict the future prosperity of Ion and the other children of Creusa and Xuthus, and to tell Creusa, "Disguise your knowledge of your son, that the king [Xuthus] may be / the happy prey of his sweet fantasy."[50]

This play has many of the elements of *Oedipus:* the foundling story, the unknowing meeting of mother and son, the speeches about their past that convince the audience of their relationship, and even the threat of murder between them before their final discovery. But here divine intervention stops the murder. And the play ends with the promise that Xuthus will never know of Ion's conception by Creusa and Apollo.

A strange ending indeed! Some critics have taken the play as a bitter attack on Apollo's intervention in mortal lives. However, Zeitlin, contrasting the play specifically to *Oedipus,* finds an admirable flexibility in its imagined Athens, specifically because of its dramatization of Apollo as giving his son to Xuthus in adoption.[51] In the Thebes of *Oedipus,* she writes,

> characters are constrained by the limits of kinship that dominate their modes of action, and they remain forever trapped in the dilemmas (or tragedies) of identity. . . . Thebes . . . cannot resort to fiction of "as if" or, at another symbolic level, create new institutions in the face of new problems. Athens, however, does precisely this in using the mythic idea of fosterage to arrive at the civic idea of legal adoption. . . . Athens may have it all ways: a child of divine parentage, a certified product of autochthonous lineage, a legitimized son of the proper social standing.[52]

Zeitlin points out that Athena makes specific reference to Athenian legal adoption when she says that Apollo gave his son as a gift "as sometimes happens when a friend gives another friend his son, that he may be master of a house."[53] Legal adoption, of course, was not supposed to involve deception, as happens in this ending, but as Creusa says, "Attributed to him [Apollo] / you'd have no claim to property or race" (ll. 1524–25).[54] Although the play takes as proverbial the hostility of a stepmother, it emphasizes the importance of other adoptive or semiadoptive relationships: Ion has received his early nurturance from the prophetess at the oracle; he calls her mother in his early, unknowing conversation with Creusa, and later greets her as "my dear mother, although not in birth"; she says farewell to him calling herself "just like the one who bore you."[55] The old tutor addresses Creusa as daughter. And Athena's adoptive relationship to Erichthonios, Creusa's father, is also glorified in the play.

Ironically, *Ion* takes a situation that seems to have been much feared by ancient Greeks, a man raising a son he thinks genetically his own who was actually begotten by another, and, by making the begetter a god, brings about the apparently triumphant ending that promises the successful alliance of the Athenians and the Ionians.[56] As Zeitlin says, "parentage itself may be a fictive category, an 'as if,' and ties of blood, although essential to one's genetic identity, are not the only relations that count."[57]

But Euripides also gives full attention to the situation of the separated birth mother and son. Ion, like many of the literary adoptees we will consider later in this book, longs to know his mother and thinks about her suffering: "her distress was equal: / her life was emptied of maternal joy" (ll. 1377–78).[58] Creusa has vivid memories of giving up her son, and the pain has clearly not gone away. Something of the ambiguity of the practice of exposure is seen when she claims to have thought Apollo would take care of his child but now assumes that he has died. If Jocasta is the exemplary birth mother for the closed-records side of the debate, Creusa is the birth mother on the open-records side—with, of course, the very significant qualification that she cannot tell her husband the truth about who begot their son.

What did these plays mean to the audience of their time? On one hand, they commented, no doubt, on Athenian religion and politics. But perhaps they were also responding to issues of domestic life. If it's not clear how guilty Jocasta feels about exposing her child, by the time of Ion, at least, there is no doubt that abandonment has marked Creusa's life. The idea that an important reason not to abandon your child is the possibility of unknowing incest appears in Roman literature of the second and third centuries, ranging from Plautus's play *Epidicus* to early Christian theologians.[59] The Oedipus legend was in the air centuries before Sophocles, but it seems to have been Sophocles who added the plague and Oedipus's search, first for the polluter and then for his father's identity, perhaps making him more clearly the paradigm for anxiety about incest related to abandonment.[60]

Although both of them deal with abandonment and substitute parents, with regard to their familial picture the two plays diverge. *Oedipus* puts its strongest emphasis on genetic relationship and on paternity, imagined simply as begetting, with a bit of concern for the adoptive father, King Polybus; *Ion*'s strongest relationship is maternity, presented not only as conceiving but also as other kinds of care. The ending either makes human begetting unimportant or attacks Apollo for treating it that way. It is not surprising that *Ion* was translated by the feminist poet H.D., who herself bore—and raised—a child out of wedlock, and that *Oedipus* is much the more canonical play.

There are many different ways to respond to *Oedipus*. I find quite moving many aspects of the play beyond adoption, such as the theme of self-knowledge, including the recognition that self-knowledge may bring responsibility and guilt. But the adoptee side of myself finds most salient the play's rejection of adoptive parents and its emphasis on "blood kinship." To other adoptees who, like me, identify with Oedipus's search, I want to critique the play's ideology and say that tragedy and genetically determined identity are not inevitable. Consider the advantages of the emphasis on nurture in *Ion* and *Oedipus at Colonus*. After your search, consider revisiting or returning to your own Corinth. (As, indeed, most adoptees do.)

I taught *Oedipus* last in the early 1970s, as I was beginning my search. I don't think I ever mentioned adoption as such, and I don't remember considering dealing with it. Could I do it now? How might the play be taught in, let us say, a college level humanities course or survey of world drama, if adoption issues were foregrounded part of the time? Might a teacher make a point of calling Oedipus an adoptee? Maybe. Should a teacher then generalize about how being an adoptee explains *Oedipus*?

In a recent narrative of his experience returning to Columbia's Literature Humanities course after many years, David Denby describes James Shapiro's class on *Oedipus*. "Hacking away at the frozen adolescent sea," Shapiro begins with a series of questions:

Whose mother told her she was found? . . . Anyone found in a basket under a bridge? . . . If you discovered you were illegitimate, would you not be the person you thought you were? Would you rather meet your twin than your natural mother?[61]

One of the students responds, "To find out who you are is a struggle you have to go through all your life." Denby calls this "a fine remark, but an answer to a different set of questions." But if you are an adoptee, whether you find out who you are by meeting your birth mother or by struggling through your whole life is a question that you might very well consider.

In this class, Shapiro is invoking adoption as a fantasy—he is particularly interested in the fact that nonadoptive parents sometimes joke to their children about having adopted them.[62] Indeed that fantasy of adoption is part of the appeal that *Oedipus* has had over the years. But just as feminist critics have pointed out the fantasies about women that literary works have appealed to in their readers, and have pointed out the discrepancy between the fantasies and women in real life, it might be worthwhile for teachers of *Oedipus* to demythologize adoption. Since adoptees in class may be slow to talk about this aspect of their lives, and may not represent much of the range of experiences (searchers are, on the average, older than first-year college students), the instructor might tell students that adoptees vary in their relation to adoption: some put much effort into searching, some do not search; some have a close relationship with their adoptive parents, some do not; some have always known they are adopted and talk about it openly, some do not. We can then locate Oedipus within these possibilities: he comes from a family where adoption is a secret, he feels loved by his (adoptive) father, he is horrified by the idea of doing anything against his family, indeed leaves them to avoid it. But when investigation of the cause of the plague in the city leads him to the choice of searching or not searching for his own origin, he chooses to search. This locates him as a particular kind of adoptee, one for whom the news that he is adopted would be traumatic even if the discovery did not also involve the news that he has committed incest and parricide, but one who is brave enough to search at whatever risk—including the risk to others.

The teacher might tell students (briefly) about the laws preventing most American adoptees from learning the names of their original parents, and the political struggles against these laws. Different as our society is from that of the ancient Greeks, the class might raise the issue of how much the rationale for these laws share with the reasons Oedipus's (adoptive) parents don't tell him of his origin and the reason Jocasta tells him not to search. Class discussions might deal, among other things, with the implications of different definitions of parenthood and identity, issues arguably central to the play as well as to contemporary adoption law. Students might also contribute ideas they have gained from observing or experiencing other kinds of variant kinship.

What would this accomplish? Students might think more about what kinship means today, in their own lives as well as in lives of their peers, and might be able to connect such issues with a close reading of the play. Adoptees, birth parents, and adoptive parents in the class might be encouraged to find that their own experience gives them special ability to notice details as they read, although they should not of course be pressured to talk about private issues in their own lives, and they may gain perspective on their own lives by contrasting their situations with those of the characters in the play. In addition, students may gain a political perspective in realizing that laws affect people's lives and can be changed, and gain a historical and cross-cultural perspective if the class discusses differences in adoption procedures across countries and centuries. And if any of these students later in life consider adopting children or giving children up for adoption, or have adult children (of either kind) who search, they will have had some preparation for dealing with the issues involved. Classes reading any of the other works discussed in this book might take similar opportunities to contextualize them with regard to experiences of adoption and kinship in their own time and ours.

How utopian, you might think, to treat literature as equipment for living, in Kenneth Burke's phrase.[63] But many of us try to give students such wide-ranging perspectives by discussing gender or race in literature. Other teachers want to affect students' worldviews when dealing with religious issues in literature. In fact, it is not at all new to engage students in thinking about "family" when discussing portrayals of families in literature. What I am proposing simply adds other dimensions to the question of what "family" means—in the classroom as well as in criticism and scholarship.

Three ❧ Adoption and
Shakespearean Families:
Nature, Nurture, and
Resemblance

In the airplane on the way to Wisconsin to meet my birth mother, I thought, "This is it—*the* recognition scene." I had spent years writing a dissertation focusing on recognition scenes in Shakespeare, in many of which characters were reunited with long-separated relatives they thought they would never see again. In those plays, family members usually mirrored each other closely. But in my own life the issue was how to have a close personal connection to someone with whom it seemed I had nothing in common except the nine months of her pregnancy, the first month of my life, and—in some unknown way—half of my heredity.

I already knew from our correspondence that Geraldine and I did not look very similar and did not share interests. Meeting her, I could find no more resemblance, no mirroring in our gestures. According to most of the stories of reunions of adoptees and birth parents I knew, in literature, in autobiographies, and in personal conversations, this is not the way it was supposed to be.

But she was glad to see me. She had bravely told her family about me, and she wanted to welcome me into that family. It was a large one, with seven sons, the five who no longer lived at home mostly still in state. I had often wished for a larger family, but having grown up as an only child, I had little idea of how to deal with one. One of her sons came home to meet me, but the evening I met several others of my half-brothers, they seemed more interested in watching their usual television than in me, and I was so disappointed that I had no idea of how to get their attention. These were not, as in a myth, my lost people. They were a challenge, people I would—from my previous everyday life—be unlikely to get close to, who had suddenly been transformed into relatives.

When I was alone with Geraldine at other times, I listened eagerly to the story of her life. There wasn't much of my thirty-three years that I could tell her. She (perhaps like her sons) didn't know how to ask, and I didn't know what I could tell her considering the restrictions of her own horizon and mine. Feminism, the main focus of my academic, personal, and political life at the time, was something she couldn't understand and was mostly against. She hadn't gone to college. She didn't read much except the Bible, and she read it as an evangelical fundamentalist with right-wing political views. I, on the other hand, was a left-wing Catholic. I had had conflicts with my adoptive mother, but after this experience, if I were to call anyone my "real mother," it would be Dorothy and not Geraldine.

My dominant impression of Geraldine was that she was tired. This may have been the inevitable result of raising seven sons in poverty in a family that believed that certain things were only women's work, or it may have been partly a constitutional lack of energy—one ominous similarity, since I am not the most energetic person myself. Either way, her life seemed confined and sad, and I wondered if I could help. Her sons and daughters-in-law seemed not to pay her enough attention. She needed friends and activities. She sat around the house too much, not even taking a walk. But improving her life much was impossible for me to do from a distance, with no one local or in her family to reinforce any of my suggestions or ideas. Or perhaps they had made some of the same suggestions without effect. I did give her a copy of *The Book of Hope*, a self-help book on dealing with depression. She found it shocking because it suggested self-assertion rather than prayer.

At first we corresponded a lot, and tried to deal with our different views in the letters. Now we correspond less, though we send cards and occasionally talk on the phone. For a long time I would spend a few days there, with my daughter, every other year. I would take Geraldine for a shopping trip and a drive to see some scenery outside the nursing home walls. Once my husband came instead of my daughter. Recently I have been taking more frequent and shorter trips by myself.

Seeing her is never as intense as was my first conversation about being raised by nonbiological parents. That conversation took place before I met Geraldine, with someone who shared a similar experience and had met his birth mother. It seems that I felt the shared story—

which was also rather different from that in Shakespeare's romances—more than the shared biology, as if the taboo against talking about being adopted was more basic than the prohibition on reunion. I maintain contact with Geraldine not just because of the hereditary link, however, but because of the relationship we have made during the more than twenty-five years since my first visit.

Near the end of his career, Shakespeare wrote three plays that conclude with the reunion of parents with grown children separated from them when very young. He had used a similar plot in one of his first plays, *The Comedy of Errors.* But three of his late plays, often called romances, muse with greater depth on the situation of a child who is born into one family and grows up in another. Shakespeare seems to have been fascinated by hereditary parent-child resemblance—or at any rate, many of his characters are fascinated, and many of their lines about this theme are his additions to his sources for the plays. These three plays, *Cymbeline, Pericles,* and *Winter's Tale,* are full of comments about the contrast between the transplanted child and her or his surroundings, and the genetic similarity revealed when she or he meets hereditary family. This was not the outcome of my reunion.

How different my story is from the plots of Shakespeare's romances, plays that appealed so much to my wish for reunion and produced visions of impossible harmony. What were the beliefs about family embedded in these plays? What were the contexts for those beliefs in Shakespeare's society? Is the family in these plays only determined by heredity, or is value given to adoptive parenthood?

In many of Shakespeare's plays, parents and children are heartbreakingly alienated from one another, in spite of a common heredity. As Miranda points out in *The Tempest,* another one of the late romances, "Good wombs have borne bad sons."[1] However, the plays I consider here present a mythology of blood as love and as identity (with the suggestion, sometimes, of "being identical to"). In the happy endings of both *Winter's Tale* and *Pericles,* a daughter miraculously re-creates her mother before her father's eyes, and even more miraculously, the mother returns in her own right in the final reunion. In *Cymbeline,* a sister and her brothers, separated in childhood, are mysteriously drawn to each other when they meet.

The mythology of blood in these plots has sometimes been taken for granted. Isn't the sense of similarity and unity inevitable in reunions of long-separated family members? Sometimes it occurs, but those of us who have experienced reunions differently know that often it doesn't. Nevertheless, the mythology of blood is not the only element in the family dynamics of these plays. All of them present nurturing by foster parents, and it could even be argued that all of them also present family as a construction. The plots always define the birth parents as the real parents, and some foster parents in two of the plays are murderous, but the plays all present alternative images of foster parents as actively benevolent.[2]

"Shakespeare's art," wrote the critic C. L. Barber, "is distinguished by the intensity of its investment in the human family, and especially in the continuity of the family across generations."[3] The romances restore that generational continuity in their family reunions, but in them and in other plays by Shakespeare, the investment in the family is so great that we can sometimes see adoption also creating, after discontinuity, another kind of continuity. As Angela Carter writes in *Wise Children,* a novel full of parodies of Shakespearean family plots, "If human beings don't have a family of their own, they will invent one."[4]

A belief in "blood" was part of the Renaissance worldview, even though there were conflicting views about how heredity worked. The writings of Aristotle, Hippocrates, and Galen, with their differing views of "seeds" and "blood," were still influential.[5] But early modern people also knew that, on the one hand, children were often very different from their parents, and, on the other hand, good or bad nurture had a significant impact on how children developed.[6] Nurture was often discussed with regard not only to teachers but also to wet nurses (who were thought to transmit moral qualities very literally with their milk) and teachers, and the concept is clearly relevant to the foster parents of these plays.[7] There was no formal legal procedure for adoption in this period; the terms *foster* and *adoptive* could be used interchangeably.

The relative benevolence of the foster parents in comparison to the biological parents increases from the first of these plays to the third. *Pericles,* written first, poses evil foster parents against good biological parents. Thinking his wife Thaisa is dead, Pericles gives the newborn Marina to his friends Cleon and Dionyza to raise, emphasizing that they should educate her according to her noble rank. Because she outshines their daughter in weaving, sewing, and singing, Dionyza plots Marina's murder, and only the chance kidnapping of pirates saves her—to be sold to a brothel. She is skillful enough to escape the brothel by her talents at sewing, singing, and persuading to chastity, and at the end of the play is reunited first with her father and finally with her mother, who turns out to be still alive in a temple of Diana.

Cleon and Dionyza clearly exemplify evil foster parents—although the term *parent* or *foster parent* is never used in the play to name the relation they have to Marina. The key word is *nurse.* Pericles plans to leave his daughter "at careful nursing" (3.1.80); when Dionyza thinks about how she will tell Pericles that his daughter is (as she thinks) dead, she says, "Nurses are not the fates, / To foster it, not ever to preserve" (4.3.14–15). This usage both connects the couple to the common practice of wet-nursing and points up their opposition to Marina's good foster parent—her nurse Lychorida.[8] The murder plot occurs after Lychorida's death; Dionyza tries to gain Marina's confidence by saying, "Have you a nurse of me" (4.1.25).

Lychorida is a shadowy figure who appears only in the scene where Marina is an infant, but she is credited with passing on to Marina the story of her birth, and an admirable image of her father's courage and patience.

> My father, as nurse says, did never fear,
> But cried, "Good seamen!" to the sailors,
> Galling his kingly hands, hailing ropes;
> And clasping to the mast, endured a sea
> That almost broke the deck.
>
> (4.1.55–59)

Furthermore, Lychorida's importance in transmitting memories is explicitly honored when Marina, unknowingly reunited with Pericles, says that her knowledge of her mother's ancestry and death is "As my good nurse Lychorida hath oft / Delivered weeping" (5.1.164–65).

The nurse's repetition of memories about Marina's parents and ancestry is in significant contrast to earlier versions of the Pericles story. In the ninth-century *Apollonius of Tyre,* it is only when the nurse is dying that she tells Marina's prototype her ancestry: the girl exclaims, "If any such thing had happened to me before you revealed this to me, I should have been absolutely ignorant of my ancestry and birth."[9] In Gower's *Confessio Amantis* (1554), Shakespeare's main source, there is no reference to what the nurse says about parentage, but in Twine's *The*

Patterne of Painefull Adventures (1594), which Shakespeare also used, and in George Wilkins's *The Painful Adventures of Pericles Prince of Tyre* (1608), probably a novelized version of Shakespeare's play, the girl thinks of the murderous surrogates as her parents, as in the ninth-century version, until the nurse, at the point of death, enlightens her.[10] Shakespeare's alteration not only gives more emphasis to the nurse as a purposeful bearer of family memory but also means that Marina knows her ancestry during her life and does not have to undergo the revision of identity necessary on discovering that people she thought of as her parents are not simply foster parents but also intended murderers.[11]

Heredity is dominant over environment in *Pericles,* but environment is not as weak an influence as generalizations sometimes assume. Not only is the nurse's image of Marina's parents important, but also nurture and nature must combine to produce Marina's superlative musical skills: Cleon teaches her, but when her talents far surpass those of his daughter, we might remember that Thaisa's father Simonides had, after all, called Pericles "music's master" (2.5.30) and said, after hearing him, "my ears were never better fed / With such delightful pleasing harmony" (27–28).[12] We might read the supremacy of nature over nurture in the way Marina's goodness escapes the bad influence of Cleon and Dionyza, as well as in the way she shows the courage and patience that the nurse has told her her father exemplified, but we could also credit Lychorida's influence. None of these points is explicitly made—the spectators can analyze Marina's virtues and talents however they wish.

Perhaps partly because the one good foster parent in this play, Lychorida, has such a tenuous presence, *Pericles'* focus on the father-daughter reunion is particularly intense. This long scene involves a complicated tension between recognition and lack of recognition, which puts the audience at the edge of their seats waiting for signs of the characters' discoveries. Like the early recognition scenes in Greek tragedy, this one contains a prolonged questioning that heightens emotions as it suspends the characters in time. When Pericles' ship comes to Mytilene, where Marina, who he thinks dead, is living, she is sent for simply as a gifted singer with no knowledge of their relationship, in the hope that she will cheer him up from his paralyzing melancholy. The dejected Pericles, unresponsive to anyone else, resists speaking to her at first—perhaps even pushes her away—then begins to talk to her slowly with incoherent echoes of her words. After a few more questions he says,

My dearest wife was like this maid, and such a one
My daughter might have been. My queen's square brows;
Her stature to an inch; as wandlike straight;
As silver-voiced; her eyes as jewel-like
And cas'd as richly.

(5.1.110–14)

But if he does guess who she is, he does not acknowledge it. Instead, he asks questions about her origin and education, to which she replies enigmatically. Yet even when she says, "My name is Marina" (145), reveals that she was born at sea, and names her dead nurse Lychorida, he still cannot acknowledge that she is really his daughter.

At various places in this long dialogue, he wonders if she is flesh and blood, or if this is a dream; and when she finally identifies herself as daughter to King Pericles, he does not respond directly to her until he has consulted with his friend Helicanus; then finally, almost one hundred lines after the first hint that he recognizes her, he welcomes her as "Thou that beget'st him that did thee beget" (5.1.200), and even after that wants confirmation about her mother's name. For the audience, his caution dramatizes his melancholy, but also the importance of her return to him. As Pericles says, "Truth can never be confirm'd enough" (206). The spectators know that his sense of her similarity to his lost wife is indeed a true guide to her identity—but the plot, in a sense, stops, to maintain suspense about whether he will trust this partial recognition and whether the questions that he asks will lead him to security about it.

No line in this scene gives Marina's reaction to her discovery that Pericles is her father, or to her reunion with him. This scene is written to make us imagine his point of view much more than hers; critics seldom discuss the question of when she recognizes him. Terence Cave argues that she "believes that she is healing a disturbed mind, so that his agitation as the truth gradually sinks in seems to her only a symptom of that disturbance."[13] This is the most likely interpretation, since she has not seen him since her infancy, and she asks him his name after he greets her as his daughter.

The imagery of the final scene makes the impossible suggestion that all the points of view could merge. The characters all speak of melting into each other. First Pericles imagines disappearing into Thaisa, then he imagines her disappearing into him, then Marina speaks of merging back into Thaisa, reversing Lychorida's early description of her as "this piece / Of your dead queen" (3.1.17–18):

PERICLES: [to the gods] You shall do well
That on the touching of her lips I may
Melt and no more be seen. O come, be buried
A second time within these arms! [They embrace.]
MARINA   My heart
Leaps to be gone into my mother's bosom.

(5.3.42–46)

These images of death and disappearance in reunion reenact and reverse the earlier apparent deaths of Thaisa and Marina.[14]

This play began with a scene in which Pericles, in his first quest for a bride, discovered that the princess he sought was living in incest with her father; the ending transforms this malignant mingling of identities in the family to a benign version. Physical ties are emphasized—flesh of flesh, heart and bosom, lips and arms. At the same time, the ending occurs in the temple of Diana: both Marina and Thaisa are emphatically chaste, and the night oblations that Pericles promises to Diana in thanksgiving sound to at least one critic, Janet Adelman, like a disturbing attempt to erase sexuality from the reunited family.[15] Marina's ancestry is now confirmed as noble, and accordingly she is married to Lysimachus, who was impressed with her purity when they met in the brothel, but little emotional weight is given to their relationship. The heart of the play is with the parent-child bond, emphasized as a bond of flesh and blood—and yet the parents and their daughter Marina are to be separated again at the end, when she and Lysimachus are to rule in Tyre while Pericles and Thaisa are to go to her family home in Pentapolis. However joyful parent-child reunion is, however long delayed, in this play it is still fragile: none of the other romances of family reunion is so emphatic that the family is again separated at the end. Perhaps this is another way to measure the strength of the threat of incest in *Pericles*.

In *Cymbeline*, the distribution of good and evil between biological and surrogate parents is somewhat more ambiguous than in *Pericles*. Imogen has a wicked new stepmother, who begins by denying that she is "After the slander of most stepmothers, / Evil-ey'd unto you" (1.1.71–72). But is Cymbeline, Imogen's father, good or bad as a parent?

He has brought up the orphaned and admirable Posthumus in his household, but upon Posthumus's marriage to Imogen, and his own to his new wife, Cymbeline banishes him and rages at his daughter. Is Belarius, who has been raising Cymbeline's sons (Imogen's brothers) as his own in the pastoral setting of Wales, good or bad as a foster parent? Belarius criticizes the insincerity of the court world, and gives the boys training in religion and morality. But he is a kidnapper. On the other hand, his kidnapping is in retribution for Cymbeline's injustice to him, and in general he seems morally superior to Cymbeline in spite of the kidnapping. When he says that the boys "take" him for "natural father" (3.3.107), there is also a pun on the way he is raising them with the virtuous discipline of living in nature. At the end the wicked queen dies, Belarius is reconciled to Cymbeline, and his sons return to him, and Posthumus, who has, in disguise, fought bravely on the king's side, is reconciled both to Cymbeline and to Imogen, whom (in a familiar Shakespearean motif) he had planned to kill because he suspected her—without cause—of adultery.

Cymbeline as a play goes in for excess. It multiplies to three the one "adoption" in a source, *The Rare Triumphs of Love and Fortune*, where a foundling brought up at court and unhappily in love with the princess discovers that his father is a banished, but noble, hermit.[16] Posthumus, Guiderius, and Arviragus are all presented as virtuous by both heredity and nurture. In the first scene we learn both of Posthumus's noble and heroic deceased father and of Cymbeline's breeding and education of the highly teachable orphan.

Characters are more emphatic about the power of heredity here than in *Pericles*. Belarius believes that his boys' true identity appears in their ambition and desire to fight. "How hard it is to hide the sparks of nature! . . . their thoughts do hit / The roofs of palaces, and nature prompts them / In simple and low things to prince it much / Beyond the trick of others" (3.3.79, 83–86). As Susan Baker has noted, however, the fact that Belarius himself knows they are princes can be seen as influencing his upbringing of them, and so one can argue that it is he who so prompts them, not nature—just as one could argue that Lychorida's image of Pericles' courage is more important in influencing Marina's courage than her heredity. But Baker with this reading is countering scores of critics who emphasize "blood."[17]

Posthumus, Guiderius, and Arviragus are praised in terms of their heredity by male characters, and the emphasis falls heavily on the male side of their ancestry. After nine lines about his father, all we hear of Posthumus's mother is this: "his gentle lady, / Big of this gentleman our theme, deceas'd / As he was born" (1.1.38–40). Belarius never mentions the mother from whom he kidnapped his boys; she enters the play only in Imogen's recollection—"This diamond was my mother's" (1.1.113)—as she gives it to Posthumus. Apart from this one example, when women figure in the discourse of heredity either as speaker or as subject, the effect is usually negative, until the last two scenes of the play. When the queen, for example, urges Cymbeline to refuse tribute to Rome by recalling his ancestor kings and their defeat of Caesar, the argument is presented as dubious. The one explicit counterexample to the principle of hereditary resemblance is the relation between the current queen and the son she brings to her marriage and wants to wed to Imogen. The Second Lord muses about the contrast: "a woman that / Bears all down with her brain, and this her son / Cannot take two from twenty" (2.1.53–55). There are strong suggestions that women's hereditary influence is either lacking or bad.

These suggestions are developed further—and perhaps finally exorcized—in Posthumus's odyssey away from and back to belief in his ancestry. When Posthumus loses faith in Imogen, he loses faith in his mother and in his connection to "that most venerable man, which I / did call my father" (2.5.3–4) and believes he is a bastard, and rails against what he calls "the woman's part in me" (20). However, when he repents of his plot against his wife—remarkably (for the time) converting her adultery, which he still thinks happened, into "wrying but a little" (5.1.5)—he regains faith in his family and prays, "Gods, put the strength o' th' Leonati in me!" (31). After his heroic performance in battle, his deceased family appears to him in a dream vision praying to Jupiter on his behalf. His mother finally appears and speaks about his painful birth. His father, confirming the restoration of Posthumus's heredity, says, "Great nature, like his ancestry, / Molded the stuff so fair, / That he deserv'd the praise o'th'world, / As great Sicilius' heir" (5.4.48–51). As Meredith Skura has pointed out, "Posthumus cannot find his parents in the flesh; he must find the idea of his parents . . . he must make what he can of the past, recreate his family in his dreams."[18]

A different kind of temporary alienation from womanhood takes place in the other plot that dramatizes the force of blood connections, Imogen's trip in masculine disguise to Wales—magnet for all the characters since it is pastoral and a port for travelers from Rome and (in

Shakespeare's own time) the titular land of the crown prince, who was invested in 1610, probably within a year of the play's first performance.[19] Her kidnapped brothers have not seen her since very early childhood, but all three at once feel a strong, though unclear, connection. Guiderius says that if Fidele (Imogen's name in her boy's disguise) were a woman, he would woo her in marriage; Arviragus says, "I'll love him as my brother" (3.6.72), and Imogen, guessing better than the others, says to herself, "Would it had been so, that they / Had been my father's sons!" (76–77). In their next scene, when Imogen/Fidele is mysteriously ill, both boys at once compare their love for "him" with their love for their father (Belarius), and Arviragus even says, "The bier at door, / And a demand who is't shall die, I'd say, / 'My father, not this youth'" (4.2.22–24).

Cymbeline's last scene is extravagantly full of many different kinds of partial, incomplete recognitions leading up to the very end. As Ann Thompson writes, this play allows "the audience to savour the recognitions and reversals at more than naturalistic length. . . . The pleasure we take . . . depends on our anticipation of the characters' pleasure."[20] But as she notes, precisely because there are so many reunions and recognitions in this scene, *Cymbeline*'s ending is in many ways funny. No matter how forceful the sense of some connection with another, characters often fail to recognize exactly what that connection is. There are so many characters to follow that the effect, opposite to that in *Pericles*, may be somewhat distancing for the audience, who know the connections the characters, one after another, are stumbling toward.

Cymbeline himself is slow to recognize the children who have been separated from him; but he does have the excuse that his sons have been raised without knowledge of him and his daughter is in boy's disguise. After his sons, in their own figurative disguise as Welsh gentlemen, join his warriors, and bravely save his Britons from defeat by the Romans; he hails them as "Preservers of my throne" (5.5.2) and creates them "knights o' th' battle . . . Companions to our person" (20–21). Introduced to Imogen in her disguise by the Roman she has been serving as Fidele, he says, "I have surely seen him; / His favor is familiar to me. Boy, / Thou hast looked thyself into my grace / And art mine own" (93–96). Note the etymological connection of "familiar" with family as the play provides another example of mysterious affinity stemming from "blood."

However, this affinity does not by itself dispel confusion. Although

Belarius and Arviragus do recognize the disguised boy Fidele as the same Fidele they thought was dead, they and their father don't recognize this page as Imogen until other characters guide them. The first to recognize Fidele as Imogen is not a relative but her servant Pisanio, who is, after all, the one who gave her the disguise to wear in the first place. After Posthumus strikes her, thinking she is an unrelated boy intruding on his grief for Imogen, whose attempted murder he is loudly repenting, Pisanio finally names her, and the revelation proceeds. Belarius eventually confesses his kidnapping to Cymbeline. When he says, "First pay me for the nursing of thy sons" (5.5.324), he alludes to the practice, discussed in John Boswell's chapter on Roman law in *The Kindness of Strangers,* of requiring the father of an exposed child to pay the expenses of the parents who had raised the child before returning him to the original family.[21] To prove that they are really the king's sons, he calls on a token such as is found in many classical recognition stories. Arviragus, he says, was wrapped in a "most curious mantle, wrought by th' hand / Of his queen mother" (363–64)—finally mentioning that woman. Cymbeline remembers, "Guiderius had / Upon his neck a mole, a sanguine star" (365–66), and Belarius—the adoptive parent again paying reverence to nature—says, "This is he, / Who hath upon him still that natural stamp. / It was wise nature's end in the donation / To be his evidence now" (367–70). Imogen is so delighted to find that the boys she already loves are her brothers by birth that when she is reminded that Guiderius will now inherit the throne she might have expected—"Thou hast lost by this a kingdom"—she replies, "No, my lord, / I have got two worlds by 't" (5.5.374–76). (These lines, among the few passages in this scene that were never cut,[22] have a close analogy in *Jane Eyre,* when Jane is much more happy to discover that the Rivers family are her cousins than she is to inherit money, and divides her inheritance among them. The Victorian audience's delight in Imogen and in these lines makes it quite likely that Charlotte Brontë knew them.)

Nevertheless, relations of adoption are given some tribute in the conclusion: Belarius's wrong in kidnapping the children is easily forgiven; Cymbeline says to him, "Thou art my brother" (401), and Imogen echoes, "You are my father too" (402). Blood relations are important in this play, but, as in *Pericles,* the blood tie does not lead to clear recognition without additional evidence, and adoptive relations are not erased.

The Winter's Tale is ambivalent about the adoptive father, referred to only as "Shepherd," in a different way than *Cymbeline* is. It is even more ambivalent about the birth father, Leontes, who, unlike any other father in the romances, threatens his child with death and commands her to be abandoned, because of his suspicion about her parentage. When the shepherd enters the play, he is highly preferable to King Leontes. Unlike his counterpart in the source, Greene's *Pandosto*, the shepherd at once decides to take up the abandoned babe, Perdita, even before he knows that gold has been left with her. For a while, as Carol Neely notes, he seems admirable in his lack of possessiveness of his children, including his acceptance of Perdita's teenage sexuality as he encourages her romance with Prince Florizel, disguised as a shepherd but obviously high-born.[23] His pastoral world seems, emotionally, a better environment for child rearing than the cold and suspicious world of the court, and this helps to present his nurturing of Perdita, even more clearly than Belarius's raising the boys, as an act of nature as well as of adoption. (This alliance of adoptive nurturing with nature will be developed more emphatically by George Eliot in *Silas Marner,* as a later chapter will show.)

The shepherd's evocation of his dead wife, Perdita's adoptive mother, shows an appreciation of her energy and sociability remarkable both because of Leontes' suspicion of his own wife's friendliness to others and because of the scantiness of the recollections of Euriphile, Belarius's deceased wife and the boys' past foster mother, in *Cymbeline*. Clearly there is more for a mother to do in this social pastoral than in the wild mountains of Wales:

> When my old wife liv'd, upon
> This day, she was both pantler, butler, cook,
> Both dame and servant, welcom'd all, serv'd all;
> Would sing her song and dance her turn; now here,
> At upper end o' th' table, now i' th' middle;
> On his shoulder, and his; her face o' fire
> With labor, and the thing she took to quench it
> She would to each one sip.

$$(4.4.55-62)$$

This figure is far from the wicked stepmother; nevertheless, the shepherd evokes her explicitly only as a hostess, and Perdita does not follow him in citing this adoptive mother as a precedent for her behavior.

Unlike Desdemona, who speaks of doing "such duty as my mother show'd" (1.3.188) she says, "It is my father's will I should take on me / The hostess-ship o' th' day" (4.4.71–72).

Thus, imaginatively the play makes still tenuous the role of the shepherd's wife in nurturing Perdita; Hermione's place is to be left unfilled until the very end. And the shepherd's benevolence to Perdita disappears when he sees that Polixenes, Florizel's father and the old friend whom Leontes mistakenly accused of adultery with his wife, is angry about the apparently cross-class betrothal. He calls Perdita a "cursed wretch" (4.4.458)—perhaps a relic of the myth of the curse on adoption, found in *Oedipus*—and plans to protect himself by telling him that Perdita is, as his son says, none of his "flesh and blood" (4.4.692). He shows Polixenes the birth tokens he found with Perdita, and this fear-motivated virtual disowning helps bring about the happy ending, as the shepherd, his son, Polixenes, and, in a different boat, Florizel and Perdita, all meet at Leontes' court, and Leontes and Perdita are reunited.

Critics have seldom noted that in the report of the recognition, Leontes "thanks the old shepherd, which stands by like a weather-bitten conduit of many kings' reigns" (5.2.55–57), and that, after this depersonalizing image, there is, nevertheless, a brief dialogue between the shepherd and his son after this scene, suggesting utopian possibilities of an extended cross-class family of biological and adoptive parents: the son says, "the King's son took me by the hand, and call'd me brother; and then the two kings call'd my father brother; and then the Prince my brother and the Princess my sister called my father father; and so we wept" (5.2.141–45). But clearly Perdita has been restored to Leontes as *his* daughter, and in the next scene, as he discovers that his wife is still alive, Perdita's other family is lost from sight. The characterization of the old shepherd, at this point, is designed to reduce interest in him, and to focus attention instead on the reunion of Leontes, Hermione, and Perdita. Leontes is regenerated and his family reconstituted; when Hermione asks her daughter, "Where hast thou been preserv'd? Where liv'd?" (5.3.124), the questions are generally taken as a sign of her love, but they can also be taken as questions whose answers would bring several different characters into the charmed circle of the family.

Descriptions of Perdita by observers often hint at the influence of heredity by suggesting that she is superior to her surroundings:

Florizel's father, himself a king in disguise, says, "Nothing she does or seems / But smacks of something greater than herself, / Too noble for this place" (4.4.157–59), and Florizel himself tells his father's friend Camillo, "She's as forward of her breeding as / She is i' th' rear 'our birth" (4.4.581–82). Although in other plays of Shakespeare it is clear that aristocratic heredity does not inevitably produce intelligence or moral nobility, the standard reading of this scene stresses influence of Perdita's heredity over her environment. For Shakespeare's audience, the argument goes, the royalty of this young woman emerges though she thinks she is a commoner. There are particularly complex moments when Perdita consciously plays a royal role (first, queen of the harvest, later, princess of Libya), and the audience knows that this role corresponds to her true rank. However, the play allows a more open reading of adoptee and class identity; in Shakespeare's time, Perdita was played by a commoner boy, who was able to imitate the gestures that suggested aristocracy as well as femininity. Furthermore, Baker has pointed out that the shepherd knows about her aristocratic birth, because of the clothes and gold left with her, and though he has not told her, might be imagined as having influenced her by having higher expectations of her.[24] (A partly environmental reading of the superiority of an adoptee to her surroundings will be developed by the narrator in *Silas Marner*, as I will discuss in another chapter.)

Many other speeches in *Winter's Tale* explicitly emphasize heredity in commenting on physical resemblance—and while the issue of marital fidelity is in *Pandosto*, this emphasis on resemblance is not.[25] After Leontes is first reunited with Perdita, but before he knows that Perdita is his daughter, he says that he thought of Hermione, "Even in these looks I made [admiring Perdita]" (5.1.228). When the old shepherd has produced the tokens he found with the child, observers who describe the achieved certainty that the lost daughter has been found stress "the majesty of the creature in resemblance of the mother" (5.2.36–37). In several other comments, Leontes makes father-child physical resemblance the test of a mother's fidelity to her husband. At the beginning, he is worried about whether his son looks enough like him to prove Hermione's faithfulness ("They say we are / Almost as like as eggs. Women say so, / That will say anything" [1.2.129–31]). He greets Florizel for the first time by saying, "Your mother was most true to wedlock, Prince, / For she did print your royal father off, / Conceiving you" (5.1.124–26).

A textual emphasis on physical similarity has a complicated effect in the theater; Anne Barton remarked of Shakespeare's *Twelfth Night* that it would be an extremely rare theater company that would have two characters as similar as Viola and Sebastian are supposed to be; so, in many cases of family resemblance in these plays, the play's language is in tension with the stage picture in which the actors are not really identical, and given this problem, it is interesting that Shakespeare sometimes added such emphasis to his source.[26] Perhaps the issue is analogous to the issue of how the Elizabethan audience saw boy actors as female characters: most of the time most of them focused on the female character, but for some of them most of the time and most of them some of the time (cued by textual self-consciousness) awareness of the actor's sex might surface occasionally. The plays are providing much material today for reflections on gender as a construction; they may also provide some material for reflections on family relationships as a construction as well. The audience, guided by the dialogue and the plot, will want Marina to look like Thaisa, and Perdita to look like Hermione, and will probably imagine that they look similar, if this is at all possible. Sometimes these mothers and daughters are doubled in performance, which means that the experience of the hereditary resemblance in the reunion scene is less of an imaginative construction; but then the audience would still have to use its imagination about the other figure who is brought into the play to perform the mother in middle age.

One moment in *The Winter's Tale* particularly exemplifies the ideology of resemblance as a sign of family relationship: the moment when Paulina enumerates all the details in the baby girl's face that are like Leontes' to prove Hermione's faithfulness. When Paulina refers to the baby as having "the trick of 's frown, his forehead, nay, the valley, / The pretty dimples of his chin and cheek, his smiles, / The very mold and frame of hand, nail, finger" (2.3.101–3), she is describing details that the audience must find impossible to see; indeed, most likely the baby would have been "played" by a doll, not a live baby at all. This passage briefly pictures Leontes as himself an infant (there is no other passage I know of in Shakespeare where the "pretty dimples" of an adult male are mentioned); more significantly here, it evokes the persistent tendency to *look for* details of resemblance between family members, and to imagine them into existence, especially in relation to babies. Clearly it is part of a still dominant ideology that babies are supposed to look like someone else in the family, and if that resemblance is not obvious, it will be imagined. In the theater, the question of what members of the audience believe about the baby's similarity to Leontes could be like the question of whether they believe the idealistic Gonzalo or the villainous Antonio about the island in *The Tempest*. Paulina may be credible in her description to the extent that she seems to be morally reliable in general; yet already in Jacobean times it must have been obvious that even if the baby was not as identical to Leontes as she claimed, it would not necessarily have meant that Leontes did not beget it. Some might well consider any exaggeration on Paulina's part justifiable as an attempt to save the baby and Hermione from Leontes' rage. This would then suggest how the desire to preserve a child—not just by confirming its paternity, as here, but also by flattering parents' frequent desire to see themselves re-created—may generate the ability to imagine resemblances between child and parents. Ultimately Leontes' recognition of Perdita as his daughter takes place offstage, and the play subordinates the question of whether Perdita looks like him; the emphasis on her resemblance to her mother, which has nothing to do with fidelity in marriage, testifies to the fact that Leontes has regained his belief in Hermione.

The recognition scenes of these plays in general tend to develop the perspective of the genetic fathers much more than the perspective of any one else in the large family constellation. We see the anxieties of Pericles and Leontes, and we hear their joys in much more intense language than their children's. There is no attention to how Perdita, Guiderius, and Arviragus feel about discovering a different set of parents, or how they come to terms with those they earlier thought of as their only parents. (In his rewritten last act of *Cymbeline,* George Bernard Shaw imagines that Guiderius would say, "We three are fullgrown men and perfect strangers. / Can I change fathers as I'd change my shirt?" and then refuse to inherit the throne.)[27] Nor are they much concerned with the feelings of the foster parents, though the foster fathers receive somewhat more attention than the foster mothers. With the exception of the shepherd's wife and Euriphile (significantly both deceased), foster mothers are characterized in a way congruent with the general cultural prejudice against stepmothers.[28] And although birth mothers are recovered in two of these plays, the final reunion is clearly seen from their husbands' points of view, not theirs.

Many of Shakespeare's plays can be discussed with reference to an absent mother. Romance is the genre in which he gives mothers, comparatively, the most attention, and an idealized image of motherhood is evoked most vividly in the return of Hermione in *The Winter's Tale*.[29] Her silence to Leontes may be, as Gail Paster suggests, a sign of her diminishment by patriarchal discipline (she would be justified in reproaching him, as she does at the beginning of the play for lesser faults); yet in her words of affection and attention to Perdita, suggesting that it is through concern for her daughter alone she has preserved herself, she is the mother that any separated daughter would want.[30] The fact that Hermione speaks only to Perdita, and indeed says that it was because of hope to see her that she remained alive, appeals to the fantasy that any child might have, that it was she her mother loved best after all. When she asks, "Where hast thou been preserv'd? Where liv'd?" (5.3.124), she is, in a sense, the perfect mother, because she wants to know about the other family without criticizing them, giving her daughter room to assimilate the complexity of her experience.

The idealized birth mothers Hermione and Thaisa contrast sharply to the evil foster mothers, Dionyza and Cymbeline's nameless queen. While Stephen Collins relates the negative view of stepmothers in the Renaissance to a general misogyny, these plays show that misogyny could be part of a polarized view of women.[31] Hermione and Thaisa, in their return, are as idealized as a dead or absent mother is likely to be by a child who lives with an unsatisfactory substitute. And indeed they are accompanied in the romances by a third idealized birth mother, appearing only in a dream-vision, Posthumus's mother, who died at his birth.[32] Perhaps the point is to focus dramatic attention on the birth mother (recovered at the end of *Pericles* and *Winter's Tale*) by removing motherly competition from her. When women do foster maternally in Shakespeare—Lychorida, Paulina—they are no threat to the prerogatives of the birth mother. Indeed, they present her or her memory to her daughter.

The recognition scenes of all these plays emphasize bodily connections in the family. The characters' words are often, among other things, stage directions indicating that characters should embrace. Rediscovered relatives are introduced to each other as "Flesh of thy flesh" (Pericles says this of Marina to Thaisa [5.3.47]) or "The issue of your loins . . . and blood of your begetting" (Belarius thus returns Cymbeline's sons [5.5.332–33]). The plays are full of the imagery of birth, pregnancy, and conception—most often in literal references to characters' origins.[33] This imagery reinforces the plays' mythology of "blood" and their emphasis on biological relatedness. But it is often used metaphorically, and sometimes the point of the metaphor is to make the reunion of parents and children into a rebirth or a reconception. Pericles, seeing Marina, says, "I am great with woe, and shall deliver weeping" (5.1.109). Cymbeline, recognizing his sons upon Belarius's proof, says, "O, what, am I / A mother to the birth of three? Ne'er mother / Rejoiced deliverance more" (5.5.370–72). And Pericles welcomes Marina as "Thou that beget'st him that did thee beget," using of her generative power a word primarily used of male actions. These images stand out because of the intense moments in which they are uttered, but birth/pregnancy imagery is also used at other times—Camillo alludes to folklore about pregnancy when he describes his desire to see "Sicilia" (a name that refers to both his king, Leontes, and his country) as "a woman's longing" (4.4.671) and Imogen describes her desire to see Posthumus by saying, "Never long'd my mother so / To see me first, as I have now" (3.4.2–3). Though good mothers here are largely absent or dead, imagery of biological maternity is frequent in the words of both male and female characters.[34] Concern with the link between generations is so strong that images of pregnancy and childbirth appear frequently partly because they are the most vivid way to picture that link, and occasionally images of begetting also figure. But the plays also show, and use for images, child rearing as well as childbearing. A memorable line when the young Pericles declares his love of Thaisa puts "fostering" and "blood" together and suggests fostering may be seen as just as basic.

> SIMONIDES: What, are you both pleased?
> THAISA: Yes, if you love me, sir.
> PERICLES: Even as my life my blood that fosters it.
>
> (2.5.88–90)

In each of these plays, the characters raised in a second family are described by others as extraordinary. Marina and Perdita speak exceptionally well and outshine others in beauty and talents; Guiderius and Arviragus are brave, ambitious, yet gentle and civil. Marina transcends the brothel, and Perdita surpasses all expectations for shepherdesses. Belarius comments on the boys whom he has raised, "How hard it is to hide the sparks of nature," and many critics have analyzed these plays in terms of the supremacy of heredity. The tendency of the romance genre to idealize its central characters (found also in the portrayal of Imogen and Miranda, raised by the fathers who begot them) here uses the lost child theme among its strategies. But in spite of all the blood-and-birth imagery, much of these plays' presentation of heredity could be seen as a construction mediated by the good foster parent. Belarius knows the boys are princes; the old shepherd infers that Perdita, found with fancy clothes and gold, comes from a wealthy and perhaps aristocratic background; and Lychorida passes on to Marina the image of Pericles' bravery. Perhaps each of them makes a connection comparable to Paulina's emphasis on the similarity between Leontes and his infant. Is modern psychology necessary to imagine this? The only concept required is the self-fulfilling prophecy, a dynamic arguably exemplified in many of Shakespeare's plays. Nevertheless none of these plays makes this aspect of the foster parent's role explicit, and only the dead Lychorida receives tribute for the memories she has passed on.

The family separations and reunions in Shakespeare's plays have many possible relations to early modern family psychology. Adoption was not part of the legal code under that name in Renaissance England, but there were many different ways in which children were raised by people who did not give birth to them, and the word might even be used, as it is when the countess in *All's Well that Ends Well* says, "Adoption strives with nature, and choice breeds / A native slip to us from foreign seeds" (1.3.142–43).[35] The word was also familiar from various biblical passages, especially in the Epistles of Paul, where Christians are referred to as adopted children of God.[36] But the events in the plays also connect with everyday family experience in Shakespeare's time. Gail Paster writes, in *The Body Embarrassed*, that Perdita's experience is "a version, romantically heightened, of what happened soon after birth to countless babies in the wet-nursing culture . . . inexplicable extrusion from the birthing chamber, enforced alienation from the maternal breast, and a journey to the unknown rural environment of a foster family lower in station than its own. Even though the birth parents knew where they had placed their baby and occasionally visited it, the physical and social separation of the two environments was virtually as complete as it is here."[37] A similar analysis could be made, though with more qualifications, of Marina's, Guiderius's, and Arviragus's experiences. Perhaps these events glamorize also the many other family separations common in Shakespeare's culture; from about ten years of age on, upper-class children might be sent to other families to learn manners and to bond dynasties, middle-class children to learn trades and professions, and lower-class children to become servants.[38] Here these ordinary separations are transformed into the more dramatic separations of abandoning, kidnapping, and shipwrecking. Perhaps these romance plots also provided a fantasy transformation for the more permanent separations caused by frequent mortality, which was much higher than ours for both parents and children, and highest, it seems, in London, where the plays were performed. At the beginning of the seventeenth century, the life expectancy in London was only 22.3 years, and "by age twenty forty-seven percent of women born in London had suffered the death of their fathers."[39] Furthermore, infant and child death rates were, in general, high in early modern Europe. "An infant in the first four months of life had in general a 20 to 40 per cent chance of dying before his or her first birthday. . . . the chances of surviving to age twenty were in general no better than fifty-fifty."[40] Shakespeare's own son Hamnet had died at the age of eleven.

Members of the original audiences in different family circumstances probably differed to some extent in their responses to these plays, just as do members of the audience in different circumstances today. Paster has argued, for example, that the emphasis on the difference in behavior between Perdita and her foster family and on characters' identification of her with nobility "offers a powerful counternarrative for the specific fears and repressed anxieties of the wet-nursed child."[41] We could imagine that the play could also soothe anxieties of parents of wet-nursed children. Similarly, the emphasis on resemblances between biological family members might have reinforced the sense of solidarity between those who had been wet-nursed or fostered out in childhood and their parents.

On the other hand, what of the many audience members whose parents had died early and who had been raised by stepparents? How important was it to them to emphasize their connections with their deceased parents? How much did their stepparents take on parental roles in their imagination? The orphaned Posthumus, who has been raised by Cymbeline, is left without a household again when he is banished for marrying Imogen; in absence from her, his suspicion of women alienates him from her as well as the memory of his parents ("That most venerable man which I / Did call my father was I know not where / When I was stamp'd" [2.5.3–5]).[42] How much does this dramatize anxieties of the time? For some members of the audience, who could never hope for a reunion in real life, Posthumus's dream-vision of his family could have served as a reassurance of their continued connection with their family, but Posthumus's marriage to Imogen reconnects him with his foster-father Cymbeline as well as with her. In *All's Well*, Helen's strong bond with the Countess of Rousillion, her foster mother as well as Bertram's mother, coexists with her frequent references to her dead father (even though at 1.1.84 she claims to have forgotten him to emphasize her obsession with Bertram).

Adults raised by stepparents could have enjoyed the wish fulfillment of the reunions with birth parents presented in these plays, but on the other hand they might also have drawn another kind of satisfaction—as could parents who were raising stepchildren—from the fact that actors seldom have as much similarity as the characters they are playing are supposed to have. The doubleness of effect—characters are biologically related, and the text tells us to see them as similar; actors are not related, and probably don't look very similar—is analogous to the doubleness in the meaning of family terms such as *father, mother* that stepfamilies and adoptees have to deal with. The term *role* is used in connection with parenthood, in ordinary language today, almost as much as it is used in relation to sex and gender. Is there a theatrical aspect to parenthood? Or is this usage a sign of inauthenticity? What are the strengths and limitations of the formulation, "The real parents are those who act like parents"? Leontes does not act like a parent when he commands Perdita to be exposed. Does Pericles when he leaves Marina at Tharsus? For much of the rest of both plays, penance is the only way these fathers have of acting like a parent.

The plots of these plays, somewhat like contemporary American adoption law, are largely structured to limit a family to one "real" set of parents, male and female, and the conclusion of *Pericles*—following the play in which the good foster parent, Lychorida, appears only briefly and the wicked foster parents are more vivid—stays closest to this model. But knowing something about the frequent uses of nursing, fostering out, and other varieties of child care beyond the nuclear family in Renaissance England, as well as the high infant death rate, may help to explain one of the most vexed aspects of this play: why is Pericles not only grief-stricken, but also virtually immobilized and apparently also in need of prolonged penance after he hears about his daughter's death from Dionyza, since he acted in good faith believing that she and Cleon were responsible people?

It may well be that parents whose children died while in someone else's house had a particularly complicated sense of self-blame. They were following the accepted pattern in their society, but was that why their child had died? Within England, Gottlieb notes, while wet-nursing was often criticized, sending children away after seven was not openly questioned. But at least one Italian observer felt that this showed "the want of affection in the English."[43] When Pericles assumes that he must give Marina to others to raise in their home, instead of taking her and Lychorida or another nurse with him—the years he stays away pass quickly in Gower's act 4 chorus—perhaps those whose children had died, or who feared their children might, while away, had particular reasons for interest in his story. Both the death of children and their boarding out might well have been especially frequent in 1608–9, the probable first year of *Pericles*' performance; plague closed the theaters part of that time.[44] Perhaps it is because such ordinary behavior on his part—rather than the insane jealousy of Leontes, for example—preceded disaster, that *Pericles* was, apparently, one of the most popular Shakespearean plays of its day.[45]

While adopted children in these three plays all have happy endings, there are at least two other places in Shakespeare where the concept of adoption appears with negative connotations. When Brabantio gives up on his daughter Desdemona, after her defense of her marriage to Othello, the disgusted father says, "I had rather to adopt a child than get it" (1.3.194). The idea, if not the word, is repeated by another disgusted father, Leonato of *Much Ado about Nothing,* when his daughter's fiancé has broken up their wedding by accusing her of unchastity, and this speech may gloss Brabantio's meaning:

> Why had I not with charitable hand
> Took up a beggar's issue at my gates,
> Who, smirched thus and mir'd with infamy,
> I might have said, "No part of it is mine;
> This shame derives itself from unknown loins"?

$$(4.1.130-34)$$

The second passage, and more elliptically the first, convey the sense that because parents identify more closely with children of their own blood, it is easier to disown an adoptee—as indeed the old shepherd does with Perdita when she has offended Polixenes.

These are striking passages to find in a culture where adoption was not regulated by law, and their presence is particularly interesting because adoption is not part of the plot of these plays, and because their world seems closer to that of Shakespeare's audience than do the worlds of the romances, which are all, in spite of references the audience would have found contemporary, placed in the distant past. They suggest that the adopted child could be a second-class child, of whom not much was expected, who could be easily disowned—an image closely related to the idea of the adoptee as cursed. The fantasy elements of *The Winter's Tale* contain and then reject this view.

Perdita, thought to be illegitimate and brought up from childhood by another family, unconnected to her first family, and unaware of her own origin, is the character in these plays whose situation is most similar to that of modern adoptees under the closed-record system; she is probably also the most familiar, since *Winter's Tale* is the play among these three that has in recent years been most performed and taught. However, many adoptees reading Shakespeare might identify with a figure very different from those I have been discussing: Edmund in *King Lear,* a play much more often taught and performed than the three romances together. *Lear,* unlike *Oedipus* or the romances, confronts birth out of wedlock, significant in this discussion as one of the key social phenomena that the modern institution of adoption was designed to correct, and one of the sources of the emphasis on secrecy involved in that institution in the United States, where birth records are legally unavailable to most adoptees.[46] Although a full treatment of illegitimacy in Shakespeare is beyond the scope of this book, I want briefly to discuss the topic in relation to the image of the possibly or certainly illegitimate adoptee, using further the contrast between Perdita and Edmund as representative figures of the literary adoptee and the literary bastard. Illegitimacy is handled differently in *Lear* than in modern adoption, but there is enough continuity in the issues for an adoptee to find Edmund's words and situation resonant. Indeed, the contemporary adoptee activist group Bastard Nation reprinted Edmund's most famous speech, quoted below, in an early issue of its newsletter under the heading "Shakespeare on Bastardy."[47] Edmund is introduced in the first scene of the play by Gloucester, his father, who immediately identifies him as a source of shame: "His breeding, sir, hath been at my charge. I have so often blush'd to acknowledge him, that now I am braz'd to 't" (1.1.9–11). Gloucester jokes that "there was good sport at his making, and the whoreson must be acknowledg'd" (1.1.23–24), but he has not really seen much of Edmund, and thinks he can keep him under control: "He hath been out nine years, and away he shall again" (32–33). Like many other critics, I read these lines as intended to show Gloucester's insensitivity, and suggesting his contribution to Edmund's sense of injustice. We never see the family where Edmund spent those nine years, and it is not clear whether his mother, who is never named, is still alive.

Edmund's most notable speech, which relishes imagining his conception in a way rather similar to his father's, challenges the law that disinherits for birth out of wedlock. This is one of those moments in Shakespeare when momentarily a cultural outsider challenges the assumptions that exclude him or her:

> Why bastard? Wherefore base?
> When my dimensions are as well compact,
> My mind as generous, and my shape as true,
> As honest madam's issue? Why brand they use
> With base? With baseness? Bastardy? Base, base?
> Who, in the lusty stealth of nature, take
> More composition and fierce quality
> Than doth within a dull, stale, tired bed
> Go to th' creating a whole tribe of fops
> Got 'tween asleep and wake? Well, then,
> Legitimate Edgar, I must have your land.
>
> (1.2.6–16)

Edmund is protesting a general cultural prejudice against bastards, a belief in their moral evil and their physical and mental disability, and the law forbidding them from inheriting.[48] Belief in their disability he can easily refute, but suspicion of their moral condition he confirms. At the time the play was written, the stigma of illegitimacy had recently increased. Inheritance law had been tightening up so that provisions previously made for children born out of wedlock were lessening; on the other hand, largely because of economic difficulties that made the responsibilities of married fatherhood seem too great, the number of births out of wedlock were increasing.[49] A few years earlier, Shake-

speare had written *Measure for Measure,* in which at least one character feels that illegitimacy is getting so out of hand that fornication
should be punished by the death penalty.

Edmund's speech begins, "Thou, nature, art my goddess" (1.2.1). It
is a commonplace of criticism now that the beginning of the speech is a
kind of pun on the use of "natural" to mean illegitimate, as well as a
contribution to the play's dramatized debate between different concepts
of nature and of human nature—a debate that will continue in later literature, often in connection with adoption, as we will see in the chapter
on George Eliot. The discrimination Edmund speaks against here can be
seen as the historical antecedent of the discrimination that adoptees
experience when their birth certificates are sealed and they cannot get
information about their medical and other family history. This connection (though without explicit reference to Edmund) was made when
Bastard Nation took its name. Lack of this information may seem triv-
ial by contrast to economic disinheritance—though on occasion it can
be lethal—but the most significant tie is in the persistence of the possibility of cultural stigma that can be taken seriously enough to provide
both legal and psychological consequences.

Edmund is never adopted, but there are details in the play that hint
parodically at substitute families for him: when he betrays his father
(for trying to help Lear) to the duke of Cornwall, Cornwall, soon to
blind Gloucester, says, "I will lay trust upon thee; and thou shalt find a
dearer father in my love" (3.5.25–26). Edmund then develops liaisons
with both Regan and Goneril, usually now played by women old
enough to suggest, in those so minded, an Oedipal scenario but also
linked with him because both of them have been called bastard by
Lear.[50] At the end they kill each other over him; mortally wounded himself when he discovers this, he says, "Yet Edmund was belov'd"
(5.3.243). No matter how bitterly or mockingly he speaks, it is hard not
to read this as a wish for a kind of life different from the "lusty stealth
of nature" and "fierce quality" he earlier gloried in, and this suggestion
of a change in Edmund is confirmed when he says, "Some good I mean
to do, / Despite of mine own nature" (247–48) and tries, though unsuc-
cessfully, to stop the death he had ordered for Cordelia. In the London
National Theatre production of 1997, he also tries to hold on to
Goneril's dead body, but is pulled away.

Recently Garry Leonard has compared the passive image of the
adoptee in Albee's plays to the energetic image he sees in Edmund as

indicating the destructiveness of the closed adoption system.[51] Perdita, by contrast, spends much of the play in a closed adoption system of her own, neither as passive as Albee's adoptee nor as rebellious as Edmund; she adapts, doing gracefully and creatively what is expected of both adoptees and females. It seems to be a difference already established in the Renaissance that the image of the bastard is mostly gendered masculine and the image of the adoptee is more often gendered feminine. In Renaissance drama, 90 percent of the bastards are male (including Shakespeare's Caliban, Don John in *Much Ado about Nothing,* and the Bastard, as speech headings usually name him, in *King John*).[52] As a word of insult, *bastard* is much more often applied to men, then and now—though Leontes applies it to the infant Perdita, everyone knows that he is wrong in doing so. The only males in Shakespeare for whom both birth and foster parents are alive are kidnapped: Guiderius and Arviragus. Both Marina and Perdita are transferred to foster parents in circumstances—for all their differences—somewhat more like that of the adoptee today. There have usually been more girls adopted than boys, and organizations of adoptees usually contain more women than men; the founders of Bastard Nation wanted an organization that would draw more men—one of the reasons they chose their name—and they seem to have succeeded.[53]

Perdita herself has been called a bastard, not only by Leontes but also, in effect, by the old shepherd upon first seeing her: "Sure, some scape. Though I am not bookish, yet I can read waiting-gentlewoman in the scape. This has been some stair-work, some trunk-work, some behind-door-work" (3.3.70–73). Then he moves outside the realm of leering or gossip to the realm of sympathy, anticipating the language— "O, she's warm!" (5.3.109)—used to describe Hermione's rediscovered life: "they were warmer that got this than the poor thing is here. I'll take it up for pity" (3.3.73–74). However, like a bastard, Perdita is, for much of the play, denied inheritance from her genetic parents, and she also, at least once, voices a belief in social equality that is sometimes associated with the subversive voice of the bastard:

> I was about to speak, and tell him plainly
> The selfsame sun that shines upon his court
> Hides not his visage from our cottage, but
> Looks on alike.

> (4.4.443–46)

Yet her occasional alliance with nature leaves many social and cultural categories untouched: Perdita is uncomfortable with flowers called nature's bastards because of her own view of what is rightfully part of nature:

> the fairest flow'rs o' th' season
> Are our carnations and streak'd gillyvors,
> Which some call nature's bastards. Of that kind
> Our rustic garden's barren, and I care not
> To get slips of them . . .
> . . . .
> . . . For I have heard it said
> There is an art which in their piedness shares
> With great creating nature.
>
> (4.4.81–88)

The defense that Polixenes uses of the grafting that created these flowers is a defense that can also be made of adoption as itself natural. The defense can be made as well of cross-class marriage, which Polixenes will soon, ironically, reject for humans when he finds out his son is engaged to this apparent shepherdess.

> nature is made better by no mean
> But nature makes that mean. So, over that art
> Which you say adds to nature, is an art
> That nature makes. You see, sweet maid, we marry
> A gentler scion to the wildest stock,
> And make conceive a bark of baser kind
> By bud of nobler race. This is an art
> Which does mend nature, change it rather, but
> The art itself is nature.
>
> (4.4.89–97)

Both characters link themselves to nature: Edmund links himself and nature and bastardy in opposition to "custom," while Perdita—who of course does not know she is adopted—links herself and nature in opposition to bastardy and "art." Nature is a key issue in conceptualizing both the adoptee and the bastard, for both fit into some definitions of nature and not to others.

Both mix parents in an unconventional way—whether by having both birth and adoptive parents, or by having parents who are imperfectly "mixed" because of not being married—or, if one person is both, in both ways.[54] Both the adoptee and the Renaissance bastard are outsiders on the inside to the family in which they are raised because they violate the norm that children should be born of sexual reproduction to the parents who raise them.[55] And since both of them have biological links to other parents, they both may raise questions about the relative importance of heredity and environment.

While for Edmund his individual nature is more the issue than his inherited nature, Shakespeare's characters often see similarities between bastards and their birth fathers: for example, in *King John,* the title character and his queen both see physical resemblance between the character known as the Bastard and Richard Coeur de Lion, and are eager to knight him and sign him up for a soldier and change his name from Philip Faulconbridge to Richard Plantagenet. In *Titus Andronicus,* Aaron emphasizes the similarity to himself—especially in blackness—of his infant son by Tamora.

But occasionally such resemblances, like those involved in the adoption plots of the romances, could be interpreted as mediated by environment. Might it have influenced Lady Faulconbridge's upbringing of Philip that she knew he was begotten by a king? Might Edmund's evil come not so much from his mother's viciousness, as Edgar later charges, as from Gloucester's neglect? When Prospero greets Caliban, the bastard who is in a sense his foster child, as "Thou poisonous slave, got by the devil himself / Upon thy wicked dam" (1.2.321–22), he is demonizing the birth parents even more literally than usual, but there is no reason for the audience to take his curse as a statement of fact within the world of the play. Prospero, who has in effect raised him, insists that he is someone "on whose nature / Nurture can never stick" (4.1.188–89). But his descriptions of Caliban are among the lines in Shakespeare most often considered as self-fulfilling prophecy. Could those much-debated lines "This thing of darkness I / Acknowledge mine" (5.1.278–79) have as one of their meanings partial acceptance of responsibility for Caliban's behavior?

And as with adoption, onstage discussions of physical resemblance in bastardy are inevitably in tension with a stage picture in which the actors are not really identical. The audience will want Aaron's infant to look like Aaron, but the family resemblance they perceive is, like adoption, a construction. Heredity is mediated by imagination on the stage, as in Shakespeare its effect is often mediated by the character who, in a tragedy, sends the child away, or in another genre, raises the child as someone special or passes on the family stories. With bastardy as well as with adoption, in studying Shakespeare's treatment of heredity we are dealing with his treatment of ideas and prejudices about heredity rather than with his treatment of heredity itself.

Alison Findlay ends her book about bastards in Renaissance drama by discussing the affinities between bastards and theater; there are affinities between adoptees and theater as well. The plot of adoption or fostering and reunion is theatrical because it is the matter of fantasy. As Marina says, "If I should tell my history, it would seem / Like lies disdain'd in the reporting" (5.1.118–19). Furthermore, the theme of multiple identity, which adoptees incarnate, is an inherently theatrical one. Perdita by no means glories in this condition, nor does she even know about it for most of the play, but she might say about it, as she says about a more limited adventure, in which she will pretend to have yet another set of parents, "I see the play so lies / That I must bear a part" (4.4.657–58). Adoption, like plays where kings are sometimes deposed and are always played by commoners, can destabilize classes and hierarchy; if we see the self as defined by genetics, then the adoptee is, in a sense, unconsciously acting when behaving as the child of adoptive parents; if we see the self as defined by environment, then the reunited adoptee is acting a role in behaving as a child to birth parents. If neither defines the self to the exclusion of the other, adoption, like theatrical cross-dressing—or indeed like any successful acting—reveals again the extent to which the self is a construction.

Like Shakespeare's recognition scenes, recent narratives of reunions between adoptees and their birth relatives almost always include some words about physical similarity. Sometimes they are inevitable because the similarity is so obvious. But they are, also, part of the script expected at such occasions, and they may also be an attempt to strengthen the relationship, like Paulina's words to Leontes. Shakespeare's plays are among the texts that wrote these scripts.

But unlike his plays, many searches provide meetings in which similarity is not so obvious. Even if physical similarity exists, contrast of personality or values may be the strongest impression. Reunions—or subsequent meetings—often frustrate any wish to find spiritual kin with whom communication is effortless. In my contact with my birth mother,

I had to accept her differences, see what I could learn about her as she is, work on bridging the gap between us. It was not so different from any other relationship, except that it was a larger gap than in most, and—even though Geraldine has other children, and I had another, closer, mother—we each somehow had irreplaceable roles in each other's lives. Perhaps physical similarity could be seen as a metaphor for that bond.

Before my work on adoption in literature, I wrote about a different kind of genealogy, women writers' uses of Shakespeare.[56] Like adoption, and like adoptees' relationships with birth parents, study of George Eliot's and Charlotte Brontë's rewriting of Shakespeare's plots and cultural image involves bridging a gap, in this case a gap between historical periods and genres whose literary relations are not often discussed. Partly because Shakespeare's plays are so much concerned with families, including adoptive families, women writers' interests in Shakespeare often coalesce with interest in adoption; for example, as I will discuss later, *Silas Marner* and *Daniel Deronda* can both be read as stories about why the plot of *Winter's Tale* doesn't always work. But perhaps the greatest significance that my previous writing has for my thought about adoption is in providing another model for how adoptees can construct their own genealogies. Writers look back on earlier literature and create their own literary tradition by what they write. Adoptees also can construct their own genealogy in deciding what is meaningful to them in both of their families as they know and imagine them. Thus I write Geraldine into my genealogy—not just in our physical connection, not in any of our obvious beliefs and interests—but most importantly in our basic openness to relationship.

Four ❧ Adoption in the Developing British Novel: Stigma, Social Protest, and Gender

In the survey of English literature that I took in my sophomore year of college, the only novel we read was *Tom Jones*. We never considered Tom as an adoptee. Ironically, the teacher of this course, Mrs. Giovannini, was known to be an adoptive mother.

The course was not generally considered exciting. My roommate and then best friend recounted to me a conversation in which Mrs. Giovannini mentioned her daughter sleeping in class. "She's her mother's daughter," my roommate joked. Embarrassed by her reflex witticism, she said to me that "the awful thing is that she isn't her mother's daughter." I, who had told her I was adopted and was used to thinking of my adoptive mother as simply my mother, said nothing.

How many children had Mrs. Giovannini? Was Tom Jones Squire Allworthy's son or not? What was my friend saying about me? And whose daughter was I?

Many historians and literary critics associate the rise of the nuclear family with the rise of the novel. Christopher Flint has even argued that the patterns of narrative "formally manifest" the social mechanisms of the family.[1] But while Flint argues that there is affinity because "Both narrative and genealogy usually develop in linear fashion," in many novels, including those to be discussed in this chapter, genealogy is much more puzzling and jagged than linear in its presentation.[2] Disturbed genealogies and displaced children are common in the eighteenth- and nineteenth-century British novel. While these novels may show the family in pieces, they also show various family-making processes at work, depend for much of their effect on assumptions about the family, and suggest the importance of some elements of the family by showing unhappiness resulting from their absence.

The focus on displaced children in the eighteenth- and nineteenth-century novel was not simply an artifact of narrative structure. During the time of the Industrial Revolution, more children *were* displaced. In late-eighteenth-century England and into the nineteenth century, the illegitimacy rate was on the rise. There was an abrupt series of increases after 1836; Laslett suggests that it was triggered by the English Poor Law of 1834, but a general rise in illegitimacy occurred across Europe at this time.[3] The novels discussed in this chapter and the next responded both to the increased sentimentalism of the family for those who could afford it and to the increased fragmentation of the family for those who could not.

Readers knew the traditional plot in which genealogies are clarified and birth parents are found. For one thing, they read Shakespeare, who was idealized and frequently read and performed in the late eighteenth century and the nineteenth. *Cymbeline* was very popular with the Victorians, and *Winter's Tale* was known well enough to have an impact too. But even more importantly, readers knew the story of Moses' adoption and many fairy tales that deal with similar themes. Moses as a foundling was on the official seal of the London Foundling Hospital; and depictions of his adoption were in Gibbs's 1836 Kitto Bible and in paintings given to the hospital by Francis Hayman and by Hogarth.[4] Like my roommate (a good friend whose place in my life has been much more positive than this story suggests), they probably thought of birth parents as the only real parents. At the same time they knew that children could be raised by other people, and apparently they were more interested than Sophocles' or Shakespeare's audiences in the psychology of this process. Although there was no legal form for adoption in England in this period, informal adoptions, in which the word was used, did occur. These de facto adoptions, as George Behlmer calls them, were sometimes beneficent and sometimes not.[5] As Penny Martin writes, "Anybody could give or sell a child to somebody else and anybody could take on a child—without it acquiring any legal rights within a new family."[6]

Many of the novels I shall discuss have been considered under the category of orphan literature. Oliver Twist, Pip of *Great Expectations*, and Jane Eyre are orphaned. Evelina's mother is dead, as is Esther Summerson's father, and for most of the book their living parents do not acknowledge them.

But Oliver, Pip, Jane, Esther, and Evelina, as well as others I shall discuss, are all at some point adopted, though not through a legal procedure. Considering them as adoptees allows us to see them more contextually. We can compare their relationships with their surrogate parents. We can look at similarities between Oliver Twist and Tom Jones, or among Evelina, Fanny Price, and Esther Summerson. We can explore the impacts of heredity and nurture as they are juxtaposed in these novels and consider the allusions to, and revisions of, traditional adoption plots.

The genre of the novel provides an opportunity to develop the possibilities of adoption plots much further than the drama or the fairy tale. Omniscient and first-person narration give a chance to explore more complexity and development of feeling, about relatives by both birth and adoption, and about the condition of being displaced and different. Such feeling is less likely to be expressed on stage (the speeches in a play have to be relatively short, with less room for the musing of a character to himself in solitude). Often novels present themselves as making a more "realistic," contemporary gloss on a literary pattern: sometimes novels use the expected plot of family discovery as a myth, structuring readers' expectations that the novel can play off against. We may anticipate a reunion that never happens. Or perhaps it happens with results very different from those the characters or the audience expects. Using part of the reunion plot can lead to the conclusion that the adoptive family turns out to be more important than the myth of discovery suggests.

At the same time, the novel may go against a different kind of audience attitude, based more on the social stratification of the historical world than on drama and fairy tale. One of the main impulses of the novel has been an attack on stigma.[7] Many eighteenth- and nineteenth-century novels dramatize the adoptee's struggle against stigma, most often the stigma of illegitimacy but sometimes simply the stigma of being a poor dependent, not a birth child of the family. Frequently, minor characters articulate prejudices against the adoptee (or the future adoptee). Sometimes the narrator, or another character, explicitly argues against those prejudices. Usually the prejudiced characters are caricatures who are clearly undercut. Tom Jones and Oliver Twist fight back against this stigma—very literally. Most female adoptees, such as Esther Summerson, Evelina, and Fanny Price, respond to prejudice by trying very hard to be good. The one female adoptee who initially follows the male pattern is Jane Eyre, who fights back against the attacks from her cousins and her Aunt Reed. The one male adoptee who follows the female pattern is Daniel Deronda, as we will see in the next chapter.

In *Tom Jones* and *Oliver Twist* explicitly and in some other novels less explicitly, adoption plots are occasions for novelists to explore questions about human nature: Are people basically good? How much of character is heredity, how much is environment, how much is a matter of the individual? Dickens's narrator argues with philosophers, and Fielding's characters, especially the tutors Thwackum and Square, stage philosophical arguments in which both the conservative Thwackum and the Enlightenment-oriented Square are wrong because they both neglect "natural goodness of heart."[8] The word *nature* and its derivatives are threaded through the fabric of these novels. Evelina, for example, says of her relationship with her birth father, "Must I now be deaf to the voice of Nature if I could endure to be abandoned without regret?"[9] Esther's reunion with her mother in *Bleak House* involves "the only natural moments of her [birth mother's] life."[10] In both of these examples, as often in Shakespeare, nature refers to an inevitable emotional impact of biological relationships. This view, as also in Shakespeare, can be expressed in negative terms, as when Brownlow in *Oliver Twist* calls Oliver's legitimately born half-brother "unnatural" (332) because of his behavior.[11] On the other hand, *nature* can be deliberately revised to refer to nongenetic relationships. Estella refers to "my nature; the nature formed within me"[12] in analyzing the influence on her of her adoptive mother, Miss Havisham.

Tom Jones and *Oliver Twist*: The Stigmatized Boy and Human Nature

Tom Jones, written in 1749 soon after the establishment of the Foundling Hospital in London by Sir Thomas Coram in 1739, is very much involved in attacking the stigma on bastardy, which was one of the main reasons for the abandonment of foundlings and the controversy about care of them. The rich and generous Squire Allworthy finds an infant in his bed and decides to raise him (this is referred to as adoption on pp. 116, 355, and 774). The family assumes that he is the child of a woman who recently worked in his household as a nurse and a schoolmaster whose servant she had been. Allworthy defends Tom against the prejudices of Mrs. Wilkins, his maid, who says that "it is, perhaps, better for such creatures to die in a state of innocence, than to grow up and imitate their mothers, for nothing better can be expected of them" (35); against the attacks of his sister Bridget's husband, who quotes the Bible and the legal term "children of nobody" (70); and against the attacks by Bridget's son, Blifil, who picks fights with Tom, calling him such names as "beggarly bastard" (112). When Tom falls in love with Sophia, her prejudiced parents oppose the match and design her for Blifil.

While Tom womanizes with many others as well and gets himself thrown out of the Allworthy house, throughout he is characterized as a man of good nature and generosity. He talks Allworthy and a constable out of sending Molly Seagrim to the workhouse because of her pregnancy; Tom takes the blame for their affair, though Fielding presents Molly as his determined seducer (151, 166). He persuades another man to marry a poor young woman he has made pregnant. This good deed is directly contrasted with his companion's casual woman-blaming: "She was a little hungry, it seems, and so sat down to dinner before grace was said, and so there is a child coming for the Foundling Hospital." Tom retorts, "Prithee, leave thy stupid jesting. Is the misery of these poor wretches a subject of mirth?" (667).

After a brief scare suggesting that he might have unknowingly slept with his mother, the end of the novel reveals that Tom is actually the now dead Bridget's son from a premarital affair. Learning this, and other information about Tom's love of him and the deception of others, Allworthy is reconciled to Tom, who at the end of the novel is happily married to Sophia.

Illegitimacy is a key issue in this as in several other novels I discuss in this chapter. Since the solution to the plot comes from a letter from a deceased woman, Fielding could have made it contain the information that Bridget and her lover had been secretly married, but he did not choose to do so.[13] Tom is presented as a kind of case study of the unfairness of the stigma of bastardy, since the characters who maintain that stigma are so ridiculous and ill-willed. Tom's promiscuity is often mingled with affection and concern for the women involved; he is fre-

quently presented as submitting to their seductions, which are understandable since he is so handsome and charming. The defense of bastardy here is in many ways an attack on what is considered cold and
prudish moralism. The characters' language usually generalizes so
much that it is clear Fielding aims not just to defend Tom but also to
comment on a social issue.

How foundlings and illegitimate children should be treated was a
topical question at the time *Tom Jones* was published. Fielding's friend
Hogarth was a strong supporter of the Foundling Hospital and encouraged his artist friends to donate paintings to the hospital, which
became, in effect, London's first art gallery.[14] From 1747 on, visitors
came to observe the children and the paintings at the same time. Fielding, a London judge as well as a novelist, was proud of such British phil-
anthropy, and the defense of Tom can be seen as an intervention against
those who believed that the Foundling Hospital encouraged immoral-
ity. Nevertheless it is not clear that the novel is consistent about the
treatment of foundlings without upper-class ancestry. We never hear
about what happened to Molly Seagrim's child, after she is saved from
Bridewell and goes back to her family, although we hear that another
man might have been the father. Should we assume that it was cared for
in her family?[15]

The treatment of women in this novel is troubling in ways that made
it a strange choice for a sophomore survey at a woman's college in 1962,
just before feminist criticism. Tom is without an adoptive mother, so
that Allworthy can appear in more patriarchal preeminence. Tom's
(unacknowledged) mother Bridget is made fun of at the beginning
because she is apparently an "old maid" over thirty (one of the reasons,
presumably, for the use of her first name in the twentieth-century
British novel *Bridget Jones's Diary,* by a more recent Fielding, Helen).
She dies offstage of the gout, while the most sympathetic characters of
the novel, including Tom, are concerned, instead, about Allworthy's
severe illness. No one ever suggests, after the secret is disclosed or
before, that Tom looks like her or has anything in common with her. As
van Boheemen says, her "dissembling hypocrisy is the origin of all
Tom's troubles," but these crimes are punished more obviously in her
also dissembling son Blifil than in her; the novel avoids focusing on
her.[16] As for the minor female characters, Fielding enjoys making them
ridiculous in fighting with each other or some other way. So many
women are ridiculed here that the ridicule may be defensive;

van Boheemen may well be right in saying that the feminine is fearsome to Fielding.[17]

Heredity in general is given surprisingly little emphasis in *Tom Jones*. Near the end, Allworthy finally discovers that Tom's genetic father was a young man named Summer, who had formerly lived in his house: "a finer man, I must say, the sun never shone upon; for, besides the handsomest person I ever saw, he was so genteel, and had so much wit and breeding" (831). Before dying of smallpox, this man, whom Allworthy had treated as a son and who was himself the son of an admired friend, a clergyman, had begotten Tom. The reader can certainly infer that Tom has inherited Summer's looks and wit, but no one ever comments on this; Tom is told about his heredity offstage, so to speak, and we never hear him display interest in his genetic father. The main effect of this revelation is that it solidifies Tom's relationship with Allworthy, who now names him his heir; this new status removes Squire Western's opposition to Tom's marriage with Sophia. In all likelihood, as John Sutherland has shown, Summer—whose name was frequently given to illegitimate children because many were conceived at summer festivals—was having an affair with Bridget Allworthy and Jenny Jones at the same time, in an anticipation of Tom's own promiscuity, but like other aspects of his resemblance to Summer, this is not made explicit.[18] In the penultimate paragraph of the novel, Fielding emphasizes nurture over nature: "Whatever in the nature of Jones had a tendency to vice has been corrected by continual conversation with this good man, and by his union with the lovely and virtuous Sophia" (870).

One character in the novel does imply a strong negative influence of heredity on Tom, but this man is so lacking in credibility that he is simply referred to as "the pettifogger" (375), and his story about Tom is one that readers know to be false: "he's the bastard of a fellow who was hanged for horse-stealing. He was dropped at Squire Allworthy's door, where one of the servants found him in a box so full of rain-water, that he would certainly have been drowned, had he not been reserved for another fate."

Another passage of the novel emphasizes further that Fielding is more interested in the paternity of the mind than of the body: he develops at great length the image of the author as father of his book—"the care, the fondness, with which the tender father nourishes his favourite, till it be brought to maturity, and produced into the world" (494)—and he praises such "paternal fondness" for its distance from "absolute instinct" and closeness to "worldly wisdom." This attitude is in keeping with the sensibility of his time. In the early and middle eighteenth century, under the influence of John Locke and the Enlightenment, authors were more likely to view the child as a tabula rasa and emphasize the importance of education; hence the adoptive parents' potential for developing the child was great. Later on there would be more focus on the child's own feelings and insight, as well as the child's own distinctive inborn hereditary tendencies.[19]

Charles Dickens, who will be the dominant figure in this chapter, was influential in developing the nineteenth century's view of childhood; his novels are full of orphaned or partly orphaned children, with critique of their treatment by society and surrogate parents a major emphasis. Dickens's commitment to arousing his readers to more sympathy with mistreated children seems to have developed from his sense of injustice at the hard labor in a blacking factory that he did as a child of twelve, because of his family's poverty.[20] Like Fielding, who titled his novel *The History of Tom Jones, a Foundling,* Charles Dickens gave his first novel of childhood, published in 1837, a subtitle indicating that he is describing an exemplary case: *Oliver Twist: The Parish Boy's Progress.* In the third edition, Dickens explicitly indicates his debt to Fielding, and aligns himself with Fielding particularly in an interest in portraying nature: "It is Nature for all that" (lxi). In both books the protagonist is repeatedly attacked for his illegitimacy and fights back; in both he is emphatically good at heart but sometimes (in different ways) is confused into going astray; in both he is fostered by a kindly man with more links than he knows with the child's birth family, who formalizes the relationship at the end of the book.

Furthermore, if Fielding's subtitle and his friendship with Hogarth underlines the likelihood that his first audience read *Tom Jones* partly in relation to the controversy over the Foundling Hospital, there is also external evidence of Dickens's interest in the condition of such displaced children, and an internal pointer to the same institution.[21] Dickens subscribed funds to the Foundling Hospital while writing *Oliver Twist:* furthermore, the name he gave to Oliver's benevolent patron, John Brownlow, was the name of the Hospital's secretary, who had recently (1831) published *Hans Sloane, a Tale Illustrating the History of the Foundling Hospital in London,* and was to publish a history of the hospital that went into at least four editions.[22] However, there are contrasts between the novels, some of which point to changes between eighteenth-century and Victorian culture.

In Dickens's novel, at the beginning we see Oliver's birth in poverty and his time in a workhouse. Escaping from the workhouse, he falls into the parody family of the head thief Fagin. Mr. Brownlow, to whose house he is sent to steal, believes in Oliver's goodness at heart and realizes that he looks much like the deceased daughter of a friend. When Oliver goes on a errand for him, Fagin catches him again. Oliver escapes Fagin and is cared for by Rose, who has turned down her would-be fiancé because she thinks her illegitimate birth would ruin his political career. Near the end of the novel, we learn that Fagin's plot to use Oliver was assisted by Oliver's half-brother, known as Monks, in order to get the larger inheritance he is entitled to if Oliver has "stained his name" (351). As Oliver, still good, returns to Mr. Brownlow, it is revealed that Oliver's mother was indeed his friend's daughter, and also Rose's sister. Not only is Oliver vindicated in his final fostering by Mr. Brownlow, but also Rose can marry the man she loves because he decides to give up his political hopes to avoid the obstacle to his marriage.

In his preface to the third edition, Dickens said, "I wished to shew, in little Oliver, the principle of Good surviving through every adverse circumstance, and triumphing at last" (lxi). On one hand, as Catherine Waters says, this "involves a critique of nineteenth-century political and economic theories concerning socially determined development."[23] On the other hand, Dickens also emphasizes, much more than Fielding, the miseries of the poor, the workhouse orphan, and worst of all, the child who is not only a poor workhouse orphan, but also illegitimate. Oliver is looked down on by everyone from the charity-boy Noah, who can look down on few other people, to the workhouse manager, Mr. Bumble, who looks down on many. And the attacks on Oliver are more likely than in Fielding to include attacks on his mother and to make an explicit attack on his heredity. Noah calls Oliver's mother, about whom he knows nothing, "a regular right-down bad un" (36), and Mr. Bumble says, turning against her the persistence for which the reader would be inclined to praise her, "that mother of his made her way here, against difficulties and pain that would have killed any well-disposed woman weeks before" (41) and later refers to him as "born of low and vicious parents." Like Tom, Oliver fights back at insults, but the effect is slightly different because he is more explicitly defending an insult to his mother and not just to himself. Doubling the treatment of prejudice against illegitimacy, Dickens near the end shows how Monks's mother tried to destroy Rose: she told her first foster parents "the history of the sister's shame, with such alterations as suited her; bade them take good heed of the child, for she came of bad blood; and told them she was illegitimate, and sure to go wrong at one time or other" (355).

Dickens, countering the social prejudice against illegitimacy, makes this child born out of wedlock more moral than any of the other children in the novel: "nature or inheritance had implanted a good sturdy spirit in Oliver's breast" (5). As Goldie Morgentaler argues, Dickens suggests his goodness is inherited from his parents because of the combination of their middle-class background and their love. Because his parents loved each other, Oliver has been "shielded by the grace of his heredity," unlike his half-brother, Monks, who is the product of a marriage that is legal but loveless. Dickens is here using the Victorian belief that "such matters as the state of mind of the parents and the degree of their affection at the time of conception had a bearing on the personality of the engendered child," a belief that goes back to views held in the Renaissance and before about the impact of the circumstances of conception.[24]

The strong emphasis on the physical resemblance between Oliver and his mother is another contrast to the situation in *Tom Jones*. Dickens uses the portrait in Mr. Brownlow's house to dramatize this; thus Oliver can see his mother's picture and respond to it without understanding the nature of his response. We are told that he looks at it with "awe" (71), but we never know if he thinks about his own similarity to the painting.[25] As Michael Ragussis has pointed out, Mr. Brownlow's relationship with Oliver, at the conclusion, stresses Oliver's connections with his dead relatives: Brownlow "traced in him new traits of his early friend, that awakened in his own bosom old remembrances, melancholy and yet sweet and soothing."[26] George Eliot will use a similar theme of memory in portraying Silas Marner as reminded of his sister when caring for little Eppie. She will also develop further the theme of the adoptive father nurturing the child in nature, and show more hands-on care in Silas.[27]

As Morgentaler writes, the strong resemblance between Oliver and both of his parents may go beyond probability, but it reflects the current theory of "blended heredity. . . . Each parent was thought to pass on all of his or her characteristics through the blood, and the resulting child was therefore a blend of the two endowments."²⁸ Mendel would not publish his findings until 1866, and even then was widely ignored; the complex interaction of recessive and dominant characteristics was not widely known. Dickens's repeated emphasis on strong parent-child physical similarity repeats a theme that, as the previous chapter has shown, was frequent in Shakespeare, a writer Dickens loved and paid tribute to in many different ways.²⁹ While physical similarities of parents and children had been commented on occasionally since at least the time of Sophocles, Dickens's stress on this theme both influenced and epitomized Victorian sentimentality about the family.

Tom Jones's loss of his mother through her pretense enables comic plotting, and her death takes place offstage; in *Oliver Twist*, by contrast, as Carolyn Dever notes, maternal loss is not just a structural device but a psychological phenomenon, and we find the "complete articulation of the psychologized, sentimentalized plot of the dead mother."³⁰

Bleak House, Jane Eyre, and the Tradition of Good Adopted Girls

Eighteenth- and nineteenth-century British novels fight against stigma on female adoptees in two different ways. *Bleak House, Evelina,* and *Mansfield Park,* for example, emphasize the female protagonist's goodness and gratitude to her adoptive father, and show the inadequacy and even destructiveness of most of the living maternal figures. In *Jane Eyre,* on the other hand, the protagonist fights back much like Oliver and Tom; Mrs. Reed's cruelty doesn't suppress her emotionally, and instead of a beneficent adopted father there are a number of helpful substitute mothers and sisters. Jane finds literal and spiritual kin in her cousins Diana and Mary, and kinship imagery is used metaphorically to make her relationship with Rochester seem like another version of the discovery of a lost family.

In *Jane Eyre* (1848), Charlotte Brontë effectively gives a first-person voice of protest to a child who mourns a lost family and is mistreated by her guardians. After the death of her parents and the uncle who adopted her, Jane is an outsider in her aunt's family. She feels "like nobody there, . . . a heterogeneous thing . . . an interloper not of her [aunt's] race, . . . an uncongenial alien."³¹ Her cousin John attacks her specifically on the basis of her poverty, and as the novel begins, she fights back for the first time, acting, she thinks, "like any other rebel slave" and, others think, "like a mad cat" (6). Without an Allworthy to defend her, she is sent away to Lowood school, another place where she is considered, by the schoolmaster Brocklehurst, "not a member of the true flock, but evidently an interloper and an alien" (61). Here, at last, she finds a kind role model in a teacher, Miss Temple, whose career she later follows; since Temple was a name common among foundlings who had been left at the Temple Court, Miss Temple might have had experiences similar to Jane's. After Miss Temple marries and leaves the school, Jane takes a position as a governess at Thornfield, in which she is once again in an ambiguous position in relation to a household, the unconventional one of Mr. Rochester, his ward Adele, and his house-keeper Mrs. Fairfax—once again an outsider on the inside, left out of the secret all the other adults know, never sure how close to Rochester she really is. While in the bad days of her relationship she worries that she is just an employee, on the good days she uses the language of kin-ship. "I felt at times as if he were my relation, rather than my master. . . . I ceased to pine after kindred" (142). "I feel akin to him. . . . I have something in my brain and heart, in my blood and nerves, that assimi-lates me mentally to him" (171). This language of kinship is not just Jane's. Rochester too, in testing her feelings, asks, "Are you anything akin to me?" (250). Nevertheless, when she finds him offensive, she tells him off, as she tells off his condescending rich associates, and when his marriage is revealed and he invites her to live with him anyway, her morality joins with her fear of being a powerless dependent and pro-duces a vision in which another kind of kinship wins out: the moon becomes her foster mother, or takes on her deceased mother's spirit, and says to her, "My daughter, flee temptation" (320). She leaves.

This choice precipitates the part of the novel that uses the folklore plot of discovery of lost kindred most literally—when Jane finds a place to stay, her unknown and unrecognized benefactors ultimately turn out to be her cousins—and, unlike the Reed cousins at the beginning of the novel, the Rivers cousins, at least the women, are congenial to Jane. With Diana and Mary she feels absolute compatibility; St. John is ide-alistic like her, but much colder. Under pressure from him to marry her and accompany him as a missionary to India, Jane leaves to find out Rochester's situation.

As most readers will remember, she finds his first wife dead and him blind, maimed, reformed, and still in love with her, and she marries him. But what readers may not remember is that her final words about their relationship complete the kinship theme. When she claims to be "flesh of his flesh and bone of his bone" (455), she is not just alluding to the relationship of Adam and Eve in language repeated in traditional Christian marriage ceremonies; her words also recall the story of Eve's "birth" from Adam's side; the use of this image by a character for whom kinship and its lack or presence has been so important is overdetermined. Metaphorically, Jane has found her true kin in Rochester.

Brontë treats loss of parents in several of her other novels. In *Shirley*, Caroline believes that her mother is dead; actually, her new friend, Mrs. Pryor, turns out to be her mother. And in *Villette*, Lucy's parents are dead and she receives some maternal care from her godmother. It is easy to connect this theme with Brontë's own life, given the early death of her own mother and the impact in her youth of her housekeeper and her aunt. But *Jane Eyre* clearly touched a chord in its society that still resonates today.

Jane was a new kind of heroine, one of the few assertive displaced girls in Victorian fiction, and indeed one of the most assertive heroines of any family configuration. But her status as an assertive adoptee is particularly striking because of its contrast to the other kind of female adoptees, who are defined chiefly by their gratitude. For example, in Frances Burney's *Evelina*, the title character, whose mother died in childbirth, has been raised by her mother's tutor, Mr. Villars, while her birth father refuses to acknowledge her. The novel is told in letters, and here is an example of the way she writes her adoptive father: "Surely never had orphan so little to regret as your grateful Evelina! Though motherless, though worse than fatherless, bereft from infancy of the two first and greatest blessings of life, never has she had cause to deplore their loss; never has she felt the omission of a parent's tenderness, care, or indulgence" (259). She experiences stigma, though in a milder form than Tom, Oliver, or Jane, in the insensitivity of "polite society," but instead of fighting back against it, she writes about it in her letters, and, at best, leaves the room.

Similarly, in Jane Austen's *Mansfield Park*, Fanny Price, adopted at ten by her richer aunt and uncle, lacks self-confidence and is grateful for very small gestures. Like Evelina, she experiences insensitivity rather than hostile attacks, and also like Evelina, she does little to defend herself; she doesn't even have the solace of letters. Austen gives a psychological analysis of Fanny's shyness, pointing out that in her adoptive household Fanny loses the importance formerly felt to her brothers and sisters.

A few years after *Jane Eyre,* Dickens created another self-sacrificing adoptee heroine, Esther Summerson of *Bleak House,* on whom this section of the chapter will focus because of the novel's psychological treatment of Esther, her relationship with her birth mother, and her pronounced contrast with Jane. Esther is raised by a stern "godmother," her aunt Barbary, who emphasizes the disgrace of her birth and conceals the child's survival from her mother; upon Barbary's death she is sent to school for six years and then hired by Mr. Jarndyce to be companion to the orphan Ada, one of the potential heirs involved in the enormous long-running lawsuit Jarndyce versus Jarndyce. Jarndyce, her "protector, guardian, friend" (144), eventually tells her about his letter from her aunt, criticizing the "distorted religion which clouded her mind with impressions of the need there was for the child to expiate an offence of which she was quite innocent" (289). In church she sees Lady Dedlock, whose face is for some reason "like a broken glass to me, in which I saw scraps of old remembrances" (305). Lady Dedlock realizes that Esther is the daughter she thought was dead, and they have one brief intense meeting in which the mother asks forgiveness and announces that she will keep their relationship secret and they will never meet again. Esther tells Mr. Jarndyce the story, and he proposes marriage to her, which makes her feel both gratitude and loss. Meanwhile, Esther's birth father has died in poverty after working as a scrivener under the name of Nemo; evidence is discovered linking his handwriting to that in love letters to Lady Dedlock, who flees to his grave, where she is discovered dead. Eventually Jarndyce gives up his claim to an engagement because he realizes that Esther really loves a young doctor, Allan Woodcourt, whom she marries near the end of the novel.

Like *Oliver Twist, Bleak House* is among other things a protest against attaching a stigma to illegitimacy.[32] Here the protest extends further to the accompanying coverups that separate birth relatives from each other. *Oliver Twist* focused, to a large extent, on physical hardships of an illegitimate boy; *Bleak House,* looking at the experience of a girl born out of wedlock turning into a woman, and using the first person, focuses more on psychological hardships. The beginning of Esther's story gives a detailed picture of one version of bad adoptive parenting:

> She was always grave and strict. . . . I felt so different from her, even making every allowance for the differences between a child and a woman; I felt so poor, so trifling, and so far off; that I never could be unrestrained with her. . . . I had never heard my mama spoken of. (63)

In a theme often found in adopted children even today, her birthday is a focus of stress, "the most melancholy day at home, in the whole year" (64). Like Jane Eyre—from whose novel Dickens quite likely learned something about presenting a first-person narrative of a displaced girl—she feels different not only from her aunt but also from her peers: "Why am I so different from other children, and why is it my fault?" (65).[33]

Esther's "godmother" explicitly voices the stigma that hangs particularly over Esther as a female because of the sexual double standard: "It would have been far better, little Esther, that you had had no birthday; that you had never been born! . . . Your mother, Esther, is your disgrace, and you were hers. The time will come—and soon enough—when you will understand this better, and will feel it too, as no one save a woman can." But she heightens the stigma by speaking as if Esther were the only child born out of wedlock in her society. "You are different from other children, Esther, because you were not born, like them, in common sinfulness and wrath. You are set apart" (65).

Unlike Tom or Oliver, or indeed Jane, Esther does not respond violently to such an attack. She has other ways of coping. She invests her doll with personality so that she will have some kind of companionship, and tells her everything.[34] Her aunt gives her a moral lesson: "Submission, self-denial, diligent work, are the preparations for a life begun with such a shadow on it" (65). She takes her aunt's lesson to heart, and even claims to be "fervently grateful to her" (66). Is Dickens thus trying to make Esther more acceptable to Victorian readers who complained that Jane was insufficiently grateful?[35] Esther's further words make clear that though she is influenced by her aunt, she also protests against her attitude: "I confusedly felt guilty and yet innocent." Unlike her aunt, she understands the importance of love and kindness; she "would strive as I grew up to be industrious, contented, and kind-hearted, and to do some good to some one, and win some love to myself if I could."

Esther thus fits much more into Victorian ideals of womanhood than Jane does. Although important traces of it remain, Brontë broke out of the Victorian gender schema in much of her novel. This is one of the reasons that post-Victorian readers have generally enjoyed Jane more. Consider, for example, the dominance of *Jane Eyre* in the interpretation of women writers presented in the pioneering feminist study *The Madwoman in the Attic;* the number of different movies made of *Jane Eyre* by contrast to only one recent filming (for the Arts and Entertainment channel) of *Bleak House;* the special session at the 2002 Modern Language Association meetings under the title "I'm Still Here: The Persistence of *Jane Eyre,*" about the novel's continuing cultural presence; and the number of other novels in which characters remember reading it.[36] Both of the girls go away to school, and feel less alone; Esther enjoys "seeing in those around me, as it might be in a looking-glass, every stage of my own growth and change there" (74). Both young women become teachers in their school. But while Brontë uses this section to dramatize Jane's further struggle against injustice, and the conflict between her attitude and Helen Burns's self-sacrifice and nonviolence, Esther is already a model of sympathy. Though she is still different—the only student in the school who helps instruct the others, because of the understanding that she would have to earn her living as a governess—this does not bother her because she now receives love: "in course of time I had plenty to do, which I was very fond of doing, because it made the dear girls fond of me. . . . At last, whenever a new pupil came who was a little downcast and unhappy, she was so sure—indeed I don't know why—to make a friend of me, that all new-comers were confided to my care" (73). While both leave the school to become companions to younger girls, Jane takes the risk of advertising, and Esther's new position is provided for her. Jane is charmed by Adele, Rochester's ward, but emphasizes that the child is not angelic and that she herself is sometimes bored; Esther, by contrast, virtually (and virtuously) falls in love with Ada: "such a beautiful girl . . . in a few moments we were sitting in the window-seat, with the light of the fire upon us, talking together, as free and happy as could be . . . my darling—it is so natural to me now, that I can't help writing it" (77–78).

Recent critics have often commented on the rhetoric of modesty in

Esther's narrative, and her announced discomfort: "It seems so curious to me to be obliged to write all this about myself!" (73–74). She praises other people for accomplishments that we infer are largely hers, and is grateful to everyone. She says of the other children, "They said I was so gentle; but I am sure they were" (73), and of Ada, "It was so delightful to know that she could confide in me, and like me! It was so good of her, and so encouraging to me!" All these passages make her fit into the Victorian ideal of how girls and women ought to speak.[37] But at the same time, Dickens writes this character somewhat in Jane Austen's mode in *Mansfield Park,* emphasizing that her upbringing contributes to this modesty. Very close to the introduction of Esther's narrative, she points this effect out to the reader: "This"—her sense of distance from her godmother—"made me, I dare say, more timid and retiring than I naturally was" (63). Austen repeatedly emphasizes Fanny's sense of being important to no one; Esther knows that she "was to no one upon earth what Dolly was to me" (65) and explicitly links this lack with her hope to win love by her good works. She reminds us of this psychology, and the way in which her feelings of embarrassment at her appearance after her disease are also overdetermined, again when ambivalent feelings emerge at the thought of marrying Mr. Jarndyce: "how often had I considered within myself that the deep traces of my illness, and the circumstances of my birth, were only new reasons why I should be busy, busy, busy—useful, amiable, serviceable, in all honest, unpretending ways" (668).

As in other novels, the stigma of birth recurs with regard to Esther's marriage possibilities. Evelina's marriage to Lord Orville seems to be threatened by his sister, a "Court Calendar Bigot." Esther, with her usual modesty, is puzzled by the obsession with birth and ancestry that emerges in Mrs. Woodcourt, the mother of her friend Allan; she "talked so much about birth, that, for a moment, I half fancied, and with pain—but, what an idle fancy to suppose that she could think or care what *mine* was" (292).

Like many adoptees, Esther has several names. *Esther* comes from the orphaned girl who names a book of the Bible, who is adopted by her cousin Mordecai. Summerson is identified as a fiction, but has a number of dimensions. The novel explicitly identifies it with Esther's provisions of warmth and sunshine for others;[38] yet it is associated with the foundling tradition; it echoes Tom Jones's birth father's name Summer, and similarly recalls the conception of foundlings during summer festivals. Her aunt had written to Mr. Jarndyce that "if the writer were to die before the child became a woman, she would be left entirely friendless, nameless, and unknown" (289); Esther says that in the many nicknames that he gives her—"Old Woman, and Little Old Woman, and Cobweb, and Mrs. Shipton, and Mother Hubbard, and Dame Durden . . . my own name soon became quite lost" (148). While arguably these names are intended as affectionate compensations for her early lack of love, they also serve as a denial of her youth and, given Victorian assumptions, of her sexuality. They also fit with the side of Jarndyce that wants to marry her himself instead of freeing her for a livelier union.[39]

Her birth parents are presented as figures who really have lost their names: her birth father, once called Hawdon, is now known as Nemo, which means "No One," and fits, as the novel develops, with the legal term identifying an illegitimate son as *filius nullius,* Latin for son of no one.[40] Her mother has lost her first name, being identified only as Lady Dedlock throughout the novel, except in one reference to the appearance of the name Honoria in her correspondence with Hawdon, mockingly made by Mr. Swallweed (787).

Lady Dedlock, this detail reinforces, has lost her honor, but what the novel emphasizes even more is that she has lost her nature in denying her relationship with Hawdon and Esther.[41] On the first page in which she is introduced in the novel, she is identified as "Lady Dedlock (who is childless)" and described as "put quite out of temper" by seeing a poor family, "a child, chased by a woman, running out into the rain to meet the shining figure of a wrapped-up man coming through the gate" (56). The first-time reader does not know why this picture should bother Lady Dedlock, but retrospectively the pain produced by her secrecy and self-repression becomes clear. When she finally acknowledges herself to Esther, their conversation involves "the only natural moments of her life" (566; the indirect discourse makes ambiguous the source of this judgment, whether Esther or her mother, but presumably they agree on it). When her housekeeper pleads for her to help her son, accused of murder, we are told "she is not a hard lady naturally . . . but so long accustomed to suppress emotion, and keep down reality; so long schooled for her own purposes, in that destructive school which shuts up the natural feelings of the heart" (812).

More than any other novel discussed here, *Bleak House* develops the feelings between a mother and a daughter separated at birth as they see each other without clear understanding and move toward acknowledgment. We see this from Esther's point of view; interestingly, though Esther has often mentioned her sense of being different from others, when she finally sees someone who looks like her, she takes a long time to mention that resemblance, as if the idea is too new, or suggesting possibilities too epochal, to admit. It is Lady Dedlock's look at her, not her looks, that she discusses: "Shall I ever forget the manner in which those handsome proud eyes seemed to spring out of their languour, and to hold mine!" (304). Yet the image of mirroring occurs, even if displaced: her face seems, mysteriously, "like a broken glass to me, in which I saw scraps of old remembrances" (305). Seeing Lady Dedlock's face in church, Esther hears the prayers uttered in her godmother's voice, and sees herself as a child, but she does not understand why. Why does Dickens insist on this lack of recognition, though other characters such as Guppy and Jo see their similarity or confuse the two? Partly to create suspense, but partly also to dramatize the distance from nature society has created in both of these characters: Esther is shy and wouldn't dare to presume this connection for herself; Lady Dedlock is reserved because of pride. Class difference, social custom, and the shame that Victorian society attributes to their true connection, if out of wedlock, keeps them apart. Consistent with this theme of social obstacles to relationship, the language that Esther uses is often similar to the language traditionally used by the secret romantic lover, much as in Petrarchan poetry: "I do not quite know, even now, whether it was painful or pleasurable; whether it drew me towards her or made me shrink from her. I think I admired her with a kind of fear. . . . I had a fancy . . . that what this lady so curiously was to me, I was to her—I mean that I disturbed her thoughts as she influenced mine . . . but when I stole a glance at her, and saw her so composed and distant and unapproachable, I felt this to be a foolish weakness" (372). The sentiment in this passage, when Esther sees Lady Dedlock in church, is remarkably similar to the sentiment in the passage in *Middlemarch* where Will sees Dorothea in church; Petrarch's first sight of Laura, the legendary genesis of Petrarchan love poetry, was traditionally in the same place.

Esther never admits that she sees a similarity to herself in Lady Dedlock until after Lady Dedlock reveals herself as her mother—and the way she phrases the similarity is by emphasizing its loss; having been badly marked by smallpox, she feels "gratitude to the providence of God that I was so changed as that I never could disgrace her by any trace of likeness; as that nobody could ever now look at me, and look at her, and remotely think of any near tie between us" (565). It is just after this thought that she first in the narration calls Lady Dedlock her mother. When she first sees Lady Dedlock at this accidental meeting, a new phase in their relationship is marked by a change in her mother's face that Esther does not want to name: "a something in her face that I had pined for and dreamed of when I was a little child; something I had never seen in any face; something I had never seen in hers before." This something, most likely, is the sign of the emotion that Esther thinks of as motherliness; it is appropriate to her inhibitions that Esther cannot name it yet. It is Esther's disease that has invited this greater concern for her in Lady Dedlock; but what leads to Esther's recognition that this is going to be their moment of acknowledgment is the token of Lady Dedlock's own interest in Esther, the handkerchief that Esther had used to cover a dead baby in what might be considered her own gesture of motherliness.

Esther wants to stand with her mother against the world, but her mother refuses. The emotional mood of their reunion gives the reader the feeling that they should be together, as they would be if they were in a plot like that of Shakespeare's *Winter's Tale* or *Pericles*. Lady Dedlock insists that she must keep her secret and not see Esther again; the plot as well as the language suggests that this is an unnatural choice. Parallel to Esther and her mother the novel places George and his mother, Mrs. Rouncewell. While they have been apart since, as a young man, George decided he wasn't good enough for his family, Mrs. Bagnet, the novel's representative of the good middle-class mother, reunites them when George is in prison. Unlike George, Esther cannot publicly take her place beside her mother.

The meeting of Esther and Lady Dedlock is one of the places where the Victorian novel seems to speak directly to the recent debate about open adoption records. Lady Dedlock is the birth mother evoked by the closed-record side, who feels that her life would be ruined if her past became visible, except that Dickens frames her position to make the reader feel the tragedy of this insistence. Some might feel that in her society such secrecy is painfully necessary, but for others this shows another cost of stigmatizing illegitimacy and dramatizes the wrong-headedness of those who would like to return to Victorian values.

Once again, the novel does not give Esther a choice about what to do.[42] The relationship must be a secret, except that she is allowed to tell

Mr. Jarndyce. The meeting sends her into the closest thing to despair; but after receiving letters from Ada and Jarndyce, she is cheered, and Ada takes on a maternal role for her at this point.[43]

Unlike the similarity between Evelina and her mother, the similarity between Esther and hers is only one of appearance, not one of temperament. Part of the point of the novel, indeed, is how environmental influences have affected both of their temperaments as well as keeping them apart.[44] Dickens uses the plot of their separation and temporary reunion to a large extent as a social commentary: "What connexion can there be, between the place in Lincolnshire, the house in town, the Mercury in powder, and the whereabout [sic] of Jo the outlaw with the broom, who had that distant ray of light upon him when he swept the churchyard-step? What connexion can there have been between many people in the innumerable histories of this world, who, from opposite sides of great gulfs, have, nevertheless, been very curiously brought together!" (272). This commentary is comparable to Austen's emphasis on the sadness of the contrast and alienation of Fanny's poor mother from the richer aunt who adopts her in *Mansfield Park;* the gap between the rich and the poor in her society had divided them so much that "the ties of blood were little more than nothing."[45] But since Victorian society felt particularly strongly about the intense bond of motherhood, to show that connection broken and made unconscious was a particularly strong social protest, here as, in a different way and country, in *Uncle Tom's Cabin.*

Dickens surrounds the plot of this broken family not only with the reconstitution of the blood-related Rouncewells but also with various other domestic arrangements in which the bereaved and orphans bond together. Jenny, the poor woman with whom Lady Dedlock changes clothes in her final flight, lost, early in the novel, the child whose corpse Esther covers with her handkerchief. She helps to take care of her friend Liz's child and says, "It's my dead child . . . that makes me love this child so dear, and it's my dead child that makes her love it so dear too, as even to think of its being taken away from her now" (367). George, who has lost touch with his family, takes care of literal orphans and encourages them to help each other out: he brings Phil and Jo together, saying, "Here is a man, sir, who was found, when a baby, in the gutter. Consequently, it is to be expected that he takes a natural interest in this poor creature" (697), and at the end, after he is reunited with his family, George still takes care of Phil. And Esther helps to take care of Ada's son Richard, after his father has died: "I call him my Richard! but he says that he has two mamas, and I am one" (934).

Esther's gratitude to Jarndyce has much in common with Evelina's gratitude to Mr. Villars. In both cases the women often claim that because of their guardian they do not feel the stigma or desertion related to their displaced status. When Esther recalls her godmother's words about the disgrace of her mother, she says to Jarndyce that "to him I owed the blessing that I had from my childhood to that hour never, never, never felt it" (290). When she suggests that Mr. Jarndyce might be able to help her mother, she says that he has "been the best of fathers" to her (568).

But since Jarndyce's adoption of Esther is not something regulated by law (as it could not be in Victorian England), there is an ambiguity about what kind of relations they are, even more than with Evelina and Villars. The ambiguity is intensified by Esther's difficulty in understanding her own feelings—understanding, for example, her need for anything else in marriage apart from a relationship of gratitude. When she calls Jarndyce "the Guardian who is a Father to her" (291), she can see some discomfort in his face, presumably because his feelings for her are not only fatherly. When he proposes marriage to her, in the odd mode of asking her, as she says, "would I be the mistress of Bleak House" (666), she feels she must accept out of affection and gratitude. Still she feels "as if something for which there was no name or distinct idea were indefinitely lost to me" (668). Esther's reticence here can be seen as generically Victorian, yet it can also be attributed in part to the specific circumstances of her early upbringing, in which sexuality is first introduced to her by her aunt as the cause of her and her mother's disgrace.[46] (We will find a similar caution in Daniel Deronda's attitude about sex, for analogous reasons.) Dickens helps to make this connection when Esther thinks, a few paragraphs later, "the deep traces of my illness, and the circumstances of my birth, were only new reasons why I should be busy, busy, busy—useful, amiable, serviceable, in all honest, unpretending ways" (668).

When Allan Woodcourt proposes to her, Esther again emphasizes her gratitude to Jarndyce, "the best of human beings" (890), though she has a brief realization that she would rather marry Woodcourt. But she finally gets the marriage to Woodcourt without ever having to make a choice: Jarndyce observes her feelings about Woodcourt and not only tells her that he is releasing her from her promise to him, but gives

Woodcourt a Bleak House of his own, furnished just as Esther likes, so that she can still be "the mistress of Bleak House." Esther continues to express her gratitude to Jarndyce till the end, yet there is still something ambiguous in their relationship. "To Ada and her pretty boy, he is the fondest father; to me, he is what he has ever been, and what name can I give to that? Yet while I feel towards him as if he were a superior being, I am so familiar with him, and so easy with him, that I almost wonder at myself" (934).

Everything seems happy in her life at the end. But at the same time, the excess of Esther's modesty (she cannot believe that people love her for her own sake; she feels gratitude that people love her in spite of her appearance) reveals to the modern reader that she is still marked by her early upbringing, though to most Victorian readers it probably gave the final confirmation to her ideal qualities.

Bleak House on the one hand and *Oliver Twist* on the other show some of the gender polarities of Victorian culture. A reader could be expected to sympathize with a boy who fights back under stigma, but if a girl were to be a novel's heroine, she would usually behave in a more self-denying way. *Jane Eyre* broke that expectation openly, but *Bleak House* and *Mansfield Park* complicate it because they show adopted girls whose habit of self-denial is not simply a virtue but also a character deformation.

Great Expectations: Male and Female Adoptees

In *Great Expectations* Dickens considers a male adoptee (as I will call him because he has substitute parents, though one is his sister) brought up with stigma, and shows that he has more psychological difficulties than Oliver and Tom had; he juxtaposes him with a female adoptee who has responded to her upbringing by becoming neither a good girl like Esther nor a rebel like Jane.

The orphan Pip, cared for by his sister (roughly) and Joe Gargery the blacksmith, her husband (lovingly), helps an escaped convict, and some time after is summoned by the rich Miss Havisham to visit her house and meet her adopted daughter Estella. Pip is much impressed by the life of the rich, and scorns his relatives and his friend Biddy in his frustrated love for Estella.

More explicitly than any of the other novels discussed thus far, *Great Expectations* deals with the impact that different forms of adoption have on the adoptee's identity.[47] The novel juxtaposes Pip's adoptive relation to his sister, to Joe, and to the convict Magwitch, with Miss Havisham's adoptive relation to Estella, and Pip's fantasy adoption by Miss Havisham.

Although Pip was born in wedlock, his position as an orphan being raised by parents other than those he was born to makes him feel stigmatized because of his sister's treatment of him, "as if I had insisted on being born in opposition to the dictates of reason, religion, and morality, and against the dissuading arguments of my best friends" (22). He is told little or nothing about his dead parents;[48] his sister mocks him for going to the churchyard and complains about what a burden he has been. Even Joe says to Pip, of his earlier self, "if you could have been aware how small and flabby and mean you was, dear me, you'd have formed the most contemptible opinions of yourself!" (47). His sister's friends also emphasize his position as outsider in the family: when Mr. Pumblechook says, "be grateful, boy, to them which brought you up by hand" (24), he is referring to the same feeding by porridge that Oliver Twist endured, and Pip takes it to refer to his sister's frequent blows. Pip's relation to her is so disturbed that we never learn her name.

In response to his sister's treatment, Pip neither fights back violently like Tom and Oliver when insulted nor attempts to be supergood, as Fanny and Esther do. He knows that she is unjust, and it affects him: "Through all my punishments, disgraces, fasts and vigils, and other penitential performances, I had nursed this assurance; and to my communing so much with it, in a solitary and unprotected way, I in great part refer the fact that I was morally timid and very sensitive" (62).[49] He seeks refuge outside the Gargery household; in the churchyard at his dead parents' tombs he is accosted by Magwitch, and, used to obeying unreasonable threats, he gets the convict food and a file, thus preparing for Magwitch's later adoption of him.

In contrast with his wife, Joe is always kind to Pip. He may even have married her, at least partly, to help Pip. Rather than insisting on a title suggesting family authority, Joe wants Pip to consider him "ever the best of friends" (47). There is no courtesy family title for Pip to use for Joe (76). On the other hand, subordinate as Joe is to his wife, the only name she is ever given is Mrs. Joe. This family thus reverses the expectations that the blood relative will be more caring than the relative by marriage, that a woman would be more nurturing than a husband, and that giving up a name in marriage means subordination.

Raised by a brutal father, Joe is illiterate and too protective of women to defend Pip from his sister's harshness, but he, together with another orphan, Biddy, provides Pip with enough kindness to mitigate her sternness, and encouragement to proceed with his education. The interest that Miss Havisham takes in him promotes his belief that he can get beyond his own household, which is heightened by the news that he is "adopted by a rich person" (159).

Raised by this money to education in London, Pip sees his position as adoptee as comparable to that of Miss Havisham's adopted daughter Estella, and tries to fit into the aristocracy and to distance himself from Joe. Aspiring to Estella since childhood, he hopes that he may be destined for her, and ignores Biddy.

Rather than the aristocratic Miss Havisham, however, it turns out that his benefactor is Magwitch the convict, who has made money in Australia and returned secretly. Pip is crushed by this news—instead of someone near the top of society, he owes his position to someone who would be near the bottom except for the fact that he has made money.

Magwitch and Miss Havisham are parallel figures, both of them wronged, and adopting someone else partly to make up for that wrong.[50] In both cases the adoption has bad effects. Miss Havisham trains Estella to look down on everyone, and Magwitch's money, with Miss Havisham's influence, enables Pip to look down on Joe and Biddy.

In the presentation of Miss Havisham's relationship to Estella, the novel gives another cautionary picture of how an ill-willed adoptive parent can deform a child. Unlike Esther's adoptive mother, Estella's focuses not on the child's inherited guilt but on how the child can be the adoptive mother's surrogate in the world, to punish the men who love her as revenge for her own jilting. Estella reproaches Miss Havisham, "I am what you have made me. Take all the praise, take all the blame; take all the success, take all the failure; in short, take me. . . I was no party to the compact . . . for if I could walk and speak, when it was made, it was as much as I could do" (308–9).

And yet the novel does not finally present Estella as irredeemable. Pip reports Estella as speaking of suffering as stronger than "all other teaching" (or than "Miss Havisham's teaching," in the original version of the ending), and helping her to "understand what [his] heart used to be" (492, 493).

What is adoption's power over Pip? The influences on him are diverse: no single person has as much influence as Miss Havisham's on Estella; his sister's harshness is mitigated by Joe and others. The novel's outcome requires not only his misery with his sister, but also Magwitch's secret gift and Pip's fantasy that it comes from Miss Havisham. Of all the novels discussed in this chapter, this novel comes closest to giving an adoptee a choice with regard to affiliation with adoptive parents, but as it turns out, all Pip can do is drop the affiliation with Magwitch by refusing his further legacy; he cannot go back to the affiliation with Joe by working on the forge and marrying his old orphan friend Biddy, as he thinks of doing.[51] His birth parents are long lost to him by death, and close association with Joe and Biddy is lost to him by his failure to recognize their worth sooner; the most he can do is keep up "a constant correspondence" (488) with them, while he works away at the position in the East that the education Magwitch has paid for has enabled him to reach. In the second version, when he meets Estella and believes that they are to be reunited, the ending permits him to have it both ways, giving him the woman he aspired to, now humbled and changed. She speaks of "the remembrance of what I had thrown away when I was quite ignorant of its worth" (492) in terms that could summarize his attitude toward Joe.

In the detective story unraveling of Estella's heredity, this novel adds to the parallel with Pip because in both cases the original parents are unrecoverable. Estella is the child of the lawyer Jaggers's servant Molly, whom he has successfully defended against the charge of murder, and of Magwitch. Pip gradually discovers the connection between Molly and Estella by noticing the similarity in their hands and eyes. One effect of these connections is to emphasize to Pip the links between people of different classes that he had thought so separated. As in *Bleak House,* Dickens uses adoption to show how people of different parts of society are bound together in ways rarely visible. He emphasizes this theme by presenting Pip's explicit thoughts about how embarrassed before Estella he is at his connection to Magwitch, how he thinks of them as such opposites. As Pip learns more of the story, he uses imagery from Joe's forge to describe the connections: seeing the similarity between Estella and Molly, he thinks "how one link of association had helped that identification in the theatre, and how such a link, wanting before, had been riveted for me now" (396). Even though Miss Havisham does not know who Estella's mother is, he thinks "the connection here was clear and straight" (406). Dickens here animates the "dead metaphor" of "links of association," and the image works in keeping with the valuation of Joe in the novel. The importance of "links" testifies to the value of the world of the forge, where literal links are made.

The specifics of Estella's ancestry and formation emphasize the power of adoptive parenting over nature in its influence on individual character, even more than in Estella's words recently quoted. Her birth mother married young and killed out of jealousy: Jaggers refers to Molly as having "gipsy blood. . . . it was hot enough when it was up" (398). Jaggers has been able to control her; she is described as a wild beast tamed under his influence. Pip is particularly struck by an action of her fingers that is like knitting without anything to knit. Knitting is making connections (with yarn instead of the steel of Joe's forge), and the family connections Molly has made cannot be acknowledged.[52] This knitting/not knitting parallels her role as a mother who is not a mother. Furthermore, readers' possible recollections of Dickens's previous novel, A *Tale of Two Cities,* with the famous Madame Defarge, who knit as she cheered on the guillotine, would have fit with the presentation of Molly as potentially threatening.

By contrast to her hot-blooded mother, Estella is repeatedly seen as cold; Miss Havisham eventually confesses, "I stole her heart away and put ice in its place" (405). Estella says that she is unable to understand what love means; this lack of understanding, she says, "is in *my* nature. . . . It is in the nature formed within me" (366). In keeping with this assessment, Pip observes "in some of her looks and gestures . . . that tinge or resemblance to Miss Havisham which may often be noticed to have been acquired by children, from grown persons with whom they have been much associated and secluded, and which, when childhood is passed, will produce a remarkable occasional likeness of expression between faces that are otherwise quite different" (240).

Adoption in this circumstance is presented as powerful, and the knowledge of Estella's heritage presents a quandary. If Molly had not concealed her child and given her to Jaggers to find a home, she presumably would have been convicted, and what sort of life would Estella have had? As Jaggers says, he sees children "being generated in great numbers for certain destruction . . . being imprisoned, whipped, transported, neglected, cast out, qualified in all ways for the hangman" (419). This is, indeed, the story of Estella's father's childhood, parentless, "tramping, begging, thieving" (350). So, bad as Estella's life with Miss

Havisham has been, life without Miss Havisham might have been worse.

All the other mysteriously born characters in the novels I discuss here learn the solution to their mysteries. Estella alone is kept in ignorance, maintaining the absence from the original compact of which she has complained. We see again some of the assumptions behind the closed adoption records. Jaggers believes that telling would hurt everybody; it does not occur to him that it could simply be revealed to Estella without telling anyone else: "I think it would hardly serve her, to establish her parentage for the information of her husband, and to drag her back to disgrace, after an escape of twenty years" (420). In this dimension, like other adopted women in Dickens's novels, like the adoptee in the closed-records system, she is represented as passive.

Like some other adopted characters, such as Esther in *Bleak House* and Daniel Deronda, she has a sense of difference from her caretaker: from her early childhood, she says to Miss Havisham, she remembers "looking up into your face, when your face was strange and frightened me!" (309). This could refer to Miss Havisham's face being strange in her eccentricity and wild regret, but, since she uses the past tense, it could also refer to her sense of being unrelated, feeling different from Miss Havisham in the years soon after her adoption, in spite of the similarity that Pip would eventually see. And Estella's mysterious marriage to Bentley Drummle, lower in class than Miss Havisham, could again be attributed to her continued sense of being an outsider in the household, no matter how much she had assimilated herself to it, and therefore seeking to marry someone else who was from a lower class, with whom she might fantasize that she might belong better.[53] (Oddly, he even has the violence associated with her birth mother.) Still, even in the fantasy world in which Pip marries Estella at the end of the novel, I find it hard to imagine Pip telling her her story.[54]

Conclusions

In all of these novels, adoptees' identities are at issue in a very literal sense. Even their names may be a perplexing topic. Not quite sure what she should call either him or herself, Evelina writes to her adoptive father, "I cannot sign to you Anville, and what other name may I claim?" (69). Oliver Twist's name is created at random by Bumble.

The sense of problematic identity is often connected with a drama-tized difference from those around them, whether in appearance, psy-chology, social status, or all three. Jane Eyre, Esther Summerson, and Daniel Deronda (and in a different way, Fanny Price, adopted at a later age from parents she remembers) are the adoptees for whom the sense of difference from those around them is most fully articulated. This is dramatized as physical difference for all these characters except Fanny, but for all of these four there is a sense of psychological difference as well.

But, as the term *adoptee* suggests more than "orphan," for most of these characters there exist others whom they are in some way more like, to whom the novel will lead them. Both Esther and Daniel will finally meet the mothers who resemble them, but for neither, any more than for Fanny Price, will this lead to the idyllic family reunion pre-dicted by the romance pattern. For Esther this is complicated further because it takes a long time to reveal that the woman whose appearance so fascinates her, with whom she feels so strangely linked, is indeed her mother, while a number of other characters confuse them.

Jane, on the other hand, will eventually find similar people of three kinds, though physical similarity is not emphasized as much as in some of the other novels. Least problematic are Mary and Diana Rivers, who she feels resemble her in their interests and temperament. Their brother, St. John, finds her sufficiently similar that he wants her to help him as his wife in his mission to India, an idea both appealing and threatening to Jane. But finally it is Rochester with whom her discovery of kinship, though metaphorical, feels the most intense. The discovery of her literal relatives, though not her parents as in *Pericles, Winter's Tale,* and *Evelina,* makes it possible for her to marry. Submerged in the imagery in which Rochester is Adam and Jane is Eve born from his side, and Rochester is also Lear to Jane's Cordelia, come back to save him in his misery, is a fantasy in which Rochester is Jane's father and her mother, and she is his mother.

In a number of plots the physical resemblance in the birth family is something we are told more by someone who observes it than by some-one who participates in it. Evelina's similarity to her dead mother is the crucial proof to her father that she is not an impostor. Dickens juxta-poses both Oliver and Esther to a portrait of their mother with a like-ness observable to others but not commented on explicitly by the chil-dren themselves. Pip discovers the physical similarity between Estella and Jaggers's servant Molly and learns the story of their relation, but never tells Estella.

In other plots physical resemblance is never noted, but spontaneous affection occurs between characters who later turn out to be blood relations. The commitment to Tom Jones that Squire Allworthy shows could be part of his general beneficence; his sister Bridget's interest could be part of what would be considered womanliness, but both turn out also to foreshadow their relationship to Tom. When Evelina sympathizes with the poor orphan Macartney, who turns out to be her brother, when Jane Eyre meets the Rivers sisters, when Oliver meets Rose, who turns out to be his aunt, the instant sense of affinity—in two of these cases also a matter of both being orphans—seems to have predicted their shared heredity.

However, in many of these novels there are counterexamples to show that shared heredity need not mean affection. Tom and Oliver are hated by their half-brothers Blifil and Monks; Evelina feels no affinity for her grandmother or her relations the Branghtons; and Fanny, devastatingly, having felt out of place with her rich aunt and uncle, also feels out of place when visiting her poor parents, brothers, and sisters. And of course all these novels contain families untouched by adoption in which relatives are at odds.

What of other kinds of resemblance beyond physical appearance among birth relatives? In most of these novels, these are developed only in a rather general way. Oliver and Rose are both virtuous; Jane feels a similarity of interests with the Rivers sisters, and they certainly resemble her temperamentally more than her other cousins the Reeds, but more specifics are rarely commented on. When Dickens gives Estella a birth mother who is a tamed murderer, we are left to wonder about the relevance to Estella's own psychology. Most of these novelists spell out many fewer specific similarities between adoptees and their birth families than the typical adoptee search narrative of recent years. Perhaps the best-known Victorian exception to this rule is George Eliot's depiction of heredity in *Felix Holt* and *Daniel Deronda*.

But even Eliot's novels, like the others, place more emphasis on the influence of adoptive parents, whether for good or for ill, than do Shakespeare's romances. In the previous chapter I found possibilities for reading the romances to see the impact of expectations and family stories, but this is an "against the grain" reading, not the meaning they most obviously convey. But the stress is quite different in these novels.

Squire Allworthy may occasionally err, but his generosity to Tom is much more discussed in the novel than, for example, the old shepherd's generosity to Perdita in Shakespeare's play. (And if the reader is tempted to think that the novel still presents this generosity as biologically based because he is Tom's uncle, think about how little emphasis Shakespeare gives to the generosity of uncles in whose household acknowledged nieces and nephews live, such as Leonato in *Much Ado.*) Many of the adoptive parents who are not related by birth are even more idealized than Allworthy: Brownlow, Evelina's adoptive father, Jarndyce. In writing her adoptive father, Evelina refers to herself as "creature of your own forming" and calls him "parent of my heart" (369). Perhaps, however, some of the characters express their gratitude in a way that reveals ambivalence to the reader. For example, of her "fate peculiarly cruel," Evelina remarks, "most benevolently have you guarded me from feeling it" (167–68).

The adoptive parents who are not idealized are still influential, even though not in ways they wanted. *Great Expectations* particularly shows this irony when Estella says to Miss Havisham, "I am what you have made me." The bad influence of Esther Summerson's godmother, in emphasizing her shame, continues throughout the book in the emphasis on Esther's diffidence. Several novels contrast adoptive children reared by different people in different ways, for example, Fanny versus the Crawfords.

In almost all of these books, one could argue, birth relatives are important and adoptive relatives are important too. Representing a group of characters related by both birth and adoption permits psychological and social exploration; it often dramatizes class differences, and, especially in Dickens, it emphasizes the unexpected connectedness of people in different classes, thus criticizing social divisions.

In the group of novels discussed here, it is quite striking that the admired adoptive parents are almost all male: Joe in *Great Expectations,* Villars in *Evelina,* Thomas Bertram in *Mansfield Park,* Jarndyce in *Bleak House,* Allworthy in *Tom Jones,* and Brownlow in *Oliver Twist* (which mitigates the pattern a bit with the presentation of Rose). Adoptive mothers are almost always presented with a dominant emphasis on criticism—consider Lady Bertram, Aunt Barbary, Miss Havisham, Pip's sister, Mrs. Reed. Some male adoptive parents are critically presented as well, but there are no good female adoptive parents as important in the novels as several of the good adoptive fathers are.

(Beyond the novels I focus on, there are exceptions to this generalization: consider, for example, Betsy Trotwood in *David Copperfield* and Lucy Snowe's godmother in *Villette*.) However, there are nurturing women, especially in the novels by women: Miss Temple, who helps Jane survive Lowood and becomes her model; Mary and Diana, her cousins; Lady Howard, who helps Evelina; Jenny, in *Bleak House*, who helps to take care of her friend's child; Mrs. Rouncewell, the model mother of the same novel.

Why are there, nevertheless, so many unpleasant adoptive mothers in these novels, all familiar enough in British literature to be influential? To some extent this is a special case of the negative presentation of mothers in Victorian fiction, what Marianne Hirsch has called "maternal repression," involving "absence, silence, and negativity."[55] Lady Bertram fits to some extent into the pattern of the "absent mother," but Barbary, Mrs. Reed, and Miss Havisham are all too present during the formative years of the central characters of their novels. Hirsch says that in Victorian fiction "multiple and surrogate mothers, like Jane Eyre's, are better able . . . to help daughters avoid the traditional temptations of romantic love, of marriage, and of objectification than a biological mother might be."[56] But clearly not every surrogate mother will do this. Or they may, like Aunt Barbary, disable a girl's self-confidence without even offering her the possible, if illusory, compensations of romantic love.

The novels I discuss here are particularly focused on the impact of children's upbringing, and since in our culture women have been most immediately involved in child rearing, this is one reason why surrogate mothers appear, rather than surrogate fathers, in narratives in which the treatment of children in early life harms them. This is most obvious in the way Dickens presents the different kinds of damage to Esther by Aunt Barbary, to Estella by Miss Havisham, and to Pip by Mrs. Joe. On the other hand, in order to provide happy endings for their characters, most of these novels need an adoptive father with social power, who has often been looking after the growing child from a distance—Villars, Bertram, Jarndyce, Brownlow, Allworthy. For day-to-day nurturing that is beneficent, the outstanding figure in these novels is Joe. His low social position makes a marked contrast with the status of the other men, and links him in some ways with Silas Marner, to be discussed in the next chapter. The mother substitute who comes closest to these fathers in both nurturing and importance is probably Rose.

Birth parents play smaller roles than adoptive parents in most of these novels. Birth mothers are dead in *Great Expectations, Evelina, Jane Eyre,* and *Oliver Twist.* Birth fathers are dead in all those novels except *Evelina,* and also in *Tom Jones.* The Prices play small, disappointing roles in *Mansfield Park,* after Fanny's reunion with them has been much anticipated. Both birth parents die during the course of *Bleak House,* the novel that gives the fullest sympathy to a birth mother. Molly in *Great Expectations* is a kind of pendant portrait to Lady Dedlock, at the other end of the class system but with a similar doom to shame and secrecy. Bridget in *Tom Jones* is a comic caricature. Evelina's birth father seems to be a negative character through most of the novel; then suddenly near the end we learn that misinformation accounts for his rejection of Evelina, and he now accepts her.

These patterns are quite different from the configurations in Shakespeare, if we remember the idealized pictures of birth mothers in *Winter's Tale* and *Pericles,* the flawed birth fathers central to both of those plays, and the subordinated lower-rank adoptive fathers of *Winter's Tale* and *Cymbeline.* One could find resemblances only in the dead birth mother and evil stepmother of *Cymbeline* (a play the Victorians loved) and the evil foster mother and good nurse of *Pericles.* The hints about the importance of caregivers' expectations in Shakespeare have turned into much clearer pictures of the impact of early environment. Harmful surrogate parents are themselves more psychologized in these novels. Rather than simply wanting to kill others' children to help their own, Aunt Barbary and Miss Havisham, even Aunt Reed, have moral agendas in their treatment of their adopted children, agendas that in some cases build on commonplaces of Victorian culture.

The novels I discuss in this chapter are important because they show how frequently the developing novel portrays adoption in a way that recognizes the importance of both heredity and nurture, protests against stigma, and mourns social divisions. The aspects of these novels that move me most are Fanny's sense of being out of place in both her families, the tragic difficulties of Esther's relationship with her birth mother, and Jane's fantasy family relationships with both the Rivers sisters and with Rochester ("He is akin to me"). I was in some ways a good girl like Fanny or Esther, but without their practical abilities and with more of Jane's recalcitrant spirit, evident mainly in my tendency to argue on behalf of open rebels. On the other hand, my family configuration was unlike that of most of these novels, with a distant, unhappy father and a loving adoptive mother. Perhaps because these novelists were more interested in critiquing adoptive mothers than adoptive fathers, and in critiquing flaws much larger than those my mother had, the pictures of adoptive households here do not particularly resonate with me. Nor do any of these novelists, unlike Eliot, present adoptive parenting in detail that I could identify with as a parent.

Many of the themes in these novels anticipate those in George Eliot's. Silas's and Rufus's care of their adoptees is similar in spirit to those of adoptive fathers like Brownlow, though Eliot's characters are much less idealized and much more limited. Daniel's questioning about his identity is a more thoroughly developed (and cross-gendered) version of Esther Summerson's, with ethnic and religious difference added on. Physical resemblance appears when he and Eppie finally meet their birth parents.

But in at least one way Eliot's novels are structured differently. In the three I discuss in the next chapter, the plots are all set up to suggest that the adoptee has a choice between two different ways of life, associated with two different sets of parents. In each case the choice is weighted to emphasize that the one chosen is better and therefore the choice is inevitable—but it is still more of a choice between different families than occurs in any of the other novels. I would argue that Eliot is probing more deeply into these questions. She plays around with words like *father* and *nature* much more in *Silas Marner* than any of the others do, demanding much more that the reader think about what fatherhood really is. This topic is hinted at by the great importance of the influence of adoptive parents in the other novels, but not developed into a possible redefinition, as in Eliot. She also shows Silas and Rufus giving more hands-on care to their adoptees than is the case with any of the adoptive parents in the other novels. And in *Daniel Deronda* she deals with the issue of adoptees' relation to cultural traditions in a way none of these novels attempt.

Five 🔊 Choices of Parentage, Identity, and Nation in George Eliot's Adoption Novels

When I was in my late twenties, my adoptive mother and I were discussing my then unknown birth mother, and she said something like, "She couldn't marry him because he was Jewish."

"What?" I exclaimed. This was a new element in the story.

"No, I was thinking about someone else," she took back the revelation. But within a few days she decided that I was old enough to handle the truth and acknowledged that my birth father was indeed Jewish.

Well! I was a committed, if left-wing, Catholic, but . . .

I went to a Holy Day service at the University's Hillel that year, and I started to research Jewish history to revise my dissertation chapter on *The Merchant of Venice* for publication. Some time after I met my birth mother, and shortly after the television miniseries on the Holocaust, I wrote my second letter to my birth father, and he responded with the article about himself I described earlier in this book. And no accompanying message except what was implied.

I have written him several times since then, never receiving a letter or even another newspaper article. Before my daughter was born, I wrote him yet again, asking about hereditary diseases. No word. More recently, I tried the approach of writing without mentioning my relationship to him, presenting myself as a researcher on immigrant Jews in Brooklyn. No answer from him, but a phone call from his wife, who left a message with my husband wanting to know how I got his name. I called, got the answering machine, left a message with my phone number, and eventually he called back. He didn't recognize my name. "You sent me an article about yourself a long time ago," I said.

"I don't want to talk about it," he said, and hung up.

In the early 1980s, I read *Daniel Deronda* for the first time. This, I felt, was *my book*! I had never before read any novel that discussed in such detail an adoptee's curiosity about ancestry, discovery that that ancestry was Jewish, nor finding a biological parent only to learn that a relationship with that parent was impossible.

But if the book was fascinating, it was also challenging. Personally, it was challenging because, in spite of the similarity in our stories, I could not follow Daniel into Judaism, and I wanted to understand why. Intellectually, *Daniel Deronda* was challenging because its plot is so different from the plots of Eliot's two other novels in which an adoptee must choose between biological and adoptive ancestry. Their adoptees make decisions opposite to Daniel's. In *Silas Marner* and *Felix Holt,* Eliot redefines parenthood to emphasize nurturance rather than genetics; in *Daniel Deronda* genetic parenthood is presented as "the real thing," and, reinforcing the picture of adoption as falsehood, Daniel's adoptive father seems to think more about how Daniel helps his image than about Daniel's feelings. In all three works, the adoptee's climactic choice is presented as the inevitable result of previous events in the novel, and the right thing to do. Though *Deronda* is especially interesting because of its detailed treatment of an adoptee's subjectivity, hidden Jewishness, and abortive reunion, this chapter will place it in the context of Eliot's whole career and in particular of her other fictions of adoption.

While adoption has been a common event in the English novel, George Eliot is the only well-known novelist who repeatedly structures her books to lead up to an adoptee's choice of heritage. Her one poetic drama, *The Spanish Gypsy,* written close in time to *Deronda,* has a similar structure—the main character changes her life when she discovers that her birth father is a Gypsy. And adoption also figures importantly in *Scenes of Clerical Life* and *Romola.*

Why was Eliot so interested in adoption? Why do *Silas Marner's* Eppie and *Felix Holt's* Esther choose their adoptive parents over their biological parents, while the adoptees in her last two works of fiction choose to identify with their heredity? What has been the effect of her fictions of adoption? Eliot's representations of adoption and adoptees are plot devices, and as Bernard Semmel points out in *George Eliot and the Politics of National Inheritance,* are ways of dealing with the nation's cultural past and recent social change.[1] While these contexts are important, I will analyze the novels in relation to adoption and not simply take their adoptions as allegories of other issues.

As the previous chapter has shown, many other British nineteenth-century novelists use adoption plots for psychological and social exploration: to dramatize struggles against stigma, to show class differences, and to emphasize the unexpected connections of widely separated characters. The number of adoptions in nineteenth-century novels is particularly striking because the institution was not legally formalized at that time. Figures on the frequency of informal adoptions are impossible to obtain (partly because of the difficulty of determining what counts as adoption, if it is informal), and historians differ significantly in their guesses.[2]

Neither George Eliot nor any other major novelist who dealt with this issue was adopted in any of the usual senses. Nor were most of their readers. We are dealing to a large extent with adoption as the precondition for the family romance plot, adoption in its mythic dimension—the fantasy that people develop to deal with uncongenial parents by imagining better parents elsewhere. It is indeed as this fantasy—related to Eliot's experience of alienation in her own family of origin—that adoption enters into her most directly autobiographical novel, *The Mill on the Floss*, when Maggie imagines the Gypsies as her "unknown kindred."[3]

Literal adoption occurred in Eliot's own circle and also, from a very early point, interested her in her reading. Her friend Charles Bray, who influenced her young adulthood enormously, adopted his own out-of-wedlock child, Nelly, with his wife Cara's consent, as Godfrey, in *Silas Marner*, might have done had he been willing to confess to Nancy.[4] Eliot—as I will call her for convenience, although she did not use this pseudonym until later—speaks about this child in a May 1845 letter and, later, sympathizes with Cara Bray on Nelly's death at nineteen: "There is no such thing as consolation, when we have made the lot of another our own as you did Nelly's."[5] While working on *Middlemarch* much later, Eliot came across a story somewhat similar to this one in Plutarch's *On the Virtues of Women* and recorded it in her notebook: "Stratonica, wife of Degetanus, being barren persuaded him to take another woman, & educated their children tenderly & magnificently."[6] During her preparatory reading for *Middlemarch*, she also took note of one of the classic analyses of adoption as a fiction, in Henry J. S.

Maine's *Ancient Law.* This book is distinctive for the view that "without the Fiction of Adoption which permits the family tie to be artificially created, it is difficult to understand how society would ever have escaped from its swaddling clothes and taken its first steps toward civilization."[7] She summarizes from Maine, "Kinship conceived as the sole ground of community in political functions (The substitution of *local contiguity* a startling revolution). Hence adoption & the fiction of a common progenitor."[8]

The most immediate variety of adoption in George Eliot's milieu, however, was her own relationship to G. H. Lewes's sons. In 1859, when she and Lewes made a mutual commitment that would have been marriage except for the peculiarities of Victorian restrictions on divorce, Lewes's oldest son, Charles, then sixteen, wrote her a letter addressing her as "Mother."[9] Eliot was forty, the same age Silas Marner is when little Eppie wanders into his home. Her commitment was so great that when Charles came to live with them, she and Lewes moved to a home in town, although she preferred the country, because Charles needed to live near his work. These biographical details are surely among the reasons why *Silas Marner,* as Eliot put it, "thrust itself" on her to interrupt her work on *Romola* (GEL 3:360). She was thinking about child rearing, and in particular about the rearing of a child not born to her. Rosemarie Bodenheimer traces in detail George Eliot's relation to her three stepsons, and notes that "her focus on children brought up by substitute parents, and her privileging of fostering over kinship, was a dominant feature of her imagination from 1860 to the end of her career; the experience of her stepsons gave her the authority for those imagined lives."[10]

I want to extend Bodenheimer's convincing analysis here. If not yet a dominant feature of her imagination, adoption was of interest to Eliot even before 1860; the unfortunate heroine of "Mr. Gilfil's Love Story," the second story she published (in 1857), is a poor Italian girl adopted by an English aristocrat. This apparently is a transformation of the story of a collier's daughter educated as a singer by Lady Newdigate, of the family for whom Eliot's father had worked (GEL 3:21n). Even earlier, in 1855, she took notes on a story in which "a man of wealth in Rome adopted a poor boy he had found in the street" who turned out to be a great villain.[11] Her prospective role as stepmother to Lewes's sons may have already been on her mind; both of these plots suggest fear that adoption could be disastrous. But in 1860, when two of the boys have actually lived with her and Lewes in London, she feels impelled to write *Silas Marner,* her most positive picture of adoption. As Bodenheimer also notes, adoption takes on an importance in Eliot's fiction that goes far beyond her reflections on her step-parenthood. She analyzes adoptions across class, race, nation, and culture, and contrasts nurturing and self-centered parental relationships. In the way that adoption dramatizes the need to deal with other people's differences from oneself, it becomes a paradigmatic test for her central concern with sympathy.[12]

Silas Marner rewrites the plot of many novels and plays in which a character is reunited with biological parents and returns to them. Godfrey Cass refuses to acknowledge Molly, the wife he has secretly married. When she dies, their daughter Eppie wanders into the home of the poor, isolated weaver Silas. Silas raises her with much love; she flourishes, and through his concern for Eppie, Silas develops ties with other people. After many years, childless by his acknowledged wife, Nancy, Godfrey reveals himself to Silas and Eppie as her father, and asks her to return to him. He says, "I have a natural claim on her that must stand before every other" (169). But Eppie does not agree.[13] In *Silas Marner,* adoptive parenthood is the crucial parenthood.

In one sense, the novel is a dramatized child custody case. But instead of the legal system, Eppie herself—and the readers—must decide which family she should choose. How does her rejection of heredity in favor of nurture become the right and inevitable choice in a novel full of descriptions and imagery of natural growth?

At stake is the meaning of two key words, *father* and *nature.* Both represent important concerns for Eliot. She had written about a compelling father-daughter relationship in *The Mill on the Floss,* was working on one in *Romola,* and was much interested in the approach to nature in the science of her day as well as aesthetically. As *father, nature,* and their variants sound repeatedly in the dialogue and narration, child rearing comes to define both. The novel challenges the opposition between adoption and nature and presents adoptive relationships as natural in themselves. Indeed, in a letter to her publisher as she is completing *Silas,* Eliot describes as its intended emphasis "the remedial influences of pure, natural human relations" (GEL 3:382). Perhaps partly to help engage a reader more skeptical about adoption, she grounds Silas's first association for Eppie—after he discovers that she is not a heap of gold but a golden-haired child—in the memory of his long-dead little sister, after whom he names her.

Long before the novel explicitly engages with prejudices against adoption, its language, like the plot, encourages the reader to see parenthood as not only genetic and the nurture of adoption as natural. Dolly, the book's authority on child rearing, says to Silas, "You'll have a right to her if you're a father to her, and bring her up according" (123). She predicts that with Silas, "The child 'ull grow like grass i' May" (121). Silas's raising Eppie is compared to the way "some man who has a precious plant to which he would give a nurturing home in a new soil, thinks of the rain and sunshine, and all influences, in relation to his nursling, and asks industriously for all knowledge that will help him to satisfy the wants of the searching roots" (131). He acts like a parental bird: "the stone hut was made a soft nest for her, lined with downy patience" (129). Silas goes out to the meadows with Eppie, she plucks flowers, they listen for birds: nurturing his adoptee, Silas puts them both in close contact with nature. Eppie at sixteen is "the freshest blossom of youth" (138) with a suitor who woos her partly by promising to bring her flowers from the gardens where he works. They will be doing more transplanting and nurturing, as metaphorically Silas did.[14]

In the crucial confrontation scene, from Nancy's point of view Godfrey is the "real father" and "father by blood" (171) and Silas is "foster-father" (171); she thinks "there's a duty you owe to your lawful father" (173). On the other hand, from Eppie's point of view, Silas is the "long-loved father" and Godfrey is the "unfamiliar father" (note the pun on *family* in "unfamiliar") (171). Pointing up the irony in the term "real," Eppie thinks of Silas as "a father very close to her, who loved her better than any real fathers in the village seemed to love their daughters" (147). As Silas says to Godfrey, "It's me she's been calling her father ever since she could say the word" (170).

Though Godfrey maintains, "I have a natural claim on her that must stand before every other" (169), the novel contests this argument. And when he gives up that claim, it is with an image of an accomplished natural process: "While I've been putting off and putting off, the trees have been growing—it's too late now" (174).

In addition to presenting Eppie's relationship with Silas as natural, the novel also tries to support it by treating the Raveloe community's valorization of heredity and its dominant ideas of what is natural critically. In a comic exaggeration of restrictive views, the town of Raveloe welcomes Doctor Kimble "as a doctor by hereditary right," a response accompanied by the belief that "Kimble was inherently a doctor's name." Since he has no son, the practice may "one day be handed over to a successor, with the incongruous name of Taylor or Johnson. But in that case the wiser people in Raveloe would employ Dr. Blick of Flitton—as less unnatural" (98).

More centrally, in Nancy's early refusal to adopt Eppie, whose heredity she does not know, the novel engages explicitly with prejudices against adoption. Nancy believes that "to adopt a child, because children of your own had been denied you, was to try and choose your lot in spite of Providence; the adopted child, she was convinced, would never turn out well, and would be a curse to those who had wilfully and rebelliously sought what it was clear that, for some high reason, they were better without" (156). She recalls an acquaintance's story about an adopted "child" who became a criminal: "That was the only adopting I ever heard of: and the child was transported [to Australia, for punishment] when it was twenty-three" (157). Notice her reference to the twenty-three-year-old as a child, and with the pronoun "it"—generally not used of human beings, at least not of human beings past early childhood.[15]

Eliot encourages the reader to criticize Nancy's bias against adoption, associating it with the past: "Adoption was more remote from the ideas and habits of that time than of our own" (155–56). She links it with other examples of Nancy's "unalterable little code. . . . she insisted on dressing like Priscilla, because 'it was right for sisters to dress alike'" (156). Then she suggests that Nancy's thinking is "nearly akin to that of many devout people, whose beliefs are held in the shape of a system quite remote from her knowledge" (157). Prejudice against adoption is thus associated with system. The paragraph ends by commenting that "human beliefs, like all natural growths, elude the barriers of system," which suggests that a too rigid system like Nancy's or that of the more educated "devout people" is unnatural. Furthermore, Eliot criticizes Nancy's prejudices by the implied contrast between the admirable Eppie and the transported twenty-three-year-old, as well as by the sadness and guilt that both Nancy and Godfrey feel when Nancy finds out the truth about Eppie, and Godfrey realizes that Nancy might have been willing to adopt her if she had known of his parenthood earlier.

Although this is a novel that favors adoption, it does show some effects of heredity on Eppie. Eppie's hair and eyes are like Godfrey's, so much so that Molly plans to use this resemblance as proof of their relationship. We are told that, as Eppie grows up, she "cannot help being rather vexed about her hair, for there is no other girl in Raveloe who has hair at all like it, and she thinks hair ought to be smooth" (138). What she sees as unruliness is also associated with nature: "the hair ripples as obstinately as a brooklet under the March breeze." With Eppie's limited perception, she does not understand that her curly auburn hair would, by many people, be regarded as more beautiful; in this detail the novel includes a remnant of the traditional romance of separated family members, which emphasizes their physical similarity by contrast to others—even perhaps a trace of the ugly duckling story, in which the cygnet must find the swans to avoid being judged by ducks' standards. However, throughout the novel, among the many characters who have some acquaintance with both Eppie and Godfrey, no one but Molly, in this heredity-conscious town of Raveloe, perceives their resemblance until the very end. Only after Eppie has rejected them does Nancy observe to Godfrey that she has "just your hair and eyes: I wondered it had never struck me before." The great social gap between the two figures has prevented anyone not already aware from thinking about whether the two auburn heads might have some connection.

To add to that social gap, there was available in Eliot's England a view of national composition that would make Silas's adoption of Eppie virtually a transracial adoption. Scott and Disraeli had emphasized the differing heritage of the Saxons and the Normans in the making of England in a way that encouraged nineteenth-century England to regard the poor as descendants of the Saxons and the rich as descendants of the Normans.[16] Disraeli's *Sybil* had as its subtitle *The Two Nations,* which referred to the rich and the poor, between whom, he wrote, "there is no intercourse and no sympathy; who are as ignorant of each other's habits, thoughts, and feelings, as if they were dwellers in different zones, or inhabitants of different planets; who are formed by a different breeding, are fed by a different food, are ordered by different manners, and are not governed by the same laws."[17] Eppie's transfer from Godfrey's world to Silas's has been so complete that no one imagines she might have been part of Godfrey's world. While the novel refuses the apparent reconciliation of the classes that her return to Godfrey would suggest—in the traditional romance plot—it is partly to point out that rich and poor, Godfrey and Eppie, are already bound in important but unrecognized ways.

However, in *Silas Marner* the bond of child-father kinship is most importantly a matter of responsible action—or, as Susan R. Cohen writes, "creative human affection"—more than of biology.[18] Even Nancy, in spite of her prejudice against adoption, eventually concedes, "It's natural you should cling to those who've brought you up" (173). She then falls back on duty to define Godfrey's tie to Eppie, but his own behavior has discredited this appeal. While Eliot uses the tradition of showing the adopted child as different from the other children in her environment, she makes a point of attributing as much of the difference here to Silas's loving care of Eppie as to her upper-class heredity. "The tender and peculiar love with which Silas had reared her in almost inseparable companionship with himself, aided by the seclusion of their dwelling, had prevented her from the lowering influences of the village talk and habits" (146). While Eppie's "delicate prettiness" must to some extent come from her heredity, Eliot emphasizes the influence of Silas's "perfect love" and its "breath of poetry" on her "refinement and fervour." Nevertheless, Eppie presents her choice of Silas not just as a choice of an individual family, but also as a choice of class: "I wasn't brought up to be a lady, and I can't turn my mind to it. I like the working-folks, and their houses, and their ways. And . . . I'm promised to marry a working-man" (173). (No one mentions the fact that her choice of life is also closer to her mother's class, and her mother's influence on her heredity is never discussed.)

As Rosemarie Bodenheimer has noted, Silas's rearing of Eppie is idealized in many ways that can be seen as transmutations of Eliot's own experience as a stepmother—and many of our own experiences of child rearing. There is no problem when Eppie interrupts Silas's work; there is no problem when Silas doesn't discipline Eppie. The novel is in many ways a fantasy, and a fantasy particularly appealing to someone who values nonbiological parenting. The transfer of Eppie from her mother to Silas is, as Bodenheimer writes, "performed when both adults are unconscious," thus eliminating conflict. Furthermore, both biological parents are, in different ways, clearly unworthy, and out of the picture for most of the novel.[19] Silas is completely open with Eppie about her history: "It would have been impossible for him to hide from Eppie that she was not his own child" (146). Though he is modest here in his claim on her, she thinks hardly at all about any other father; she wants to know more about her mother, but does not know enough to worry about her mother's addiction to drink or opium, and what of this she might have inherited. It is, however, very important that the parents were married—her mother's wedding ring is very precious to her. The ring is necessary to the plot because Godfrey's relationship to her mother must be serious enough to be an obstacle to the higher-status marriage he wants, but it also saves Eppie from stigma.

Molly Farren, Eppie's mother, is almost as absent from the novel as she can possibly be. There is no suggestion that Eppie has inherited anything from her. Godfrey's secret marriage to her is described as the consequence of "a movement of compunction . . . on a pliant nature . . . an ugly story of low passion, delusion, and waking from delusion" (30). Eliot devotes two pages of chapter 12 to Molly's point of view, which is no prettier. As she walks through the snow to confront the Cass family, "Molly knew that the cause of her dingy rags was not her husband's neglect, but the demon Opium to whom she was enslaved, body and soul" (107). As Nancy Paxton observes, Eliot is emphasizing the idea that maternal altruism must be cultivated; it is not an automatic instinct that always prevails.[20] Molly does have good impulses: the sentence quoted above, for example, continues, "except in the lingering mother's tenderness that refused to give him her hungry child."[21] Cold and tired, Molly thinks of getting comfort from "the familiar demon in her bosom; but . . . the mother's love pleaded for painful consciousness rather than oblivion—pleaded to be left in aching weariness, rather than to have the encircling arms benumbed so that they could not feel the dear burden" (108). But the negative picture of Molly dominates: in effect the birth mother is being sacrificed to save the reader's sympathies—to some small extent for Godfrey, and much more for Silas. Eliot even goes so far as to associate the beginning of Eppie's exalted basking in love and poetry with the moment she leaves her dead mother, before she actually meets Silas: "this breath of poetry had surrounded Eppie from the time when she had followed the bright gleam that beckoned her to Silas's hearth" (146). Considering how often *Silas Marner* has been required school reading, how many adoptees have formed pictures of their birth mother based on it? How many birth mothers who came back to school with the assurance that no one would ever know where they had been, could tell no one why they hated this book?

The family romance, discussed by Freud, analyzed by Frye and others, and repeated in many tales, novels, and plays, including *The Winter's Tale,* casts the birth parents as rich nobility and the adoptive parents as poor commoners.[22] In real life, the situation is more likely to be the opposite. Molly's poverty is the detail of this novel that resonates most with the actual circumstances of most historical and recent birth mothers.

How does ideology of class register in the novel? In the insistence that even Molly knew that Godfrey is not really the cause of her problems, the novel is class-biased and conservative. Nevertheless, in other ways the novel uses the adoption plot to protest against the split between classes. This protest is made very subtly. No one thinks about the similarity between Godfrey's and Eppie's hair, in spite of the fact that they live fairly close together (Godfrey eventually becomes Silas's landlord).[23] However, Aaron, the gardener Eppie marries, does, once, make the protest more explicitly. Discussing the excess of flowers owned by the Casses, he says "there's never a garden in all the parish but what there's endless waste in it for want o' somebody as could use everything up. . . . there need nobody run short o' victuals if the land was made the most on" (140).

Near the end of *Silas Marner,* Aaron transplants the superfluous flowers to make a garden for Eppie, where she can nurture them as Silas nurtured her after her own transplant. Just as Eliot rewrites Shakespeare's *Winter's Tale* in making Eppie choose her adoptive father, she rewrites the passage in *The Winter's Tale* in which the unknowing adoptee Perdita rejects grafted flowers; instead the novel supports the argument of Perdita's interlocutor Polixenes, which Eliot quotes elsewhere: "This is an art / Which does mend nature, change it rather, but / The art itself is nature."[24]

Romola, on which Eliot was already working when she began *Silas Marner,* presents a very different picture of the results of adoption. Romola's husband Tito had been, as a little boy, "rescued . . . from a life of beggary, filth, and cruel wrong, [and] . . . reared . . . tenderly," by Baldassare, whom Tito, as an adult, refuses to ransom from slavery.[25] When Baldassare is freed, he pursues the ambitious Tito for vengeance and, like the adoptive father in Eliot's notebook, kills him. But as if Eliot needed to place a positive picture of adoption next to the picture of an unsuccessful one, right after Tito's death Romola rescues a Jewish child whose family has died of the plague, cares for him while she serves the plague-stricken village, leaves him with another adoptive mother there, and seeks out Tessa, who has had two children by Tito believing that they were married, so that she can help Tessa raise those children. This is all narrated in a few idealizing pages—the Jewish child is baptized Benedetto (blessed) without any thought of a problem in changing his religion, and Mamma Romola, as he calls her, tells Tessa's little Lillo of the baseness of "a man to whom I was once very near" (675), without the hint that she is one day to tell him that this was his father.

In *Felix Holt,* her next novel, Eliot once again explores a father-daughter adoption, with many similarities to the one in *Silas Marner,* but in a more realistic tone and with a more extended look at the class and national issues that discovering heredity can involve. Esther's original father, Bycliffe, an aristocratic English prisoner of war, dies without ever seeing her. Her mother, Annette, a Frenchwoman who goes to England to seek him out, finds refuge in her hunger and poverty with a poor Dissenting minister, Rufus. French and Catholic, she seems blind to Rufus, but he loves her silently with the passion of a delayed first love, and provides for her and little Esther, to the shock of his parishioners. Passively she accepts his love and agrees to marry him, and when she dies four years later, Esther becomes his responsibility.

As in *Silas Marner,* Eliot suggests a class contrast between adopted daughter and father; we first see Esther through the eyes of Felix, whose quest to bring about political reform by educating workers is a central concern of the novel, and who eventually provides some moral education for Esther: "a very delicate scent, the faint suggestion of a garden, was wafted as she went. . . . he had a sense of an elastic walk, the tread of small feet, a long neck and a high crown of shining brown plaits with curls that floated backward—things, in short, that suggested a fine lady to him."[26] Because she speaks some French from her early life with her mother, Rufus has sent her to school in France, to prepare her to support herself by language teaching. But he does not anticipate how her governess position will affect her. Unlike Eppie, Esther experiences several conflicting kinds of environment: after her time with Rufus, "all her native tendencies towards luxury, fastidiousness, and scorn of mock gentility, were strengthened by witnessing the habits of a well-born and wealthy family" (159). While *Silas Marner* emphasizes the idealization that Silas's love of Eppie brings, *Felix Holt* presents the love of a poor adoptive father from the viewpoint of a daughter raised in a more pretentious environment. The novel vividly portrays her ambivalence about Rufus: "Esther had affection for her father: she recognised the purity of his character, and a quickness of intellect in him which responded to her own liveliness, in spite of what seemed a dreary piety, which selected everything that was least interesting and romantic in life and history. But his old clothes had a smoky odour" (161). Extending this ambivalence, through most of the book Esther is troubled by self-division: "Her life was a heap of fragments, and so were her thoughts" (264).

Rufus is less idealized than Silas not only from his daughter's point of view but also from other perspectives; he refuses to give Esther more than a sentence of information about her mother, because "He had not the courage to tell Esther that he was not really her father: he had not the courage to renounce that hold on her tenderness which the belief in his natural fatherhood must help to give him, or to incur any resentment that her quick spirit might feel at having been brought up under a false supposition" (162).

Thus, though memories of her mother are more vivid than Eppie's, they are not vivid enough: "she had no more than a broken vision of the time before she was five years old . . . when a very small white hand, different from any that came after, used to pat her, and stroke her. . . and when at last there was nothing but sitting with a doll on a bed where mamma was lying, till her father once carried her away" (161).

The psychological question of which way Esther's attitude to Rufus is going to turn is closely connected with the plot question of what she will find out about her heredity; these questions fuse when Esther learns that she is heir to the Transome estate and must decide whether to accept it.

When Rufus learns that Esther might profit "if the law knew who was her father" (350), he tells her the next day. This openness transforms their relationship:

> her mind seemed suddenly enlarged by a vision of passion and struggle, of delight and renunciation, in the lot of beings who had hitherto been a dull enigma to her. And in the act of unfolding to her that he was not her real father, but had only striven to cherish her as a father, had only longed to be loved as a father, the odd, wayworn, unworldly man became the object of a new sympathy in which Esther felt herself exalted. (354)

As in *Silas Marner,* the language plays with the question of who should be called father. The characters are introduced in chapter 5 simply as father and daughter; but the passage about Rufus's failure to tell the story describes him as "not really her father." When Christian, her dead birth father's acquaintance, discusses Esther with Rufus, he makes a point of calling her Rufus's "daughter, step-daughter, I should say" (351). But Rufus's answer to him refers to "my daughter's birth," and Christian follows him in saying, "It is for your daughter's interest" (352). When Rufus tells Esther the story for the first time, the narrator refers to "her step-father's long-pent-up experience" (354). After the passage that describes Rufus's confession (see above), where the question of what is real fatherhood is posed partly by the ironical uses of "only," the two of them are mostly "father" and "daughter" again, both in their words to each other and in the narrator's references. Once Esther speaks of the other man as her "first father" (356), and for a while she still thinks of him as her "real father." But Silas is her "present father." And for the rest of the book *father* and *daughter* are the words they and the narrator use.

Unlike the situation in *Silas Marner,* there is no competing father alive, no relative to question the importance of Esther's bond to Rufus in terms of duty. Esther's dilemma about whether to accept the inheritance of the Transome estate becomes a choice of which world, which class identity, she wants—whether she should marry Harold Transome, who is interested in her mostly because he hopes to keep a claim to the estate that is now legally hers, or Felix Holt, who by contrast has vowed that he will never be rich and would refuse to marry her if she accepted the inheritance. The possibilities that she might accept the inheritance and not marry anyone, or that Rufus could move with her to Transome Court, are briefly raised and then denied.

As in *Silas Marner,* nature imagery is an important preparation for the adoptee's choice, but here it is associated with Felix (rather than Rufus) and, more explicitly than in *Silas Marner,* with opposition to social convention and to the artificiality of Esther's previous values. Earlier in the novel, Esther's thoughts of Felix in his absence, "mixed with some longings for a better understanding," are analyzed thus: "in our spring-time every day has its hidden growths in the mind, as it has in the earth when the little folded blades are getting ready to pierce the ground" (292). In the afternoon of the day on which Rufus tells her about her heredity, Felix takes Esther for a walk through the fields. The issue is not simply nature, but spontaneous, unconventional nature, as the epigraph, drawn from Coriolanus's attack on custom, emphasizes: "walking alone with Felix might be a subject of remark—all the more because of his cap, patched boots, no cravat, and thick stick. Esther was a little amazed herself at what she had come to. So our lives glide on: the river ends we don't know where, and the sea begins, and then there is no more jumping ashore" (360). Felix's emphasis on nature revises the language of blood, so that its favorable sense no longer refers only to aristocratic heredity: "I have the blood of a line of handicraftsmen in my veins, and I want to stand up for the lot of the handicraftsmen as a good lot, in which a man may be better trained to all the best functions of his nature than if he belonged to the grimacing set who have visiting-cards, and are proud to be thought richer than their neighbours" (366). Like a hero of pastoral literature, Felix chooses to withdraw from "the push and the scramble for money and position" and prefers to observe "how beautiful those stooping birch-stems are with the light on them" (362). He believes that his choice is understandable because of "my history or my nature" (360), suggesting that they point in the same direction.

Harold, on the other hand, chooses a kind of progress opposed to nature, cutting down trees and memories. Esther perceives that "the utmost enjoyment of his own advantages was the solvent that blended pride in his family and position, with the adhesion to changes that were to obliterate tradition and melt down enchased gold heirlooms into plating for the egg-spoons of 'the people'" (529).

In Bycliffe, Esther's genetic father, aristocratic rank was combined with nobility of character. Rufus recalls from his wife's words that he was "beautiful to the eye, and good and generous; and that his family was of those who have been long privileged among their fellows" (356). But that combination of aristocracy and generosity is lost to Harold and the other Transomes, who currently hold the estate that should have gone to Bycliffe and are portrayed in devastating terms. Mrs. Transome suffers the consequences of her long-ago affair with Jermyn, her lawyer, in his mishandling of her estate as well as in Harold's determination to sue him for it; she is miserably unhappy in her relations with both men as well as with her apparently senile husband, whom she scorns. Esther knows that Harold has "a padded yoke ready for the neck of every man, woman, and child that depended on him" (538). And to further undercut the Transome family, Esther's discovery of her heredity is paralleled with Harold Transome's discovery, near the end of the novel, that Jermyn is really his genetic father—so Harold is not even a legitimate heir of the Transomes, even apart from the fact that their claim legally belongs to the Bycliffes. The Transomes' false position, and Harold's doubly false position as a Transome, are presented as corresponding to their moral defects.

The novel emphasizes Esther's divided feelings about marrying Harold. She is drawn to him by what the narrator calls "native tendencies" (548), associated with her aristocratic ancestry, but these are tendencies "against which she had once begun to struggle." She sees marrying Harold as the road to "a life of middling delights" instead of the "high mountain air" (547) of Felix and his life of both nature and aspiration. She also feels "generous sympathy for the Transomes" (548) and, motherless herself, responds to Mrs. Transome's desire to mother her.

Two dramatic events push her in the other direction. One is Felix's imprisonment for inciting a riot, when he was actually trying to calm the crowd. She visits him in prison and is irresistibly drawn to speak in his defense at his trial. The other is the talk with Mrs. Transome, after Harold's paternity has been exposed, in which Esther sees the "tragedy of this woman's life, the dreary waste of years empty of sweet trust and affection" (597). This vision destroys any appeal that life as another Mrs. Transome might have had for her.

How does this novel ultimately imagine Esther's identity as an adoptee? Esther's last conversation with Felix in the novel, where their life together is pledged, touches on issues in her heredity: they joke about her curls, of which she says "they cost nothing—they are natural" (601), and she plans to teach French, at least to him. But she identifies herself not as the "delicate creature" he calls her but as "very healthy. Poor women, I think, are healthier than the rich" (602). Eliot has used the adoption/discovery plot to emphasize Esther's choice of the class of her adopted father rather than of her biological father. (While her work as a French teacher comes from Rufus's decision to encourage her to do more work in her mother's language, in her refusal of delicacy she is choosing against, at least, Rufus's image of her mother as "of delicate nurture" (165).

Esther's choice against taking her hereditary place stands out in a novel where heredity is such a repeated theme. We hear of "blind hereditary Tories" (152), "sound hereditary British manner" (190), "hereditary bias and class interest" (195). In the cases of both Esther and Harold, the physical similarity across generations is dramatic, and it is not only physical. When Esther begins to behave more sympathetically to Rufus, he says, "Child, what has happened? you have become the image of your mother to-night" (245). To someone who has seen them both, "Esther's features and expression, and still more her bearing, now she stood and walked, revived Bycliffe's image" (348). When Jermyn tells Harold, during a fight, "I am your father," and Harold looks at Jermyn's face in a mirror "with his own beside . . . [he] saw the hated fatherhood reasserted" (581). Harold has long wondered why he had "the trick of getting fat" (90) when his father was so thin; Harold and Jermyn roll their fingers in the same way, and Jermyn thinks that Harold "has inherited a deuced faculty for business" (286). Harold has unknowingly behaved in an entrepreneurial manner similar to that of the biological father he hates—a foundling who is probably also illegitimate (see 125). Esther is drawn toward a life associated with her heredity and with her upbringing in France, but ultimately rejects it. Heredity is influential, but not all-determining. And the use of the word *hereditary* in phrases like "the old hereditary printer" (373) sometimes seems like mockery, as in *Silas Marner*.

In both *Silas Marner* and *Felix Holt,* Eliot is reversing the old plot in which the adopted child discovers an aristocratic background that permits marriage into an aristocratic family. Marrying Felix is more complicated than marrying Aaron in *Silas Marner,* however; Felix, who has studied in Glasgow, is cosmopolitan; he often seems out of place among the workers, and there are divisions in him corresponding to Esther's divisions, even though her relationship with him is supposed to bring her wholeness. Although Felix's language has some affinities with that of actual reformers of his time, who included watchmakers and weavers in their ranks, he is clearly presented in an idealized mode.[27] Following him as a moral guide thus provides a miraculous solution to Esther's identity problems as an adoptee.

Esther's story in *Felix Holt* also plays off against and reverses the story of the biblical Esther, which valorizes heredity. Her name echoed in Eliot's own time by Dickens's Esther Summerson of *Bleak House* (1852–53), the original Esther was an orphan raised by her cousin Mordecai. Explicitly recalled when Eliot early in the narrative refers to her character as Queen Esther, the biblical Esther married King Ahasuerus, who did not know she was Jewish. When the king plans to

exterminate the Jews in his country under the influence of his evil coun-
selor Haman, Mordecai asks her to plead with the king. In the climactic moment of this book, Esther speaks out, revealing her ancestry, and
asking the king to spare the lives of her people. The king relents. Eliot
and many of her readers would have known this story not only through
the Bible but also through the Racine play and the Handel opera.[28]

In Eliot's Esther's climactic moment, she too speaks out to save
someone. When Felix is in trial for his behavior during the riot, Esther
intervenes to tell what she knows about his wish to quiet the disturbance and to testify to his kindness and what she calls his noble nature.
While this does not sway the judge, it persuades a number of influential
men to sign a memorial that ultimately brings about Felix's pardon.
Furthermore, Esther's act consolidates her decision that her place is
with Felix and his moral leadership rather than with Harold and his
wealth, a decision for a life closer to her adoptive father's than her biological father's. While the biblical Esther spoke at the same time for her
adoptive parent and her hereditary community, which he shared, this
Esther chooses her adoptive community. But both Eliot's Esther and the
Bible's make a decision that is also seen in religious terms. The narrator
suggests that Esther's choice can give "unity to life, and [make] the
memory a temple where all relics and all votive offerings, all worship
and all grateful joy, are an unbroken history sanctified by one religion"
(551). Her final decision respects both her ministerial adopted father
and Felix's secular religion of moral education.

Eliot's last novel, *Daniel Deronda,* published in 1876, likewise gives the
title character a choice of identities, but this time heredity, rather than
nurture, is compelling. Daniel has been raised as the nephew of an English gentleman, but his help to a poor Jewish girl, Mirah, leads to the
discovery that he is himself Jewish by ancestry.[29] His mother, a former
opera singer who felt stifled by Judaism and by his birth, had placed
him with his guardian so that he would be free from Judaism and she
would be free to sing; thwarted in her career anyway, Leonora tells him
her story out of guilt but does not want a continuing relationship with
him. Though disappointed in his mother, Daniel is so committed to his
newfound identity that at the end he leaves England to help begin a Jewish nation in Palestine. Daniel's development is presented in counter-
point with that of Gwendolen, who marries disastrously to save herself
from poverty, and to whom he becomes a mentor.

From early in the novel Daniel wonders about his origins more consistently and intensely than Eppie and Esther.[30] Reading Renaissance church history, the thirteen-year-old Daniel discovers that *nephew* could be a euphemism for *illegitimate son*. He at once applies this to himself, with a sudden sense of loss, disillusionment with his beloved guardian Sir Hugo, and "the idea that others probably knew things concerning him which they did not choose to mention, and which he would not have had them mention."[31] Although as an adolescent his "tastes were altogether in keeping with his nurture" (143), he notices that no one in the gallery of family pictures looks like him. He is embarrassed and angry when his uncle asks him if he would like to be a great singer, because he knows that singing is not a career for gentlemen like his uncle. While curious about his heredity, Daniel never asks his uncle about it, both because he thinks his uncle wants secrecy and because he doesn't want to "bring himself near even a silent admission of the sore that had opened in him" (145). As a consequence, Daniel seems reserved when other boys talk about their families. His speculations about his heredity are turned into persistent silent questions about whom he looks like and into sympathy for his unknown mother, who he feels was wronged, and by extension for all women.

The novel also prepares for Daniel's choice by showing Sir Hugo's lapses of sensitivity. Sir Hugo is a kindly man, a much more appealing adoptive parent than most of the adoptive mothers discussed in the previous chapter but more critically presented than most of the adoptive fathers. He keeps Daniel's heredity secret, and this focuses the novel's critique of him specifically on that secrecy about Daniel's difference from himself.[32] Earlier in Daniel's life, Sir Hugo had told him, "You lost your father and mother when you were quite a little one" (139), and a little later, encouragingly, "The best horse will win in spite of pedigree" (138), which presumably reinforces Daniel's sense that his own pedigree is bad. Otherwise he never discusses the matter until he is forced to do so late in the book. The narrator tells us that he is pleased that Daniel is generally thought of as his son: "his imagination had never once been troubled with the way in which the boy himself might be affected, either then or in the future, by the enigmatic aspect of his circumstances. . . . what could be more natural [that word again] than that he should have a beautiful boy like the little Deronda to take care of?" (148).

Nevertheless, Sir Hugo does not choose to be called Daniel's father or foster father, and the novel does not play much with variations on the word *father,* in describing him. Instead, the narrator suggests that Sir Hugo regards him as a possession, at best a pet, at worst an object: "a convenience in the family . . . this substitute for a son" (192–93). Most devastatingly, Daniel himself realizes that Hugo regards children as "a product intended to make life more agreeable to the full-grown, whose convenience alone was to be consulted in the disposal of them." Daniel half-excuses Hugo with the thought that this attitude "was massively acted on at that date of the world's history" (612), but this observation adds to Eliot's social critique, hinting at obliviousness to children in families made more conventionally than Hugo's and Daniel's.[33]

Unlike Silas's child-rearing, furthermore, Sir Hugo's care for Daniel is seldom described with imagery of natural growth. Late in the novel, when Daniel is wondering about how to behave if his ancestry is Jewish, he does describe his upbringing as giving rise to "Feelings which have struck root through half my life" (430). But along with his affection for Hugo, there has grown in Daniel an "early-rooted feeling that his birth had been attended with injury for which his father [Hugo] was to blame" (237).

Nature imagery, by contrast, is much more intense in the language used by Mordecai (Mirah's brother) about the restored Jewish nation he envisions: "Is it rational to drain away the sap of special kindred that makes the families of man rich in interchanged wealth, and various as the forests are various with the glory of the cedar and the palm?" (451). Daniel longs to be part of an organic social unit, and Mordecai, convinced they are related, offers him one: "Have we not quivered together like the leaves from a common stem with stirrings from a common root?" (489). When he discovers his Jewish birth, Daniel picks up this imagery in speaking to his mother: "Your will was strong, but my grandfather's trust which you accepted and did not fulfil—what you call his yoke—is the expression of something stronger, with deeper, farther-spreading roots" (568).[34]

The imagery of roots in this novel, unlike the nature imagery of *Silas Marner,* does not emphasize the conscious choice of the nurturer. Where imagery of active nurturing occurs, *Deronda* is clearly dealing with a different issue than the child rearing of *Silas.* He speaks of "the men who had the visions which, as Mordecai said, were the creators and feeders of the world—moulding and feeding the more passive life which without them would dwindle and shrivel into the narrow tenacity of insects" (586).

The imagery suggests, furthermore, that while his mother, Leonora, provided "natural parentage," she herself is associated not with nature, but rather with the mythic and preternatural. Leonora is ill, and her disease appears to be terminal and caused by guilt. Eliot describes her as "a Melusina, who had ties with some world which is independent of ours . . . a mysterious Fate rather than the longed-for mother" (536), "a sorceress who would stretch forth her wonderful hand and arm to mix youth-potions for others, but scorned to mix them for herself, having had enough of youth" (565), "a dreamed visitant from some region of departed mortals" (571).

We might compare the treatment of Leonora with that of Eppie's birth father, Godfrey. Godfrey's failure to acknowledge his daughter is presented as rather ordinary, while Leonora, most often referred to as "the Princess," has behaved in an extraordinary way. Godfrey is punished by having no children in his marriage, but Leonora, though she has children, sounds emotionally removed from them as well as Daniel, as if she had been cast out of the world of human connection. This difference results partly from the different emotional weight carried by birth mothers as opposed to birth fathers.

Could any woman live up to the image of the lost mother that this novel evokes? Before Daniel's early life is revealed, several characters in its other main plot participate in staging a scene from *The Winter's Tale,* in which a lost mother appears to come to life out of a statue and speaks in a way that fulfills all needs of her now-grown child. As the scene appears in *Deronda,* however, the child is missing, and Gwendolen, who is playing the role of Hermione, shrieks in terror at the sudden appearance of a dead face at the moment when she should act out her return to life. The nightmarish transformation of the Shakespeare's happy ending foreshadows the way Daniel's mother too finds the role of the returning mother too difficult to play.

Our culture is full of successful reunion plots like that in *The Winter's Tale.* Daniel has made up similar plots in his own daydreams. When he finally sees his mother, he thinks, "He had lived through so many ideal meetings with his mother, and they had seemed more real than this!" (535). In his fantasies she has been sacred: "To Daniel the words Father and Mother had the altar-fire in them, and the thought of all closest relations of our nature held still something of the mystic power which had made his neck and ears burn in boyhood" (402).

At the same time his idea of his mother has also been associated with fear since he was thirteen, when he first thought of himself as Sir Hugo's son born out of wedlock. Seeing a "forsaken" girl about to attempt suicide, he thinks "perhaps my mother was like this one" (162). Furthermore, as he learns that this girl, Mirah, is searching for *her* mother, the fear spreads. He assumes his mother is a "fallen woman" and probably a prostitute. For Daniel, sexuality is dangerous, and thus he distances himself from his own.

When he finally meets Leonora, he learns that both his pictures of the fallen woman and his pictures of the "ideal meetings" are false. A respectable woman whose passions have been devoted to her art, Leonora was once a true star. She speaks with convincing fervor of "the slavery of being a girl. To have a pattern cut out—'this is the Jewish woman; this is what you must be; this is what you are wanted for; a woman's heart must be of such a size and no larger, else it must be pressed small, like Chinese feet; her happiness is to be made as cakes are, by a fixed receipt'" (541). This scene suddenly introduces a different world—for previously women's complaints about restrictions have appeared only in the mouth of Gwendolen, who is often framed as frivolous. Leonora had the discipline and musical talent Gwendolen lacked. And yet after the fascination with which the book has depicted Jewish culture, Leonora too can sound shallow when she complains, "I was to love the long prayers in the ugly synagogue, and the howling, and the gabbling, and the dreadful fasts, and the tiresome feasts, and my father's endless discoursing about Our People, which was a thunder without meaning in my ears . . . I wanted to live a large life, with freedom to do what every one else did, and be carried along in a great current, not obliged to care" (540). Note the self-contradiction in the desire for both freedom and conformity; they are presumably linked in her mind because she equates freedom with assimilation to gentile England.

Eliot, so often interested in the physical similarities between relatives, points them out in this scene; Daniel, whose face in the mirror had for him long been associated with the thought of someone else he resembled and had never seen, now finds that similar face. But physical resemblance is combined with opposition of values, in an irony Eliot also uses in novels where the related characters have always lived as a family. She articulates this most memorably in *Adam Bede,* where she calls Nature the "great tragic dramatist" who "knits us together by bone and muscle, and divides us by the subtler web of our brains . . . and ties us by our heart strings to the beings that jar us at every movement."³⁵ Daniel has longed for familial and communal identity, and a sense of duty—Leonora felt oppressed by her father and her inherited Judaism, and was happy only as an opera star in a life she describes as "a myriad lives in one" (537) with "no bonds" (547). Among the many images she uses to explain her rejection of Judaism is one associating it with an animal nature that she scorns: "I was not, like a brute, obliged to go with my own herd" (544).

Daniel at his most dispassionate can make "room for that effort at just allowance and that admiration of a forcible nature whose errors lay along high pathways, which he would have felt if, instead of being his mother, she had been a stranger who had appealed to his sympathy" (542). Indeed his very sympathy for her is painful. He offers to help her, but she can accept little from him and can give him no unblocked emotion in return. "Is it not possible that I could be near you often and comfort you?" he asks, and she responds, "No, not possible . . . I have a husband and five children. None of them know of your existence" (547). So this formerly brave and unconventional woman keeps on maintaining secrets and lies.

In their second and last meeting, it is clear that she feels deeply troubled. She is preoccupied with her dead father, who wanted a grandson and who, she feels, is now getting his revenge in Daniel's love of Judaism. She hopes that in giving Daniel his family history, she will lose her obsession with her father's judgment against her. In spite of her hatred of Judaism, she invokes its ritual prayer for the dead; "if you think *Kaddish* will help me—say it, say it. You will come between me and the dead. When I am in your mind, you will look as you do now— always as if you were a tender son,—always—as if I had been a tender mother" (569). But when she begins to imagine what their life would have been like together, her choice seems inevitable: "you would have hampered my life with your young growth from the old root" (571). Leonora confesses, "I am not a loving woman" (571). Daniel is left with "a grave, sad sense of his mother's privation. . . . All his boyish yearnings and anxieties about his mother had vanished. He had gone through a tragic experience which must forever solemnize his life, and deepen the significance of the acts by which he bound himself to others" (571).

What a nemesis George Eliot places on the birth mother! But her powerful lines have the eloquence of the determined female artist/individualist. Eliot's own history suggests that she was drawing on some of her feelings in writing the dialogue between Daniel and Leonora. Her ability to project herself into both speakers significantly contributes to this scene. Rosemarie Bodenheimer has suggested a more specific biographical resonance in Eliot's relationship with her stepchildren. By the time Eliot wrote *Daniel Deronda,* her two younger stepsons, Thornie and Bertie, had both died. Unlike Charles, they had lived with her only briefly. Thornie came home to die while she was writing *Middlemarch.* Thornie had been, according to Lewes's journal, "shipped off to Natal, well equipped with funds, outfit, and letters, to seek a career for himself there."[36] Bertie had followed him to the Transvaal. Bodenheimer demonstrates that Eliot and Lewes occasionally wondered about their behavior with regard to these stepsons, and concluded that they had done the best they could have. Her conjecture that Eliot was emotionally somewhat removed from these stepsons puts a different light on Leonora's withdrawal.[37]

But the significance of this episode in the book is not limited to its connection to Eliot's biography. What it provides is, among other things, one of the most detailed pictures in literature of a confrontation between adoptee and birth mother. Possible issues in these meetings— guilt, forgiveness, family history, secrecy, and alternative pasts—are explored with a profundity provided by no other work of literature that I know. In *Oedipus,* Jocasta kills herself before she and her son can have this conversation. Nor does literature provide such talks with birth fathers. In *The Winter's Tale,* Perdita and her mother express happiness at being reunited, but when the family is miraculously restored, neither confronts Leontes about his earlier decision to get rid of his daughter. Even in Eliot's own *Silas Marner,* when Eppie discovers that Godfrey is her birth father, the scene ends with a much shorter dialogue between the two of them.

It may seem ironic that a work where the adoptee chooses hereditary identity has the most explicit confrontation with a birth parent. Perhaps it is not ironic but logical. If this were a reunion that reconstituted a family, the novel might end in the let-bygones-be-bygones spirit of Shakespearean conclusions. But since Leonora does not want to continue her relationship with Daniel, the more important heredity is to Daniel, the more she must account for her behavior. Two aspects of hereditary identity are at stake for Daniel—being a Jew and being a son. Although his mother will not acknowledge him publicly, he can still regain his heredity by identifying as a Jew.

In *Silas Marner* and *Felix Holt* the adoptee chooses her adoptive father over biological ancestry. In *Deronda* the adoptee chooses biological ancestry, even though his biological mother rejects him again. Did Eliot simply change her mind about what aspect of identity was more important for the adoptee? I have suggested that in *Felix Holt* she was using adoption to dramatize the demand for a choice between two ways of life. Given the similar structural use of adoption in the later work, are there any other similarities in her treatment of adoption in these novels in spite of their different outcomes?

The most consistent element in Eliot's treatment of adoption is the critique of the English aristocracy's attitude toward children, those they adopt and those they beget. Godfrey Cass is negligent, Sir Hugo is generous but insensitive, Mrs. Transome hated her first-born son, and Harold shows little concern for his. Turning away from a rich but cold world, in each case the adoptee chooses the group that is more oppressed, whether because of class or poverty (in *Silas Marner* and *Felix Holt*) or race/ethnicity (in *Deronda*).

The adoptee also always chooses the group or person more associated with religion or religious imagery or language.[38] Eppie's Silas has returned to religion, wanting to do what is best for her. Esther's choice of the dedicated Felix and the devout Rufus is described in religious language. Daniel chooses a Judaism associated strongly with religious mysticism and ritual; the institutional Christianity that he leaves is dismal. The Reverend Mr. Gascoyne, for example, urges Gwendolen to the financially advantageous but loveless and ultimately disastrous marriage to Grandcourt. In spite of Eliot's own dissent from any organized religion, in these novels she presents the heritage with spiritual value as preferable to the heritage with material value. The successful adoptions are into households that have a religious sense of community, though the faith in which Silas has Eppie baptized and the faith that provides a common ground between Rufus and Felix do not have much specific propositional content.

Each novel is in part a rejection of the dominant upper-class English culture and a critique of certain kinds of family dynamics, especially secrecy and treating children as possessions and conveniences. In *Silas Marner*, the biological father is secretive, while Silas is completely open. Rufus abandons secrecy with Esther when he believes that knowing her history might help her. In *Deronda* the adoptive father Sir Hugo tells the truth only when forced, after Daniel has for a long time lived with a completely false picture of his heredity. The adoptive father Silas provides hands-on care; Rufus cared for Esther during her mother's illness; Sir Hugo enjoys being with Dan, but the novel doesn't show much of his role as a caregiver. On one level the adoptee's choice in *Silas* and *Deronda* may be a consequence of deficiencies in parenting. In *Silas Marner* Eppie's choice is a reward for Silas. But Hugo's flaws in parenting do not completely account for Daniel's choice, since his biological mother does less for him than Sir Hugo does, and is hobbled by her own continuing wish for secrecy.

While the movement from *Silas Marner* to *Daniel Deronda* might suggest that Eliot came to value heredity later in her life, a more thorough look at her novels and her letters shows that she always believed in the potential importance of both nurture and inheritance. As early as *Scenes of Clerical Life,* Eliot presents Caterina's difficulties in the Cheverel household in part as a consequence of their failure to understand her (stereotypically Italian) passionate nature. In a letter written close to this time, she notes as a limitation in the natural philosopher Buckle that he "holds that there is no such thing as *race* or *hereditary transmission* of qualities," and in a letter on *Adam Bede* she comments on the influence of his "peasant blood and nurture" (GEL 2:415, 3:60). Still, as she moved from one novel to another, the aspect of influence that she emphasized changed.

From the first to the third of the novels discussed in this chapter, the adoptive father becomes less idealized, the adoptee feels more different, and national contrasts grow more significant. *Silas Marner* is an idyll or a fable, *Felix Holt* a political novel, and *Daniel Deronda,* in its adoption/discovery plot, a kind of epic. By the time of *Deronda,* Eliot was less interested in redefining family relationships to valorize adoption than in other issues. As the ideas of nationalism and blood increasingly preoccupied nineteenth-century Europe, Eliot wrote novels that meditated more on the problematics of adopting across difference.[39] The greater the emphasis on ethnic and cultural difference, the more the adoptee is likely to choose genetic identity. Eppie notices her physical difference from Silas and the other girls of her town, but no one else does, and it is clearly much less important to her than her love for Silas and Aaron and her related feeling: "I like the working-folks, and their houses, and their ways" (173). *Felix Holt* invokes national difference: Esther's mother is French, and Rufus sends her to a French school. Her differences from Rufus are linked in part to the national differences between the French and the English (which come in Esther's case from environment as well as from heredity) as well as with her genetic father's aristocratic ancestry. These differences strain Esther's relationship with Rufus, and Felix's mediation is required to mend it. In *Deronda* the issue of racial difference, as Eliot considered it, is central. In a letter to Harriet Beecher Stowe, to whose work in *Uncle Tom's Cabin* Eliot felt an affinity, she describes the novel as an effort to counter "the usual attitude of Christians towards Jews" and "to treat Jews with such sympathy and understanding as my nature and knowledge could attain to. . . . There is nothing I should care more to do, if it were possible, than to rouse the imagination of men and women to a vision of human claims in those races of their fellow-men who most differ from them in customs and beliefs" (GEL 6:301–2). One of the people who had most influenced Eliot in the particular concerns of *Daniel Deronda* was a friend who died just as she was beginning the novel and provided a model for Mordecai—Emanuel Deutsch, a scholar who gave her Hebrew lessons, emphasized the continuity between Judaism and Christianity, and wrote about his strong emotions on finally visiting Jerusalem.[40]

As an apparently ideal English gentleman doing research on Judaism, Daniel evidently was intended to inform Eliot's readers and disarm their prejudices.[41] One of her points is that Daniel benefits from learning not only about his birth parents, but also about his connection to a valuable cultural tradition and community. Indeed, when Eliot used the word "race," the meaning was partly cultural because of her Lamarckian belief in the inheritance of acquired characteristics (what we now call culture)—experience transmitted by heredity.[42] The most important part of Jewishness for Daniel is not simply biology, but the Jewish culture that his mother has rejected. And it is Mordecai and Mirah, whom he marries at the end of the novel, who consolidate this part of his identity. Although Daniel says, "I am finding the clue of my life in the recognition of my natural parentage" (643), Mordecai's "spiritual parentage" [Daniel's term] is at least as important.[43] Named after the biblical Mordecai, adoptive parent to the biblical Esther, Mordecai passes on his vision to Daniel; even their names signal their affinity because both their namesakes in the Bible are, like these characters, dreamers and interpreters of prophetic dreams. So in some ways *Deronda* too can fit Bodenheimer's generalization about Eliot's privileging of fostering over kinship. Sir Hugo is an inadequate foster parent for Daniel, but Mordecai is the spiritual parent he really needs. As Gillian Beer says, Eliot recognizes, in herself and her culture, the "drive back toward origins, the Oedipus story" and counters it "with an equally intense movement toward differentiation, expansion, lateral kinning, fostering and foster parenting, and sympathetic generalisation, which all create new and multiple relationships."[44] Daniel leaves behind his loss of childhood fostering (of the sort that Rufus and Silas give) to pursue the fostering that Mordecai provides—meeting his need for vocation, tradition, and identity.

With the combination of his heredity and Mordecai's "spiritual parentage," Daniel is able to enter into a Jewish culture that is enough of an "imagined community," in Benedict Anderson's term, to become a nation. The novel includes explicit parallels between Jewish and Italian nationalisms. Mirah sings "O Patria Mia," Leopardi's grand ode to Italy (414), and Daniel takes Mazzini's struggle for a united Italy as a model for the possible rebirth of a Jewish nation (457). But other kinds of nationalism are evoked too: Scottish—suggesting a parallel between the situation of Scotland and the Jews in England developed by Sir Walter Scott—and American.[45] Early in his life Daniel "easily forgot his own existence in that of Robert Bruce" (143), a hero of Scottish nationalism, and tells his tutor that he would like to be a "leader, like Pericles or Washington" (147).

Daniel's desire to be such a leader—and his eventual commitment to political leadership at the end of the novel—had special meaning in England at the time of the novel's writing. Benjamin Disraeli, a Jew converted at a young age to Christianity but still maintaining a strong identification with Judaism, was prime minister. As Ragussis has shown, Daniel is a kind of fantasy transformation of Disraeli, whose emphasis on what Jewishness and Christianity have in common is echoed in some of the dialogue in Eliot's novel. In Eliot's early letters she had strong criticisms to make of the "fellowship of race" (GEL 1:246)—referring to Judaism—in Disraeli's novels, but Eliot's views about Judaism and race changed later in her career. Deronda and Disraeli "both are descended not only from English and Italian Jews but from those Iberian Jews persecuted and banished in the late fifteenth century," Ragussis points out.[46] He argues convincingly that the plot of *Daniel Deronda* "functions symbolically to liberate Disraeli to do what his critics accused him of doing, under cover of being the leader of

Protestant England—to represent his own ancestral people, to seek their best interest."⁴⁷ And he demonstrates that the preparation for leadership Deronda receives from his double identity—Jewish ancestry, Christian English education—rewrites a frequently hostile comparison often made between Disraeli and the prototypical adoptee Moses.

Before Eliot wrote *Daniel Deronda,* she wrote another work in which the adoptee chooses to follow heredity in a way that confers leadership of a previously unknown people—*The Spanish Gypsy.* Here, as in *Silas Marner* and *Felix Holt,* the adoptee, Fedalma, is female. In this poetic drama, Eliot loads the dice in favor of heredity even more than in *Deronda.* Fedalma has no living adoptive parent. The conflict is between the Gypsy father from whom she was stolen and a Spanish fiancé. Before discovering her father, she already dances with a Gypsy-like freedom that transgresses the codes for Spanish women. In her "Notes on the Spanish Gypsy and Tragedy," Eliot argues that the importance of race in the plot is "a symbol of the part which is played in the general human lot by hereditary conditions in the largest sense, and of the fact that what we call duty is entirely made up of such conditions; even in the cases of just antagonism to the narrow view of hereditary claims [perhaps this is where she would place Eppie's antagonism to Godfrey's claim], the whole background of the particular struggle is made up of our inherited nature."⁴⁸

Following heredity requires Fedalma to renounce her fiancé, and Eliot says that she developed an interest in such a plot by considering a portrait of the Annunciation, which she imagines as depicting a woman chosen because of her heredity [Mary was of the House of David, as predicted by the prophets for the ancestry of the Messiah] "to fulfil a great destiny, entailing a terribly different experience from that of ordinary womanhood." For all human beings adjusting to necessity, "partly as to our natural constitution, partly as sharers of life with our fellow-beings," Eliot says, "Tragedy consists in the terrible difficulty of this adjustment."

A woman whose destiny cannot be the "ordinary lot of womanhood": a reader who knows Eliot's life cannot help but think about how autobiographical these reflections are, as well as how relevant they are to the restrictions that requirements of the "lot of womanhood" place on each of her heroines. On one level, the situation of Fedalma, as of most of her female characters, can be taken as an allegory for the conflict between a woman's individuality and social expectation, marriage, or love.⁴⁹ On a more literal level, however, the drama, in its tragic mode, portrays how wrenching the conflict between adopted and genetic identity can be, especially if the only living parent is associated with both genetic identity and a historically oppressed group.

But *Silas Marner, Felix Holt,* and indeed, *Daniel Deronda* were not written in a tragic mode, though *Deronda* comes closest. While *The Spanish Gypsy* requires Fedalma to renounce the fiancé she still loves, each of the novels promises the adoptee a marriage that in an idealized way meets her or his needs. Furthermore, in each one the adoptee makes at least one gesture toward the *other* identity—biological or adoptive, the identity that is not chosen. Eppie allows Godfrey to pay for her wedding, though no one knows why. Esther keeps her natural curls and can improve Felix's French accent. *Daniel Deronda* goes furthest to articulate the multiple loyalties of the adoptee's situation at the end. In *Deronda,* Daniel says to his mother, "The effect of my education can never be done away with. . . . The Christian sympathies in which my mind was reared can never die out of me. . . . I will admit that there may come some benefit from the education you chose for me. I prefer cherishing the benefit with gratitude, to dwelling with resentment on the injury. I think it would have been right that I should have been brought up with the consciousness that I was a Jew, but it must always have been a good to me to have as wide an instruction and sympathy as possible" (566–67).

To use a modern phrase, Daniel is a cultural hybrid.⁵⁰ As Gillian Beer says, he is "enriched by the multiple past, both genetic and cultural."⁵¹ Though he wants to found a Jewish nation, he knows that he cannot return to a pure Judaism from the past: "I shall call myself a Jew. . . . But I will not say that I shall profess to believe exactly as my fathers have believed. Our fathers themselves changed the horizon of their belief and learned of other races" (620). Daniel's words, the narrator's, and even Mordecai's value both nation-building and diversity. "We English are a miscellaneous people" (85), says the narrator, invoking the late Victorian commonplace that English people came from a variety of ethnic traditions—even if not as various as today.⁵² Mrs. Meyrick, the best mother in the novel, possesses a "happy mixture of Scottish caution with her Scottish fervour and Gallic liveliness" (484). Klesmer, similarly, is a "felicitous combination of the German, the Sclave [Slav], and the Semite." When Mordecai describes his vision of a Jewish nation, he imagines it as carrying "the culture and the sympathies of every great nation in its bosom" (456), not only as "purified" but also as "enriched by the experience our greatest sons have gathered from the life of the ages. . . . Only two centuries since a vessel carried over the ocean the beginning of the great North American nation. The people grew like meeting waters—they were various in habit and sect. . . . What had they to form a polity with but memories of Europe, corrected by the vision of a better?" (458).

Much as I would like to stress Daniel's hybridity, however, his final discussions of his identity seem more unified than this term suggests. His upbringing outside Judaism is placed in a very Jewish context: he has been prepared, "as Moses was prepared, to serve [his] people the better" (641). He identifies himself without qualification as a Jew, "enjoying one of those rare moments when our yearnings and our acts can be completely one, and the real we behold is our ideal good" (640), and compares himself to "the stolen offspring of some mountain tribe brought up in a city of the plain, or one with an inherited genius for painting, and born blind—the ancestral life would lie within them as a dim longing for unknown objects and sensations, and the spell-bound habit of their inherited frames would be like a cunningly-wrought musical instrument, never played on, but quivering throughout in uneasy mysterious moanings of its intricate structure that, under the right touch, gives music" (642). These images of the unified self and the musical instrument finally played are very similar to those Eliot uses of Esther when she defends Felix in court and thereby aligns herself with her adoptive father more than with her heredity ("some hand had touched the chords, and there came forth music that brought tears" [chap. 46; 573]. Both novels show a longing for a unified identity, and use imagery to suggest it has been achieved. But in both, the chosen identity, the alliance with a subordinate group and the vocation to help them, is actually more complex.

Daniel's resolution of his identity reconciles several potentially conflicting ideological currents of the time. On the one hand, racial and biological concepts of nationhood were becoming more widespread, and the revelation of Daniel's original parentage, with the discovery of his "ancestral life" and "inherited [frame]" appeals to such concepts. On the other hand, Daniel's choice of Judaism, like the choices of Eliot's earlier adoptees, can also be seen as an act of sympathy, though in David Marshall's phrase it is more obviously "far-reaching" than theirs.[53] As Eliot emphasizes, it is partial, not universal sympathy, but the same is true of Eppie's choice of Silas and the poor instead of God-frey and the rich. But in *Deronda* we see more of the way that sympathy brings what is distant close, and the special paradox that the strangers to whom sympathy brings Daniel close are in some ways already close to him without his knowledge.

As Beer points out, there are many links in Eliot's novels between sympathy and adoption.[54] With both, Eliot explores relationships that are not confined to the biological family. Using adoption permits her to explore two kinds of what Judith Modell has called "kinship with strangers," both adoptive kinship and the kinship of the adoptee with unknown relatives.[55] Arguably, adoption can be seen as a kind of para-digmatic gesture of sympathy—taking on responsibility for another—which often then presents the adult adoptee with the further challenge of where he or she will, in turn, offer sympathy. But if adoption is an act that Eliot often associated with sympathy, her portrayal of some adop-tive parents enacts what could be called either a critique of sympathy or a critique of apparent sympathy unaware of its object's real needs. While Silas and Rufus show sympathy, Eliot's earliest portrayal of adoption shows its lack when Lady Cheverel brings Caterina up partly because "it would be a Christian work to train this little Papist into a good Protestant, and graft as much English fruit as possible on the Ital-ian stem" (*Clerical Life,* 103). Similarly, Sir Hugo's wish to raise Daniel doesn't bring an understanding of Daniel's feelings.

Sympathy has often been gendered as feminine; why do Eliot's adop-tion triangles generally include adoptive fathers and not adoptive moth-ers? There is little of the play with different meanings of the word *mother* that there is with *father*.[56] Eliot does not exclude women from nurturing outside the family. Romola adopts both Benedetto and Tito's children by Tessa, Dolly helps Silas bring up Eppie, and Mrs. Meyrick provides a temporary home for Mirah. But Eliot does not focus on the relationship between a woman and her adopted child from infancy to adolescence or older. Perhaps this omission derives from the tradition in classical literature that adoption is a contract between men, or draws on the greater centrality in Shakespeare's romances of adoptive and genetic fathers rather than mothers, or aims at giving sympathy more cultural prestige by attributing it to men, in whom it is taken to have a less bio-logical basis.[57] Whatever the causes, in all three novels, *Silas Marner, Felix Holt,* and *Daniel Deronda,* the focus on an adopting father dra-matizes more emphatically the continued loss of the birth mother.

Raised by men, Eppie, Esther, and Daniel all wonder about the woman who bore them in a way they might not if they had adoptive mothers. Furthermore, because Silas and Rufus don't have wives and are less social than Sir Hugo (who marries late in the novel), their relationship with their daughters involves more emotional need and dependence on the fathers' part. The maternal absence poses the question of how much the fathers will take on maternal nurturing—Silas does so much more than Sir Hugo.

In exploring parental relationships complicated by adoption, Eliot moves away from the celebration of maternal instinct common in her society. The women who nurture outside their family, the men who adopt, and the unmaternal mothers such as Leonora, all provide implicit arguments against the view that nurturing is an instinctive capacity determined by women's biology alone.[58] Biology is not destiny in Eliot's mothers or in Eppie or Esther's choice of family.

Daniel is the only one of Eliot's adoptees with a living birth mother and a dead birth father and the only one whose dead grandfather is a strong presence. This gender distribution is inextricably entwined with the novel's complex consideration of Judaism and of women's experiences versus cultural ideas about women. Daniel must have a Jewish mother to be Jewish by blood, and his mythic image of what his birth mother will be like is rather like the traditional Jewish image of woman; Leonora does not fit into either. His grandfather's love of Jewish traditions and, especially, longing for a grandson, are presented in the novel as at the same time oppressive to Leonora and appealing to Daniel.

While most of Eliot's adoptive parents are male, most of her adoptees are female. However, both Eliot and her critics often call Daniel feminine, or attribute to him qualities conventionally considered feminine. Following a long cultural tradition, the novel encourages thought about analogies between prejudices and restrictions against women (from which Gwendolen suffers) and prejudices against Jews (from which Daniel is apparently protected by his upbringing, but which occur in many characters' casual statements).[59] The analogy has its positive dimension as well as its negative one; Daniel values Judaism for its transmission of emotion rather as Eliot values cultural femininity ("gentleness, tenderness, possible maternity suffusing a woman's being with affectionateness, which makes what we mean by the feminine character" GEL [4:469]).

In her own earlier life, Eliot had dealt with restrictions against women, but her late letters, especially, emphasize her solidarity with women as a group in a way that could be compared to Deronda's attitude toward being a Jew. One might say that her novels had become the woman's homeland she could create, except that Eliot's solidarity with women never implied, either literally or metaphorically, a separate land for women. Eliot could not have the kind of heroic nation-founding life that Daniel chose, and the novel reminds us that no woman could. And when, in *The Spanish Gypsy,* she imagines a female adoptee who becomes committed to leading the oppressed people of her birth, it is in tragic terms.[60]

The heroic position Daniel reaches at the end of the novel is the transformation of several different kinds of outsider status that he has occupied. Whether as adoptee or as bastard, he cannot inherit his uncle's estate. This exclusion also puts him in a position similar to that of women in his society. He shares his inability to inherit his uncle's estate with his uncle's daughters.[61] The novel closely links exclusion related to birth status—seen in the condition of Gwendolen's husband's illegitimate children as well as in Daniel's assumed bastardy—with exclusion related to gender. Before he receives his inheritance, Daniel, as what one might call a "closed-record adoptee," is in a feminine position in other ways as well. The very situation of being transferred from one family to another, of having their name changed, gives adoptees early in their life an experience of forced adaptability similar to what is expected of women when they are married; Daniel's too diffuse sympathy and his passivity continue this adaptability until his final commitment to build a Jewish nation.

What are the effects of George Eliot's representations of adoption? No doubt the most widely read of her novels that deal with this topic has been *Silas Marner,* which makes a case for the benefits and the naturalness of adoption, the redefinition of family by nurture rather than by genetics, more emphatically than any well-known novel before the twentieth century. But the topic had not been an important focus of writing on this novel until Susan Cohen's article from 1983.[62] Many adoptive mothers and fathers, and quite likely other parents, have identified with Silas, but I wonder how many adoptees—teenagers who read the novel in high school, or others who read it later—have identified with the idealized Eppie. The negative picture of the birth mother and birth father may be the most vivid impression they received from it.

Daniel Deronda is the Eliot adoption novel whose readers have left the most extensive record of their responses. Though most of these responses have focused on its representation of Jewishness, they are inextricably entwined with its representation of adoption as well. Many critiques of the book that now sound obviously anti-Semitic also oppose the idea of the adoptee choosing a hereditary identity.[63] On the other hand, from 1876 on, Jewish readers reviewed the book enthusiastically, and some identified Daniel's political aims—for which Eliot had drawn on ideas of her friend Emanuel Deutsch—with their own hopes for a Jewish colony in Palestine. In the 1880s on, the book was translated into German, Hebrew (several times), and French. In the words of Terence Cave, on whose research I am drawing, "Large numbers of Jews in Germany and eastern Europe were thus reading a version of the novel for seventy years after its first publication. They associated it with the dream of a national home, which began to take more concrete form in the 1890s with the establishment of the European Zionist movement."[64] Even Susan Meyer, who finds strong elements of anti-Semitism remaining in the novel in spite of Eliot's intentions, observes that "small streets in Tel-Aviv, Jerusalem, and Haifa have even been named after George Eliot."[65] Though *Deronda*'s ending was a fantasy in its own time, arguably the novel has had real historical effects. But the multicultural quality of Mordecai's fantasy nation, modeled on a diversity associated with the United States, is seldom remembered, just as modern Israel, with laws enforcing a particular kind of Judaism, is far from the secular state envisioned by Theodor Herzl.

What does *Deronda* say to readers about adoption? It makes a powerful plea to adoptive parents not to treat their children as insensitively as Sir Hugo. Elements of Daniel's characterization that some critics have found implausible—his failure to question Sir Hugo about his heredity, his apparent asexuality, his extended sense of responsibility—correspond to behavior found by psychologists in someone who has taken on the role of the "good adoptee."[66] The novel's exploration of pain possible in a cross-cultural adoption—together with the joy possible in affirming a newly discovered culture, even without a continuing relationship to a close biological family—could resonate with many adoptees as well as with those who have lost and found traditions for other reasons. In focusing on the loss and recovery of Jewishness, the novel deals with an identity particularly targeted by prejudice—and particularly ambiguous about whether it is ethnic or religious—and more hidden even than most heredities in adoptive families. (I am not the only adoptee whose Jewish ancestry was the most secret part of my history.)

Like the much less successful *Spanish Gypsy, Daniel Deronda* relates adoptees' discovery of their heredity to a drastic redefinition of their personal and national identity and their vocation. In the simple terms of slogan, the novel makes a powerful case for the view that adoptees must learn their heredity to know who they really are. Furthermore, it demythologizes the fantasy of the ideal birth mother as well as the purely negative image of the fallen woman, the promiscuous and lazy slut. Leonora has made Daniel suffer, but she has a heroism of her own. And, painful as the meeting with her is, Daniel survives.

But if it demythologizes the birth mother, the novel provides other idealized images that help Daniel achieve heroic stature: his mythic grandfather, Mordecai, and Mordecai's vision of a new nation. Though the grandfather appears in the novel only through others' memories, though Mordecai dies at the end of the novel, and though the new nation is only a hope, their images are powerful enough to conclude Daniel's part of the novel with a sense of triumph.

Few if any adoptees today will have the chance to find heroism in rebuilding their ancestral nation. But many will concur with Daniel's desire to know his heredity and hereditary culture, and would like adoptive parents to understand this desire. Yet it is important to historicize beliefs about race, nation, and ethnicity in the novel. Ideas about hereditary racial characteristics common in Eliot's time have been generally discredited by the way similar ideas were used by Hitler.[67] The progressive nationalism of the late nineteenth century, which united smaller groups into larger nations, has become the rather different nationalism that has been devastating many lands and people in Eastern Europe, Africa, and Asia. Belief in hereditary ethnic/racial/national characteristics—as opposed to belief in the importance of cultural history—is an idea that needs to be analyzed rather than assumed.

Is closed adoption like colonialism, like forced conversion, or neither? That depends to a large extent on the atmosphere in the adoptive family and the behavior of the birth parents. Is meeting birth parents like decolonization? It breaks a silence, unveils a hidden knowledge, but for many of us it provides new questions about identity, rather than answers. The equivalent of decolonization—joining the culture(s) of one's birth parents—may be difficult or impossible in this context; the turn of some postcolonial theorists to embrace cultural hybridity rather than an original purity may be a better model. Important as it was to me to learn my heredity, I feel uncomfortable with the unqualified claim that adoptees need to know their ethnicity to know who they are. I would prefer to argue for open records in terms of history rather than identity. Yet I am also uncomfortable with the thought of a couple I have heard of, who adopted a Russian baby and called him Ryan.

I do not remember having thoughts about my birth mother as often as Daniel did when growing up, but I too developed reticence, caution about sexuality, and even a belief in my wide-ranging sympathy leading to a sense of inaction in a way similar to Daniel's, and I was drawn to the book partly because of this characterization of him—an ironical attraction partly since many readers consider the characterization of Daniel a failure. The novel presents him as having qualities culturally considered female, another dimension of my identification with him as well as of what I have argued elsewhere is Eliot's own. From many standpoints, he seems too idealized, but on the other hand this may well have made him appeal to me more, since he could have some of my limitations and yet become heroic.

He chooses to be a Jew—and I am, now, an Episcopalian with ecumenical interests, who would list Jewishness as one of many ethnicities in my ancestry. This is the personal side of my insistence that his identity decision in the novel is more than a matter of discovering his heredity. What have I learned from studying this book about why our choices are different?

I can hear some readers objecting to the naïveté of this approach to literature. He is a character in a novel; his choices are determined by literary constraints of the plot. I live outside novels. Nevertheless, many works of fiction that touch readers most lead them to expect that their lives will follow plots like those in the fictions. Some may even, as in the case of the eighteenth-century German novel *The Sorrows of Young Werther,* which is thought to have inspired a number of suicides, lead impressionable readers to imitate the plot of the novel. I have shown in earlier chapters the long-standing literary tradition of the plot in which discovery of ancestry leads characters to a new identity, apparently forgetting the family in which they were raised. This plot still circulates outside literature as a fantasy in the nightmares of some adoptive parents and the daydreams of some adoptees. It is not surprising, then, that the imaginative fullness of *Daniel Deronda* has led me to more thought about differences between its plot and the plot of my life.

There are obvious differences. However feminine, Daniel is a male character. His Jewish heredity is on both sides; his Jewish parent is willing to meet him and give him the legacy of his grandfather in family history. My adoptive mother was a better parent than Sir Hugo; my birth mother is more accepting of me, and braver about telling her family, than his. But perhaps these contrasts need not have been conclusive. Crucially added to them was the difference in our ideological situation. Unlike Daniel at the point of discovering his ancestry, as Eliot presents him, I already had a sense of Christianity as a religion with meaning for me; furthermore, I was already involved in a political movement, feminism. More clearly than Eliot's, my own attitude toward being a woman is something like Daniel's about being a Jew—though no more than Eliot do I believe in a promised land for women.

If my birth father had welcomed contact with me, I might have had a more difficult task of identity reconfiguration. Nevertheless, I have not become an evangelical in spite of the welcome I received from my birth mother.

Unlike Daniel's, my discoveries of ancestry have led to my affirmation of my previous religious tradition, though in a move I will discuss in the afterword, I see that tradition as liberal Christianity more than as Roman Catholicism. Reflecting on his narrative, I see my decision to remain Christian as a choice, but it is a choice conditioned by so many differences between us that it also seems inevitable. But just as Daniel's is presented as in some ways a Judaism with a difference, mine is now a Christianity with a difference, aware of both anti-Semite and Jew among my ancestors, aware of the fantasies about Jews that may have contributed to my conception and even perhaps to some of the ways my adoptive parents thought about me.[68] The histories of the Jews, of anti-Semitism, of religious persecution and toleration (which affected my adoptive parents too, in other ways) are all part of my history. With this conclusion, the agnostic George Eliot, deeply interested in religious history, would agree.

Six ❧ Commodified Adoption, the Search Movement, and the Adoption Triangle in American Drama since Albee

In the previous chapters of this book, I have been bridging a large historical gap in reading earlier literature from my perspective as, among other things, an adoptee of twenty-first-century America. In this and the chapters that follow, the gap is smaller, as I discuss works written during my lifetime and about my own society, and in some cases even commenting directly on a movement in which I have participated. This chapter will move from the novels that provide so much representation of individual consciousness back to drama, but to a mode of drama very different from the classics by Shakespeare and Sophocles. Most of the plays I discuss are, arguably, more interesting in their commentary on the social issues of their immediate time than for any other reason. I am not treating them at great length, but rather looking for clusters of concerns and selectivity of emphasis. Nevertheless, one writer stands out in this chapter. Edward Albee, one of the few playwrights influential at midcentury and still today, was involved in the beginning of the adoptee rights movement, portrayed adoption in one of his earliest plays, and has turned to the topic again in some of his most devastating recent works.

Edward Albee, American Adoption, and Commodification

In 1953, Jean Paton, a forty-one-year-old adoptee and social worker, placed an ad in the *Saturday Review of Books*.

Were you adopted before 1932? Your experience may assist
research in adoption from the point of view of experienced adult.[1]

This ad—explicitly aimed at adult adoptees, contrary to the continuing
picture of the adoptee as a child—produced sixty-four responses, and
forty of the respondents filled out questionnaires that Paton sent. These
questionnaires became the basis for Paton's pioneering 1954 book *The
Adopted Break Silence,* which showed a great diversity of viewpoints
on adoption.[2] Some had been happy in their adoptive family; some had
not; they were also mixed in attitudes about birth parents. Paton had to
self-publish this book, since there was then little market for discussions
of adult adoptees' experiences.

One of the respondents to Paton's ad was a twenty-five-year-old
unknown and virtually unpublished writer named Edward Albee, obviously very unhappy with his adoptive family, whose home he had left
four years before.[3] Five years after answering this questionnaire, Albee
would burst upon the theater scene with *The Zoo Story,* which began
his career as the leading American playwright of what came to be called
the Theater of the Absurd.[4] In 1960 he wrote a play, *The American
Dream,* in which Mrs. Barker of the Bye Bye Adoption Service drops in
on Mommy and Daddy and Grandma.

Mrs. Barker's organization is the first adoption agency in any of the
works discussed in this book. For the first time we are considering texts
from a culture in which infant adoption is legally formalized, and from
a nation that has a special affinity with the institution of adoption. Barbara Melosh has recently written, "Adoption has been accepted more
readily and practiced more widely in the United States than in any other
comparable industrialized nation." She attributes this to our openness,
fluid class and social structure, diversity, optimism, and "belief in the
malleability of human nature and the beneficence of institutions."[5] But
some of the plays I shall discuss—such as *The American Dream*—represent adoption in very different ways, and it can also be argued that
adoption is important in American literature partly because of its use-
fulness in representing key American themes of ambivalence about the
past and the family.[6]

In recent American drama about adoption, questions about the
meaning of family and parenthood and the relative importance of
heredity and environment raised in earlier literature continue to be
important. As in earlier literature, playwrights often use adoption plots

to bring together characters that differ greatly, especially in class. But the plays I will discuss here comment more specifically than nineteenth-century literature on adoption practices in their society. When they employ the plot of search for birth parents, they are not only following a structure as old as *Oedipus,* but often responding more specifically to the open-records movement and to adoptees' searches reported in their own newspapers. And the critique of adoption practices as commodification of children, briefly suggested in *Daniel Deronda,* becomes a major concern.

In the United States, formal adoption with protection of children's interests began in Massachusetts in 1851, and by the beginning of the twentieth century most of the states had established a similar legal procedure.[7] (Adoption would not be similarly formalized in Britain, where keeping inheritance rights in the "blood family" seemed more important, until 1926.)[8] Until the 1920s, the number of adoptions remained relatively small, but then they began to increase, apparently because of Progressive Era reforms.[9]

During this time adoptive parents and adult adoptees could generally find out information about heredity. Nevertheless, in the 1930s the procedure began of issuing new birth certificates that listed only the names of adoptive parents. The main reason was to protect adoptees from the stigma attached to adoption and, especially, to illegitimacy.[10] The original birth information was at this point supposed to be available to adoptees when they came of age. However, after World War II, when there was a large increase in the number of middle-class women who placed their children for adoption, and also an increase in the number of childless couples seeking to adopt, state officials and social workers began to tighten up, and gave less information both to adoptees and to adoptive parents.[11] The hope was that adoptees could be raised as a kind of genetic blank slate, erasing any possible stigma for them and both sets of parents. This would seem to fit with the general emphasis on assimilation in the 1950s—but of course, even though there was an attempt to match adoptees to their parents, some adoptees needed medical information that was unavailable, or, perhaps for reasons of looks or temperament, felt out of place, especially in a family or a subculture where heredity was still felt to be important.

And there must have been many people who did feel heredity was important. For one novel of the period so popular that it became both a stage play and a film was *The Bad Seed,* in which the environmentalist is stupid and the villain is the eight-year-old child of an adoptee; she has inherited the gene for being a sociopathic murderer from her birth grandmother.[12] One of the chief messages of the plot is that adoption is dangerous because the adoptee may bear the seeds of hereditary evil— if not in her own life, in her children's. This was not the dominant attitude about adoption in the 1950s, but it had been earlier in the century, and probably many people in the audience at least thought they knew someone who had a similar prejudice.[13] Thus one of the few plays that breaks the silence about discussing adoption—and could be seen as arguing that the adoptee ought to know more about her heredity—reinforces its stigma, promoting further silence. I was about the age of the Patty Duke character at the time, and have a vague memory of hiding the book, though not of reading it—perhaps a symbol of how taboo discussing adoption was in our house.

Roughly the same time *The Bad Seed* was popular, Albee's *American Dream* was also telling a story about adoption in the family, though here it is the adoptive parents who are murderous, rather than the birth mother and the adoptee's child. This play first presents Mommy as a consumer constantly demanding satisfaction, or at least a ritual attempt to meet her demands. Twenty years ago, we eventually learn from Grandma, Mommy and Daddy adopted an infant, or, in the play's language, "the lady, who was very much like Mommy, and the man, who was very much like Daddy, . . . *bought* something very much like a bumble" from Mrs. Barker.[14] But the bumble kept doing things wrong, from the parents' viewpoint—bumbling, you might say—with nightmare results. In such novels as *Bleak House* and *Great Expectations,* adoptive mothers were the ones responsible for deformation of adoptees; this pattern is repeated here, since mothers are generally considered more responsible for how a child is raised, although there is an adoptive father who is also to blame for his passivity. When the child "only had eyes for its Daddy" (99), its mother gouged out its eyes, and after further mistakes and offenses, Grandma says, "they cut off its you-know-what" (100). Then its hands, and its tongue. Furthermore, "it didn't have a head on its shoulders, it had no guts, it was spineless, its feet were made of clay" (101). Not surprisingly, it eventually died, and as Grandma says, "you can imagine how that made them feel, their having paid for it, and all. . . . they wanted satisfaction; they wanted their money back" (101).

In Jean Paton's book, one of the anonymous unhappy adoptees

writes, "The child has little to do with choosing who adopts him and he should not be made to feel like some merchandise to be sent back (or, in this case, away), if, after many years, it does not satisfy."[15] Was this Albee? The similarity in this language to that of the play could point to a commonality of symbolics among adoptees in dysfunctional families; still, I think most likely this writer was Albee, and, perhaps under the encouragement of the questionnaire, images that would eventually become *The American Dream* were beginning to form in Albee's mind. Mel Gussow's recent biography emphasizes from beginning to end the importance to Albee of his feelings about being adopted; one detail he does not mention is that Albee kept in touch with Jean Paton when he became successful as a playwright and sent her copies of his plays; indeed the copy of *Tiny Alice* that Albee sent her in 1965 included a handwritten dedication to her organization, Orphan Voyage.[16]

Albee was not the first writer to relate adoption to commodification. Already in the 1920s, when he was adopted, there were more couples wishing to adopt than there were healthy white infants available, and some worried that wealthy parents, like Albee's, were using their financial power to circumvent agency requirements and get children more quickly. In an article from 1930 the *Saturday Evening Post* called adoption "a big bull market," with "Baby securities" promising "investors" plenty of "dividends" paid out in "toothless smiles and endless giggles." In 1924 an Oklahoma department store had a display of bassinets—and borrowed babies up for adoption from a local child-placing society to display in them.[17] Writings intended to help children understand their own adoption or to help parents explain adoption to their children sometimes follow the commodification model in a way that may sound more disturbing. The journal *Hygeia*, in 1942, for example, suggested that adoptive parents explain to children that parents who get children by birth "just have to be good sports and pretend there never was such a perfectly beautiful baby before. But that's what happens to folks who have to order sight-unseen. Now in your case, we saw a lot of children. We looked them over and suddenly we actually saw just exactly what we wanted—right size, right sex, right sound and everything."[18] There was a similar emphasis in the famous book for adopted children, *The Chosen Baby* (1939). By the time Albee wrote his play, some psychologists were criticizing this language. In fact, though there were now relatively more children available for adoption, parents were more likely to be choosing an agency that proposed one specific child to them. But the myth remained, and perhaps because of the consumerist identity of American society as a whole in the 1950s, it continued to have resonance. Mommy and Daddy can easily be seen as bitter caricatures of the repressive, consumerist family of the 1950s and early 1960s, and their adoptive status, in the fact that it literally involved their giving money to get a child, as a metaphor for a more general condition in which parents treat children as commodities and try to mold them to requirements. Surely this was one of the reasons that many people besides adoptees found the play a devastating critique of the family. Biographical critics, knowing that Albee is himself gay, can see in it a critique of homophobic parents being unable to accept their child's sexuality, the reason for Albee's break with his own parents.[19] But adoptees have special reason to be interested in it.

Does conceiving and giving birth to a child, or nurturing it, make a parent? If nurture is more important, adoption can be real parenthood. But Mommy and Daddy in *The American Dream* are parents by neither definition, only by virtue of money and adoption law. At several points, the characters refer to the problems of seeing under artificial light, which recalls the theme of adoptive parenthood as pretense, opposed to natural parenthood.[20] More directly, the lack of nurture Mommy and Daddy provide is established by Grandma's account of how they destroyed their child. At the end of his play, Albee provides for Mommy and Daddy an apparently healthy and good-looking young man, whom Grandma identifies as the American Dream of the title, and who is probably the identical twin of the one who died. Upon seeing him, Mommy says, "Now this is a great deal more like it! . . . Who says you can't get satisfaction these days!" (124–26; ellipsis mine). The *Hygeia* writer would be shocked, but Mommy's attitude is an extrapolation of his picture of the advantages of adoption.

There are other ways in which this play can be seen in relation to adoption history. The adoption was arranged not by a social worker but by "a dear lady . . . who did all sorts of Good Works" (97). At the time that Albee himself was adopted, social workers believed in blood ties and family preservation rather than adoption; he was placed by the Alice Chapin Adoption Nursery, which was founded not by a social worker but by a physician's wife.[21] And, as Garry Leonard has pointed out, when Grandma refers to the child as a "bumble of joy" (97), the word echoes the name of Dickens's Mr. Bumble of *Oliver Twist,* who oversees a workhouse for orphans and "colludes with those running the institution to maximize the profits from money given by the state to the workhouse . . . by starving the children, and . . . when possible, by selling them."[22] Commodification again.

The character referred to as the American Dream has a long monologue in which he elaborates on his loss of feeling—and consequently his inability to relate to others—in his eyes, his heart, his groin, his hands. This reinforces the idea of his correspondence to the physically mutilated boy. But among his losses he gives relatively little attention to his birth parents. Matter-of-factly, he begins his story, "My mother died the night that I was born, and I never knew my father; I doubt my mother did" (113–14). His major emphasis is on his loss of his identical twin brother. "We . . . we felt each other breathe . . . his heartbeats thundered in my temples . . . mine in his" (114). According to Gussow, among the many questions related to his adoption that Albee himself often wondered about was whether he had a brother or sister, perhaps a twin, stillborn or alive.[23] He had questions about his birth parents as well, but they do not enter into the play. The concern of the play is with an adoptee's identity and how it has been destroyed by his adoptive parents.

At this point—1960—few people in the United States except for Jean Paton were talking about the people who are now called birth parents. In fact, in the late 1950s a licensed adoption agency in Washington, D.C., organized and controlled by adoptive parents, surveyed its adoptive parent members. This organization's name, the Barker Foundation, is oddly echoed in the name of the "dear lady" of *The American Dream*, Mrs. Barker. They found that only half whose children were ages six to eight had told them anything about their biological parents, and most of them felt that "adopted children should have virtually no information about their biological parents during early childhood."[24]

Albee's own parents did not give him any such information. Ironically, the records were relatively open during the time that he was growing up. His parents had kept his adoption papers, but never told him that they had them; he learned his birth mother's name only upon finding the papers when his adopted mother died, in 1989.[25] According to Gussow, he was haunted by a line from James Agee's loving memoir about his parents—they "will not ever tell me who I am."[26] Albee's parents had kept him in ignorance in a more literal sense, and a less affectionate way. By the time he answered Jean Paton's questionnaire, adoption records were more generally closed, and many other adoptees, whose adoptive parents might have been willing for them to have information, could not receive it because of adoption agency policy.[27] Some adoptees whose adoptive parents were much more nurturing than Albee's still felt that their lack of information about their history and contact with "blood relatives" made them feel mutilated, using images close to those in *The American Dream*.[28]

The Open-Records Movement

Because of these protests and others, soon the general invisibility of adoptees and, even more, of birth parents would begin to change. In the 1960s and early 1970s adoptee writers and activists Betty Jean Lifton and Florence Fisher pursued long and difficult searches for their birth mothers, and then wrote about them for a larger audience than Paton had gained.[29] The greater publicity of the adoptee rights movement from the 1970s on resulted from many factors. There now were more adoptees who had experienced denial of their requests for information. In many geographical areas and population groups adoption and illegitimacy had lost some of their stigma. Researchers such as the psychiatrist Arthur Sorosky and his coworkers Annette Baran and Reuben Pannor published studies promoting open records and open adoption in both popular and professional journals.[30] And there was now an international interest in the history of minority and subjugated groups. The open-records movement, active in many countries, could draw on the language of decolonization and civil rights protest. Many adoptees arguing for open records used analogies with the loss of names in slavery and the search for family history in Alex Haley's *Roots*.[31]

In 1975, England officially opened records to adoptees at the age of eighteen.[32] However, in the United States, the adoption rights movement met a backlash that sealed records even in some states, like Pennsylvania, that had been partially open. But during this same time adoption as an institution has been changing in other ways. Because the stigma of illegitimacy is somewhat less, contraception is more available, and since 1973, abortion is legal, fewer healthy infants are available for adoption—at least fewer healthy white infants, those most actively sought. More babies and children have been adopted cross-culturally, making adoptive families more obvious, and more people have been establishing new kinds of adoption in which the adoptive parents and birth parents have some kind of contact from the beginning. Both of these changes are consistent with the idea that adopted adults have a right to information about their heredity, and searches and legislative struggles continue. In the 1990s and the next five years, nine states passed laws that—with varying qualifications—opened their adoption records to adult adoptees.

Celebratory versus Oedipal Adoption Plots

With the greater visibility of adoption in the contemporary society, it is sometimes used theatrically for a celebratory close. At the end of Wendy Wasserstein's *Heidi Chronicles* (1989), the feminist art historian Heidi holds her Panamanian daughter Judy triumphantly as if they were a Madonna and Child statue.[33] Heidi has always looked forward to motherhood, but has not married; the key men in her life either begrudge her professional identity, or are not available for marriage because they are gay. International adoption is presented as the triumph that finally permits her to combine love and her career. The utopian ending of the American musical *Ragtime* involves the adoption of the black orphan Coalhouse Junior by the WASP Mother and the Jewish Tateh. After all the intergroup conflicts the play has dramatized, including the racially motivated killing of Coalhouse Junior's parents, the musical suggests, bringing tears to my eyes, yes, we can all not just get along but become a family. There is an analogous celebration, with a little more look at family tensions, at the end of *Widows and Children First,* the third play in *Torch Song Trilogy,* where the youth who has been staying in foster care with the two gay men on whom the play focuses decides that he wants them to adopt him.[34]

But in a number of different recent plays adoption is not simply the happy ending. In several darker plays, the representations of the adoptee's lack of knowledge of ancestry draw more on the *Oedipus* tradition than on realistic representations of the search movement. Two recent examples use a plot similar to that of *Oedipus* to deal with social shame and to attack inequalities. The British musical *Blood Brothers,* which, as of this writing, has been continuously playing in London since 1988, repeats from Sophocles the prediction of familial murder and the fruitless attempt to avert it. A poor woman bears twins, and her rich, childless neighbor adopts one of them: the chorus tells us that if the two boys ever meet, they will kill each other. The play emphasizes the unhappiness of the rich family and the warmth of the poor mother, who looks longingly on the son she has given up. But the inevitable class hostility arises (this is Britain), and in the last scene, after they find out about the brotherhood, the poor brother accidentally (apparently) shoots the other and is shot by the police. The musical uses the adoption plot to protest against the split between the rich and the poor.

Even closer to *Oedipus* is Rita Dove's play *The Darker Face of the Earth,* which deals with race, arguably the fault line in American culture as class is in Britain. At the beginning of this play, set in the nineteenth century, a white woman bears a child by one of the slaves on her plantation; he is sent to a slave market and returns to the plantation as an adult. He unknowingly kills his birth father and sleeps with his birth mother. The truth is revealed in the middle of an at least temporarily successful slave rebellion; she kills herself and he is proclaimed the leader.[35]

Clearly the way in which relinquishment for adoption divides people formerly connected, whom the audience will intuitively feel belong together, fascinated both Willy Russell and Rita Dove as they used elements from *Oedipus* for social commentary. Following the assumption predominant in *Oedipus* that the "blood tie" is the only real tie, in *Blood Brothers* the adoptive relationship is presented as false and unhappy and the birth mother is treated with sympathy; in *Darker Face* Amilia is promised that Augustus will be brought up by kind people, but from his own speech it seems that the closest thing Augustus has to an adoptive parent is a generous slave-owner. These works portray relinquishment for adoption as the tragic error that perpetuates and dramatizes the divisions of society; they bring birth parents to visibility and are not interested in reflecting on the possibilities of adoptive parenthood.

Plays about Birth Mothers

A drama in which social criticism focuses even more on the situation of the birth mother is *Top Girls,* written by the British playwright Caryl Churchill in 1982.[36] Here, uniquely among these plays, the adoption is an informal one, within the extended family, the adoptive mother is the poorer sister, and the economic and emotional issues are contextualized with more widespread contemporary issues of child care and the history of restrictions on women, as women from different centuries in the first act remember giving up their children. This play contains a truncated search plot; Angie suspects that her professionally successful aunt is her mother, but she never receives acknowledgment. While this play is not formally a tragedy and does not end with the violence of *Blood Brothers* or *Darker Face*, it presents a less tangible social violence in which the birth mother's prosperity is futile given her emotional hollowness, and all three characters in the adoption triangle, plus most other characters in the play, are miserable. This play has been widely performed in America, but its representation of an adoption in which the adoptive parents and children live in poverty is increasingly distant from the way adoption is visualized in the United States.

By contrast to *Top Girls*, Carol Schaefer's *Sacred Virgin*, a recent off-Broadway American play by and about a birth mother, contextualizes adoption very specifically within the history of attitudes toward the "unwed mother."[37] In this play, Bridget, an acting student in her late thirties who seems emotionally blocked, remembers her time in the unwed mothers' home that has finally sent her a letter, which she cannot bear to open, from her lost son, Liam. Before her acting class, she role-plays her feelings about him with David, another actor in the class who is himself an adoptee. When she decides to open the letter, she finds that he has recently killed himself, in despair because of his separation from her. David resolves to find his birth mother, and in the play's final moment he and Bridget embrace.

Like *Top Girls* this play presents a collective experience: This play gives us not only Bridget's own experiences as a birth mother, but her memories of Sarah, Cathy, and Mary, from the Mercy Home, as well as another birth mother, Mary from her acting class. In her memories, there is a friendly sense of exchange among the girls, in spite of the fact that they are forbidden to tell one another their last names. They giggle as the boyfriend of one of them sneaks them a bag of Christmas snacks through the window. They share confidences about their sexual experiences and the effect of their pregnancy on their bodies.

When she tells the other students in her acting class about her experiences, some of that friendly sense of confidence and support is repeated. Most of the others don't know about unwed mothers' homes, and Bridget gives them a social history lesson. For some of them life seems very different now: Sophia says, "You would not believe when I lost my virginity! It took me until I was almost seventeen to know how to say no" (act 2, p. 5). Echoing the emphasis in *Top Girls* on continuity of women's problems throughout history, Mary, on the other hand, just returned after an obviously painful month away, says, "Times haven't really changed all that much. Not from Shakespeare's time. Not from twenty years ago. Families still freak out when a daughter becomes pregnant. But now their daughter doesn't have to let them know. She can take care of the problem" (act 2, p. 10). Mary, who has been away for a month, has had an abortion, but when she acts out her experience, she mimes it as giving up a baby for adoption.

One of the main ways in which this play differs from *Top Girls* and others I will discuss is in its emphasis on the influence of religion and shame on the birth mothers. In *The Sacred Virgin,* the economic issue is mentioned only briefly: "Johnny's parents thought it best we not marry, since we were not financially stable and hadn't finished college" (act 2, p. 5). Bridget's trauma is closely linked with shame—"I believed if I kept my son he would have been called a bastard the rest of his life"—and the Catholic culture of the unwed mothers' home. It is not a coincidence that the play contains unwed mothers in two different generations named Mary, or that the first memory scene in the Mercy House is set on Christmas Eve, or that a piece of stained glass depicting the Madonna and Child is one of the most important props. These religious images not only comment ironically on the fate of the unwed mother in a culture that honors the Virgin Mother, they also predict the fact that like the Mary of Christianity, Bridget must deal with her son's death. Liam turns out to be a sacrifice to the social institutions of shame and adoption. Nevertheless, Bridget finds a spirituality to help her cope with the loss. Anna from her acting class has said, "A broken heart is a heart broken open" (act 2, p. 11), and in her final soliloquy Bridget says, "Strange, this peace just knowing his name. . . . My son is now enveloped in pure love" (act 2, pp. 15–16).

Sacred Virgin's rather melodramatic ending puts the central adoptee back in the position of the dead son in *The American Dream,* although the institution of adoption rather than the particular insensitivity of his adoptive parents is to blame in this case, and although the play tries to remedy the bleakness by ending with Bridget's peace, David's resolve to search, and his embrace of Bridget. The letter that Liam writes portrays him as an adoptee who still remembers the trauma of lying in his bassinet alone in a tiny room after he has been given up for adoption. "I scream in rage for you. . . . I died in that little room. My soul died" (act 2, p. 14). It is as if the play were trying to dramatize Nancy Newton Verrier's theories about adoptees' lifelong pain because of the memories of early separation in *The Primal Wound,* without recognizing her qualification that the memories are unconscious for adoptees separated at such an early age.[38]

All of these plays—*Blood Brothers, Darker Face of the Earth, Top Girls,* and *Sacred Virgin*—have bleak endings, though there are gestures toward hope in *Darker Face* and *Sacred Virgin.* All the plays besides *Sacred Virgin* are concerned with other social issues in addition to adoption, and this may have helped them gain recognition. Given the lack of literature and drama that focuses in depth on the situation of the birth mother, it is unfortunate that *Sacred Virgin*'s melodrama limits its appeal. The play has won raves from some activists of the open-records movement, but even in that group it has critics, especially with regard to the last segment. The vividness of Liam's memories of his early infancy is improbable in the realistic framework the play has maintained up to the appearance of his letter, and if his suicide because of his relinquishment for adoption touches the audience, then Bridget recovers too quickly.

Plays about Searching Adoptees

Plays that focus on the adoptee's search rather than the birth mother's and allude explicitly to the search movement may have happier endings.[39] Two surprisingly similar plays about searching adoptees from the early 1990s are Lanford Wilson's *Redwood Curtain* and John Olive's *Evelyn and the Polka King.*[40] In both the adoptee, a girl of seventeen or eighteen, from a rich family, near the beginning of the play confronts a seemingly burned-out man she thinks is her father, hoping to find out more about herself. In both plays, the plot brings the adoptees together with characters from widely different worlds—in Wilson's a homeless Vietnam vet, Lyman, who fits some of the description she has of her birth father; in Olive, an apparently washed-up polka player, Hank. Both these male playwrights make the daughter's relationship to the birth father crucial; though in *Redwood Curtain* he turns out to be dead, in *Evelyn and the Polka King* he is the real focus of the play.

These, like a number of recent adoption plays, position both the adoptee and the theater audience as torn between two sets of parents. We can see why the adoptee feels alienated from the family she knows, but we can also see that the new world she confronts poses problems for her as well. In both plays the adoptee thinks she has been treated as a commodity, and her adoptive parents are the unappealing rich. Evelyn's adoptive father is a banker who has literally stolen ninety-four million dollars during the savings-and-loan buyout. He is named Starkweather, which might recall the mass murderer of that name. Geri's adoptive mother and her rich friends talk about food all the time, even when they are pretending to be interested in concerts.

Olive's play makes the audience learn about her birth father's world as Evelyn does; she begins to appreciate her birth father and her Polish roots at the same time as the audience members are encouraged to sing along with the chorus of his polka band, "Kielbasa, beer, and sauerkraut!" (39). On the other hand, Hank learns to wake up to the present, enjoy Evelyn, play polkas again, and write new ones. In *The Redwood Curtain*, the happy ending also involves music; the half-Vietnamese Geri, disillusioned with her ability as a pianist when she associated it with her adoptive father, Laird, returns to playing when she discovers that he was also her birth father.

Both plays are odd mixes of sociology and fantasy. *Redwood Curtain* locates Geri in relation to television shows about what her aunt Geneva calls "hopelessly arrogant young men and women claiming their right to know their biological parents at whatever cost to everyone else" (66). It locates Lyman in relation to other Vietnam veterans hanging out in the forests of California, and Geneva in relation to stock takeovers and clear-cutting of redwoods. Yet Geri has magical powers that can produce thunder and lightning, and intuitive semihallucinatory knowledge about Vietnamese culture and her ancestry: she thinks that her birth mother owned a flower shop, and that turns out to be true.[41] *Evelyn* quotes from a sociologist on the relation of polka music to the fate of the white urban middle class, but its plot is built on a highly improbable adoption certificate with the birth father's full name (although he didn't even know about the child) and only initials for the birth mother, and the idea that Evelyn is on the lam with a suitcase full of the millions her adoptive father stole and can give the money away with no bad consequences.

Evelyn and the Polka King is really a father-daughter love story. Not for Hank such refinements as "birth father"; when he hears her story, he is immediately moved and gives her a new name, Junior. He has just given up drinking, and the past that she wants to know about is also the past that he wants to recover from his previous alcoholic haze. Evelyn at first looks down on the birth father who is so enthusiastic about her, hates the idea of having "polka blood" in her veins" (32), and uses him as a means to find her mother. But in the process of searching, she comes to depend on him, and learns more about people outside the rich South. She gives the stolen money away to impoverished Polish farmers, a home for retarded adults, a family in Oshkosh (another Polish town) whose child needs an operation, a Slovenian church. Though she has expected that finding her birth mother, Wanda, would be the key to her identity, when she discovers that Wanda has been in a mental institution and is still fragile, Evelyn is only briefly upset about it, and begins to mother Wanda instead. She eventually returns to her adoptive parents and begins to appreciate that "Daddy's . . . actually being . . . brave" (63) about going to jail. But she decides to go to college at Northwestern, near Hank in Chicago, not too far from Wanda in Wisconsin. She doesn't turn out to be obviously much like either of her birth parents, though she says "fuzzy water" (8) as Hank does. But her life is clearly expanded from meeting them.

Redwood Curtain is a somewhat darker play, and takes more seriously the idea that finding a birth parent who is mentally disturbed has implications for the adoptee. Geri is uncomfortable with the solitary life she has had as a pianist, and associates it anxiously with Lyman's antisocial behavior. Then when she discovers that Laird was her birth father, she is upset because she knew him as sad and usually drunk. Feeling that she must follow her father's footsteps, she worries, "Not a very promising path he's laid out for me to follow" (94). But then she discovers that he was melancholy because he missed her birth mother and, like Geri herself, was unhappy in the money-oriented milieu of her adoptive mother. At the end she learns that before the war he was a much happier man. So she can identify with the earlier Laird. (Given the fact that so much is made of her Vietnamese identity, it is a surprise that the parent she discovers and identifies with turns out to be the upper-class Anglo one she already knows.)

Finally the adoptees' searches benefit other characters as well. New starts are possible for many of them. Evelyn rejuvenates Hank and takes Wanda to visit to Chicago. Geri has the persistence to make a connection with the taciturn Lyman, getting him to tell the truth about her birth, and finally drawing him into sit and listen to her play piano. She also gives Geneva, dispossessed from her family's past, the possibility of a new career as her manager. The adoptive parents don't particularly benefit, except that Mr. Starkweather, about to go to jail, may now have a better relation to Evelyn; he and the adoptive mothers are simply sketched or caricatured and never appear.

Both of these plays, like so much other literature, meditate on nature in relation to adoption—but here it is often to emphasize damage to nature and what the adoptee and others have lost. In *Redwood Curtain,* Geri, having lost her history, is fascinated with the twenty-thousand-year-old trees that are about to be cut down. Olive's play includes the environmental damage theme but ends differently. As Hank tries to search for Wanda, he remembers a small town with pine trees; when they find the town, it's different: "those houses weren't there, it was all woods then" (58). That the environment has been damaged is part of what Evelyn tells Hank as she gets him to wake up to the present: "the acid rain, and the skin cancer every time you go outside, and, oops, the trees're gone" (she comes from Texas) (6). He decides to write a polka about the damage to the ozone layer, to take the polka beyond Polish traditional themes and audiences. But the "Ozone Polka" he actually writes is not the angry protest he promised but a strange combination of environmental consciousness, humanism, and fatalism, to confirm his claim that the polka takes anger away: "The earth giggles when we polka on her. I've faced it now, and I've decided that, maybe, we're not long for this planet. But I tell you, I'd still rather be a human being than almost anything else I can think of. . . . OH, IT'S TIME TO PARTY NOW / THE EARTH WON'T MISS US ANYHOW" (62). The environmental message here is subordinate to Hank's theme "change or die": "And I'm doing it, one day at a time. If I can change, we can all do it, one polka step at a time" (61).

The greater importance of birth parents in these plays may result partly from the fact that now many adoptees have made contact with their birth parents or are working to change laws that prohibit this contact, more adoptions are made with some contact from the beginning, and many birth parents themselves have conducted searches or gone public for legislation. However, it is ironic that these plays focus on birth fathers when it is birth mothers who have actually been much more visible as part of the movement, and it is, in general, birth mothers who are sought first by adoptees and are more likely to want contact than birth fathers. The focus on birth fathers in these plays partly reflects the difficulty women playwrights are still having in getting their work performed. The adoption rights movement involves many more women than men, but the contemporary search plays most widely known reflect the structure of the theatrical world more than the composition of that movement.[42]

Two recent plays that appear to be closer to the search movement deal with adoptees looking for their mothers. In neither case does the play actually show the mother, though one character in each play finds hers. Both of these plays are in a more experimental mode, and use ethnic music and dancing, though to very different effect. *Mask Dance,* written by Rick Shiomi of Minneapolis's Theater Mu, and performed there in 1995, based on interviews with a number of Korean adoptees, focuses on three teenagers who have been adopted into the same family, and another Korean adoptee in her early twenties, P. K., a performance artist.[43] From the very beginning this play emphasizes that adoptees can react in very different ways: Karen values an old Korean doll from their childhood and Lisa doesn't. Carl, their brother, is more alienated from the family, and also, initially, hates "that Korean stuff [Mom] tries to shove down our throats."[44] P. K. and Lisa talk about the racism that they experienced; Karen seems better adjusted, and Carl more reticent. The crisis comes when Lisa attempts suicide, feeling alone because Karen and Carl, who are older, have left home. They all come together to help her feel less alone, and the adoptive parents decide to move to the city so Lisa will be closer to the others.

After this greater family solidarity is established, in the last phase of the play, Lisa and Carl go to Korea, and each of them has a disappointing experience. Carl learns that he was found in a plain brown basket, the nurse he remembers has died, and the train station he remembers is going to be torn down. Lisa visits her birth mother and her husband and children in a small apartment, and realizes that she is American and doesn't want to stay, as she is invited to. Karen, who has been more interested in Korean culture all along, surprisingly refuses to accompany Carl and Lisa. She doesn't want to lose her image of herself as a lost princess, and feels justified when she hears their experiences, but at the end of the play is planning to visit with a college tour group. The play emphasizes the solidarity of the adoptees, especially Carl, Lisa, and Karen, who found each other in the orphanage and insisted on staying together when they were adopted. Some of the variety insisted on at the beginning disappears by the end when Karen decides to go on her trip, but there are still differences: she doesn't commit herself to visit the orphanage or Lisa's birth mom; Carl is still more distant from the parents because he is "still sorting a lot of things out" (385).

In keeping with the adoptees' double identity, this American domestic drama moves into a different style with the presence of two characters called Spirit, described as "Asian Spiritual character with half-white face," and Mask Dancer, described as "Asian Movement Character wearing Chwibari Mask." Chwibari is identified later in the play, by P. K., as "the playboy . . . the prodigal son . . . sometimes the monk gone bad. . . . He's a real prankster" (372). The play begins with Korean drumming and unnamed performers dancing traditional Korean mask dances, and then comes a duet between Spirit and Mask Dancer. These characters sometimes speak for one of the adoptees, and often intervene in the narrative later; for example, at one point the Spirit holds Carl's hand to keep him from walking out on a conversation with his sisters; after Lisa's attempted suicide, the Masked Dancer helps Carl reach her against the opposition of other figures. They do a dance to exorcize Karen's troubled spirit. And the characters' responses to the mask mix the "realistic" plot with the Mask Dance theme: after he reaches Lisa, Carl picks up a Chwibari mask and shows interest in it, though earlier he had refused to try it on, and at the end of the play—before the last two dances—Lisa and Karen give him a similar mask as a housewarming present.

Lauren Weedman's 1999 play *Homecoming* focuses, like most of these plays, on just one adoptee, and it gives a detailed picture of her relationship with her adoptive family, but also uses music and dance in a way that could be seen as a parody of their use in *Mask Dance*. After an initial "Freedom Dance" to Aretha Franklin's "Think," the play begins with the main character's first meeting with her adopted grandmother and ends with her first phone contact with her birth mother.[45] The birth mother never appears.

Like the adoptee herself during the play, who is constantly wondering about her ethnicity, we are left in doubt about what the birth mother looks like. The grandmother fears, at the beginning, that she might be black, and this possibility is hinted at by the use of Aretha Franklin and other black music between scenes, the adoptee's sometime membership in the Black Student Union, and suggestions from her black boyfriend's mother. In *Mask Dance* the Korean music at the beginning represents the adoptees' ethnicity, with which they have, in a sense, come to terms at the end; from most of the script, *Homecoming* might be about an adoptee coming to terms with the fact that she is biracial, or at least still wondering if she is. But the author Lauren Weedman, who plays the character Lauren Weedman, is actually very fair-skinned. So when she performs, the idea that Lauren or her mother could be black most likely seems improbable, maybe even comic. With a darker performer, the effect would be quite different.

Clearly, the racial issue here is a metaphor for Lauren's sense of alienation from her adoptive family. In the beginning her grandma sets her on the floor on a "dog towel" (scene 1, p. 3); later she is the only family member without a lock on the door. Her sister is constantly claiming that family relations mean less to the adoptee because she has more of them, though she doesn't know them. But the theatrical irony is that this is a one-woman, autobiographical performance piece, so that the adoptee herself plays the roles of all the difficult people in her adoptive family, as well as her friends, black and others, and herself. One person playing the role of many different people in turn is not only splendidly theatrical, but also embodies the sense of chameleonic identity that many adoptees feel.

This is a funnier play than any of the other search plays I have mentioned, as well as more involved with details of the search process, though it works a switch on the usual procedure because Lauren's adoptive mother, Sharon, is the one who pursues the search. Through Sharon it explores the official rules about closed adoption records in Indiana, a support group meeting, and the search underground. It shows the difficulty people have with language about birth relatives: Lisa speaks of "your birthmom or your natural-mom or I don't know what you call her" (scene 2, p. 9). Her adoptive mother, Sharon, insists that she is searching for Lauren's BM (initials with a scatological double meaning), but when she finally reaches her on the phone, she says, "I'm her mother—well you're her mother" (scene 13, p. 44).

Though it's a funny play, *Homecoming* touches on a lot of important issues of Lauren's identity confusion. In her first attempt to get information from Sharon, long before Sharon starts to search, she says, "Well, I feel like I can't tell what I look like" (scene 2B, p. 12). Sharon says, "You are what we are" (13) and tries to remember her ethnicity: "You're German-English." Her sister says, "I hope you'll always remember that I consider you my real sister. And I always have. Okay? Did I ever tell you how for a long time I thought you were a foster child that was just staying with us for a while until your family came to get you?" (scene 3, p. 16) As the search progresses, Lauren has a scene of fantasies about her birth mother. Does she smell like fresh cookies, or does she walk away trying to deny responsibility? Is she a fat Italian who thinks Lauren is too skinny, an Irish dancer, or a new age blue vapor, or a Hispanic she can call "Mi Corazon"?

But much of what carries this play is the obvious affection with which the quirky adoptive mother, Sharon, is portrayed. She asks her teenage daughters for an okay to put a clause in her will that they accept her visiting them as a ghost. Near the end she puts on a wig and fake glasses so she can go undercover on the phone to do the search. Eccentric as she is, she loves Lauren as best she can.

When Sharon asks at the adoption agency if Lauren had head injuries as a child, the answer is another question, "Is she a teen-ager?" (scene 6, p. 23). The conflicts between them have much in common with the conflicts between mother and daughter in any family. The mother looks incredibly weird to the daughter, whose perspective we generally share, but the daughter has moments of rebellion that the audience may well see from her mother's point of view. The *New York Times'* enthusiastic review of this play was appropriately titled, "Seeking Her Birth Mother, Loving Her Adoptive One."[46]

All four of these plays deal with the social tension around adoption by affirming the search. Whereas Albee's adoptee was passive, these are quite active, even if Sharon does some of the detective work for Lauren. The plays by Olive and Wilson deviate usefully from the myths by making clear that what the adoptees find is neither an ideal other family nor on the other hand a disaster; Olive in particular shows some of the issues of working out a new relationship with a birth father who is very different. *Mask Dance* presents the trip to Korea as important in the "will to face the past," even if what is found is disappointing. Karen's refusal to go is a turning away from the others that needs to be exorcised and reversed. *Homecoming* leaves many issues to be resolved, ending with a phone reunion that makes only the slightest of gestures toward the question of what kind of relationship the adoptee and birth parent will actually have.[47]

In all four of these search plays, the adoptee is younger than the typical age of actual searchers.[48] This positions her as younger than almost everyone in the expected theater audience and identifies her search with the typical adolescent search for self, as explicitly happens in *Homecoming*. On the one hand, this could be seen as trivializing adoptees' searches; on the other hand, it makes it possible for people without adoption in their families to connect with the characters. Quite likely there are fathers whose daughters have always been in their family who feel some of what Hank feels as he tries to appreciate his daughter and deal with her scorn. But I would imagine most adoptive parents, particularly adoptive mothers, would really dislike the plays by Olive and Wilson, and so, I think, would most birth mothers and fathers, unless they could identify with Hank, who has a charm of his own. And I don't think I am the only adoptee to be annoyed by the picture in *Redwood Curtain* of Geri as having magical powers and magical knowledge about her ancestry. *Homecoming* and *Mask Dance* are probably the best of these plays for communicating to people outside adoptive families something about the experience of growing up in one, as well as of searching. The fact that Sharon is so obviously eccentric—though also loving to her daughter—may help relieve her from the duty of representing all adoptive parents. *Mask Dance* also gives a sympathetic picture of the adoptive mother. She has a moving scene in which she tells Karen about the moment when she stopped mourning her hypothetical unborn children, and decided to adopt.

Although *Mask Dance* uses cultural traditions specific to Korean culture, many of the issues it deals with are those faced by transnational adoptees from many different countries, larger versions of the problems of domestic adoptees with which most of these plays concern themselves. Like *Homecoming*, it draws in more of the audience because of its theatricality.

Plays of Struggle over the Baby

While other playwrights were developing the theme of the adoptee's identity in a far different way than Albee had in *The American Dream*, Albee himself was returning to the adoption issue after many years during which it was mostly submerged, and writing his first well-attended plays in years out of a look at the perspective of other members of the adoptive triangle. After a partial reconciliation with his mother and her subsequent death, he wrote *Three Tall Women*, which for the first time gives a relatively sympathetic picture of her. This play presents her at three different ages as three different characters who discuss their memories and expectations, and thus considers her disillusionment, losses, and physical pain as well as her prejudices. When the son refers to her throwing him out of the house as firing him, the play makes something of the same critique of adoption as trying to build a family with money made in *The American Dream,* though this acknowledged portrait of his mother never makes explicit her adoptive status.[49]

Albee spoke for open records when giving the keynote address at the annual meeting of the Congress for Equal Rights in Adoption in 1995, and a few years later wrote *The Play about the Baby.*[50] First produced in Germany in 1997, it ran in New York for most of 2001 and mystified many in its audience, though reviews were excellent, but to those familiar with the institution of adoption, one of its referents is obvious. This play is about a younger couple who have a child and are then persuaded by an older couple that they did not. This persuasion is an exact parallel to the advice that birth parents often still receive, to go on with their lives and put their past behind them as if nothing has happened. Having begun with a focus on the pain of the adoptee, switched his focus to see that the adoptive mother also has sufferings, Albee now for the first time looks at adoption from the birth parents' point of view.

About the Baby joins two other recent plays that consider relinquishment and adoption at a time close to that of the baby's birth—*Emma's Child* and *The Baby Dance.* Albee's is the least sociological and most abstract. "Man" simply announces, "We've come to take the baby" (28). Woman takes it while Man is talking to "Boy" and "Girl." She briefly returns the blanket, which is all we have seen of the baby, and then reveals that there is no baby there (as of course, in the theater, there never literally was). Boy and Girl had no intention of giving up their child; there is no specific reference to institutions of adoption. The closest parallel suggested is kidnapping by Gypsies, but Man and Woman are not Gypsies (though they claim to be at one point), and there is no hint that they plan to raise the baby themselves (nor, particularly, that they plan to kill or sell it).

The birth parents are presented mostly in terms of naïveté, youth, playfulness, and innocent sensuality—except when they are in uncomprehending pain. The older characters, Man and Woman, have the long speeches, during which they question not only the younger characters' parental status but also their other memories, their fidelity, and their sexual identities. They are defined not only in terms of their cruelty but also in terms of their greater experience of life; Man says, "If you don't have the wound of a broken heart, how can you know you're alive?" (36). Most of the audience would be old enough to be uncomfortably forced into identifying with Man and Woman at some moments. Man says to Boy and Woman to Girl, "I am your destination" (36, 37), and this line, though a reversal of one used romantically earlier by Boy of Girl ("She's my destination" [18]), also suggests that the older characters represent what the younger will turn into later in their lives. This play is not only about birth parents' loss of their child, but also about the loss of youth's simple confident pleasures experienced in growing older.

Emma's Child, by Kristine Thatcher, and *The Baby Dance,* by Jane Anderson, both more sociologically realistic, focus on the question of what happens to a proposed adoption if the baby is, or might be, damaged in some way.⁵¹ Both plays deal with the new world of adoption, in which birth parents appear to have more choice and deal with adoptive parents more directly. And in both plays the would-be adoptive mother wants to take care of the child in spite of its defects and her husband does not. *Emma's Child,* by Kristine Thatcher, focuses much more on the potentially adoptive parents, the possibilities for nurture of a deformed child, and the theme we have seen presented so often, that nurture rather than genetics defines real parenthood. *The Baby Dance,* by Jane Anderson, gives a more thorough picture of the sociological contrasts between the birth parents and the adoptive parents, and, like *The American Dream,* presents adoption as commodification.

Emma's Child presents Jean and Henry as a couple under stress from the pressures of infertility and preadoption procedures, but, ultimately, caring for each other and for others. When the baby, Robin, turns out to be hydrocephalic, she continues to visit him, changes his diaper, lets him practice sucking on her finger, massages him, exercises his arms and legs, brings him a Walkman, and learns from the nurses how to hold him and feed him. She enjoys hopeful signs as his condition improves slightly and eventually he smiles. She even wants to take a sabbatical from her university job so that she can visit him regularly if he is moved to a more distant hospital. Meanwhile, we discover that Henry's reluctance to do anything for Robin is not from simple coldness, but from the belief that the baby is suffering as he himself did during a painful operation for cancer. In spite of small improvements,

Robin dies and Jean and the staff mourn him, but at the end Jean and Henry have won another birth mother's approval and are going to try again.

Throughout the play Robin legally belongs to Emma, but after the birth she disappears. Jean has no right to make any official decisions about Robin's care—about an operation, a change of hospitals, or resuscitation—but Emma can't be reached. The one decision she has made, the Do Not Resuscitate order, prevents the hospital staff from taking extraordinary means to save him when his heart stops beating, means that by that time Jean would have endorsed. The play offers a protest against the assumption suggested by the title, that this is Emma's child. Emma has given up on him and Jean has not, so should he not be considered Jean's child?

Emma is not condemned for her lack of persistence. Henry gives a quick sociological sketch of her difficulties: "Emma lives on welfare with her alcoholic father and her two-year-old son" (47). But the play does not explore her life or the difficult potential relationship between her and Jean. And Michelle, the second birth mother, who turns up at the end, becomes a kind of wish-fulfillment figure for Jean and Henry when she says, as she leaves the play, "Ever since I got pregnant, I feel like I've been baby-sitting. Watching over this child for somebody else. She isn't mine . . . I've taken care of her for somebody else" (74). Older, more educated, and less oppressed than Emma, she even likes the fact that they have two different religions.[52]

Jean is not perfect. She can easily be seen as someone who always tries too hard. She prepares for a social worker's visit by filling the living room with too many flowers. As they wait for the arrival, she nags her husband about his clothes, and begs him for the cigarettes she has just asked him to keep from her. But the play is an affirmation of her spirit, and her husband's too. At the interview with Michelle, when Jean is, for a moment, too drained to respond to the question, "What can you give this child?" her husband puts in, "Time," and gives her his hand. This gesture enables her to go on: "Time, effort, yes. . . . My hands. My voice. My lap. Stories. Music. . . . We have a wonderful home, and a great big garden. I want to go on my hands and knees across that garden with my child" (73–74). As in *Silas Marner,* the nurturing of adoption is associated with nature.

The Baby Dance gives a much harsher picture of adoption, though some of the lines that present the characters at their worst are cut in the

1998 adaptation for television—changes perhaps made partly for the differently positioned audience, which would include more people similar to the birth mother, and partly because in the meantime Anderson and her female partner had adopted a child. (Thatcher was a fairly recent adoptive mother when she wrote *Emma's Child*.) As in several of the search plays, the audience is positioned between two sets of parents. Its would-be adoptive parents are richer (in the movie business instead of teaching and writing), they adopt independently rather than using an agency, and when they give flowers to the birth mother, the flowers are an expensive and inappropriate gesture rather than the result of their hard work in the garden. Class contrast is emphasized, and Rachel is less a nurturer than a preacher: she tries to get pregnant Wanda, who lives in a stiflingly hot trailer, to drink bottled water, take prenatal vitamins, avoid caffeine, and play classical music (in 1998 she doesn't try the classical music, and more emphasis is placed on her painful infertility treatments, which have resulted in many miscarriages). Wanda and her husband use the money Rachel wants them to spend on air conditioning and their phone bill to repair their car and pay bail for Wanda's mother, who takes care of their other four kids. Meanwhile Rachel lectures Wanda against prejudice and in favor of compassion to welfare mothers because, as she says, "poverty causes a lot of despair which breaks down the family unit" (18).

Though Wanda doesn't follow middle-class maternity health rules, she loves her children, including the one she is carrying. When Rachel proposes breaking off the contract, Wanda talks about how happy the child will be with her own pool in her own backyard, and persuades her not to break it off. In spite of all its strain, the two women could have a semifriendly relationship; not so their husbands. Richard resents Al's height and fertility, and even when not fighting him is oblivious to his need for respect. Each of them accuses the other of caring too much for money and not enough for people; Al's anti-Semitism emerges, since Richard seems to fit his stereotype of the rich Jew who exploits everyone else.

Such class-related conflict could happen with many adoptive and birth parents today because the adoption of healthy white babies is getting more and more expensive, birth parents are in general choosing wealthier adoptive parents, and the gap between rich and poor in our society is growing drastically.[53] This particular case, however, is made somewhat more difficult by Ron, the sleazy lawyer go-between, as well as by the requirements Rachel and Richard have for their child. Another pregnant woman, a premed student also using Ron as a lawyer, might have been more compatible with them, but she is only four feet eleven, and Richard, a short man himself, agrees with Ron that that is too short. When Richard is annoyed by the financial demands from Wanda's husband Al, Ron talks like a drug dealer: "You're still gonna get the rush, you're gonna get the rush when you hold the baby" (55).

While Robin of *Emma's Child* is unambiguously disabled, the nameless infant of *The Baby Dance* may actually be all right, but she has some oxygen deprivation during the delivery, which leaves the *possibility* that she is developmentally damaged. Richard will not adopt her with this uncertainty. "I want a child I can teach the alphabet to and take on hikes. I didn't go through all of this for a kid who might sit in a corner and rock her knees all day" (72). Rachel protests, "We *have* a child, that other child does not exist, I want *this* child," but Richard says, "Honey, she's not the only one." We are looking at the other side of the chosen baby story, the side of the child who is not chosen.

For the 1998 television adaptation, the baby's total abandonment is clear. The would-be adoptive parents take a plane home to Los Angeles. The birth mother sits in her truck, shows on her face that she thinks for a moment of reclaiming the baby, but does not. The baby is never given a name, and the space on the hospital bassinet that should hold her mother's name is vacant.[54] She is no longer a valuable commodity. Obviously the warning in this play holds not just for adoption but also for new reproductive technologies like surrogate motherhood and genetic engineering. Ron, the intermediary who encourages Rachel and Richard to abandon the baby and provides no counseling or other help for Wanda, is symptomatic of the fact that adoption practitioners are absolutely unregulated, which may make an unscrupulous one even more dangerous in the age of the Internet.

Emma's Child deals with a situation somewhat similar to that in *The Baby Dance,* but Robin is not presented as commodified in the same way as the nameless little girl, even though in both cases there is some discussion of the parents' requirements and of the challenge the disabled baby is to their image of what parenthood would be like. Not only is their wealth less, but also Jean and Henry go through an agency, rather than through an independent lawyer who presents them with pictures of birth mothers he thinks might appeal to them. It follows that Jean and Henry are closer to home, and it is more possible for Jean, who seems to have a better relationship with her husband anyway, to keep on visiting the child when he doesn't want to. Jean's experience contradicts the view of Richard that "there will be no joy with a child like this" (72).

Furthermore, *Emma's Child* gives a less bleak picture by including caring hospital staff: verbal Laurence, who appreciates the classical music Jean wants Robin to listen to, and Mary Jo, who doesn't, but still finds Jean an article claiming that hydrocephalics can have normal intelligence. They are overworked and tell her that hospital volunteers don't pick up babies like Robin, but nevertheless they give a larger picture of a nurturing society, in spite of problems with the administrative bureaucracy that determines many hospital decisions.

I value *Emma's Child* for its ability to imagine such nurturing, and for its tribute to the persistence that enables Jean to go on to another adoption possibility—while Rachel seems to give up. It also provides a more three-dimensional picture of the would-be adoptive father and of other males than *The Baby Dance,* and extends its treatment of commitment to explore male-female relationships as well. Nevertheless, by contrast to *The Baby Dance* it seems somewhat evasive of potential problems in adoption today.

Like *American Dream, Baby Dance* deals both with the general issue of commodification in American society and with specific modes of commodification that adoption can involve. The mode of this play, however, is realism rather than Albee's grotesque surrealism. Richard, who wants "the magic of taking [his child] to her first play" (72), is not so different from the expected theater audience, even if he has more money, and neither is Rachel, who could raise the child she has seen if her husband could accept her, but not alone. Wanda and Al—already stretched with four children and only a trailer to live in—have relinquished her, and have no resources for dealing with another child, let alone one who might have special needs. And so, very likely the child will remain in foster or institutional care, perhaps to be mutilated figuratively as the bumble in Albee's play is—offstage—mutilated literally. Commodifiable children may be wanted by too many parents— others by too few. As the gulf between the rich and the poor grows in our society, so will this gulf. These conditions for adoption are not inevitable; in England, unlike the United States, adoptions are treated as a social service with no fees involved, although individuals can circumvent national policy by adopting internationally (or, as in *Top Girls,* by giving up the baby informally, placing the adoptive mother in poverty). In *The Baby Dance,* the abandonment of the baby by both rich and poor prospective parents may be seen as an allegory, but the conditions it allegorizes are intimately involved in the real life parallels to its story.

Is there any special affinity between adoption and nonrealistic modes of drama? Garry Leonard has argued that there is in Albee, that many of his plays "present the existential absurdity of growing up within the process of the closed-record adoption system."[55] *The Play about the Baby,* written after Leonard's article, extends scrutiny to the absurdity of living as a birth parent in a system where the birth is supposed to be forgotten. Institutions that require erasure of the past indeed lend themselves to portrayal in a mode different from usual conventions of realism. Furthermore, the play with identity involved in adoption procedures that involve the adoptee taking on a new name, new parents, and perhaps even a new country has affinity with the theatricality of Weedman's *Homecoming,* in which the performer plays every role in her story. Dramatizing cross-cultural adoption leads several playwrights to theatrical uses of magical realism, such as Wilson's in *Redwood Curtain* and Shiomi's in *Mask Dance.* On the other hand, *Emma's Child* and *The Baby Dance,* in both of which the adoptee's perspective is present only by implication, stay very much within the mode of realism, though in different ways. In these plays the question of identity, or of reality, is less important than the question of who should or can take care of the child. In neither of these plays does adoption actually occur.

Drama is the literary form in theory most capable of showing many different viewpoints on the same situation. But, after surveying recent American plays about adoption, I am struck by how difficult it is for plays to represent three positions on the adoptive triangle in depth. Most, indeed, focus on only one point of view. Albee has represented characters in all these positions over the course of his career, but in his early plays the audience sees from the viewpoint of the adoptee, and the adoptive parents are caricatures and the birth parents invisible.[56] *Evelyn and the Polka King* and *Redwood Curtain* ignore or caricature the adoptive parents. *Homecoming* doesn't try to represent the birth mother (and doesn't consider the birth father). *Emma's Child* gives a fully imagined adoptive mother and father, but only a sketch of two birth mothers, one of whom is impossibly matched to her requirements in the play. *Sacred Virgin* presents a detailed picture of several birth mothers, but only stereotypes of the adoptee, and doesn't consider adoptive parents. *The Darker Face of the Earth* presents the birth mother and her adult son in depth, but does not consider him as an adoptee. *Mask Dance* shows several adoptees and an adopted mother with sympathy, and there is a brief narrative of the difficulties of Lisa's birth mother, but we don't see her. Though I find its social commentary telling, at least four of the five characters in the theatrical version of *The Baby Dance* are satirically treated types. But in its TV adaptation, where the last scene is the nameless baby crying, it comes close to the ability of Caryl Churchill's *Top Girls* to show the pain of characters on all three sides of the triangle. All of these plays present adoption in more depth than do those listed at the beginning of this chapter, which use it as a celebratory close—although in *Ragtime*, at least, we know the stories of the birth parents before their death and the stories of the adoptive parents before the adoption.

Unlike the novel, which is usually read silently and individually, the drama is an inherently public genre; it is one of the few forums in our society where people with every relation to adoption, including total ignorance, can potentially see something of how it appears to others with different perspectives. American theater now presents many other representations of adoption in contemporary life beside that in *The Bad Seed*. These plays have helped to keep adoption in public discussion and, in most cases, added a dimension to the representations in news media and television. I hope for more plays to extend our awareness of adoption's complexity, diversity, and connections with other aspects of society.

Seven ❧ Nurture, Loss, and Cherokee Identity in Barbara Kingsolver's Novels of Cross-Cultural Adoption

My daughter once joked that she must have been born to soccer players from Latin America. In reality she was born to my husband and me, two of the most unathletic people to live in Pittsburgh in the late twentieth century and early twenty-first. Yet, physically, she is recognizably my daughter, as much as a strong young woman at ease in her body can look like a middle-aged one whose favorite sport is walking.

In thinking about raising a daughter markedly different from myself—though in our case it is not a question of heredity-related differences—I have had the figurative companionship of the large number of parents in the United States who have adopted cross-culturally. Many of their adoptions, involving obvious ethnic differences, pose issues about the relative importance of environment and heredity. In two recent novels, Barbara Kingsolver takes on these questions about adoption. In a way surprisingly like George Eliot, with whom she shares an interest in science, she moves from a novel that redefines family to emphasize nurture to another one that uses an adoption and search plot to emphasize contrast between cultures as well as dramatize the loss of culture to the adoptee not in contact with birth heritage.[1]

In *The Bean Trees* (1988), Taylor's adoption of the abused child she calls Turtle is seen as an unproblematic good for Turtle; in *Pigs in Heaven* (1993), Turtle's Cherokee relatives and how she will deal with anti-Indian prejudice must be reckoned with. Both of these novels, unlike Eliot's, turn on legal child custody, but like Eliot's the novels prepare for the conclusion partly by the way they present the adoptive parent's nurturing, in the first case, and the history of the adoptee's hereditary culture, in the second. Unlike Eliot's, however, and unlike any of the previous works I have discussed except *Emma's Child,* these novels represent in depth the perspective of an adoptive mother. They also represent, more directly than most previous novels dealing with adoption, the effect of the traumatic loss of a parent on a young child and the attempt to heal that trauma.

In *The Bean Trees,* Taylor, a poor white woman from Kentucky, on her way west to find a better life, is handed a small child by an Indian woman who says it's her dead sister's; "there isn't nobody knows it's alive, or cares" (18).[2] This encounter is close to the one of *Silas Marner,* in that conflicts about whether to adopt are removed from the narration. As in *Silas,* nurturing a child integrates the adoptive parent into a new social system, and, again, adoptive nurturing becomes a natural process. The novel even includes a reference to *Silas Marner,* as an answer in a crossword puzzle.

But together with the emphasis on nurturing, *The Bean Trees* pays more respect than *Silas* to the importance of hereditary ties—particularly in oppressed groups. Not only is Taylor's small fraction of Cherokee ancestry brought into play in her relation with her daughter, but her adoption is contrasted with the experience of two Mayan refugees from Guatemala, Estevan and Esperanza, whose daughter was forcibly kidnapped to be adopted by their oppressors.[3] Taylor meets Estevan and Esperanza because her mentor, employer, and friend Mattie shelters them as part of the sanctuary movement. Mattie's care for the abused refugees parallels Taylor's care for the abused child. On the other hand, Estevan and Esperanza, in their indigenous ethnicity, figuratively represent Turtle's dead birth parents, and the close bond that Esperanza, in particular, develops with Turtle, suggests the bond of physical similarity that is missing in Taylor's close relationship with Turtle.

Nevertheless, *The Bean Trees* champions nurture throughout. Taylor's narrative teems with examples of how parental expectations influence children. She repeatedly recalls her own mother's encouraging pride in her—"no matter what I did, whatever I came home with, she acted like it was the moon I had just hung up in the sky and plugged in all the stars" (10)—and contrasts her success with the misery of characters such as Jolene Hardbine, who got pregnant too young because, she says, "my daddy'd been calling me a slut practically since I was thirteen, so why the hell not?" (9). The novel even includes a cat who is good because one owner calls it Snowboots and thinks he is good, and bad because the other owner calls it Pachuco, a name for a "bad Mexican boy" (74).

The novel also highlights nurturing by images of natural growth, often in improbable or unpromising circumstances. Turtle gets her name because her hands cling to Taylor in a clasp that reminds her of the bite of a mud turtle, "like roots sucking on dry dirt" (22). In the backyard of Mattie's tire store, fruits and vegetables grow luxuriantly from old tires. The night before the trip to Oklahoma, a homely, spiny plant bursts out in enormous flowers for one night of the year; it is the night-blooming cereus. When the three-year-old Turtle finally speaks, her first word is "bean," and her early vocabulary is mostly names of vegetables. These details further associate her recovery from trauma with natural growth. She is so fascinated by plants that she can see the similarity between the beanlike pods of wisteria and ordinary beans, and gives wisteria the name that becomes the title of the book. Near the end Taylor and Turtle discover that beans and wisteria are indeed both legumes, and learn that "wisteria vines, like other legumes, often thrive in poor soil" (227). Microscopic bugs called rhizobia live underground on the wisteria's roots and get fertilizer for the plant from the nitrogen in the soil. Taylor makes explicit a comparison between the plant symbiosis that maintains wisteria and the human communities that she sees and experiences in the novel. Rhizobia are

> a kind of underground railroad [a term also used, in this novel and historically, for the sanctuary movement as well as for the antislavery safe houses of the nineteenth century] moving secretly up and down the roots.[4]
>
> "It's like this," I told Turtle. "There's a whole invisible system for helping out the plant that you'd never guess was there." I loved this idea. "It's just the same as with people. The way Edna has Virgie, and Virgie has Edna, and Sandi has Kid Central Station, and everybody has Mattie. . . . Put them together with rhizobia and they make miracles." (227–28)

When she speaks of miracles, Taylor is thinking of her friends as well as of rhizobia.

Taylor's sense of community leads her to a redefinition of family. When she moves in with Lou Ann, who has a new baby and needs to cut down on expenses, at first she rejects the idea that they are a family and is uncomfortable with the way they seem to fall into conventional gender roles, with Lou Ann doing the child rearing and cooking and Taylor the paid work outside the home. But at the end when Lou Ann says to her, "You and Turtle and Dwayne Ray [are] my family. . . because we've been through hell and high water together" (231), Taylor concurs.

In addition to surrounding adoptive child-care and child growth with imagery of nature and foregrounding the importance of nurture in families begun by birth as well as by adoption, the novel stresses the similarity of the relationship between Taylor and Turtle and relationship of a mother and daughter begun by birth. Contrary to the popular use of language, the implications are, Taylor is an adoptive mother *and* a natural mother *and* a real mother. As an unintentional parent, she is similar to that of many mothers by birth. She tells a coworker, "She's not really mine. . . . She's just somebody I got stuck with" (52) and Sandi, whose child's father has disappeared, identifies with those words. Taylor's anxiety about child rearing is juxtaposed with Lou Ann's, which is even greater because of the sense of danger her mother has passed on to her.

Taylor's mother Alice, from the beginning a model of nurturance, repeatedly speaks of similarities between her and Turtle. When Taylor says of Turtle, "You never know what she's going to say," and Alice says, "Well, she comes by that honest," Taylor protests against the phrase: "if it acts like you, it proves it's legitimate. . . . I'm just sensitive, you know, since she's not blood kin" (223). But Alice redefines "honest" and makes explicit the point about the importance of nurture as opposed to heredity. "I don't think blood's the only way kids come by things honest. Not even the main way. It's what you tell them, Taylor. If a person is bad, say, then it makes them feel better to tell their kids that they're even worse. And then that's just exactly what they'll grow up to be." After this Taylor herself can revise conventional language about kinship: "Turtle's my real daughter. I adopted her" (223). She confidently defines herself to Turtle near the end: "I'm your Ma, and that means I love you the most. Forever" (225). When she gets the adoption certificate, she shows it to Turtle, saying, "That means you're my kid . . . and I'm your mother, and nobody can say it isn't so. I'll keep that paper for you till you're older, but it's yours. So you'll always know who you are" (232).

However, *The Bean Trees* does not leave heredity totally out of the question. Taylor is one-eighth Cherokee, the only ethnicity that she ever mentions, and she sometimes affirms her relationship with Turtle as a kind of ethnic solidarity. In one of the earliest times she acknowledges a bond with Turtle, speaking to someone trying her out for a place in a commune, she says, "Her great-great grandpa was full-blooded Cherokee. . . . On my side. Cherokee skips a generation, like red hair" (71–72).

Even before meeting Turtle, Taylor takes advantage of the ride through Cherokee country in Oklahoma to think about what this heredity means to her. Seeing two Indian women in a picture postcard, she identifies "the long, straight hair and the slender wrist bones" (15) as Cherokee traits she has inherited, and notes that one is wearing her "two favorite colors, turquoise and red." Taylor's love of bright colors is, she has said, a family trait shared with her mother, and when she bathes Turtle, she acts out this bond by dressing her in a turquoise-and-red T-shirt. "Indian colors," she says. The shirt comes from "one of Mama's people," and bears the message of self-confidence she has derived from her mother's nurturing: "DAMN I'M GOOD" (23). Thus the emphasis on Cherokee affinity by heredity and the emphasis on nurturing are combined.

As positively as Taylor's relationship with Turtle is described, near the end of the novel Turtle's loss of her birth mother emerges as a significant issue. This becomes clear on the trip to Oklahoma, in which Taylor drives Estevan and Esperanza to their new home, hoping that she will find some of Turtle's relatives in that area. There is no trace of anyone she met on her earlier trip. Instead, Turtle begins to respond to cemeteries by crying, "Mama." And when she buries her doll and repeats the same word, her fascination with planting becomes revealed as the transformation of watching the burial of her mother.

Taylor acknowledges and shares Turtle's sadness at the permanence of loss in death, and resolves to make her adoption of Turtle legal in whatever way she can. She asks Estevan and Esperanza to impersonate Turtle's parents for a notary. The act that they put on functions in the novel in many more ways than deceiving the judge to get official papers. Estevan and Esperanza in their indigenous ethnicity resemble Turtle's dead birth parents—Taylor says they have "the same high-set, watching eyes and strong-boned faces [she'd] admired in . . . the Cherokee Nation" (92–93). The novel suggests that their impersonation both helps Turtle to deal with her loss and helps them to deal with their loss of their own daughter. As Esperanza says to the judge, "We love her, but we cannot take care for her. . . . We move around so much, we have nothing, no home" (214), she is reenacting the kidnapping of her own daughter and her choice not to approach the corrupt Guatemalan police about it.

The effect of this leavetaking is heightened because of the close bond that Esperanza has developed with Turtle, who so much resembles her kidnapped daughter Ismene. This bond has increased the tension between Taylor's valuations of different forms of family life and her desire for the unique position of mother to Turtle. In this respect, Esperanza, with her physical similarity to Turtle and her own lost daughter, is particularly appropriate for representing the emotional challenge to Taylor of Turtle's birth mother. Taylor can accept Turtle calling all women "Ma" before their first name, but is more uneasy about Turtle calling Esperanza "Ma," even if she knows "Esperanza" is too difficult a word for her. But when she sees Esperanza holding Turtle before the judge she says, "Here were a mother and her daughter, nothing less. . . . I couldn't have taken her from Esperanza" (215). In the middle of this scene, Estevan gives Turtle a kind of blessing that is also a blessing for Taylor: she must be "good and strong, like your mother." At this one point, Taylor acknowledges the possibility of many mothers, as she wonders "which mother he meant. . . . I was touched to think he might mean me." It is significant then that her final affirmations of her relationship with her daughter emphasize that "you've only got one Ma in the whole world" (225). In Turtle's vegetable-soup song, which now includes names of people, too, she says, in the last line of the novel, "I was the main ingredient" (232). In two successive scenes near the end, then, characters relive a previous loss by relinquishing a substitute. Turtle reenacts the loss of her first mother by burying her doll, as Taylor grieves with her.[5] Then Esperanza reenacts the loss of her daughter by giving up Turtle to Taylor, which also helps Turtle reenact her own loss again. While earlier she responds to trauma by retreat into catatonia, at this point she comments on Esperanza's tears ("Try, Ma?") and has "the sniffles" (215). In both cases the novel suggests that these rituals work.[6] Turtle returns to thinking about beans and is willing to leave her doll behind. Esperanza's face shines "like a polished thing, something old made new" (216). Estevan, who is already established as an intelligent and educated English teacher, gives the process a name: "catharsis." We are suddenly in the world of Greek tragedy.[7] This word names the purgation or purification of pity and fear that Aristotle thought tragedy should accomplish. Theatrical imagery has already framed the adoption-hearing scene: Esperanza "was first in line for the Oscar nomination" (213). But there is a certain strangeness in Estevan's use of the word "catharsis," even if Kingsolver has plausibly made Taylor herself not know the word.

Why does Kingsolver bring in the concept of catharsis at this point? The application to Esperanza does stretch Aristotle's concept, which has been interpreted in literary criticism to apply to the purgation of the audience, by some, and the character, by others, but not to the actor. Kingsolver is suggesting not only the use of the word in aesthetics but also the use of the word in psychiatry: the German equivalent of "the cathartic method" was one of Freud's own terms for his method of bringing repressed material to consciousness by encouraging his patients in revisiting the past.[8] What Turtle does with her doll is like what previously traumatized children may eventually do in play therapy.

But using a word from classical Greek theater theory also helps to activate the literary allusion in the name Ismene. Ismene is, perhaps, imaginable as a Guatemalan or Mayan name, but in a context in which *catharsis* appears, it must be relevant that it is also the name of Antigone's sister. Antigone, a Greek tragic heroine who chose to go against state law to bury her brother, is still honored by dissidents in many different countries; she has been associated, for example, with the Mothers of the Plaza de Mayo, whose children were kidnapped by the Argentine government between 1976 and 1983, and a feminist bookstore in Tucson, Kingsolver's home when she wrote this novel, is called Antigone Books.[9] In Sophocles, however, Ismene was the traditionally submissive woman who rebuked her sister for her daring. If Kingsolver's Ismene, the missing child, adopted into a prosperous fascist family and apparently without knowledge of her past, is comparable to Sophocles' Ismene, then at some level Turtle, her physical double adopted into Taylor's subversive working-class family and obsessed with burial, is a version of Antigone. Antigone is the prototype of the characters in the novel involved in the sanctuary movement, who are committing civil disobedience to protect refugees persecuted in their own country and illegally escaping through the United States to Canada. But she is also reflected in Turtle's obsession with burial. In many ways the novel tries to show how public and domestic issues are connected; Antigone is one of the classical figures for such a link made when the state makes a law that threatens an individual's sense of family. Indeed, in *Antigone's Claim: Kinship between Life and Death,* Judith Butler sees her as a figure for all those who maintain nonnormative kinship, including adoptive relationships and multiple families.[10]

The use of the term *catharsis,* by associating human actions with both theater and healing, also helps link another central issue of the novel to aesthetic theory. Most of *The Bean Trees* defines parenting as nurturance and treats adoptive parenting as real parenting, championing it against the view that it is just "pretend parenting." But here, as the issue of loss emerges, the view that adoptive parenting is pretense is treated indirectly. In Taylor's discussion with Estevan, the pretense most immediately at issue is not adoption but Turtle standing in for Ismene. Taylor says that Esperanza seems "as happy as if she'd really found a safe place to leave Ismene behind. But she's believing in something that isn't true" (220). Estevan calms Taylor's objections, saying "in a world as wrong as this one, all we can do is to make things as right as we can." The imagery defends the pretense in the courtroom in part by making it a theatrical performance that heals, using a word—catharsis—from both theatrical and medical language. Estevan's defense of this substitution works at the same time to defend the other aspects of pretense here—the Mayans representing the Cherokees to make the adoption legal. His defense of this substitution is a substitution for a defense of the other substitution. Perhaps through him Kingsolver is also defending her own novel as another pretense that heals.

Does pretense work in *The Bean Trees?* What judgment does the novel ask us to make of the adoption, and what should we think of the novel's strategies? At the end, Taylor is more prepared to raise Turtle in many ways. She has developed a support community now identified as a family, with Lou Ann. She has help from Mattie, who is used to caring for traumatized children. She knows that Turtle needs special attention. Although at the very beginning she considered returning the "Indian child" to "its rightful owner" (22), she now knows that Turtle isn't an "item of commerce" (178). She has heard from Lou Ann—whose usual insecurities give her occasional wisdom about parenting more force—"your kids aren't really *yours.* They're just these people that you try to keep an eye on. . . . everything you ever get is really just on loan" (231).[11] She has some sense of the impact on Turtle of looking different from her surroundings, coming from her observation of how Esperanza and Estevan look different—more relaxed, even taller—when they are in the Cherokee Nation and everyone around them looks

Indian (204). She has a sense of Cherokee tradition as valuable, involving, for example, the beautiful places of the Ozark Mountains and the Lake of the Cherokees, as well as the government of the Cherokee Nation.

Kingsolver, it seems, has tried to meet many of the possible objections specific to cross-cultural adoption by giving Taylor some Cherokee ancestry, by showing that even Esperanza and Estevan recognize that Taylor is a good mother and give her a kind of indigenous blessing, and by presenting a caregiver who feels powerless to help her as Turtle's only remaining birth family member. Readers for whom Cherokee history is not vivid will probably find this convincing—and I am, viscerally, still among them when I read the novel. But on the last page, when Taylor says to Turtle that she can have the adoption certificate so that, as she says, "you'll always know who you are," though Turtle nods excitedly, she keeps "her eyes fixed on something outside the window that only she could see" (232). This is a kind of anticipation of all that *Pigs in Heaven* will show Taylor of what she doesn't know and Turtle needs to learn. "If her relatives want her back, then I'll think of something" (183), Taylor has said. It is only a threat to her, not a question of divided rights. While I admire Kingsolver's ability to inform readers about the sanctuary movement and political torture in Guatemala, after reading *Pigs in Heaven* it becomes clear that in adopting Turtle, Taylor needs to know more specifically about Cherokees. I can't help loving *The Bean Trees,* but I can see why a Native American might hate it.

What of my personal experience contributes to my affection for *The Bean Trees?* I first read this novel when my daughter, Liz, was only a little older than Turtle. Like Taylor, I was inexperienced with parenting, and had spent years successfully avoiding pregnancy, though unlike Turtle's, Liz's arrival was by birth, expected, and long hoped for. And emotionally, I came from almost as much a one-parent family as Taylor did—though my mother was not quite the ideal that Taylor's is, she was a warm, nurturing person who expected the best of me. Kingsolver wrote this book when she was pregnant with her first daughter, as I later discovered, and in some ways the book offered a kind of return to the occasional euphoria of a wanted pregnancy. The repeated emphasis on the similarity between loving motherhood by birth and loving motherhood by adoption, between Taylor's motherhood of Turtle and Alice's motherhood of Taylor, drew me in to this book and reassured me. I loved Taylor's language and her personality, confident about much, aggressively identifying with the underdog as a cleaning woman's daughter who has been taught to feel she's as good as anyone, lovingly observing her daughter's growth. Because of my politics, I appreciated the way Kingsolver linked the sanctuary movement with the attempt to care for an abandoned child. I have had students who think that Taylor should have called the police about child abandonment, or should have returned home where her mother could help her with Turtle, or should have at least seriously considered giving her to Esperanza and Estevan, and also students who felt that she, or the doctor she sees, should have reported the earlier child abuse to the authorities, and were shocked by the impersonation of Turtle's birth parents that she arranges for Estevan and Esperanza. None of these possibilities ever occurred to me. When I first read the book, in spite of my own interest in my birth parents, I don't remember thinking about whether Turtle would ever want to find hers.

Thus, I have personal reasons for giving Kingsolver a chapter to herself as the main representative of twentieth-century American fiction about adoption. But she deserves that chapter also on other grounds: she has received critical and popular acclaim and, especially with *Bean Trees,* a place in high school and college curricula; she has written about adoption repeatedly; and, like George Eliot, her novels seriously debate the definition of parenthood and the claims of heredity, changing emphases as her angle of vision changes.

At the end of *Bean Trees* it seems that Turtle has a comfortable hybrid identity in which both nurture and heredity are recognized. However, in *Pigs in Heaven* Taylor must do much more to recognize Turtle's heredity. Kingsolver comments, "I had the option and the *obligation* to deal with the issue because the moral question was completely ignored in the first book."[12] This novel contextualizes Turtle's adoption with the history of forcible removal of children from Indian families, which, as late as the 1970s, affected 25–35 percent of Indian children.[13] It also portrays the Indian practice of informal adoption within a large extended family, and gives Turtle a concerned grandfather, Cash Stillwater, with a legal advocate. Annawake Fourkiller, a young Cherokee lawyer whose brother was taken from their family, emphasizes Turtle's need to learn more about her Native American identity. She stresses the power of the negative Indian stereotype as well as the need to deal with hereditary physical conditions such as lactose intolerance. But even more, she urges the importance of having an identity as part of a community, not just as an individual. Much dialogue contrasts the communal identity of the Cherokees with the critically portrayed individualistic emphasis of the dominant white culture. The support system of the earlier novel now seems too fragile by contrast to the Cherokee Nation.

Kingsolver adds to the Cherokee side of the equation by turning the bravery Taylor showed in *The Bean Trees,* especially in her stressful, vulnerable position as a single parent, into a foolhardy attempt to escape from Annawake's investigation into the staged adoption. Instead of helping admirable refugees, Taylor helps a pop-culture-obsessed counterfeiter who has renamed herself Barbie with a trademark sign, after the doll. She is useful as a babysitter but feeds Turtle junk food and steals their savings. Instead of being the attentive parent of the first novel, Taylor fails to notice that the ice cream and milk she is urging on Turtle are making her sick instead of healthy.

Nevertheless, even Annawake recognizes the value of Taylor's nurturing, and she and the Child Welfare Services ultimately allow Taylor shared custody, while they give Turtle her grandfather's last name of Stillwater and make him her legal guardian. Here Turtle's hybrid identity will cost Taylor some control; the child must spend three months of the year in the Cherokee Nation. Classically minded readers may think of the compromise between Demeter and Hades, through which her daughter Persephone spends part of the year in the underworld with her husband and part of the year with her mother. But such agreements are common in custody cases. To soften this one, however, in a reconciliatory move so improbable that it has to be set up with a scheme devised by Annawake to make them fall in love with each other, Turtle's grandfather and Taylor's mother plan to get married at the end.

The plot, which involves the revelation of Turtle's social and family history as a Cherokee and its final integration with her situation as Taylor's daughter, structures a novel in which much of the dialogue also debates the meanings of parenthood, kinship, and families. In considering where Turtle belongs, the novel enters into current controversies about the relative influence of genetics and nurturing, and also contrasts current dominant American understandings of family with Cherokee ones.

Conventionally, debates about custody in contested adoptions begin with the question of whether nurture or birth makes a parent. From the beginning, Kingsolver gives something to each side in this debate, and ultimately tries to move beyond it. While in *The Bean Trees* Turtle's ethnicity is acknowledged from the start, that novel establishes the importance of nurture and the reality of Taylor's parenthood; here nurture, while important, has less directive power, and there is more emphasis on children's own temperament as influential. Taylor wonders "where all that persistence [in Turtle] comes from and where it will go." She "has had many moments of not believing she's Turtle's mother" (10). Taylor says of Turtle, "Doesn't she walk like a queen? I swear I didn't teach her that. It's a natural talent" (128). Both Alice and the uncle who raised Annawake see their child rearing in terms of responding to the child: "When you're given a brilliant child, you polish her and let her shine," thinks Alice (127). "If you have a frisky horse you put him in a race," says Ledger (332). Similarly, Cash tells Alice that when a child is selected to be a medicine man, the training builds on a prior temperament; "the medicine man can tell from the child how they'll be" (306). When Alice looks at Taylor and Turtle together, she thinks, "they share something physical, a beautiful way of holding still when they're not moving. Alice reminds herself that it's not in the blood, they've learned this from each other" (138). Note that here the learning goes both ways: she imagines Taylor learning from Turtle, not just Turtle learning from Taylor. And here there are limits to what nurturing can do. Alice "is ready to adopt" their former waitress Barbie when she loses her job (141), but after Barbie steals their money, clothes, and furnishings, Taylor realizes, "You don't adopt a wild animal and count it as family" (214).

The bonds of pregnancy and genetic parenthood are more important in this novel than in *The Bean Trees,* not just on the level of plot but in other ways as well. In the free clinic where Taylor and Turtle go near the end to find out why Turtle has a stomachache, there is a poster picture of "one half of a pregnant woman with an upside-down baby curled snugly into the oval capsule of her uterus," which reminds Taylor of cutting a peach in half and seeing a "little naked almond inside" (293).[14] This is an image that Alice will reverse when, near the beginning of the next chapter, "naked, curled little nuts [which she is separating from their shells as Cash prepares their meals] remind her of babies waiting to get born" (298). The poster makes Turtle wonder about "the real mom that grew me inside her" (293) and Taylor, without commenting on the "real," reminds her that her "mother had died": "you remembered seeing your first mama get buried" (294). It is in this clinic that an African-American doctor explains to Taylor that she has inadvertently caused Turtle's stomachache by feeding her dairy products without recognizing Turtle's lactose intolerance, a condition frequent among people of color.[15] Not understanding Turtle's genetics has made her intended nurturing occasionally toxic.

Though nurturing controls less here than in *The Bean Trees*, its impact is still strong. The narrator says of Turtle, "She's been marked in life by a great many things, and Taylor's odd brand ["marked" revivifies the dead metaphor in "brand" here] of love is by far the kindest among them" (12). Taylor's motherhood is clear in this novel. Taylor is always spoken of as Turtle's mother. Even Annawake calls her "the mother" (65) and says, "I'm sure you are a good mother" (77).

As the novel progresses, the two versions of parenthood seem more and more similar. The fact that Taylor's motherhood is adoptive does not exclude her from a protectiveness that seems instinctive. Alice says, "She's protecting her child, like any living mother would do, man or beast" (308). Jax recalls the idea that "getting between a mother bear and her cub" is dangerous (84) and refers to both Annawake, trying to get Turtle back, and Taylor, trying to keep her, as "Mama Bear" (84, 90). Jax thinks of this conflict when he sees a coyote, either pregnant or nursing, devour a nest of dove's eggs. One mother, to help her own child, consumes the children of another.

As Jax tries to put this event in a larger context, his analysis eventually dissolves the conflict between biological and adoptive parenthood in another way. "The predator seems to be doing only what she has to do. In natural systems there is no guilt or virtue, only success or failure, measured by survival and nothing more. Time is the judge. If you manage to pass on what you have to the next generation, then what you did was right" (180). Both biological and adoptive parenthood pass on something to the next generation.

What will be passed on to Turtle? What has been passed on to her? In this concept is one intersection between the two definitions of parenthood—as genetic and as nurture. A Cherokee appearance and biology have been passed on to her. How will her nurture take this into account?

Furthermore, as Cash's role develops in the novel, it becomes clear that his relation to her has been more than simply genetic. After Taylor sees Cash with Turtle, she understands that "He's still just aching for Turtle after all this time," and this continued relationship becomes the example that she uses to define family: "That's what your family is, the people you won't let go of for anything" (328). Kind, parental Cash, with his memories of caring for his granddaughter, makes Alice's phrase "any living mother, man or beast," quoted above from the conversation in which she tells him about Taylor and Turtle, particularly appropriate. He approximates what Sara Ruddick calls the "male mother."[16]

Cash's nurturing qualities are also emphasized in his relationship with Alice. He cooks for her—something she has never seen a man do before. And at the end of the chapter they go to bed, and the description of their lovemaking moves toward a description that, remarkably, assimilates both female and male sexuality to nursing. "She is pierced with a sharp, sweet memory of nursing Taylor, and when he puts his mouth there she feels once again that longing to be drained, to give herself away entirely. Slowly Cash moves himself against her, and then very gently into her, and she feels the same longing coming through his body to hers" (302–3). "Just aching," quoted above from the following chapter, is, in part, an echo of the imagery here. If sexuality is like this— if sex is giving yourself away, as nurturing is—here is another perspective providing an intersection between procreative and adoptive parenthood. It is no wonder that the title of this chapter, and its last phrase, ending the sentence after the one just quoted, is "the secret of creation."

But for the resolution of the novel, the two Mama Bears, Taylor and Annawake, both move to a more abstract plane of motherhood, seeking that much-evoked goal, the best interests of the child. Annawake argues on the basis of Turtle's welfare instead of the tribe's. "There are a lot of things she'll need growing up that you can't give her. . . . Where she comes from, who she is. Big things. And little things, like milk" (77). The wording might remind us not just of lactose intolerance but also of the fact that Taylor could not give Turtle her breast milk.[17] Even though at this point Annawake is convinced that Turtle's identity comes from heredity and Taylor is convinced that it comes from her nurturing care for Turtle, the fact that they are discussing Turtle's identity rather than the tribe's need turns the discussion toward Western concepts.[18] While Annawake begins by identifying Turtle's fate with the fate of her brother Gabriel, adopted by a white family who mistreated him, as the story progresses she becomes able to see how different Turtle's situation is.

Meanwhile, Taylor learns to deal better with Turtle's hereditary appearance and biology. Not only does she learn about the lactose intolerance, but she gains more understanding of what it feels like to look different from most people around you. At the end of *The Bean Trees,* it seemed that she had that insight when she arrived in Cherokee Nation, but in this novel she learns it all over again and explicitly applies it to Turtle. "Since her arrival in Oklahoma, she has felt her color as a kind of noticeable heat rising off her skin, something like a light bulb mistakenly left on and burning in a roomful of people who might disapprove. She wonders if Turtle has always felt her skin this way, in a world of lighter people" (318). After she confesses that she has wronged Turtle by making her drink milk and by living "on the edge" in poverty as she tried to hide Turtle and stay independent, there is an image of rapprochement. "Taylor and Annawake gaze at each other like animals surprised by their own reflections" (321).

When Uncle Ledger, her adoptive father and the one person to whom she goes for advice, translates the biblical story of Solomon into Cherokee terms, Annawake concludes that she doesn't "want to jump for joy to see a baby cut in half" (331). Mourning for her lost brother, Annawake has been, in a sense, this novel's politically active reflection of Antigone. But unlike the original Antigone, Hegel's paradigmatic example of an individual in a tragic situation facing a conflict between two absolute but irreconcilable principles—family and state in the original—Annawake realizes that she is facing a conflict between family and family, with love on both sides, and reconciliation may be possible.[19]

In the final court scene, Annawake articulates the compromise she has reached: the child "should be called Turtle, since she's grown to be a fine little person under her adopted mother's care, and that's the name she connects with her conscious memory of herself," but "we have to reinstate her as the granddaughter and legal ward of Cash Stillwater. We recommend her legal name be recorded as Turtle Stillwater. So, we've figured out *who* she is" (337–38).

In *The Bean Trees,* the certificate of adoption was to tell Turtle who she is. Who she is here is both Turtle—the Indian-sounding name given her by Taylor because of her behavior—and Stillwater, the name that connects her to Cash and to the Cherokees. But what does it mean to have an Indian identity, and how does this relate to the possibilities for Turtle's upbringing? The novel discusses these questions from several different points of view.

One of the perspectives is in the contrast presented between the "extended" family that Cherokees have to offer Turtle and the "contracted" white one—Annawake's term (284)—she lives in with Taylor, so informal and attenuated that Turtle doesn't recognize it as one. The novel gives vivid pictures of the Cherokee family. It's exemplified by the happy, affectionate household constituted by Annawake with her brother and sister-in law, who live together with her though they are divorced, and their children. Annawake sees family as "a color, a notion as fluid as *river*. She tells Alice, 'I used to work at the Indian hospital at Claremore, checking people in. Sometimes it would be years before we'd get straight who a kid's mother was, because one aunt or another would bring him in'" (227). The child belongs to the tribe more than to one or two parents.[20]

The white family imagined most deeply is the warm loving bond between Taylor and Alice, which is nevertheless closely linked with aloneness, here equated with alienation from men. The unhappily married Alice thinks, at the beginning of the novel, that aloneness is "a defect [that] runs in the family, like flat feet or diabetes" (4) and calls it "her inheritance, like the deep heartline" (23) on her palm, but also thinks of it as something her influence has transmitted to Taylor, who is emphatically not married to her housemate and boyfriend Jax. Alice traces the individualism in her family back to her mother who "had hogs by the score but nothing much to offer her fellow man, other than ham" (27), even though during the Great Depression she honored the extended family enough that second cousins such as Sugar Hornbuckle "showed up at Minerva's door once they'd run out of everything except relatives" (7).[21] A less attractive version of the white family is Jax's. His mother was or is an alcoholic, and he doesn't know where either she or his sister is. Then there is Barbie, who has left her family, never mentions them, and has apparently replaced her family name with a trademark sign. While in *Bean Trees* Taylor sometimes sees her extended network of close friends as her family (328), in *Pigs in Heaven*—especially when fleeing from a custody battle—she feels that the family is just her and Turtle, and that "isn't enough. We're not a whole family" (291). It is no wonder that when Turtle is questioned about her family by an Indian social worker, she says, "I don't have one" (324). Taylor's discovery that Turtle feels she doesn't have a family is part of what motivates her softening toward the Cherokees and her desire for a more permanent relationship with Jax near the end.

However, while the novel portrays many happy Cherokee families, it also shows Cherokee (as well as white) families gone wrong. Alice raises the question: "So with all this love going around, how does it happen that somebody walks up to my daughter's parked car one night and gives a baby away?" (227). Cherokees do not all live the happy "natural" life. Annawake explains, "Our chain of caretaking got interrupted. . . . Federal law put them in boarding school. . . . Family has always been our highest value, but that generation of kids never learned how to be in a family." Contrary to the image of nurture as instinctive—as in the Mama Bear motif—the presence of broken Cherokee homes shows that it needs to be learned; under oppression such learning may not happen.

The images of Cherokee families are mirrored in many different images of animals in groups. The most frequent form of observation of nature here, by contrast to that in *The Bean Trees,* is not of individual plants growing or being nurtured, but of animals moving as a group, like the Vietnamese pigs trying to get into a garden full of petunias, the finches all flying to Taylor's apricot tree, and the salmon trying to swim upstream to where they were born. Alice, learning about connections among the Cherokees, wonders "if the butterflies are all related to one another too" (221). These images of animals in groups present an image of life as basically social.

The chapter in which Cash is introduced puts special emphasis on his isolation from his community by counterpointing his isolation with a flock of pigeons he repeatedly observes as a bird shoot approaches. At first he thinks of them as "shining creatures whose togetherness is so perfect it makes you lonely" (113). But birds can go wrong, and they come to mirror his current condition as well. Like Cash's daughters and his friend Rose, who ruins her eyes making bead jewelry on display at the Trading Post in Jackson Hole, they have lost their place. They want to live in Jackson Hole, but they can't. These displaced birds are echoed in the birds that shriek unhappily in the office of Mr. Crittenden, the melancholy white man who makes money from Cash's fine Indian beadwork.[22] By contrast, when he returns to Oklahoma, Cash is met by one image of harmonious living things after another, culminating with "five beagles . . . reverent as a choir, blessing his overdue return" (176).

Could Turtle be a Cherokee in isolation from the Cherokee Nation? This possibility is negated not only by the pictures of the Cherokee family and the birds, animals, and Indians out of place, but also by the novel's treatment of inadequate, even exploitative, white attitudes toward Indians. Indians are figures of fantasy identification for Crittenden, who sells their jewelry, and for Taylor's landlady Gundi, who buys it and wants to paint their land, but neither one of them has much sense that Indians are a live community.[23] Taylor observes the scanty and partial representations of Indians in popular culture: an Indian actor in a movie, "The innocent-looking girl on the corn-oil margarine." The hook-nosed cartoon mascot of the Cleveland Indians, who played in Tucson" (95). While she can critique the negative images, she has little positive to put in their place, "no idea what she should be telling Turtle about her ancestors" (206).

However, in her awareness of her own lack of knowledge, Taylor has a perception that the novel's representations of Indian identity seem to bear out. "Maybe being an Indian isn't any one thing, any more than being white is one thing" (95). What is an Indian? As the anthropologist Circe Sturm shows, this continues to be a disputed question.[24] Kingsolver's novel, like Sturm's study, shows that it's not a simple matter of biology: characters with less Indian heredity may be more committed to Indianness than the "full-blooded."[25] Alice's cousin Sugar, biologically no more Cherokee than Alice, explains, "It's kindly like joining the church. If you get around to deciding you're Cherokee, Alice, then that's what you are" (271). Annawake's mother "was a die-trying acculturated Cherokee, like most of her generation, who chose the Indian Baptist Church over stomp dances and never wore moccasins in her life" (59).[26] For Annawake, being Indian means having a sense of belonging to a place of natural bounty: "All those perch down there you could catch, any time. . . . A world of free breakfast, waiting to help get you into another day" (67). Cash, on the other hand, thinks that one of the things you have to be an Indian to know is "how to stretch two chickens and a ham over sixty relatives" (111). Franklin, Annawake's boss, grew up in an Indian/white mixed family that kept no Indian customs, and became a "born-again Indian" while studying Native American law; he "knows he isn't white because he can't think of one single generalization about white people that he knows to be true. He can think of half a dozen about Cherokees. They're good to their mothers. They know what's planted in their yard. They give money to their relatives, whether or not they're going to use it wisely" (68). While Sturm argues that "most Cherokee people still live and imagine their identity as something rooted in essence, inextricably linked to their race, biology, genetics, phenotype, blood and culture,"[27] Kingsolver is particularly interested in defining Cherokee identity in terms of behavior.[28] She may not expect us to take Franklin's generalizations as true of all Cherokees, but they suggest something of how he gives content to his identity as a "born-again Indian."

Some of the novel's most vivid pictures of what it means to be Cherokee come at the stomp dance. Around an old flame thought to contain embers as old as the Trail of Tears, members of the community greet each other and welcome Alice. They trace family connections, converse mostly in Cherokee while mixing in English words like "distributor cap" and "gall bladder," listen to the medicine chief (Annawake's Uncle Ledger), smoke the peace pipe, and dance.[29] "For the first time she can remember, Alice feels completely included" (271). Tradition is maintained, but variations exist (the young people speak more English among themselves), and there is a place for everyone. For Alice it is an experience of self-transcendence: "Alice's life and aloneness and the things that have brought her here all drop away, as she feels herself overtaken by uncountable things. She feels a deep, tired love for the red embers curled in the center of this world" (272). Describing the stomp dance through Alice's eyes is, of course, calculated to make it more comprehensible and appealing to the white reader, and the welcome the Cherokee community offers her is a kind of prefiguring of the welcome to be extended to Turtle.

In writing a sequel to *The Bean Trees,* Kingsolver relied to a very large extent on the difference that adding a more detailed picture of Cherokee life, characters, and history would make. But there is another large attitudinal contrast related to the concept of family.[30] While *Bean Trees* repeatedly emphasizes the self-sufficiency of families without fathers, here Taylor discovers that she and Turtle need not only a connection to the Cherokee Nation but also a more stable bond with Jax. The end of the novel reverses the end of *The Bean Trees,* in which Taylor establishes her unique place in Turtle's life. Here Taylor faces the fact that she has lost the "absolute power of motherhood" (341). But at the same time she has lost power, she has added relationship: "From now until the end of time she is connected to this family that's parading down Main Street, Heaven" (341). The emphasis on aloneness in Alice's family is reversed at the end as well, as Cash proves he will meet Alice's requirement of paying attention to her by shooting his television, which she hates. "The family of women is about to open its doors to men. Men, children, cowboys [Jax is in a rock group named Renaissance

Cowboys and Cash is "one step away from being a cowboy" (113)] and Indians" (343). Alice has returned to the heritage of her great-grand-mother, whom she had heard of just as somebody who died young. But she also has, for the first time in her life, it seems, a truly companionate marriage.

The Bean Trees is easier than Pigs in Heaven to read as a feminist book, with Taylor's self-confidence, Mattie's abilities and hers in non-traditional areas, and the household with Lou Ann; yet it has some of the historical problems of the feminist movement in its consideration of race and color. The only nonwhite woman is Esperanza, who is rela-tively silent in the novel, partly because of the torture she has experi-enced as well as the traumatic loss of her daughter—both of which the novel is, of course, protesting against. In order for Taylor to have secure custody of Turtle, Esperanza has to be someone who cannot mother at this time because of her refugee position, yet in order to substitute for Turtle's birth mother legally and emotionally she must look like her. From one point of view she is sacrificed to the plot somewhat as the Creole Bertha Mason is sacrificed for Jane Eyre's happiness.

On the other hand, in keeping with the greater appreciation of eth-nic, racial, and cultural difference of the more recent feminist movement and indeed the greater diversity of U.S. society today, Pigs in Heaven contains one very powerful Cherokee woman, Annawake, and many others. Much more than any character in Bean Trees, Annawake, who shares parental loss and adoption with Turtle, imagines her experience as a woman of color later in life. "Some boy will show her that third-grade joke, the Land O'Lakes Margarine squaw with a flap cut in her chest, the breasts drawn in behind the flap, and ask her, 'Where does butter come from?' On the night of the junior prom, Turtle will need to understand why no white boy's parents are happy to take her picture on their son's arm" (149). Though Annawake seems a threat to Taylor's happiness, her dynamism, intelligence, and love of her tribe, her family, her brother, and her niece are attractively portrayed. Annawake, fur-thermore, is nontraditional in Indian terms in her resistance to mar-riage, though her alternative to marriage is not living as an individual, but living with her brother's family—her brother's family, not her sis-ter's.[31] There is a symmetrical contrast between Annawake's family without other women as she was growing up and Alice and Taylor's family without men, made explicit at one point in a way that suggests the incompleteness of both. While Annawake never indicates a sexual interest in men in the novel, she does change at the end in that she decides to try to contact her imprisoned brother Gabe directly, rather than giving up on him. The possibility of reading Annawake as discovering during the course of the novel that she is a lesbian adds further to the diversity that she represents.[32]

Even though Taylor says, "I never missed having a dad" (133), men are more important in *Pigs in Heaven* than in *The Bean Trees*. The issue is not exactly sexuality or even marriage—there is more sexual feeling in her relation to Estevan in the first book than in her relation to Jax in the second, and she says, "I don't know if *married* is really the point" (327). The real point is presented as permanence—a distinction suggested in the fact that Annawake's brother and sister-in-law (as she calls them) live together and produce and raise children together in spite of the fact that they are, for some unknown reason, divorced. Taylor may not be sure about marrying Jax at the end, but she is sure about wanting him as Turtle's "official daddy" (341).

This vision of permanent families requiring men, though countered by Alice's memories of her unstable former husbands, may well reflect the move away from all-female feminist communities—except for lesbian ones—that has continued since *Bean Trees* was written (though it was already well under way at that time). It is perhaps easier to read this as related to the change in Kingsolver's own perspective, moving from the circumstances in which she wrote *Bean Trees,* pregnant in a marriage soon to break up, to the new marriage in which she wrote *Pigs in Heaven.* But it should be clear that the two men who enter the previously all-female family of Alice, Taylor, and Turtle are decidedly nonpatriarchal—Daddy and Pop-pop, not "Father." Taylor is definitely the dominant partner in her relationship with the laid-back Jax, who worships her, and Cash cares enough about Alice to give up even television for her.

And though *Pigs in Heaven* does not experiment with the two-mother family, there are still new-style families at the end. From the white standpoint, at least, Annawake's household, with her brother and sister-in-law, divorced, and their children, seems unconventional. But the unconventional family that will be formed by the shared custody of Cash and Taylor is, of course, central to the novel. The sharing of Turtle is presented in a relatively nonthreatening way because of Cash's marriage to Alice; there are many families in which a child visits grandparents for part of the summer, with no Native American heritage.

However, in those families the grandfather and the mother do not share custody, with the primary custody going to the grandfather. And of course the custom of moving the child around among relatives is more common among Native Americans than among whites.³³

Both *Bean Trees* and *Pigs in Heaven* can be seen as commenting not just on adoption custody issues, but also on American culture and the terms of its inclusion of Cherokees, as a representative case of individuals or a community marked as different. Both novels make frequent comments on the limits of the American mythology of individualism, yet in *Bean Trees* Turtle is to a large extent included only as an individual, apparently without a history. Her Cherokee identity is mainly relevant in that prejudice against her skin color is voiced by a few characters who are critiqued. Turtle is able to give her a few bits of information about aspects of Indian culture with which she identifies— for example, Indians like bright colors—but not much else. The inclusion of *Bean Trees* is close to the inclusion of transracial adoption in writers like Elizabeth Bartholet.³⁴ On the other hand, in *Pigs in Heaven,* when the family of women opens up to Cash as well as to Turtle, when the life of the Cherokee Nation is portrayed so attractively, the implication is more emphatically that the United States should welcome minority cultures and communities, not just individuals who can assimilate, whether as adoptees or as immigrants. In fact, since Cash and Taylor are given joint custody, the image may even be one of joint partnership with other cultures, not admission of them on the basis of their childlike status.

Kristina Fagan critiques the suggestions of such an allegorical reading in *Pigs in Heaven,* writing, "By individualizing this utopian racial harmony, Kingsolver avoids the task of imagining how Native people and settlers can learn to live together as large communities. This is a challenge that will need to be met on a much larger scale—involving the settlement of land claims, changes to the educational and legal systems, constitutional changes, and other daunting tasks. . . . a big part of the appeal of this novel comes from the way in which it sidesteps these big issues by working them out in a way that is apparently natural. The reader is reassured that all the ethical and cultural conflicts that the book lays out can be solved by individual acts of love."³⁵ Fagan is right to say that the ending of this novel includes a kind of utopian racial harmony worked out as an individual solution for Turtle and Taylor— though with so much emphasis on the community of the Cherokees it is not as much of an individual solution as she says. However, I question her conclusions. The utopian quality of the solution in the book requires the very particular situation that Taylor and her mother are part Cherokee, that her mother is planning to leave her husband and has a cousin in the Cherokee Nation she spent time with as a child and can locate, and then that Annawake spreads gossip to Alice and Cash about their interest in each other, in a way that works as effectively as in *Much Ado about Nothing.* The solution would not even have worked so well with most other Indian nations; the Cherokee Nation is, according to Sturm, "remarkable for having no minimum biogenetic standard, no minimum degree of blood, for citizenship."[36] For this resolution of the second novel, it was, in a sense, just good luck that a Cherokee great-grandparent, rather than one from some other tribe, was one of the autobiographical pieces that Kingsolver used in creating Taylor. As Fagan herself says, two sentences later, "[The novel's] resolution is so unusual and so particular that it does not offer a feasible approach to either interracial adoption or the broader issue of community versus individual interests." This is so obviously a manipulated happy ending that it is more like a deus ex machina, or the sudden conversions marked as "most strange events" at the end of *As You Like It,* than "a way that is apparently natural." It is a less sardonic analogue of the point in Brecht's *Threepenny Opera* where suddenly the royal messenger arrives to commute Mackie's death sentence, and we are reminded that "Saviors on horseback are seldom met with in practice."[37] Readers of *Pigs in Heaven* will not expect that transracial adoption issues will be solved in life by allowing transracial adoption only to people with parents related to the nonwhite group who will marry into it if the adoption is contested. "Utopias" need not be read in such a literal way.

On the contrary, *Pigs in Heaven* helps its readers see the complexity of transracial adoption and the tragedies of Native American history. Its readers are more likely to pay attention to a child's need for contact with an ancestral community if they have already adopted, to think more about this issue if they are considering such adoption, and to support the public policy changes that Fagan advocates.

And we should note that, while the ending may be utopian from Turtle's point of view, or from the allegorical perspective that it joins Native Americans and whites, Taylor's point of view is different. She is losing the unique maternal power and position that is so important to her. At the end of this novel, Turtle is in an "open adoption," rather than a "closed adoption" though it originates in a different way than open adoptions typically do. As Judith Modell has argued, open adoptions and blended families are contributing to a "new kind of kinship, in which genealogy is only one way of constructing parenthood." As Modell explains, open adoption is more radical than closed adoption: "eliminating the separation between giver and taker of a child, distributing the components of motherhood over several individuals, and attaching a child in different ways to different parents represent substantial revisions of familiar customs" by which closed adoption has maintained ideologies of the family, parenthood, and gender.[38] Molly Shanley argues similarly that "open adoption . . . would undercut the blood-based understanding of family bonds" because it suggests "that a child can have multiple sources of family identity and multiple mothers and fathers."[39] Like the more typical openly adopting parents that Shanley writes about, Taylor must "receive [her] child in his or her specificity and acknowledge his or her social history . . . make room in [her life] for those things that 'belong to' [her] child."[40] The novel emphasizes, as Shanley does, that "the child is no one's possession. . . . That parenthood is not a proprietary relationship is true of all families, but is easier to see when two sets of parents must cooperate (even if only in the moments of relinquishing and assuming custody) to provide for a child's needs." This is a similar vision—normalizing some of the uncertainties associated with adoption—to the one that Lou Ann articulates in *The Bean Trees*, in a passage even more confirmed in *Pigs in Heaven*: "your kids aren't really yours, they're just these people that you try to keep an eye on, and hope you'll all grow up someday to like each other and still be in one piece. What I mean is, everything you ever get is really just on loan" (231). The ideal for Taylor and for other parents in open adoptions is a more obvious version of the paradoxical ideal for any kind of parents—supply permanence for their children while giving it up for themselves.[41]

At one point in the novel Taylor mentions that she amuses herself during car trips by imagining what "improbable combinations" (102) of people would say to each other. This is a homey version of what Kingsolver announces as her goal in fiction. "I want to know, and to write, about the places where disparate points of view rub together—the spaces between. Not just between man and woman but also North and South, white and not-white; communal and individual; spiritual and carnal."[42] Is there a point of intersection in this dialogue? That is Jax's phrase to Annawake; it is also a phrase that Kingsolver uses in discussing this novel when it was still in progress.[43] The opposition between the two sides is most clearly articulated in the first exchange between Taylor and Annawake:

> "How can you possibly think this is in Turtle's best interest?"
> "How can you think it's good for a tribe to lose its children?" (76)

But the discussion moves on, even when it seems they are at an impasse. Cross-racial adoption provides a situation in which Kingsolver can work on this and other dialogues. Turtle is young enough and Taylor and Alice and Cash and Annawake open-minded enough that the intersection is possible to find; thus, even though Taylor has given up some power at the end, the novel closes with a tone of triumph.

Jay Clayton has discussed the focus on family, home, and community in recent novels by women, and has contextualized this focus in relation to feminist and communitarian theory. Kingsolver's novels can be located with those he discusses, others of which deal with adoption as well. "These novels present the family as a partial, contingent structure, vulnerable both to internal and external pressures, yet open to revision. Further, they see the boundaries of home as permeable, subject to renegotiation."[44]

But at the end of *Pigs in Heaven,* however permeable the boundaries are, Turtle's family ties both to Taylor and Jax and to Cash and the Cherokees are seen as permanent and joyous. The novel offers hope that a cross-cultural adoptee can be happily bicultural and bifamilial, though many cross-cultural and open adopters will have to put more effort into finding a community and individuals representative of that other culture, or establishing the trust of the other family, than Taylor. Perhaps this utopian quality is dependent on the fact that the adoptee in this novel remains a child. Yet perhaps today's cross-cultural adopters have learned enough lessons from the past that their children, with the many cross-cultural camps and support groups now established and, more importantly, a different consciousness in society, will also be able to integrate their identities happily. Bicultural identity is the subject of many recent books, and even the census now accommodates mixed race as a category and encourages respondents to list multiple ethnicities. The possibility of a multicultural family resulting from one or more adoptions can be seen as an image of the possibility of embracing diversity in our country.

Turtle opens Taylor up to the whole history and ongoing life of the Cherokees, helping her to see much more in an aspect of herself that she has never thought much about, but at the end of the novel there is no sense that she will move into the Cherokee community as her mother will. Some transracially adopting parents do, on the other hand, make geographic and other changes to make sure that there are, for example, African Americans in their neighborhood, schools, and friendship networks, apparently the strategy associated with most successful identity formation of such children. One says, "People may see us a white family with black children, but I point out that we're a black family with white members."[45] Parents who adopt children from overseas are less likely to be able to find a U.S. community into which they might integrate, but they may find themselves strongly motivated to learn more about their child's birth culture, developing, for example, every bit of their linguistic ability to learn Chinese.[46] The attempts that adoptive parents can make to give their children some share in their children's hereditary culture is an image of the openness that all parents need in order to deal with the fact that their child is a separate person; they must try to connect in a way respectful of that separateness. In the words of my friend and colleague Nancy Glazener, "part of what happens in parenting is an ongoing search for grounds of connection."[47]

Like Taylor's Turtle, my daughter has educated me. Yet I am aware of the differences between my situation and that of an adoptive mother, and I will return to this topic in the afterword.

～ Afterword: Locating Myself as an Adult Adoptee

In the last two years of high school, my daughter Liz spent most of her free time at friends' houses rather than at home. She stopped going on family vacations with us and hardly ever showed us anything she wrote at school. She spent her first college spring break—in a very successful year—visiting friends out of state rather than seeing us.

Is this just adolescent assertion of independence within the normal range? Does it reflect dissatisfaction with a home life that wasn't good enough? What does it bode for the future?

In contemporary America many parents worry about their relationships with their children. Has my upbringing as an adoptee made our relationship more difficult, or made me particularly anxious?

One of the themes of Jean Paton's pioneering book *The Adopted Break Silence* is that the popular image of adoptees as always children is a myth; adoptees do grow up, and the experiences of adult adoptees should be heard. While much previous literature has focused either on adoptees as children or, like George Eliot and other novelists, on adoptees near the point of marriage and/or career choice, recent psychology has begun to discuss dealing with adoption as a lifelong process.[1] And several recent novels enter this dialogue by imagining adoptees in middle or old age.

My study of adoption in literature has been most intense during my daughter's years as a teenager. It is probably for this reason that when I think of recent novels about adult adoptees, the ones that have meant the most to me have been novels in which some relationship between the adoptee and a younger person—usually a parental relationship—is crucial. However, in only one of these novels, *The Diviners*, is she a child of the adoptee by birth. In *A Gesture Life* it is the main character's adopted daughter; in *Jazz* it is a young woman who becomes a friend to both members of a childless couple (both of whom also have lost their birth parents) after the death of her friend, the man's young lover. In *Mr. Ivess' Christmas* it is the regenerated murderer of the adoptee's son.

All of these are books about memories, in which the past is revealed in complicated and circuitous ways. The main characters learn little, if any, factual knowledge by the ends of the novel they did not have at the beginning, but by the end their significant memories have emerged. These are all books about coming to terms with losses, the first loss of parents and later losses that sometimes explicitly repeat that one and are sometimes made worse because of it. These novels present the loss of parents as more of a trauma with aftereffects than do most of the other works of literature I have discussed. (In nineteenth-century novels, the worst aftereffects come more clearly from the way characters such as Esther, Estella, and Pip are treated by their adoptive parents.) For the adult characters in the novels, the search for birth parents is either impossible or in the past; it doesn't solve their problems as some literature suggests it might. But they are seeking for something. Perhaps one could call it a way to lead their lives while accepting their past and future losses. I am tempted to call it redemption, though in only one novel is religion an explicit theme.

The first of these is *The Diviners,* the last novel by the Canadian writer Margaret Laurence.[2] As far as I know, this is the only work of literature discussed in this book except Albee's plays in which the author as well as a character is an adoptee. Margaret Laurence's mother died when she was four. Her mother's sister helped her father with his young daughter, and then married him. He died when Margaret was nine.[3]

The main character in her novel, Morag, was orphaned at four and adopted not by a relative but by Christy, the town ragpicker, and his wife, Prin. Morag fights against her class position in her society and against its male dominance, and eventually becomes a successful writer. In this autobiographical novel she looks back over her career as she tries to come to terms with her past, her friends, her future, and her teenage daughter, deliberately conceived out of wedlock with an Indian friend, breaking her ties with her white husband and making her daughter repeat her own past as a social outcast. Morag reevaluates her parents and ancestry in ways particularly interesting to other adoptees: she learns that Christy's stories about her birth father played up his heroism and played down Christy's own; she decides that her own land is not really Sutherland, in Scotland, the land of her birth father's ancestors, but the Canadian town Manawaka, the land of Christy's ancestors, whom she has now taken for her own. At the end of the novel, she accepts the fact that her daughter is leaving town to visit the other side of her heritage—the land of Morag's ex-lover's family.

In Toni Morrison's *Jazz*, three of the major characters have lost both birth parents and one has lost his father.[4] All of these characters were informally adopted, mostly within the family. The novel begins after fifty-year-old Joe has killed Dorcas, his much younger lover, and Violet, his wife, has broken up the funeral. As their stories are told, all these characters reveal psychologies of loss, search, and substitution. Joe's memories of seeking out his mother when he was fourteen emerge when he talks with Dorcas, and even in the search that ends with his shooting her. Dorcas has responded to his retelling of his search by telling him her childhood memories of her mother's death shortly after her father's. Violet, also orphaned and raised by her grandmother, is preoccupied with her childlessness when Joe turns to Dorcas, and later becomes preoccupied with the dead Dorcas. This quest leads her to visit Alice, the aunt who raised Dorcas, who provides some of the mothering Violet has missed and helps her reconstruct her life as she says, "You got anything left to you to love, anything at all, do it" (112). Trying to learn about Dorcas, Violet meets another young woman, Felice, Dorcas's friend, who gives Violet and Joe both a critical perspective on her friend and knowledge that makes Joe less of a murderer (Dorcas was shot in the shoulder; she wanted to die; she wouldn't have died if the ambulance had arrived in time). At the end of the novel, the relationship Violet-Joe-Felice is a transformation and redemption of the triangle Violet-Joe-Dorcas. Instead of tearing the couple apart as Dorcas did, Felice helps their love and shows that they can now be open to the world.

The story of Joe and Violet and their two "substitute daughters" is interrupted by another story of loss and substitution, the story of Golden Gray, raised as a white boy by his white mother and her black maid, at the age of eighteen searching for his black father. On the same trip, he finds and helps a pregnant black woman, Wild, who makes a home for him and who, we eventually learn, is Joe's mother. And Violet's life, too, has been affected by Golden because her grandmother was the black maid who brought him up as an idealized white boy. Thinking partly of this influence, Violet says of Joe, "From the very beginning I was a substitute and so was he" (97). This view of human psychology is one of the key themes of the novel. It is balanced, perhaps, by Dorcas's mysterious dying words. "There's only one apple . . . Tell Joe"

(213). The image recalls the apple of Eden, with its choice interpreted as a choice of experience rather than a fall. Joe has earlier said to Dorcas, "You were the reason Adam ate the apple . . . Don't ever think I fell in love. I rose in it" (133, 135). If love is always love of a substitute, the novel suggests, it is still love; this has obvious implications for how we see the substitution involved in adoption. So does the way Violet accepts substitution as part of the imaginative remaking of the world that she finally chooses: "What's the world for if you can't make it up the way you want it?" (208). In the final description of Joe and Violet together, Violet takes on images suggestive both of the lost Dorcas and of Wild, Joe's lost mother, while Joe is described in language that echoes the description of Violet's mother and father in their best moments.

Chang-Rae Lee's *A Gesture Life* is another novel in which the main character's adoption is an influential event in his life. At the beginning, we meet him as Franklin or Doc Hata, owner of a medical supply store in a small New England town. We find out that he was born into a poor Korean family and adopted by a middle-class Japanese one, and learned very early to be ashamed of his origin and never to say his Korean birth name. This repressed past returns to set up what turns out to be his greatest trauma, which he is able to reveal only very late in the novel; while in the Japanese army, he fell in love for the first time—with a Korean "comfort woman," who begged him to kill her to save her from gang rape by the other soldiers in his company. Unable to do this, he was forced to tend her dead body and that of her unborn child. By implication, this event heightens his lifelong problems with intimacy after he moves to the United States. Retrospectively it explains much of his distance from the two women in the book who care for him, as well as his difficulties with the daughter he adopts from Korea, his anxiety about her sexuality, and eventually his repetition of his earlier trauma by forcing her to have an abortion during which he assists.

Nevertheless, in spite of his past alienation from his daughter, they are eventually reconciled, about seven years after she has a son. Hata for the first time has experiences that he thinks of as like the family joys that most people feel. It is only after this regeneration that he is able to reveal to the reader the full story of his past traumas.

At the end of the novel, however, he does not settle down in the company of his refound daughter and grandson. His last plans are to sell his house, make provisions for them and for a dying, motherless child whose father owns the medical supply store formerly owned by Franklin, and travel, "maybe farther still, across the oceans, to land on former shores."⁵ Wherever he is, he will go on a walk and "come almost home."

In Oscar Hijuelos's *Mr. Ives' Christmas*, Edward Ives, a foundling adopted by another foundling, looks Latino and feels a sense of affinity to the Spanish people of New York City, where he lives, and takes on a strong Catholic religious belief under the nurturance of his adoptive father.⁶ Like the older Ives, he goes into newspaper work. He becomes a cartoonist, marries, and has children and a reasonably happy life until his sixteen-year-old son is shot by a fourteen-year-old Puerto Rican teenager. At this point it seems his life is destroyed. But he is moved by the grief of the murderer's grandmother, takes her to support group meetings, and at the pleas of her and a priest begins to write to his son's murderer, Gomez. This is difficult for him to do, but it actually has an effect on Gomez, who learns to read and write better and is ultimately released from jail. While still resentful of Gomez, Ives meets with him and receives his gratitude.

In each of these novels, adoptees are divided between different ethnic identities, and in each of them, an adoptee moves toward more affiliation with the one less socially valued, although with one exception that affiliation is less drastic than in *Daniel Deronda*. Golden Gray, the exception, becomes black, like his birth father and the maid who helped raise him; Hata acknowledges his Korean ancestry and also the African-American side of his adopted daughter, who herself prefers racially mixed society, and at the end of the novel he is about to travel to Asia; Morag eventually identifies with her adopted father's people, and with Canada, where she grew up, rather than her birth parents' ancestry, unlike the previous characters, but in this way she is giving up identification with the more poetic Highlanders in favor of someone who is socially despised.⁷ Mr. Ives has no way of finding his ethnic identity, but he learns Spanish and makes most of his friends among Latinos.

In each novel adoptees have an intense desire for, and eventually, a relationship with someone in the next generation—in Morag's case her birth child, Pique, in Hata's an adopted daughter and her son, in Joe's and Violet's case their friend Felice—whose independence they can ultimately acknowledge along with that relationship. The novels explore Morag's desire for "someone of her own blood" (193), Violet's move from not wanting a child to sleeping with dolls to thinking of Dorcas as her lost child, and the adoption to which, we eventually realize, Hata was driven by reasons he never understood. Mr. Ives's desire for a child is communicated largely through his pregnant fiancée's perspective. Anxious as she is about the limitations a child will place on her life, "her thoughts always returned to Ives and how he had been a foundling, and how much it must have hurt him even to consider giving up the child to make her happy" (50). Mr. Ives's relationship with his son is short-circuited by death; his most emotional relationship with the next generation seems to be with Gomez, who is in a bizarre way a kind of substitute for his son.

Is there a connection in these novels between the emphasis on ethnicity and ethnic difference and the emphasis on two generations of parental relationships? On the one hand, the facts that the central adoptions in *A Gesture Life* and *Mr. Ives' Christmas* are across ethnic lines—as well as that Golden Gray is raised as white—emphasize, to different degrees, contrast and stress in the parent-child relationships. On the other hand, it also locates those relationships as part of a larger community and a larger history. In each case, the author is from the group identified with the "double identity" character's heredity. In both *A Gesture Life* and *Jazz,* the oppression of one racial group by another and its psychological effects, including internalized racism, is a major theme; in *Mr. Ives' Christmas* the Catholic religion is a bridge across cultures, passed on to Mr. Ives by his Anglo father, shared with the Latinos whom he resembles, and helping him to forgive his son's murderer. *The Diviners* concerns itself even more with ethnic difference with regard to nonadoptive issues: the Métis identity of Morag's lover and the consequent identity difficulties of their daughter.

Each of the novels explores how later intimate relationships recall earlier ones—with elements of searching, loss, rejection, and substitution. *Jazz* and *A Gesture Life,* especially, explore the echoes of the relation to birth parents in later life—the sense of loss and the search in *Jazz,* the embarrassment over their sexuality and low social level in *A Gesture Life.* Each novel involves forgiveness: Mr. Ives forgives Gomez, Violet and Joe forgive each other, so do Hata and his daughter, and Morag and Pique. All four novels also emphasize the relationship of the adoptee to a community, though they are also always in a sense outsiders within that community. In *A Gesture Life,* Hata leaves his community at the end, and for the first time he may actually return to places he lived in earlier.

One of the controversial issues among people who write about adoption is the question of how much trauma is inevitable in adoptee experience. Is the loss of a birth mother, whether through death or relinquishment, always painful and therefore a primal wound that affects the adoptee throughout life? I have serious doubts about this as a general claim, since the loss may be softened if it takes place early enough and is followed quickly by adoption in a loving and understanding family, but in all of these novels, trauma is clearly involved. The adoptee loses parents as a child old enough to remember and grieve, or to forcibly change identity and distance himself from birth parents, like Hata, or stays in an orphanage for years, like Ives, or is raised by adoptive parents with a sense of being an outsider and having a possible birth mother who is scorned by all, like Joe. In all of these novels we see the effects of these events as long lasting, even if hidden most of the time; but the characters all manage to integrate them in some ways into a life that is not defined by victimhood. Their experiences of loss and adoption are exaggerations of the experience of many adoptees who were adopted in a less traumatic way; for example, I moved directly from my birth mother to my adoptive parents when I was about a month old. Nevertheless, I find a kind of hope in the development of these characters.

For in these adult adoptee novels I find many of my own issues. Like Morag, Ives, Violet, and Hata, I longed for a child. Like Morag and Hata, I must deal with her increasing distance as she grows up, hoping that we will be able to forge a new and better relationship in her adulthood. Though I never reexperienced a frustrated search for a birth parent as explicitly as Joe in my current relationships, I have sometimes wondered about whether any relational difficulties I have in some way reenact, for example, my feelings of being rejected by my birth father. Two aspects of my own life I find uniquely among these novels in *Mr. Ives' Christmas*, in exaggerated form. Ives finds it very hard to throw away anything that ever mattered to him; the narrator calls his tendency to save objects "a practice that had something to do with his foundling beginning" (5), though I know other adoptees who are not hoarders at all.[8] And Ives has a strong faith in God's love, conveyed to him by his adoptive father, which remains important to him all his life even though the loss of his son challenges him enormously. These are the first two aspects of Ives that the narrator introduces, as if they are connected; Ives cannot throw away his Catholic faith, as he cannot throw away his old letters, drawings, and correspondence. His memory of the absolute sense of loss in the foundling home returns to him at his son's death and motivates his investment in all the objects that have taken on meaning for him, including, perhaps, the sacramental, ritual objects of Catholic tradition.

None of these novels gives the adoptee a simple solution. *The Diviners* turns away from giving Morag a clear identity with ancestors in Scotland, and she doesn't tell Christy that she thinks of him as her father until just before he dies. Motherhood is not simple for her either, and the authorship that is so much her own identity is presented as a gift that may well leave her as she grows older. *Jazz* tells and retells Joe's search for his birth mother, and the ambiguity of its results, which leave him still looking for a sign from her. At the end Joe and Violet are happy together, but this happiness is the product of much struggle, suffering, forgiveness, and compromise. Hata apparently gives up the family happiness he seems at last to have found, and denies the idea that his trip is a pilgrimage: "I won't attempt to find comfort in the visage of a creator or the forgiving dead" (356). Ives does find comfort in his imagination of a creator, and his dreams of his dead son, but the novel conveys the wrenching pain he experiences all the way to that point.

I see my renewed appreciation of my adoptive mother as parallel to Morag's of her adoptive father, and I identify with most of these characters in their ability to endure loss and reconstruct relationships. When Hata, finally reconciled with his daughter and grandson, decides to move away and travel instead, I mentally gasp and wish for reassurance that he is coming back to them; but in this book, more bitter than the others, it is not there, and once more I learn more about myself by seeing how I would have chosen differently.

These novels present hope after loss, but they deny the adoptee many of the simple "happily ever afters" of resolution. I turn to them, as to many of the other works discussed in this book, because I want to see adoption imagined in complexity and diversity. I look for the way imaginary lives are like mine, and the way they are different. I look for those touched by adoption in fiction, in the thought that others will be able to understand their own lives better by seeing the way their lives are both like and unlike the fictions I discuss.

Some of the literature I discuss shows possible difficulties in adoptive family life, and I hope that my analyses will help people who experience those difficulties feel less alone and will help others avoid some pitfalls.

But I also hope that people who belong to or observe good adoptive families will be able to read my literary analyses with less cognitive dissonance than they read criticism that takes for granted the ideology of blood in *Oedipus* and *Winter's Tale,* believes that the repression in the *American Dream* family is inevitable in adoption, and misses the emphasis on the importance of nurture in Dickens, Eliot, and Kingsolver. And I hope that analyses of the myths of reunion in earlier literature will help adoptive parents feel less threatened by the idea of their children having information about their heredity, eventually meeting their birth parents, or even growing up in open adoptions. I hope my analyses contribute to undoing the invisibility of birth parents in literature that does not mythologize them as the only parents. I hope that people in other forms of families can use insights from the literature of adoption about accepting difference in the family. And I hope that this book will also contribute to thought about other nonstandard forms of kinship. Gay marriage or partnership, for example, stands in obvious similarity to adoption as a form of kinship that does not involve a direct link between sex and procreation, and poses the question about what defines marriage, just as adoption poses the question of what defines parenthood.

Since this book began by locating my history in relation to adoption, I want to end it partly by discussing some aspects of where I now am as an adoptee. I want to look at some of the ways being adopted has affected my current close family relationships, and the way they, in turn, relate to the ways I think about being adopted. I also want to consider two aspects of identity most entangled with adoption, ethnicity and religion—both of which might seem to provide multiple possibilities for me since my adoptive and birth parents were such a diverse lot. I grew up with my adoptive parents' ethnicity and my adoptive mother's religion ascribed to me, but as an adult have been in a position to choose from many ethnicities what to identify with, and to decide which religion is my own.

As I write, putting much emphasis on my own ethnicity seems somewhat artificial, since I don't think in ethnic terms very often. Now that I know all my ethnicities, perhaps, I can take them more for granted. But since many adoptees do think in those terms, and since ethnicity appears significant in other chapters, let me take stock. If anyone asked me about my ethnic identity and gave me enough space, I would list all my possible ones, birth and adoptive, since all have influenced me. Norwegian, German, English, like Geraldine. Irish, German, English, like Dorothy. Czech, like Frank. Jewish, probably Ashkenazi, probably from the former Soviet Union, like Murray. Though I have no Czech or Irish "blood," Czech and Irish culture influenced the atmosphere in which I grew up, probably in many ways that I will never know. For my fiftieth birthday, I went to Prague with my husband, daughter, and "birth niece," two years older than my daughter. I stopped by Rocycany, the small town my adoptive grandparents came from, and thought of them as I saw the Catholic church probably of my grandmother's childhood next to the science museum my grandfather might well have valued.

James Baldwin once wrote about his relation to white culture, "I was forced to recognize that I was a kind of bastard of the West. . . . I brought to Shakespeare, Bach, Rembrandt . . . a special attitude. . . . I was an interloper; this was not my heritage. At the same time, I had no other heritage which I could possibly hope to use—I had certainly been unfitted for the jungle or the tribe. I would have to appropriate these white centuries. I would have to make them mine—I would have to accept my special attitude, my special place in this scheme; otherwise I would have no place in any scheme."[9] Baldwin's position as the outsider to tradition in some ways applies to me more as a woman than ethnically, and much of my writing before this was an attempt to appropriate my literary past as a woman. Appropriating the ethnic identities I was raised among was not as complicated for me as is the process Baldwin describes. As I discussed in the introduction, ethnicity was not an issue with much content in my adoptive family. There was enough overlap between my birth and ethnic identities that crossing them was not nearly so difficult for me as it was for Baldwin, or for people adopted transracially. And unlike Baldwin, at a time when black history was just being discovered by Americans, I can find out about Norwegian and Jewish history, even if not about the history of my birth father's family. I could construct a relation to an ethnic past as Stuart Hall discusses his son doing in adapting African traditions in his sculpting: "Our relationship to that past is quite a complex one, we can't pluck it out of where it was and simply restore it to our selves. . . . We tell ourselves the stories of the parts of our roots in order to come into contact, creatively, with it."[10]

But in my own particular situation, I cannot, emotionally, reconstruct myself as a member of an ethnic Norwegian or ethnic Jewish community. Theoretically it would be a possible choice for me to join an ethnic organization connected with any of my adopted or inherited affiliations. Pittsburgh has many such groups. But psychologically joining any of them would be, for me, a leap not worth making, since I don't have happy memories of cultural practices to be revived or, at present, a strong wish to learn new ones based on ethnic allegiance in particular; if I were joining a new singing group, for example, I probably wouldn't select one that focuses on the music of one of my ethnicities, though an adopted friend of mine is doing this partly as a link to her otherwise unknown Latin American ancestry. I am not really at home in any group defined by ethnicity, though I can enjoy many different kinds of "ethnic" music.

I teach English literature, and there is English ancestry in both my adopted and birth families, and I am now part of a denomination associated with English tradition, but I don't feel ethnically English. I could appear so, at least on paper, if I took my husband's last name, Carrier, but keeping my own appeals not just to my feminist consciousness, my wish to be identified with the writing and other achievements done before my marriage, but also to my sense of solidarity with the particular kind of outsider identification with which the name Novy marks me, no matter how little I know about Czech history. When I write about Shakespeare, I am interested in Shakespeare's relation to outsiders within the plays, and to international readers and audiences today. The question "Who are your people?" came to me in a dream, and I had no answer.

On the other hand, I like the idea of having connections with the complex history of all these traditions, finding my own heroes and heroines to celebrate in each and learning how all my parents were influenced by each. And also finding heroes and heroines in other traditions, such as struggles for women's rights, civil rights, workers' rights, religious freedom. Though as a white person I am not clearly identified by ethnicity, I still resonate to the creative multiplicity in some ethnic writers. My fantasy is to be like Gloria Anzaldúa's mestiza, who "copes by developing a tolerance for contradictions, a tolerance for ambiguity. She learns to be an Indian in Mexican culture, to be Mexican from an Anglo point of view. [I feel this need to tolerate contradictions and ambiguity with regard to religion and other issues more strongly than ethnicity at present.] She learns to juggle cultures. She has a plural personality, she operates in a pluralistic mode—nothing is thrust out, the good the bad and the ugly, nothing rejected, nothing abandoned."[11]

Nothing rejected, nothing abandoned. With the resonance of these words, I move from ethnicity to more individual issues. Once Geraldine and I were rejected by my birth father. But he was just a nineteen-year-old boy—the first time, anyway. Once I was, you could say, abandoned by Geraldine. But she didn't abandon me. She arranged for me to be taken care of by Dorothy and Frank, who she thought could give me a family life she could not. Perhaps adoptees who have lived all their lives in an environment where single parents are accepted have more difficulty dealing with their birth mothers than I do. I remember how strong and terrifying the stigma on unwed pregnancy was in my childhood. It is easy for me to understand why Geraldine felt she couldn't keep me.

I keep up with Geraldine, and visit her occasionally. Though I see us as so different, on one recent visit she said, "You're like me. Neither one of us is explosive." I didn't argue with her. If she wants to see us as similar, why deprive her of that? And perhaps she is right about this particular issue. Neither one of us seeks out conflict at this point. She has osteoporosis, anemia, and a tendency to macular degeneration, but not cancer or heart disease, and I can consider this information (which closed records would have denied me) in making health decisions. Time has led me to a greater appreciation of my brothers, especially Gordon, the second oldest, who is much better than I am at sending e-mail messages and newspaper clippings. I also remember that another one, Galen, overseas in the military when he found out about me, tried to initiate a correspondence to which I didn't respond very well. And Geraldine recalled, during my last visit, the youngest one, Ben, excitedly saying, "I have a sister!" when she told him about me.

As I returned to writing this book, I made a last attempt to communicate with Murray. I had the press send him a copy of my anthology on adoption in literature. Since nothing in the package would indicate that I had ordered it, this seemed to me a fairly cautious gesture; I expected that, as after most letters I sent, I would probably hear nothing, but he might be curious enough to read some of it. A few weeks later, the press sent me a credit for the book. By process of eliminating the other people I had books sent to at that time, I infer that he returned it to the press. I didn't expect such a drastic rejection—but I'm not astonished. I assume he wants his respectable image preserved and may even fear that I would be entitled to inherit money from him if he acknowledged me— I didn't think possessing my book would be that much evidence against him to others, but perhaps it would. I'll have to write him off. I've had bad luck with fathers, but I think of the end of Sean O'Casey's *Juno and the Paycock*, where Juno says that if her grandchild won't have a father, "It'll have what's far betther—it'll have two mothers."[12] As I have had.

I still keep up with some members of my adoptive family. My mother's brother's wife, my aunt, died a few years ago at ninety-one. I was the closest surviving relative. In her last years, I came to realize how she and my Uncle Dan had influenced my childhood. She was another Dorothy, like my mother, and I sometimes wondered if that name had unconsciously helped draw my uncle to her, but they had much else in common. They were the happiest couple I knew in my extended adoptive family, and the members of it who were the most present in my childhood. We saw them on holidays, and I remember Dan quoting poetry, giving me books, playing records, and taking us to the opera. Poignantly, they had lost a baby less than a year before I was adopted, and, reading Dan's letters after Dorothy's death, I saw him staying with my parents and taking care of me as an infant as she went to recuperate in her own difficult family. They never had another child.

Given the fact of my presence reminding them it was possible, one could say that they chose not to adopt. But one could also say that they chose, in a less drastic way, to adopt me as their niece. (My mother's other brother and his wife were not nearly as close to us.) Reclaiming my memories of Dan and finding out more helps make up for the bleakness of my memories of my father and the rejections of my birth father. My bond with my aunt—besides the fact that she seemed to be an independent woman with a career, who showed that you could be a wife without cooking—was that we both loved to learn and to read. She was always taking courses that I could talk about with her at family events.

Now my family on my adoptive mother's side consists of two cousins. First, Joann (the daughter of my mother's much older half-brother), about ten years older than me, who lives in Michigan, and has five grown children. She and I cooperated in the care of our aunt, and she was always close to my mother. I hope I will make time to see more of her in the future. I have another cousin, Julie, who has lived in Atlanta for years; I had an enlightening phone conversation with her after my aunt's death, when she told me that she had also been struck by the contrast between Dorothy and Dan, as a happy couple, and her own parents, who had more difficulties.

On the other side of my adoptive family, after one of my father's sisters died I eventually discovered that the other one's daughter—June, another older cousin—was an adoptee. Another cover-up in the family; I had no idea of this earlier. We had a pleasant day of reunion in Dayton, after a number of exchanges of greeting cards, and talked about many issues, though not much about adoption. I heard a little of what I might have guessed about that side of the family's perspective on my mother: "She was so involved in her Catholic religion." June died a few years after that.

I sometimes have the fantasy that Murray has an open-minded grown daughter who would like to meet me. And I sometimes wonder about getting in contact with Geraldine's younger sister, the one who became a Unitarian, another kind of outsider in their family.

Which leads me to religion once more. The Christian tradition, with which I still affiliate, does not see religion as involving heredity in the same way that the Jewish tradition does. But the American system has officially placed considerable effort in matching adopted children by religion, as if it were something that should be inherited, and growing up with parents of different religions still presents some kinds of definitional problems, even if not the tension that it did in my family and many others of the 1950s.[13] Although I clearly affiliated with my mother's Catholicism, I am sure that the Protestants in my family—not just my father, but also my aunts—had some impact on me. I was always interested in the ecumenical movement and in dialogue between different religions.

But dialogue with the religions in your birth family is complicated. I have attended church with Geraldine and some of my brothers, and have usually been quite uncomfortable, to a large extent because of their churches' links with what I see as extremely conservative politics. And to some extent because the emotional evangelical style is such a different language from the religious languages I know. (Black evangelical style seems more attractive to me than white evangelical style; I had a moment of insight that helped me appreciate Geraldine while attending a performance of Langston Hughes's *Black Nativity*.)

When I moved near the Jewish Community Center, to a mostly Jewish street, and expected my daughter to go to a largely Jewish public high school nearby, I had some fantasies of regaining some of the Jewish part of my identity. (Squirrel Hill, where we live, is still recognizable as the most Jewish neighborhood in Pittsburgh.) She went to after-school programs and summer camps at the JCC, where she learned something about Jewish traditions while she also went to CCD, Catholic religious education classes. (I have the recollection of her drawing a picture of a child decorated with two sets of initials, JCC and CCD.) We went as far as attending a family Purim festival, but it didn't work for us. And, much later, she didn't like Taylor Allderdice High School and insisted on transferring to a private school, where she was, she said, the fifth most Jewish student in her class (in other words, the Jewish population was tiny; she was, comparably, described as the blackest white student). I have told her that she and I are partly Jewish (as well as other ethnicities), and she has read *The Diary of Anne Frank*, and *Number the Stars*. At present I go to every Bar or Bat Mitzvah I can—which means three in the last ten years—and subscribe to *Tikkun*, a journal associated to the Jewish renewal movement, which relates Jewish tradition to both spirituality and social justice and has many non-Jewish readers and writers. I can't claim that either my heredity or my behavior makes me a Jew, but my life has been affected, in a particularly intimate way, by the complex historical relationship between Christians and Jews.

I now belong to a religious group associated, as far as I know, with no one in my birth or adoptive family: the Episcopal Church. This change came not because of my discoveries about my birth parents but because of the strictness of the current institutional Catholic Church, the transfer of my previous remarkable pastor and the dissolution of his parish, and my recognition that the small rule-stretching Catholic parishes I like are all vulnerable to closing. The Episcopal Church liturgy and tradition keeps—or has returned to—much from Roman Catholicism, and there are many former Catholics in my current parish. Our pastor is a woman, and significant members of the parish are African-American or openly gay; these are advantages as far as I am concerned. The upper-class associations that *Episcopalian* suggests are not positive associations to me, and indeed my parish has more of a middle-class atmosphere. It is something like an extended family and provides my daughter with a community in which people know her, and even chose her as the youth representative on the vestry, the church governing board.

Becoming an Episcopalian gives me a different relation to some of the religious poets I teach, like John Donne and George Herbert, who were Episcopal priests, and learning more about the Reformation, good background to my writing on Shakespeare as well, gives me more perspective on the conflicts between Catholic and Protestant in my adoptive family. Much as I resist the suggestion that my birth mother contributed to my joining this parish (they are at opposite ends of the Protestant spectrum), I have found that my family connection with evangelical fundamentalism isn't so unique in this church. It also included some people with Jewish backgrounds, including at least one other adoptee who discovered Jewish ancestry late in life. It is an open parish with a strong commitment to interreligious dialogue, located near us in Squirrel Hill. But I still read the *National Catholic Reporter,* and I am still on the mailing list for Catholic reform groups like the Association of Pittsburgh Priests. And I would prefer more time spent preaching explicitly on social issues and less on details of the biblical passages for the week. I very much enjoy singing in the choir, but I am still uncomfortable about some of the remaining "establishment" aspects of my parish. To paraphrase Anzaldúa, perhaps I move between seeing the Catholic Church from an Episcopalian viewpoint and seeing an Episcopal parish from a Catholic viewpoint. And I try to see some Christian behavior from a Jewish point of view.

People need community. Ethnicity and religion can help provide this but are not the only sources of it. I find some of it through my parish, some through my university, some through people whose writing interests are close to mine, some through political action and other support groups. Some has come through my neighborhood, some through my daughter's schools and her soccer teams and even a bit through walking our dog. Like Franklin Hata, I am a good citizen. But perhaps I am also like Franklin in settling for distant relationships in a community too much of the time.

The year after I met Geraldine, I met the man who would eventually become my husband. The most relevant aspect of our meeting, in the context of this book, is that I found out very soon that David has a much younger sister, who was adopted into the family while a toddler.

(In the 1990s, Lisa's older birth siblings found her.) But while this and other aspects of his family background made connections between David and me, our relationship continues because, among other reasons, I enjoy his quirky playfulness and sense of humor, his appreciation of beauty, his drive to learn, his willingness to admit mistakes, his resourcefulness. He is a philosopher turned art historian and art critic, and his major community is the art world. The sociologically curious reader might be interested to know that David is a nonreligious ex-Catholic born to a Catholic mother whose mother immigrated from Austria, and a Protestant-raised, nonreligious father. As I was beginning this book, we asked his parents, Louise and Walter, questions about their family past, and they spent several years of their seventies putting together a history that traced Walter's family back to Lawson Carrier, who was born in Vermont in 1813, and followed the path of westward migration and farm life. Though the genealogy is full of English- or Scottish-sounding names, one of Lawson's six children claimed to be French. There are mysteries in nonadoptive families as well!

The most important aspect of my life as an adoptee that I want to update further from my introductory chapter is my relationship with my daughter, Liz, with whom I am linked by both birth and nurture. Liz looks a lot like me. But we are very different. As I have said before, the athletic involvement unknown to me, my husband, or any other members of our families we know may be the very core of her identity now. Not for her first few years of life, but when we moved to our present street, and she learned from neighbors how to play kickball and ride a bike, and joined a soccer team, everything changed. Liz was the starting goalie for her last three years of high school. In her senior year, when the high school season was over, she played on three other soccer teams. And she is now the starting goalie on her college team, and was women's soccer rookie of the year in her first year.

In my childhood environment, I did not even know that there were extremely athletic girls. When I played sports, whether for required physical education classes or elsewhere, it was almost always difficult work for me. I was never even much of a spectator of sports after my relationship with my father got worse and we stopped watching the Cleveland Indians together. I was not the sort of parent who looked forward to watching my child's athletics as a central part of child rearing.

How does this contrast between Liz and me influence my attitude about adoption? It demystifies heredity. That is, it shows that similar heredity, even similar appearance, does not necessarily mean that people will be similar, or that their relationship will be smooth. Some adoptees think that it is only because they were adopted that they felt different from their parents. If I didn't already know how different I am from Geraldine, this difference from Liz would be enough to show me otherwise.

And it also emphasizes environment. I know a few adoptees who, on hearing about Liz, speculated about whether she had got her athletic ability from her birth father. It wasn't mentioned in the article about him that is the basis of most of my information. I don't think there were many champion soccer players in his immigrant Jewish community in the 1930s and 1940s. Murray may have had athletic potential, but it didn't show up in me. So I conclude that my difference from Liz exemplifies to a large extent the importance of environment: the specific environment of Marlborough Road, where there happened to be athletic families with children near her age when she was young, and the general environment of Pittsburgh, and the United States, and perhaps the world, in the late twentieth and early twenty-first centuries. Perhaps it is because she watched sports on television in the early years on the Sunday afternoons we thought we had to work. But it is also her own individuality—she liked watching those games, she tries harder at sports than many young soccer players.

Learning to appreciate what soccer means to Liz is, for me, like learning to appreciate a foreign culture. Though I love to watch her play because she looks so happy and does it so well (since she is a goalie, it is obvious even to someone who doesn't understand the game when she is making a difficult save), I am an improbable soccer mom—the sort who at halftime would like to find out what else I have in common with the other parents besides being a parent of an athletic teenager.

Still, in spite of how different we are, I can see that the fact that I gave birth to Liz has made some things easier for me. When she cried a lot as an infant, I did not have to worry that she was crying because she had left her birth family. When she gets cranky after not eating for a long time, I understand because I am the same way. When she procrastinates, I remember that I used to, and nevertheless became a responsible adult. I enjoy the fact that she resembles me somewhat, even as I appreciate the ways we are different.

So, on the one hand, I now know what it is like to live with a genetic relative, in the advantages it can give. On the other hand, I can see that the "blood" link does not necessarily assure harmony or understanding. Even in families where parents and children share a lot of interests, parents still have to come to terms with their children's being separate people. Even the Shakespeare professors whose children write Shakespeare dissertations have to deal with the fact that eventually those children disagree with them about the plays. Though Liz does seem to have developed politics similar to mine—which she conducts, as might be expected, in a more confrontational way—I think that my adoptive mother passed on to me more of her cultural interests than I have to my daughter, and as many of her values.

Is my parenting of Liz influenced by my own upbringing, including the way in which Dorothy responded to my being adopted? Inevitably. Will I always want more closeness to Liz than she does to me? Probably, but many other parents deal with a similar disparity. I am reminded of Margaret Moorman noting how her attitude toward her young daughter is influenced by her earlier experience as a birth mother, and comparing herself to adoptive parents who have difficulty accepting their children's independence.[14] As a parent I share experiences with many people beyond adoptees.

When I read novels about adoptive parents learning to respect a child's different culture, such as Barbara Kingsolver's *Pigs in Heaven,* I identify with the parent as well as the child. Parent-child difference occurs in all families, not just in adoptive families, and maybe one of the reasons why many readers from all kinds of families relate to literature about adoption is that they find it portraying forms of issues that they face in their own lives even if they are not involved with adoption. Having experienced both kinds of kinship, I feel more comfortable now discussing this common ground. There is a certain cultural privilege in speaking as a mother by birth and nurture about family relationships that I can use here, while if I had remained without a child, or adopted one, this book might have ended differently (or perhaps never been written).

I don't think all adoptees are more like each other than like non-adoptees, and I do not claim that all adoptees have the same psychology. The warmth, love, and openness of the adoptive family, the parents' similarity to the adoptee or the accessibility of others who are similar in interests and appearance, the inborn degree of sensitivity of

the adoptee, the frequency and openness of adoption in the environment, the attitude toward and kinds of contact with the birth parents,
the age at adoption and preceding history, the subsequent life history,
all have their effects. Adoptees all grow up in families consciously constructed in a way different from most—but what that means varies
enormously, and today they live in a world where there are many other
kinds of difference from the traditional family, which may be combined
with adoption or not—resulting from death, divorce, single parenthood, or gay partnership. My gut-level sense of difference growing up
as a closeted adoptee has had its disadvantages, but people whose sense
of difference is based on more material oppression may well feel that
focusing on the adoptive difference too exclusively is a luxury.

Like other people, I live in the tension between difference and similarity. I read partly to understand imagined people who are unlike me,
with a hope that this will also help with real people unlike me. "Can
you work with people different from yourself?" a colleague of mine
running for an office was once asked. His response was, "What other
choice is there?"—an answer especially meaningful to an adoptee.

My mother's acquaintance who wore pillows during her pretended
pregnancy tried to hide the difference of adoption, as did I once upon a
time. Members of the adoption triangle can pretend that we live in ordinary kinship. Or we can acknowledge that we are different in this way,
and then look, as I have tried to in these pages, both for the issues that
we face because of this specific kind of kinship, and the issues that we
face because of other aspects of our humanity.

Appendix: Other Adoption-Related Fiction and Drama

Works in addition to those listed here can be found in William Gage's online bibliography, *Reader's Guide to Adoption-Related Literature,* http://mem bers.aol.com/billgage/lit-list.htm (last visited November 12, 2004), which mostly includes late-twentieth- and twenty-first-century materials. There are surely many other works still. I have read only a fraction of those listed here, and some of them may include adoption only marginally or may be more accurately described as about fostering, illegitimacy, or orphanhood.

FICTION

See also chapters 4, 5, 7, and the afterword.

Conrad Aiken, *Ushant* (1952)
Louisa May Alcott, "A New Year's Blessing" (1856); "Little Genevieve" (1856); "Marian Eroll" (1858); *Jo's Boys* (1886)
Sherman Alexie, *Indian Killer* (1996)
Maria Amparo Ruiz de Burton, *Who Would Have Thought It?* (1872)
Michael Arditti, *Pagan's Father* (1996)
Paul Auster, *Mr. Vertigo* (1994)

Larry Baker, *Flamingo Rising* (1997)
Sarah S. Baker, *Coming to the Light* (1862); *The Lighthouse* (1863); *Bound-Out; or, Abby at the Farm* (1868)
Charles Baxter, "A Relative Stranger," in *A Relative Stranger* (1990)
Calixthe Beyala, *Le petit prince de Belleville* (1992)
Robert Boles, *Curling* (1968)
Dermot Bolger, *A Second Life* (1994)
T. Coraghessan Boyle, *A Friend of the Earth* (2000)
Harold Brodkey, *Stories in an Almost Classical Mode* (1988); *Runaway Soul* (1991)
Emily Brontë, *Wuthering Heights* (1847)
Rita Mae Brown, *Rubyfruit Jungle* (1973); *Six of One* (1974); *Southern Discomfort* (1982)
Rosellen Brown, *Civil Wars* (1984)
Marina Tamar Budhos, *House of Waiting* (1995)
Frederick Buechner, *The Storm* (1999)
Frances Hodgson Burnett, *Little Lord Fauntleroy* (1886)

Frances Burney, *The Wanderer* (1814)
Frederick Busch, *Long Way from Home* (1993); *Rounds* (1979)

Anne Cameron, *Child of Her People* (1987)
Angela Carter, *Nights at the Circus* (1984)
Dan Chaon, *You Remind Me of Me* (2004)
Charles Chesnutt, *The Quarry* (1999; written 1928); *Paul Marchand F.M.C* (1998; written 1921).
Lydia Maria Child, *Hobomok* (1824)
Kate Chopin, "Desiree's Baby" (1894)
Wilkie Collins, *Hide and Seek* (1852); *Legacy of Cain* (1888)
James Fenimore Coooper, *The Pilot* (1824), *The Red Rover* (1828)
Dinah Craik, *King Arthur: Not a Love Story* (1886)
Chris Crutcher, *Whale Talk* (2001)
Maria Cummins, *The Lamplighter* (1854)
Christopher Paul Curtis, *Bud, Not Buddy* (1999)

Daniel Defoe, *Moll Flanders* (1722); *Roxana* (1724)
Nicholas Delbanco, *Fathering* (1973)
William Demby, *Beetlecreek* (1950)
Anita Desai, *In Custody* (1984)
Peter de Vries, *Tunnel of Love* (1954)
Charles Dickens, *David Copperfield* (1850); *Hard Times* (1854); "Doctor Marigold" (1865)
E. L. Doctorow, *The Book of Daniel* (1971)
Margaret Drabble, *A Natural Curiosity* (1989); *The Red Queen* (2004)
Sara Jeannette Duncan, *The Story of Sonny Sahib* (1895)

Maria Edgeworth, *Ennui* (1809)
Ralph Ellison, *Juneteenth* (1999)
Buchi Emecheta, *The New Tribe* (2000)
Louise Erdrich, *Tracks* (1988); *Beet Queen* (1986); *Bingo Palace* (1994); *Love Medicine,* new ed. (1993)

Nuruddin Farah, *Maps* (1986)
William Faulkner, *Light in August* (1932); *Go Down, Moses* (1940)
Dorothy Canfield Fisher, *Understood Betsy* (1917)
Theodor Fontane, *Vor dem Sturm* (1878); *Ellernklipp* (1881); *Irrungen, Wirrungen* (1888); *Der Stechlin* (1896)
Leon Forrest, *The Bloodworth Orphans* (1977)
Margaret Forster, *Battle for Christabel* (1992)
Connie May Fowler, *River of Hidden Dreams* (1994)
Anatole France, *Crime of Sylvestre Bonnard* (1881)
Abby Frucht, *Are You Mine?* (1993)

Elyse Gasco, *Can You Wave Bye Bye, Baby?* (1999)
Martha Gellhorn, *In the Highlands* (1984)

Kaye Gibbons, *Ellen Foster* (1987)
André Gide, *The Counterfeiters (Les Faux-Monnayeurs)* (1926)
Ellen Gilchrist, *Annunciation* (1983)
Eileen Goudge, *Garden of Lies* (1989); *Thorns of Truth* (1998)

Erich Hackl, *Farewell to Sidonie* (1989)
Frances Harper, *Iola Leroy* (1892)
Jim Harrison, *Dalva* (1988); *The Road Home* (1998)
Josephine Hart, *Sin* (1992)
Bret Harte, *Gabriel Conroy* (1871)
Nathaniel Hawthorne, *Dr. Grimshaw's Secret* (unfinished, 1860s)
Shelby Hearon, *Afternoon of a Faun* (1983)
Mark Helprin, *Refiner's Fire* (1990)
Joshua Henkin, *Swimming across the Hudson* (1997)
Peter Hoeg, *The History of Danish Dreams* (1988)
Mrs. Hoffland, *Elizabeth and Her Three Beggar Boys* (1833)
Alice Hoffman, *Fortune's Daughter* (1985); *Here on Earth* (1997)
Linda Hogan, *Solar Storms* (1995)
A. M. Homes, *In a Country of Mothers* (1993)
Carolyn Hougan, *Blood Relative* (1992)
Keri Hulme, *The Bone People* (1985)

Rachel Ingalls, "Sis and Bud," in *Be My Guest* (1992)
John Irving, *The Cider House Rules* (1985)
Kazu Ishiguro, *When We Were Orphans* (2000)

Helen Hunt Jackson, *Ramona* (1884)
Henry James, *Watch and Ward* (1878); *Princess Casamassima* (1887)
P. D. James, *Innocent Blood* (1980)
Storm Jameson, *The Intruder* (1956)

Yasunari Kawabata, *The Lake* (1954)
Jackie Kay, *Trumpet* (1998)
W. J. G. Kingston, *The Young Rajah* (1876)
Rudyard Kipling, *Kim* (1901)
Heinrich von Kleist, "The Foundling," in *Erzhahlungen* (1811)

Wally Lamb, *I Know This Much Is True* (1998)
Lynn Lauber, *21 Sugar Street* (1993)
Haldor Laxness, *Fish Can Sing* (1966)
Don Lee, *Country of Origin* (2004)
Madeleine L'Engle, *The Small Rain* (1945)
Lois Lenski, *Indian Captive* (1941)
Elinor Lipman, *Then She Found Me* (1990)
Margot Livesey, *Criminals* (1995)
Andrew Lytle, *Velvet Horn* (1957)

Sara Maitland, *Ancestral Truths* (1994); published as *Home Truths* in England
David Malouf, *Imaginary Life* (1978)
Seth Margolis, *Losing Isaiah* (1993)
Pierre Marivaux, *La Vie de Marianne* (1731–41)
Charles Robert Maturin, *Melmoth the Wanderer* (1820)
Armisted Maupin, *Night Listener* (2001)
Alice McDermott, *That Night* (1987)
Maile Meloy, *Liars and Saints* (2003)
Anne Michaels, *Fugitive Pieces* (1996)
James Michener, *Chesapeake* (1986)
Laura Owen Miller, *Place of Sapphires* (1956)
Yukio Mishima, *Decay of the Angel* (1975)
Jacqueline Mitchard, *A Theory of Relativity* (2001)
N. Scott Momaday, *The Ancient Child* (1989)
Lucy Montgomery, *Anne of Green Gables* (1908) and sequels
Wright Morris, *Fire Sermon* (1969)
Toni Morrison, *Sula* (1974); *Tar Baby* (1981)
Bharati Mukherjee, *Leave It to Me* (1997); *Jasmine* (1989)
Rya Murakami, *Coin Locker Babies* (1980)
Albert Murray, *Train Whistle Guitar* (1974)

Gloria Naylor, *Mama Day* (1988)
Alice Dunbar Nelson, "Sister Josepha" (1899)
Sandra Newman, *The Only Good Thing Anyone Has Ever Done* (2002)
Susan Nunes, *A Small Obligation and Other Stories of Hilo* (1982)

Joyce Carol Oates, *Triumph of the Spider Monkey* (1976)
Frank O'Connor, "Set of Variations on a Borrowed Theme," in *Collected
    Stories* (1981)
Philip Oliphant, *Maya* (1908)
Michael Ondaatje, *In the Skin of a Lion* (1987)

Gary Pak, *The Watcher of Waipuna* (1992)
Aldo Palazzeschi, *The Sisters Materassi* (1934)
Ann Patchett, *The Patron Saint of Liars* (1992)
Susan Beth Pfeffer, *About David* (1948)
Belva Plain, *Blessings* (1990); *Daybreak* (1994)
Reynolds Price, *Kate Varden* (1986)

Rahna Reiko, *Why She Left Us* (2000)
Conrad Richter, *The Lady* (1952); *The Light in the Forest* (1953)
Ruthann Robson, *Another Mother* (1995)
Merce Rodoreda, *La place de Diamant* (1962); *El carrer de les camelies* (1966)
Judith Rossner, *August* (1983)
Jane Rule, *Against the Season* (1971)
Salman Rushdie, *Midnight's Children* (1983)

Jacques-Henri Bernardin de Saint Pierre, *Paule et Virginie* (1788)
George Sand, *Isidora* (1846); *François le Champi* (1847–48); *La filleule* (1853)
Elspeth Sandys, *River Lines* (1995)
Joanna Scott, *The Lucky Gourd Shop* (2000)
W. G. Sebald, *Austerlitz* (2001)
Catherine Maria Sedgwick, *A New England Tale* (1821); *Redwood* (1824);
    Hope Leslie (1827)
Mary Shelley, *Frankenstein* (1817)
Carol Shields, *The Stone Diaries* (1994)
Leslie Marmon Silko, *Ceremony* (1997)
Betty Smith, *Maggie-Now* (1958)
Charlotte Smith, *Emmeline, the Orphan of the Castle* (1788); *The Old Manor
    House* (1793)
Ellease Southerland, *Let the Lion Eat Straw* (1980)
Elizabeth George Speare, *Calico Captive* (1957)
Edmund Spenser, *Faerie Queene,* book 6 (1596)
Elizabeth Stoddard, *Two Men* (1865)
Noel Streatfield, *Ballet Shoes* (1937)
Hesba Stretton, *Jessica's First Prayer* (1867); *Alone in London* (1869)
Ruth McEnery Stuart, *The Cocoon: A Rest-Cure Comedy* (1915); "Saint Idyl's
    Light" (1897)

Mary Tannen, *Loving Edith* (1995)
Walter Tevis, *Queen's Gambit* (1983)
Camilla Toulmin, "The Adopted; or, Impulse not Principle" (1844)
Barbara Trapido, *Juggling* (1994)
David Treuer, *Little* (1995)
William Trevor, *Death in Summer* (1998)
Anthony Trollope, *Doctor Thorne* (1858); *Ralph the Heir* (1871); *Cousin
    Henry* (1879)
Joanna Trollope, *Next of Kin* (1996)
Mark Twain, *Adventures of Huckleberry Finn* (1894); *Pudd'nhead Wilson*
    (1894)

Lane von Herzen, *The Unfastened Heart* (1995)
Kurt Vonnegut, *Slapstick* (1976)

Alice Walker, *The Color Purple* (1982)
Susan Warner, *Wide Wide World* (1850)
Jean Webster, *Daddy Long Legs* (1912)
Edith Wharton, *The Old Maid* (1924); *Summer* (1917); *The Children* (1928);
    House of Mirth (1905)
E. B. White, *Charlotte's Web* (1952)
Patrick White, *Voss* (1957)
Robert White, *Elephant Hill* (1959)
Binjamin Wilkomirski, *Fragments* (1995)

Lynna Williams, *Things Not Seen and Other Stories* (1992)
Harriet Wilson, *Our Nig* (1859)
Leigh Allison Wilson, "The Raising," in *From the Bottom Up* (1983)
Jeanette Winterson, *Oranges Are Not the Only Fruit* (1985); *Sexing the Cherry* (1991)
Ruth Wolff, *I Keturah* (1963)
Hilma Wolitzer, *Tunnel of Love* (1994)
Shawn Wong, *Homebase* (1991)
Richard Wright, *Rite of Passage* (1995; written in 1940s)

Charlotte Yonge, *Hopes and Fears* (1859); *Countess Kate* (1862)
Shay Youngblood, *The Big Mama Stories* (1989)

Joseph Zobel, *La rue cases-negres* (1974; trans. 1980 as *Black Shack Alley)*

DRAMA

See also chapters 2, 3, and 6.

Edward Albee, *Tiny Alice* (1965)
Samuel Beckett, *Endgame* (1958)
Bertholt Brecht, *The Caucasian Chalk Circle* (1947)
Armand Charlemagne, *L'adoption villeageouise ou l'ecouteur aux Portes* (1794)
Tom Donaghy, *Boys and Girls* (2002)
Edward Fitzball, *The Floating Beacon* (1824); *The Pilot* (1825); *The Red Rover* (1829)
John Olive, *Careless Love* (1988)
P. Piis, *La nourrice republicaine ou les plaisirs de l'adoption* (1794)
Jean Racine, *Andromaque* (1668); *Britannicus* (1670); *Les freres ennemis* (1664)
David Rudkin, *Ashes* (1977)
Diane Samuels, *Kindertransport* (1995)
Ruben Santiago-Hudson, *Lackawanna Blues* (2001)
George Bernard Shaw, *Major Barbara* (1907)
Nickie Silver, *Pterodactyls* (1994)
Kathleen Tolan, *Memory House* (2005)
Oscar Wilde, *The Importance of Being Earnest* (1895)
David Williamson, *Birthrights* (2002)

Notes

CHAPTER 1

1. Nancy K. Miller, *But Enough about Me: Why We Read Other People's Lives* (New York: Columbia University Press, 2002), 1–26, 111–25.

2. Henry J. S. Maine, *Ancient Law* (1861; rpt. Boston: Beacon, 1963), 26.

3. Judith Modell, *Kinship with Strangers: Adoption and Interpretations of Kinship in American Culture* (Berkeley and Los Angeles: University of California Press, 1994), 2, quoting Maine, *Ancient Law* and commenting.

4. See Kath Weston, "Forever Is a Long Time: Romancing the Real in Gay Kinship," in *Naturalizing Power: Essays in Feminist Cultural Analysis*, ed. Sylvia Yanagisako and Carol Delaney (New York: Routledge, 1995), 88, and the essays in *Relative Value: Reconfiguring Kinship Studies*, ed. Sarah Franklin and Susan McKinnon (Durham, N.C.: Duke University Press, 2001).

5. Cf. attempts to conceal adoption in Barbara Melosh, *Strangers and Kin: The American Way of Adoption* (Cambridge: Harvard University Press, 2002), 225.

6. Katarina Wegar, in *Adoption, Identity, and Kinship: The Debate over Sealed Birth Records* (New Haven: Yale University Press, 1997), 97, observes that "between April 1993 and March 1994, the adoption theme was featured 113 times in nationwide radio and TV news programs." Many of these either directly involved the Schmidt-DeBoer case or were contextualized with regard to it. For comparison, divorce and separation, which occur more frequently, were only discussed 97 times.

7. In this book I deal with the issue of claims of both kinds of parents themselves and also with the issue of the relative influences of heredity and environment. On this second point, I am aware of recent research showing, for example, that certain hereditary tendencies are activated only in certain environments, so that treating these factors as dichotomous is too simple. However, when they are mentioned in literature, usually they tended to be treated as opposed.

8. Janet Beizer, "One's Own: Reflections on Motherhood, Owning, and Adoption," *Tulsa Studies in Women's Literature* 21, no. 2 (2002): 245.

9. Sigmund Freud, "Family Romances," in *Complete Psychological Works*, trans. James Strachey (London: Hogarth, 1959), 9:237–41. Freud argues that these fantasies are also disguised ways of manifesting the child's affection for original parents, who can be seen as appearing in them exalted in rank.

10. Though the central characters in these works were not legally adopted, the transfer to a new household while their ancestry is kept secret puts them in situations close enough to those of modern adoptees that I will use the current

terms. The happy and disastrous adoption stories correspond approximately to the two kinds of adoption novels identified by Patricia Howe in "Fontane's 'Ellernklipp' and the Theme of Adoption," *Modern Language Review* 79 (1984): 121, and developed further by Tess O'Toole, "Adoption and the 'Improvement of the Estate' in Trollope and Craik," in *Imagining Adoption: Essays on Literature and Culture,* ed. Marianne Novy (Ann Arbor: University of Michigan Press, 2001). Howe suggests that disastrous adoption plots are more frequent in German literature than in English.

11. Barbara Estrin sees the most important myth shaping our view of adoption as the one that sees identity as determined by "blood ties." While my approach is consistent with hers in many ways, I believe that the happy adoption story that erases the child's past and genetic relatives is also an influential myth. See Barbara Estrin, "Ending in the Middle: Revisioning Adoption in Binjamin Wilkomirski's *Fragments* and Anne Michaels's *Fugitive Pieces,*" *Tulsa Studies in Women's Literature* 21, no. 2 (2002): 277.

12. See Betty Jean Lifton, *Journey of the Adopted Self: A Quest for Wholeness* (New York: Basic, 1994), 146–273, for more discussion of the complexities of reunions of adoptees and birth parents.

13. Many of those discussions have focused on literature from societies without formal legal procedures for adopting children, where, however, informal adoption could take place. Some of the same books, such as *Oliver Twist,* could be considered under either category, but grouping them with literature about adoption facilitates a close look at relationships within the text, not just at the child in isolation, and also at their connections with later novels and cultural fantasies, such as the frequent pretense that adoptees are orphans; see Betty Jean Lifton, *Twice Born: Memoirs of an Adopted Daughter* (New York: Penguin, 1977), 9–13. The literary and social history of bastardy is also relevant to adoption in literature, although the position of a person born and raised by the same single mother is quite different from the position of one born outside of marriage and adopted by someone else. Some of the critics who have discussed orphans, foundlings, and bastards in literature without much reference to the social history of these conditions are Northrop Frye, in *The Secular Scripture: A Study of the Structure of Romance* (Cambridge: Harvard University Press, 1976) (mysterious birth); Edward Said, in *Beginnings: Intention and Method* (New York: Basic, 1975) (orphanhood); Peter Brooks, in *Reading for the Plot: Design and Intention in Narrative* (1984; rpt. Cambridge: Harvard University Press, 1992) (orphanhood and surrogacy); Marthe Robert, in *Origins of the Novel,* trans. Sacha Rabinovitch (Bloomington: Indiana University Press, 1980) (the bastard and the foundling); Marie Maclean, in *The Name of the Mother: Writing Illegitimacy* (London: Routledge, 1994); and Michael Ragussis, in *Acts of Naming: The Family Plot in Fiction* (Oxford: Oxford University Press, 1988). See also Marc Shell, *Children of the Earth: Literature, Politics, and Nationhood* (New York: Oxford University Press, 1993), and *The End of Kinship: 'Measure for Measure,' Incest, and the Ideal of Universal Siblinghood* (Palo Alto: Stanford University Press, 1988); and Eileen Simpson, *Orphans: Real and Imaginary* (New York: Signet, 1990).

14. Jean Paton, writing as Ruthena Hill Kittson, *Orphan Voyage* (1968; rpt. Cedaredge, Colo.: Country Press, 1980). Paton wrote most of this book in the late 1950s.

15. Betty Jean Lifton writes, "Inherent in the adoption process is the expectation that the child is to regard the birth parents *as if* dead," in *Lost and Found: The Adoption Experience* (1979; rpt. New York: Harper and Row, 1988), 14. As of 2005, only six states—Kansas, Alaska, Tennessee, Alabama, New Hampshire, and Oregon—give the American adoptee unequivocal rights to identifying information about their biological parents; see Adam Pertman, *Adoption Nation: How the Adoption Revolution Is Transforming America* (New York: Basic, 2000), 32, 82. Records are open with some reservations in Illinois, Delaware, Montana, Ohio, and Vermont.

16. See Drucilla Cornell, *At the Heart of Freedom: Feminism, Sex, and Equality* (Princeton: Princeton University Press, 1998); and Mary Lyndon Shanley, *Making Babies, Making Families: What Matters Most in an Age of Reproductive Technologies, Surrogacy, Adoption, and Same-Sex and Unwed Parents* (Boston: Beacon, 2001) for discussions of multiple parenting and the need to give up ideas that parenthood is unique ownership.

17. Rickie Solinger, *Wake Up Little Susie: Single Pregnancy and Race before Roe v. Wade* (New York: Routledge, 1992). Some today argue for the restigmatization of illegitimacy. In a pattern continuous with the history Solinger discusses, many whites easily stigmatize illegitimacy among blacks.

18. See Barbara Melosh, "Adoption Stories: Autobiographical Narrative and the Politics of Identity," in *Adoption in America: Historical Perspectives*, ed. E. Wayne Carp (Ann Arbor: University of Michigan Press, 2002), 227–30, especially on Katrina Maxtone-Graham's *An Adopted Woman* (New York: Remi, 1983); some she discusses vary this pattern.

19. "The study requires volunteers who were adopted and have never met their birthmother to submit the following information: 1. A copy of the non-identifying information or whatever documents that best describes the adoptee's birthmother at the time of the adoption. 2. A photo of adoptee at approximately the same age as adoptee's birthmother was at the time of relinquishment." Posted on Adoption News Service, July 10, 2003. This is encouraging people to imagine the impossible; the real person's appearance would inevitably be a disappointment.

20. Barbara Katz Rothman, *Genetic Maps and Human Imaginations* (New York: Norton, 1998).

21. See, for example, Sandra Patton, *BirthMarks: Transracial Adoption in Contemporary America* (New York: New York University Press, 2000), 43–45, 91–92.

22. Adrienne Rich, *Blood, Bread, and Poetry: Selected Prose, 1979–1985* (New York: Norton, 1986).

23. See Elise V. Lemire, "From Blood to DNA: The Failed Narratives of Interracial Kinship," paper presented to the Annual Meetings of the Modern Language Association, Chicago, December 28, 1999; and Rothman, *Genetic Maps*, 16.

24. See Margaret Homans, "Adoption and Essentialism," *Tulsa Studies in Women's Literature* 21, no. 2 (2002): 264, on the limitations of the cultural information for transracially adopted children recommended by social workers.

25. Mary Waters, *Ethnic Options* (Berkeley and Los Angeles: University of California Press, 1990), 91. Subsequent references will be included in the text.

26. Alan Wolfe, "The Return of the Melting Pot," *New Republic,* December 31, 1990.

27. Quoted by Henry Louis Gates in "Integrating the American Mind," in *Loose Canons* (New York: Oxford University Press, 1992), 116.

28. Enthusiasm about adoption in America of the 1920s and 30s, discussed by Vivian Zelizer, *Pricing the Priceless Child: The Changing Social Value of Children* (New York: Basic, 1985) 189–95, coincided with enthusiasm for multicultural education. Today transracial adoption is becoming popular in previously monocultural Norway, leading to many complications: see Signe Howell, "Self-Conscious Kinship: Some Contested Values in Norwegian Transnational Adoption," in Franklin and McKinnon, *Relative Value,* 203–23.

29. See Melosh, *Strangers and Kin,* 15–16.

30. Solinger, *Wake Up Little Susie,* 14–17; Melosh, *Strangers and Kin,* 12–50.

31. Solinger, *Wake Up Little Susie,* 19.

32. Ellen Goodman, *Paper Trail: Common Sense in Uncommon Times* (New York: Simon & Schuster, 2004), 138. The essay, "Meet Your Children," 137–38, originally appeared August 29, 1993. For further reflections on this issue, see Mary Watkins and Susan Fisher, *Talking with Young Children about Adoption* (New Haven: Yale University Press, 1993), 217–19. See also Beizer, "One's Own."

33. Gates, *Loose Canons,* 175. Transcultural adopters who write about this include Drucilla Cornell, "Reimagining Adoption and Family Law," in *Mother Trouble: Rethinking Contemporary Maternal Dilemmas,* ed. Julia E. Hanigsberg and Sara Ruddick (Boston: Beacon Press, 1999), 213–15; and Emily Prager, *Wuhu Diary: On Taking My Adopted Daughter Back to Her Hometown in China* (New York: Random House, 2001). On complications of international adoption, see Homans, "Adoption and Essentialism," Andrew Elfenbein and John Watkins, "Papadada: Reinventing the Family," *Tulsa Studies* 21, no. 2 (2002): 301–18, and Alice Jardine, "Dolphins, Dying Rooms, and Destabilized Demographics, Or: Loving Anna in a Transmodern World," *Tulsa Studies* 21, no. 2 (2002): 333–45.

34. I would like to think that on balance Dorothy benefited as well. It is unlikely that without me she, a devout Catholic of the 1950s and 1960s, would have divorced Frank and lived happily ever after, given the fact that after he died, she entered the convent (though she left after a year and a half). And Geraldine has spoken with surprising fondness of the atmosphere in the Florence Crittenton home, which was apparently warmer than her own parents provided. Nevertheless, all of us were scarred—especially Geraldine, who didn't feel she had a choice about where I went—by some aspects of adoption practice at the time. To give another perspective, people from families somewhat like Geraldine's have, as I think of it, "escaped" into worlds I would consider

less restrictive. I tend to doubt that I would have had as much courage as they, but who knows?

35. For a critical contextualization of international adoption, see Claudia Castaneda, "Incorporating the Transnational Adoptee," in Novy, *Imagining Adoption*, 277–99.

36. Betty Jean Lifton, *Twice Born: Memoirs of an Adopted Daughter* (New York: Penguin, 1977), 3.

37. Jean Paton, *The Adopted Break Silence: The Experiences and Views of Forty Adults Who Were Once Adopted Children* (Philadelphia: Life History Center, 1954); Paton [Kittson], *Orphan Voyage*.

38. Maxton-Graham, *An Adopted Woman*.

39. Occasionally I encounter the claim that *adoptee* has negative connotations. However, it is used by many perceptive, respectful writers and is much less clumsy than "adopted person" or "adopted people."

40. Carolyn Steadman, *Landscape for a Good Woman* (New Brunswick, N.J.: Rutgers University Press, 1987); Gayle Greene and Coppelia Kahn, *Changing Subjects: The Making of Feminist Literary Criticism* (New York: Routledge, 1993); Rachel Brownstein, *Becoming a Heroine: Thinking about Women in Novels* (New York: Viking, 1982); Suzanne Juhasz, *Reading from the Heart: Women, Literature, and the Search for True Love* (New York: Viking, 1994). Note also the 1996 MLA Forum "The Place of the Personal"; and Diane P. Freedman, Olivia Frey, and Frances Murphy Zauhar, eds., *The Intimate Critique: Autobiographical Literary Criticism* (Durham: Duke University Press, 1993).

41. See recent summaries of the controversy in Wegar, *Adoption, Identity, and Kinship*, 43–71; and Lifton, *Journey of Adopted Self*, esp. 91–108. An influential book emphasizing psychological damage continuing after adoption is Nancy Newton Verrier, *The Primal Wound: Understanding the Adopted Child* (Baltimore: Gateway, 1993). Watkins and Fisher, in *Talking with Young Children*, bridge the gap to some extent because they emphasize the reality of the adoptee's history, favor openness, interview some parents in open adoptions, but focus on studies of nonclinical populations that conclude that adoptees are for the most part as psychologically healthy as nonadoptees.

42. Wegar, *Adoption, Identity, and Kinship*, 121–23, 135–37, takes a similar position.

43. This last view is the way my student Mary Beth Magin applied standpoint theory in her excellent term paper in my Adoption Literature course of spring 2003, discussing especially Jeanette Winterson's *Oranges Are Not the Only Fruit*.

44. Judith Modell, "Natural Bonds, Legal Boundaries: Modes of Persuasion in Adoption Rhetoric," in Novy, *Imagining Adoption*, 221.

45. David Kirk, *Shared Fate: A Theory of Adoption and Mental Health* (New York: Free Press, 1964).

46. Nancy Cott, "Historical Perspective: The Equal Rights Amendment Conflict in the 1920s," in *Conflicts in Feminism*, ed. Marianne Hirsch and Evelyn Fox Keller (New York: Routledge, 1990), 44–59; Joan Scott, "Deconstructing Equality-versus-Difference: Or, the Uses of Post-structuralist Theory for

Feminism," in Hirsch and Keller, 134–48; Jane Gallop, conversation at conference on psychoanalysis and feminism, 1980.

47. See Christa Hoffmann-Riem, *The Adopted Child: Family Life with Double Parenthood* (New Brunswick, N.J.: Transaction, 1990).

48. Denise Riley, *"Am I That Name?" Feminism and the Category of "Women" in History* (Minneapolis: University of Minnesota Press, 1988). Riley has written at least one poem, "The Castalian Spring," in the persona of someone who does not wish to have her life or writing categorized with reference to the circumstances of her birth—her "sociologized self."

49. See Wegar, *Adoption, Identity, and Kinship,* 65.

50. Melosh, *Strangers and Kin,* 54–68, shows these as frequent reasons for the consistent American preference for adopting girls, in the records of the Children's Bureau of Delaware, by contrast with the more common preference of biological parents-to-be for boys. From the 1930s to 1960s, some wanted to adopt boys because they wanted more spirited or athletic children.

51. Michaela DiLeonardo, "The Female World of Cards and Holidays: Women, Family and the Work of Kinship," *Signs* 12, no. 3 (1987): 440–53.

52. Marianne Hirsch, *The Mother/Daughter Plot: Narrative, Psychoanalysis, Feminism* (Bloomington: Indiana University Press, 1989).

53. Sara Ruddick, *Maternal Thinking: Toward a Politics of Peace* (New York: Ballantine, 1989), 48–51.

54. Ruddick, *Maternal Thinking,* 51.

55. Modell, *Kinship with Strangers,* 229, 238.

56. Jackie Kay, *The Adoption Papers* (Newcastle upon Tyne: Bloodaxe, 1991), 23. See also the adoptive mother quoted in Beizer, "One's Own," 244: "I change his diapers, I feed him, I sit up with him at night when he's sick; *of course* he's my own."

57. Adrienne Rich, "When We Dead Awaken: Writing as Re-Vision," in *On Lies, Secrets, and Silence* (New York: Norton, 1979), 35.

58. For more on adoption in earlier American literature, see Carol Singley's forthcoming book, *Brave Bonds: Adoption and American Literature.*

59. See my *Engaging with Shakespeare: Responses of George Eliot and Other Women Novelists* (1994; rpt. Iowa City: University of Iowa Press, 1998).

60. Whitney Balliett, *The New Yorker,* in Albee, *The American Dream and The Zoo Story* (New York: Plume, 1997), 54.

61. See Melosh, *Strangers and Kin,* for a contrast of Native American adoptees in Kingsolver's novels with those in Sherman Alexie's *Indian Killer.*

CHAPTER 2

1. Paton [Kittson], *Orphan Voyage,* 15.

2. Lifton, *Twice Born,* 1. In these editions, she gives her childhood city, Cincinnati, the name of Corinth, where Oedipus was raised; in the 1998 edition, she drops the pseudonym.

3. Lifton, *Twice Born,* 4; see also 3, 5, 6, 83, 88, 106, 147, 149, 153, 171, 240.

4. H. J. Sants, "Genealogical Bewilderment in Children with Substitute

Parents," *British Journal of Medical Psychology* 37 (1964): 139. Lifton uses Sants in *Lost and Found,* 48–50, and Paton footnotes his interpretation of *Oedipus,* which she read after she developed her own, on *Orphan Voyage,* 15. E. Wayne Carp, *Family Matters: Secrecy and Disclosure in the History of Adoption* (Cambridge: Harvard University Press, 1998), 154–55, discusses Sants's influence and his reliance on literature and psychoanalytic theory. Sants quotes Watling's translation (Penguin, 1947), but adds the third "I."

5. Sophocles, *Oedipus Rex,* ed. R. D. Dawe (Cambridge: Cambridge University Press, 1982), commentary to l. 780, p. 171. This is more exact than "bastard," the translation in *Oedipus the King,* trans. David Grene, in *Sophocles I,* in *The Complete Greek Tragedies,* ed. David Grene and Richmond Lattimore (1954; New York: Washington Square, 1957), from which subsequent quotations of Sophocles indicated parenthetically in the text are drawn. I have also consulted the text and translation in *Sophocles,* ed. and trans. Hugh Lloyd-Jones (Cambridge: Harvard University Press, 1994).

6. Bernard M. W. Knox, *Oedipus at Thebes: Sophocles' Tragic Hero and His Time* (1957; New York: Norton, 1971). Cf. the emphasis on Oedipus's "knowingness" in Jonathan Lear, *Open Minded: Working Out the Logic of the Soul* (Cambridge: Harvard University Press, 1998), 33–55.

7. Sigmund Freud, *The Interpretation of Dreams,* in *Complete Psychological Works,* trans. James Strachey (London: Hogarth Press, 1900), 4:262.

8. Freud, *The Interpretation of Dreams,* 4:261–62.

9. I have a vague recollection of my freshman college English teacher, Sister Mary St. Francis, saying that Oedipus was adopted. But when I look at my notes for that class, I don't find that point—perhaps it seemed too obvious to note. I do find more conventional criticism and the warning, "Don't interpret a play as a fragmentary biography of a real person," and an extraordinary number of doodles, as if there were more things than usual being said that I didn't write down, and yet I had too much nervous energy to do nothing. The only other page with as many doodles was the page on Dante.

10. John Gould, "The Language of Oedipus," in *Modern Critical Interpretations: Sophocles' Oedipus Rex,* ed. Harold Bloom (New York: Chelsea House, 1988), 145.

11. Gould, "The Language of Oedipus," 158.

12. See Gerald Else, *Aristotle's Poetics: The Argument* (Cambridge: Harvard University Press, 1957), 349.

13. The first chapter of my dissertation, written when I was just beginning to be able to talk to my friends about being adopted, was on the Greek tradition behind Shakespeare's recognition scenes. My dissertation research revealed to me, among other things, that in Greek terms I did not know who I was. No wonder I decided to turn aside from tragic recognitions to comic ones in my dissertation.

14. Use of the term *blood* with regard to biological kinship comes from the ancient (false) tradition, found, for example, in Hippocrates, that semen (once thought to be produced by both men and women) is refined blood. See Lemire, "From Blood to DNA"; also Thomas Laqueur, *Making Sex: Body and Gender from the Greeks to Freud* (Cambridge: Harvard University Press, 1990), 35.

While Aeschylus's Apollo, in *The Eumenides,* frees Orestes from the charge of parent-murder by saying that the mother is not a true parent but only nurse of the father's seed, the ancient Greeks held several theories of generation, and the mother's contribution was debated. See Sarah Pomeroy, *Families in Classical and Hellenistic Greece: Representation and Reality* (New York: Oxford University Press, 1997), 96–97; and Laqueur, 55–57. I would like my readers to think here about how much more emotional force the term *blood parents* has than the term *genetic parents.* That emotional force also involves a suggestion of potential violence, actualized in particular in such popular works as the musical *Blood Brothers,* in which two brothers, one of them adopted, are doomed to kill each other if they meet, and P. D. James's detective novel *Innocent Blood,* analyzed by Wegar in *Adoption, Identity and Kinship,* 102–7. However, in Lloyd-Jones's literal translation, *blood* does not occur with reference to kinship in *Oedipus.*

15. Pietro Pucci, *Oedipus and the Fabrication of the Father: Oedipus Tyrannus in Modern Criticism and Philosophy* (Baltimore: Johns Hopkins University Press, 1992), 2.

16. Pucci, *Fabrication of the Father,* 111. The Greek construction translated "that begot me" is sometimes used restrictively and sometimes not, so Pucci's argument is not conclusive.

17. See Pomeroy, *Families in Greece,* 122, quoting from Isaeus 2.13, which is, however, later than Sophocles.

18. A. R. W. Harrison, *The Law of Athens: The Family and Property* (Oxford: Clarendon Press, 1968), 84–88.

19. Pomeroy, *Families in Greece,* 21. She emphasizes that descent lines were constantly in danger of dying out.

20. W. K. Lacey, *The Family in Classical Greece* (Ithaca, N.Y.: Cornell University Press, 1968), 145–46.

21. Mark Golden, *Children and Childhood in Classical Athens* (Baltimore: Johns Hopkins University Press, 1990), 142. However, Golden supports this with a quotation (Isaeus 2.18) in which an adopted son argues that he "cared for and respected [his adoptive father] as if he were my father by birth." If this point has to be made, Golden says, it is not to be taken for granted.

22. Golden, *Children and Childhood,* 98.

23. S. C. Humphreys, *The Family, Women, and Death: Comparative Studies,* 2d ed. (Ann Arbor: University of Michigan Press, 1993), 7, 65. Her evidence is from the fourth century B.C. *Oedipus* was first produced earlier, ca. 430–428 B.C.

24. See Richmond Lattimore, *The Poetry of Greek Tragedy* (Baltimore: Johns Hopkins University Press, 1958), 82; Peter Burian, "Myth into *Muthos:* The Shaping of Tragic Plot," in *The Cambridge Companion to Greek Tragedy,* ed. P. E. Easterling (Cambridge: Cambridge University Press, 1997), 186.

25. Jan Bremmer, "Oedipus and the Greek Oedipus Complex," in *Interpretations of Greek Mythology,* ed. Jan Bremmer (London: Croom Helm, 1987), 45.

26. Nancy Demand, *Birth, Death, and Motherhood in Classical Greece* (Baltimore: Johns Hopkins University Press, 1994), 22.

27. Demand, *Birth, Death, and Motherhood,* 6.

28. Nicole Loraux, "Kreousa the Autochthon: A Study of Euripides' *Ion,*" in *Nothing to Do with Dionysos? Athenian Drama in Its Social Context,* ed. John J. Winkler and Froma I. Zeitlin (Princeton: Princeton University Press, 1990), 188, sees such exposure as "first and foremost a denial of paternity." Golden, *Children and Childhood,* 23, and Demand, *Birth, Death, and Motherhood,* 6, note the gender issue; Golden the economic ones, 88–89. See also Mary Lefkowitz and Maureen B. Fant, *Women in Greece and Rome* (Toronto: Samuel-Stevens, 1977), directions to expose a child if it is a girl (91); as part of a marriage annulment (41); if it is "puny and ill-shaped" (54). Thanks to my colleague Nicholas Jones, and to Patricia Storace, who used the Lefkowitz and Fant anthology of documents as source for a poem in the persona of an ancient Greek who directs his wife, "If it is a girl, expose it."

29. John Boswell, *The Abandonment of Children in Western Europe from Late Antiquity to the Renaissance* (New York: Pantheon, 1988), 4–49.

30. Dawe, *Oedipus Rex,* 171; Pucci, *Fabrication of the Father,* 99–100. See also Frederick Ahl, *Sophocles' Oedipus: Evidence and Self-Conviction* (Ithaca, N.Y.: Cornell University Press, 1991), 142–43.

31. Froma I. Zeitlin, *Playing the Other: Gender and Society in Greek Literature* (Chicago: University of Chicago Press, 1996), 335; Harrison, *The Law of Athens,* 84. I am particularly struck by this etymology as a reader of English Renaissance literature because Sir Philip Sidney, in his *Apologie for Poetry,* says that poets were often called "makers," and Ben Jonson, in his epitaph "Upon my First Son," refers to his (biological) son as "his best piece of poetry."

32. Humphreys, *Family, Women, and Death,* 67. See also Elizabeth S. Belfiore, *Murder among Friends: Violations of Philia in Greek Tragedy* (New York: Oxford, 2000), 4–9.

33. Humphreys, *Family, Women, and Death,* 74.

34. Dawe, *Oedipus Rex,* 171.

35. Parental love also appears in Oedipus's words to his children at the end.

36. Cf. Meredith Skura, *The Literary Use of the Psychoanalytic Process* (New Haven: Yale University Press, 1981), 51: "The horrible deeds are not Oedipus's fault, but rather a vast Freudian slip of the universe." For more comments on Freudian readings see below.

37. Philip Vellacott, *Sophocles and Oedipus: A Study of Oedipus Tyrannus with a New Translation* (Ann Arbor: University of Michigan Press, 1971); on the other hand, Ahl, *Sophocles' Oedipus,* argues that there are many gaps in the train of evidence that convinces Oedipus of his ancestry and incest: he believes the worst, which is not necessarily true.

38. Zeitlin, *Playing the Other,* 293.

39. Lifton, *Twice Born,* 153.

40. The words translated as "foulness" and "sinner" here are all forms of the Greek word *kakos.* Lloyd-Jones translates the first as "sickness" and the second and third as "evil."

41. Lifton, *Twice Born,* 3.

42. Gould, "The Language of Oedipus," 155, 158.

43. See Wegar, *Adoption, Identity and Kinship,* 103, though she sees these

images as presenting the adoptee not just outside society but also "outside the natural order of things."

44. Some groundwork for this influence was laid by Erik Erikson, the psychoanalyst who in *Childhood and Society* and *Young Man Luther* developed the idea of the identity crisis. See Jonathan Arac, "Toward a Cultural Genealogy of the U.S. Discourse of Identity: *Invisible Man* after Fifty Years," *Boundary* 2 (2003): 195–216, esp. 206–10. Lifton discussed adoption frequently with Erikson, a "half-adoptee," as she calls him, who learned about his paternal ancestry as an adolescent. See *Twice Born*, 274–75.

45. Lifton, *Twice Born*, 267. In the 1998 version of the book, she cuts this, but keeps the earlier declaration that "she who raises the child is the mother" (219).

46. Paton, *Orphan Voyage*, 89.

47. Paton, *Orphan Voyage*, 257.

48. Sophocles, *Oedipus at Colonus*, trans. Robert Fitzgerald, in *Sophocles I*, ll. 974–78.

49. Froma I. Zeitlin, "Thebes: Theater of Self and Society in Athenian Drama," in Winkler and Zeitlin, *Nothing to Do*, 159.

50. Euripides, *Ion*, trans. Anne Pippin Burnett (Englewood Cliffs, N.J.: Prentice-Hall, 1970), 128.

51. On the other hand, Rebecca Bushnell, contrasting the two plays, notes that Ion "is no one in Athens and has no voice, except as his birth ensures it," in *Prophesying Tragedy: Sign and Voice in Sophocles' Theban Plays* (Ithaca, N.Y.: Cornell University Press, 1988), 119.

52. Zeitlin, *Playing the Other*, 337.

53. Zeitlin, *Playing the Other*, 335. The passage quoted is her translation of ll. 1532–36.

54. Euripides, *Ion*, 125.

55. Zeitlin, *Playing the Other*, 295. She is quoting ll. 1324 and 1363.

56. This is a kind of anticipation of Christian societies fearing cuckoldry but having at the center of their religion a Child being reared by his mother and foster-father—except that the biological fatherhood in this case was imagined as nonsexual and Joseph knew about it.

57. Zeitlin, *Playing the Other*, 334.

58. Euripides, *Ion*, 115.

59. Boswell, *Abandonment of Children*, 3–4, 107.

60. Charles Segal, *Oedipus Tyrannus: Tragic Heroism and the Limits of Knowledge* (New York: Twayne, 1993), 44–47.

61. David Denby, *Great Books: My Adventures with Homer, Rousseau, Woolf, and Other Indestructible Writers of the Western World* (New York: Touchstone, 1997), 111.

62. James Shapiro, personal communication, July 30, 2000. In this conversation, he also said that adoptees sometimes tell fascinating stories at this point in his class.

63. Kenneth Burke, "Literature as Equipment for Living," in *The Philosophy of Literary Form*, 3d ed. (Berkeley and Los Angeles: University of Califor-

nia Press, 1973), 293–304. Burke writes that a work of literature may be considered "the strategic naming of a situation. It singles out a pattern of experience that is sufficiently representative of our social structure, that recurs sufficiently often *mutandis mutatis,* for people to 'need a word for it' and to adopt an attitude towards it. Each work of art is the addition of a word to an informal dictionary" (300). This is all relevant to the way literature influences how we imagine adoption.

CHAPTER 3

1. This and all other quotations from Shakespeare, except as noted, are taken from *The Complete Works,* ed. David Bevington, 4th ed. (New York: HarperCollins, 1992); this is from *Tempest* 1.2.120.

2. Barbara Estrin, *The Raven and the Lark: Lost Children in Literature of the English Renaissance* (Lewisburg, Pa.: Bucknell University Press, 1985), while noting that such plots in literature "predicate that the biological parents are superior to the adoptive ones," also writes that "the good of art appears in the adoptive sections where the supremacy of inheritance is superseded by the idealization of the replacement" (14).

3. C. L. Barber, "The Family in Shakespeare's Development: Tragedy and Sacredness," in *Representing Shakespeare: New Psychoanalytic Essays,* ed. Murray M. Schwartz and Coppélia Kahn (Baltimore: Johns Hopkins University Press, 1980), 188.

4. Angela Carter, *Wise Children* (1991; New York: Penguin, 1993), 180.

5. See Laqueur, *Making Sex,* 25–43, and his explanation (55–57) of how the encyclopedist Isidore of Seville, still influential in the Renaissance, simultaneously holds "that only men have sperma, that only women have sperma, and that both have sperma" (55). See also Janet Adelman, "Making Defect Perfection: Shakespeare and the One-Sex Model," in *Enacting Gender on the Renaissance Stage,* ed. Viviana Comensoli and Anne Russell (Urbana: University of Illinois Press, 1999), 23–52; and Francois Jacob, *The Logic of Life: A History of Heredity,* trans. Betty E. Spillman (1973; Princeton: Princeton University Press, 1993), 25. See Laqueur, 38, on "seeds" as refined blood; see also Aristotle's belief that the fetus feeds on menstrual blood, which accounts for the resemblance of children to their mothers, in Ian Maclean, *The Renaissance Notion of Woman* (Cambridge: Cambridge University Press, 1980), 37. For a classic, influential text of another dimension of belief in "blood," the natural love of parents for their children, combined with a description of how Nature uses women's blood to feed the seed, see Plutarch, "On Affection for Offspring," in *Moralia,* 16 vols., trans. W. C. Helmbold (Cambridge: Harvard University Press, 1970), 6:343–53. For still other Renaissance notions of blood, see Gail Kern Paster, *Body Embarrassed: Drama and the Disciplines of Shame in Early Modern England* (Ithaca, N.Y.: Cornell University Press, 1993), 64–112.

6. Children's difference from their parents was sometimes explained as the influence of the maternal imagination: see Clara Pinto-Correia, *The Ovary of*

Eve: Egg and Sperm and Preformation (Chicago: University of Chicago Press, 1997), 128–30. For other explanations related to the condition of both parents at conception, see Paster, *Body Embarrassed,* 167–72.

7. For the early modern comparison of teachers to gardeners, see Rebecca Bushnell, *A Culture of Teaching: Early Modern Humanism in Theory and Practice* (Ithaca, N.Y.: Cornell University Press, 1996), 73–116. On the influence of wet nurses, see Valerie Fildes, *Breasts, Bottles, and Babies: A History of Infant Feeding* (Edinburgh: Edinburgh University Press, 1986), 168–78. See also Paster, *Body Embarrassed,* 197–201, on early modern wet-nursing and its transformations in drama.

8. Dionyza's words resonate ominously with some contemporary cases of infanticidal nursing, mostly of illegitimate children: see Keith Wrightson, "Infanticide in Earlier Seventeenth-Century England," *Local Population Studies* 15 (1975): 10–22. Thanks to Frances Dolan for sending me a copy of this article.

9. See Elizabeth Archibald, *Apollonius of Tyre: Medieval and Renaissance Themes and Variations* (Bury-St. Edmunds: D. S. Brewer, 1991), 145.

10. See Geoffrey Bullough, ed., *Narrative and Dramatic Sources of Shakespeare,* vol. 6 (New York: Columbia University Press, 1966), 396–405, 445–53, 518–29. Wilkins's Pericles alone motivates this secrecy, by telling the nurse that Marina should be "brought uppe as the daughter of Cleon and Dyonysa, lest that the knowledge of her highbirth, should make her growe prowd to their instructions" (524).

11. Unlike Marina's prototype in these sources, Perdita, Guiderius, and Arviragus have no lines commenting on their discovery of a different set of parents, and the foster parents and birth parents in each play make alliance by the end.

12. F. D. Hoeniger, introduction to *Pericles,* ed. F. D. Hoeniger, Arden Edition (London: Methuen, 1963), lxxviii, notes that Pericles' role as music teacher is emphasized in the sources.

13. Terence Cave, *Recognitions: A Study in Poetics* (Oxford: Clarendon Press, 1988), 289.

14. As Janet Adelman points out, they also rearticulate, benignly, "the deadly mergers of the beginning—the collapse of mother, wife, and daughter in Antiochus's daughter's body and the attendant collapse of Pericles's masculine identity." *Suffocating Mothers: Fantasies of Maternal Origin in Shakespeare's Plays, "Hamlet" to "The Tempest"* (New York: Routledge, 1992), 197.

15. Adelman, *Suffocating Mothers,* 197–98.

16. Geoffrey Bullough, ed., *Narrative and Dramatic Sources of Shakespeare,* vol. 8, *Romances* (New York: Columbia University Press, 1975), 22–23. The number is four if we count Imogen's relationship with her stepmother as an adoption.

17. Susan Baker, "Personating Persons: Rethinking Shakespearean Disguises," *Shakespeare Quarterly* 43 (1992): 312.

18. See Meredith Skura's "Interpreting Posthumus' Dream from Above and Below: Families, Psychoanalysts, and Literary Criticism," in Schwartz and Kahn, *Representing Shakespeare,* 212–15.

19. Bullough, *Narrative and Dramatic Sources*, 8:6–7.

20. Ann Thompson, "Cymbeline's Other Endings," in *The Appropriation of Shakespeare*, ed. Jean Marsden (New York: St. Martin's, 1992), 207–8. Thompson also has some fun with reviewers' habit of "counting the number of separate explanations or revelations: I have found totals of fourteen, twenty-four and just about every number in between" (204).

21. John Boswell, *The Kindness of Strangers: The Abandonment of Children in Western Europe from Late Antiquity to the Renaissance* (New York: Vintage, 1988). Such a requirement is also present in a number of the newly discovered private adoption contracts in early modern France discussed by Kristin Elizabeth Gager, *Blood Ties and Fictive Ties: Adoption and Family Life in Early Modern France* (Princeton: Princeton University Press, 1996), 101–2.

22. Thompson, "Cymbeline's Other Endings," 212.

23. Carol Thomas Neely, *Broken Nuptials in Shakespeare's Plays* (New Haven: Yale University Press, 1985), 202.

24. Baker, "Personating Persons," 312.

25. Fawnia's "natural disposition did bewray that she was borne of some high parentage" (Robert Greene, *Pandosto*, in Bullough, *Narrative and Dramatic Sources*, 8:175), but specific resemblances do not, for example, strike her father, and thus he pursues her without suspecting that his love is incestuous. Shakespeare also added discussion of the physical resemblance between the Bastard and his father to his historical source for *King John*. See Phyllis Rackin, *Stages of History: Shakespeare's English Chronicles* (Ithaca, N.Y.: Cornell University Press, 1990), 187, 190.

26. Anne Barton, "*As You Like It* and *Twelfth Night*: Shakespeare's Sense of an Ending," *Shakespearian Comedy*, Stratford-upon-Avon Studies 14, ed. D. J. Palmer and Malcolm Bradbury (New York: Crane, Rusak, 1972), 176.

27. Shaw, "*Cymbeline* Refinished" (1937), quoted in Thompson, "Cymbeline's Other Endings," 213.

28. On that prejudice, see Stephen Collins, "'Reason, Nature, and Order': The Stepfamily in English Renaissance Thought," *Renaissance Studies* 13 (1999): 312–24; see Neely, *Broken Nuptials*, 174, on the desexualization and sanctification of mothers in the romances through real and mock deaths. The foster mother in *Pandosto* begins as a misogynist caricature who threatens to cudgel her husband "if hee brought any bastard brat within her dores," though eventually she nourishes "it so clenly and carefully as it began to bee a jolly girle, in so much that they began both of them to be very fond of it" (Greene, *Pandosto*, in Bullough, *Narrative and Dramatic Sources*, 8:174, 175).

29. See Adelman, *Suffocating Mothers*, 9–10 and passim, for a detailed analysis of the varying roles of mothers and fantasies about mothers in Shakespeare's canon. Hermione and Thaisa are less idealized early in the play than after they reappear. Only two other plays, *Romeo and Juliet* and *Merry Wives of Windsor*, include mother-daughter relationships; in both, those relations are rather cool and distant, to tragic effect in *Romeo and Juliet*.

30. Paster, *Body Embarrassed*, 179.

31. Collins, "Reason, Nature, and Order," 320–21. On polarization in

views of women, see for example, Mary Beth Rose, *The Expense of Spirit* (Ithaca, N.Y.: Cornell University Press, 1988), 4–5.

32. Compare the presence of the idealized mothers Ceres and Juno in the masque of *The Tempest.*

33. Doreen Delvecchio and Antony Hammond give a list of examples in *Pericles:* see their introduction to *Pericles, Prince of Tyre,* ed. Delvecchio and Hammond (Cambridge: Cambridge University Press, 1998), 47–49. See also Neely, *Broken Nuptials,* 191–92; and Marianne Novy, *Love's Argument: Gender Relations in Shakespeare* (Chapel Hill: University of North Carolina Press, 1984), 171–74.

34. For an interpretation of the cross-gendered imagery emphasizing male nurturance, see Novy, *Love's Argument,* 174; for the view that it involves male appropriation of female procreative power that excludes women, see Adelman, *Suffocating Mothers,* 197–98 (which also emphasizes the repression of sexuality); and Marilyn Williamson, *The Patriarchy of Shakespeare's Comedies* (Detroit: Wayne State University Press, 1986), 165.

35. Bevington glosses this passage as referring to grafting, a metaphor also used of adoption in some twentieth-century writing, such as *Perspectives on a Grafted Tree,* ed. Patricia Irwin Johnston (Indianapolis: Perspectives Press, 1983).

36. See Gal. 4:5–7 and Rom. 8:12–17. Gager has speculated that, in spite of clerical hostility to adoption discussed by Jack Goody, "the Christian theology of 'adoption through baptism' might very well have aided in sustaining adoption traditions for families interested in having a non-natal child to stand as their heir" (*Blood Ties,* 69; see also 44–46). Perhaps some ambitious historian will discover records notarizing adoption in England as Gager has done in France. But see Goody, *The Development of the Family and Marriage in Europe* (Cambridge: Cambridge University Press, 1983), 72–75, 99–102.

37. Paster, *Body Embarrassed,* 273.

38. Beatrice Gottlieb, *The Family in the Western World from the Black Death to the Industrial Age* (New York: Oxford University Press, 1993), 160; these customs are discussed with specific reference to the late sixteenth and early seventeenth century in Ivy Pinchbeck and Margaret Hewitt, *Children in English Society,* vol. 1 (London: Routledge and Kegan Paul, 1969), 25–26. Gottlieb claims that apprenticeship often began around age seven, but Ilana Krausman Ben-Amos finds that ten, twelve or later were much more likely ages, though younger children could be boarded out for such reasons as schooling, outbreaks of plague, poverty, or parental death; see her *Adolescence and Youth in Early Modern England* (New Haven: Yale University Press, 1994), 54–64. Her view of the ages of apprentices is supported by Paul Griffith, *Youth and Authority: Formative Experiences in England, 1560–1640* (Oxford: Clarendon Press, 1996), 33. Lawrence Stone discusses what he calls a "mass exchange of adolescent children, which seems to have been peculiar to England," in *The Family, Sex, and Marriage in England, 1500–1800* (New York: Harper and Row, 1977), 107. Lori Humphrey Newcomb discusses *The Winter's Tale*'s source, *Pandosto,* in relation to the widespread institution of adolescent service, in "The Romance of Service: The Simple History of *Pandosto*'s Servant Readers," in *Framing Elizabethan Fictions: Contemporary Approaches to Early Modern Narrative Prose,*

ed. Constance Relihan (Kent, Ohio: Kent State University Press, 1996), 117–39. I am grateful for a prepublication copy of this essay, which now has been revised into a chapter in Lori Humphrey Newcomb, *Reading Popular Romance in Early Modern England* (New York: Columbia University Press, 2001).

39. Heather Dubrow, *Shakespeare and Domestic Loss: Forms of Deprivation, Mourning, and Recuperation* (Cambridge: Cambridge University Press, 1999), 162. She deals with the relation of the romances to the threat of parental death on pp. 166, 189–93. See also her comments on parental death, step-parenting, and theatricality on pp. 165 and 170. I am grateful for a prepublication copy of this chapter, which is expanded from "The Message from Marcade: Parental Death in Tudor and Stuart England," in *Attending to Women in Early Modern England,* ed. Betty S. Travitsky and Adele F. Seeff (Newark: University of Delaware Press, 1994).

40. Gottlieb, *Family in Western World* , 133. Frances E. Dolan, *Dangerous Familiars: Representations of Domestic Crime in England, 1550–1700* (Ithaca, N.Y.: Cornell University Press, 1994), 168, has argued that *Winter's Tale* in particular is a displaced, aestheticized resolution of anxiety about infanticide.

41. Paster, *Body Embarrassed,* 276.

42. See Adelman, *Suffocating Mothers;* and also Skura, "Interpreting Posthumus' Dream."

43. Daniele Barbar, *Italian Relations* (1551), in *How They Lived,* ed. Molly Harrison and O. M. Royston, vol. 2 (Oxford: Blackwell, 1963), 267–68; quoted in Gottlieb, *Family in Western World,* 162. She notes criticism of this pattern eventually developing in England, beginning with William Penn, and argues that "some people were genuinely puzzled by why they were doing what was expected" (161).

44. See Hoeniger, introduction, xxv.

45. Hoeniger notes, "There are few plays by Shakespeare for which as much evidence is available to testify to their popularity on the stage during the early decades of the seventeenth century" (introduction, lxvi–lxvii).

46. On the connection between sealed records and illegitimacy, see Wegar, *Adoption, Identity, and Kinship,* 36.

47. *Bastard Quarterly* 1, no. 4 (1998): 8. Thanks to Marley Greiner for the reference.

48. See Alison Findlay, *Illegitimate Power: Bastards in Renaissance Drama* (New York: Manchester University Press, 1994), 128, on Goneril and Regan as "bastardised."

49. Peter Laslett, "Long-Term Trends in Bastardy in England," in *Family Life and Illicit Love in Earlier Generations,* ed. Laslett (Cambridge: Cambridge University Press, 1977), 113–15, on the increase in the illegitimacy rate; on changing social attitudes, see Pinchbeck and Hewitt, *Children in English Society,* 200–206. See also Michael Neill, " 'In Everything Illegitimate': Imagining the Bastard in Renaissance Drama," *Yearbook of English Studies* 23 (1993): 270–92, esp. 273.

50. Findlay, *Illegitimate Power,* 128.

51. Garry Leonard, "The Immaculate Deception: Adoption in Albee's Plays," in Novy, *Imagining Adoption,* 116.

52. Findlay has calculated this figure; she believes that the main reason is that women already suffered from the inability to inherit under the law, so loss of inheritance because of bastardy was less dramatic for them (*Illegitimate Power,* 5). This point is also made by Neill, "In Everything Illegitimate," 275.

53. On the larger number of female adoptees who search, see Wegar, *Adoption, Identity, and Kinship,* 65. Shea Grimm deplores the lack of men in previous adoption reform organizations, and boasts that "Bastard Nation's membership is over 30 percent male," "Birth of a Nation," *Bastard Quarterly* (spring 1997) 1, no. 1:1.

54. Neill discusses the connections between the idea of bastardy and forbidden mixture ("In Everything Illegitimate," 277–78).

55. The term *bastard* identifies someone as outside of a family. It probably derives from the Old French *bast,* meaning "pack-saddle," and thus "distinguishes the placeless pack-saddle child from the offspring of the marriage bed" (Neill, "In Everything Illegitimate," 273).

56. Novy, *Engaging with Shakespeare.* See also the anthologies I edited, *Women's Re-Visions of Shakespeare: On Responses of Dickinson, Woolf, Rich, H. D., George Eliot, and Others* (Urbana: University of Illinois Press, 1990), *Cross-Cultural Performances: Differences in Women's Re-Visions of Shakespeare* (Urbana: University of Illinois Press, 1993), and *Transforming Shakespeare: Women's Re-Visions in Literature and Performance* (New York: St. Martin's, 1999).

CHAPTER 4

1. Christopher Flint, *Family Fictions: Narrative and Domestic Relations in Britain, 1688–1798* (Stanford: Stanford University Press, 1998), 16. He discusses the controversies in both disciplines, as does, more briefly, Susan Greenfield, *Mothering Daughters: Novels and the Politics of Family Romance, Frances Burney to Jane Austen* (Detroit: Wayne State University Press, 2002), 14–17.

2. Flint, *Family Fictions,* 20.

3. Peter Laslett, "Introduction: Comparing Illegitimacy over Time and across Cultures," in *Bastardy and its Comparative History,* ed. Peter Laslett, Karla Oosterveen, and Richard M. Smith (Cambridge: Harvard University Press, 1980), 13.

4. Toni Bowers, *The Politics of Motherhood: British Writing and Culture, 1680–1760* (Cambridge: Cambridge University Press, 1996), 7–14.

5. George K. Behlmer, *Friends of the Family: The English Home and Its Guardians* (Stanford: Stanford University Press, 1998), 272–300.

6. Penny Martin, *Victorian Families in Fact and Fiction* (New York: St. Martin's, 1995), 135.

7. Cf. Ragussis, *Acts of Naming,* 38: "The history of fiction charts an attack on the name as stigma."

8. Henry Fielding, *Tom Jones,* ed. John Bender and Simon Stern (New York: Oxford University Press, 1996), 111. Subsequent references will be parenthetically included in the text.

9. Frances Burney, *Evelina,* ed. Kristina Straub (New York: Bedford, 1997), 200. Subsequent references will be parenthetically included in the text.

10. Charles Dickens, *Bleak House,* ed. Norman Page (New York: Penguin, 1971), 566. Subsequent references will be parenthetically included in the text.

11. Charles Dickens, *Oliver Twist,* ed. Kathleen Tillotson (Oxford: Clarendon Press, 1966), 332. Subsequent references will be parenthetically included in the text.

12. Charles Dickens, *Great Expectations* (New York: Holt, Rinehart, Winston, 1948), 366. Subsequent references will be parenthetically included in the text.

13. Christine van Boheemen, *The Novel as Family Romance: Language, Gender, and Authority from Fielding to Joyce* (Ithaca, N.Y.: Cornell University Press, 1987), 47, suggests this possibility. See also Homer Brown, "Tom Jones: The Bastard of History," *Boundary 2,* vol. 7, no. 2 (1979): 201–33.

14. See *Enlightened Self-Interest: The Foundling Hospital and Hogarth,* ed. Rhian Harris and Robin Simon, catalog of an exhibition at the Thomas Coram Foundation for Children (London: Draig Foundation, 1997).

15. T. G. A. Nelson, *Children, Parents, and the Rise of the Novel* (Newark: University of Delaware Press, 1995), 174–75, claims that the child is "presumably left on the parish," but he thinks that Molly is sent to Bridewell, whereas in fact she is discharged to her parents (167). The point remains that Fielding does not clarify what happens.

16. Van Boheemen, *Novel as Family Romance,* 80.

17. Van Boheemen, *Novel as Family Romance,* 79.

18. John Sutherland, *Can Jane Eyre Be Happy? More Puzzles in Classic Fiction* (New York: Oxford University Press, 1997), 23.

19. See Peter Coveney, *The Image of Childhood,* rev. ed. (New York: Penguin, 1967), 29–51.

20. See Grahame Smith, "The Life and Times of Charles Dickens," in *The Cambridge Companion to Charles Dickens,* ed. John O. Jordan (Cambridge: Cambridge University Press, 2001), 4; and Robert Newsom, "Fictions of Childhood," also in Jordan, 92–93.

21. Laura Berry, *The Child, the State, and the Victorian Novel* (Charlottesville: University of Virginia, 1999), shows that *Oliver Twist* also contributes to the debate over the New Poor Law.

22. Norris Pope, *Dickens and Charity* (New York: Columbia University Press, 1978), 179; Ruth McClure, *Coram's Children: The London Foundling Hospital in the Eighteenth Century* (New Haven: Yale University Press, 1981), 253, 307. The connection between the two Brownlows was pointed out by Laura Schattschneider in "Mr. Brownlow's Interest in Oliver Twist." *Journal of Victorian Culture* 6, no. 1 (spring 2001), 46–60. See also Jenny Bourne Taylor, "Received, a Blank Child: John Brownlow, Charles Dickens, and the London Foundling Hospital," *Nineteenth-Century Literature* 56 (2001): 293–363.

23. Catherine Waters, *Dickens and the Politics of the Family* (Cambridge: Cambridge University Press, 1997), 31.

24. Goldie Morgentaler, *Dickens and Heredity: When Like Begets Like* (New York: St. Martin's, 2000), 39. Morgentaler contextualizes this with the

Victorian belief that "such matters as the state of mind of the parents and the degree of their affection for one another at the time of conception had a bearing on the personality of the engendered child." This belief goes back to views held in the Renaissance and before about the impact of the circumstances of conception. Dickens revises Shakespeare's Edmund's argument relating his superiority to his bastardy because he was conceived with "fierce quality" and not " 'tween asleep and wake."

25. Morgentaler discusses in detail the relation between portraiture and heredity in Dickens, taking this incident as a point of departure; she calls Oliver's emotion about the portrait "mystical heredity. . . an intuition of kinship" (*Dickens and Heredity*, 40), but in fact Oliver does not know why he is responding so strongly.

26. Ragussis, *Acts of Naming*, 41–43.

27. See Waters, *Dickens*, 36, on the final "pastoral retreat" and the "restorative powers of nature and imagination."

28. Morgentaler, *Dickens and Heredity*, 43.

29. See Morgentaler, *Dickens and Heredity*, 35, for more examples of Dickens portraying parents and children as similar in appearance. As Morgentaler shows, however, Dickens would present parent-child resemblance in a more complicated way in some of his later novels, for example, in *Dombey and Son*, as an ideal related to paternal egotism (53), and in *David Copperfield*, as a matter of learned behavior (68). See Valerie L. Gager, *Shakespeare and Dickens: The Dynamics of Influence* (Cambridge: Cambridge University Press, 1996) for more on Dickens's intense relationship with Shakespeare.

30. Carolyn Dever, *Death and the Mother from Dickens to Freud: Victorian Fiction and the Anxiety of Origins* (Cambridge: Cambridge University Press, 1998), 7, 23.

31. Charlotte Brontë, *Jane Eyre* (London: J. M. Dent, 1993).

32. "A Progress" is the title of the chapter in which Esther is introduced, echoing the subtitle of *Oliver Twist, A Parish Boy's Progress*, as well as Defoe's *Pilgrim's Progress*, still very influential at this time.

33. See Newsom, "Fictions of Childhood," 99, which describes *Bleak House* as "virtually an anti-*Jane Eyre*" and suggests that Brontë influenced "Dickens' turn to first person narratives," although he claimed that he had never read *Jane Eyre*.

34. See the discussion of the doll in Dever, *Death and the Mother*, 88.

35. See Dever, *Death and the Mother*, 90.

36. Sandra Gilbert and Susan Gubar, *The Madwoman in the Attic* (New Haven: Yale University Press, 1979). The use of *Jane Eyre* in Jeanette Winterson's *Oranges are not the Only Fruit*, an autobiographical novel about an adoptee, is especially interesting.

37. See for example Anny Sadrin, *Parentage and Inheritance in the Novels of Charles Dickens* (Cambridge: Cambridge University Press, 1994), 64; and Dever, *Death and the Mother*, 102.

38. See Ragussis, *Acts of Naming*, 90.

39. Van Boheemen, *Novel as Family Romance*, argues that it is only after

Esther has acknowledged her dead mother that "the taboo on her sexuality is lifted," and that her confession of her attraction to Alan is "avoiding the mistakes of her mother," 122.

40. See Ragussis, *Acts of Naming*, 253n.

41. A similar name is used satirically in *Tom Jones*, 178, where Mrs. Honour, Sophia's maid, emphasizes that her birth, in marriage, is better than Tom's.

42. See Dever, *Death and the Mother*, 84.

43. See Ragussis, *Acts of Naming*, 101, on Ada's symbolic maternity here.

44. See Jonathan Arac, *Commissioned Spirits: The Shaping of Social Motion in Dickens, Carlyle, Melville, and Hawthorne* (1979; New York: Columbia University Press, 1989), 132, on environmental influence on Esther's diffidence parallel to environmental influence on Phil and Jo.

45. Jane Austen, *Mansfield Park* (Boston: Houghton Mifflin, 1965), 325.

46. See Dever, *Death and the Mother*, 90.

47. Morgentaler argues that in *Great Expectations* Dickens "discard[s] heredity as a determining force in human development" (*Dickens and Heredity*, 72). Possibly Pip's identity as parentless is emphasized further by Pocket's nicknaming him Handel, since the historical Handel was a governor of the Foundling Hospital and frequently conducted and played music there. See McClure, *Coram's Children*, 70.

48. As Waters shows, his images of them deriving from the shape of the letters also accord with Victorian stereotypes of masculinity and femininity (*Dickens*, 151).

49. Waters comments on the oddness of Pip's association of these two different women, and also on Mrs. Joe's social pretension (*Dickens*, 154–55).

50. Waters makes this point, saying that Magwitch wants "to make Pip a gentleman so as to revenge himself upon the moneyed social class he holds responsible for his victimization" (*Dickens*, 158). She also notes that the fact they are both victimized by Compeyson highlights this parallel, and that "by adopting personal schemes of vengeance in response to the experience of social injustice, Miss Havisham and Magwitch inevitably embrace the ideology they struggle against and are defeated" (171).

51. Waters comments on the novel's construction of Pip's choosing between gentility and domesticity in terms of the contrast between Estella and Biddy (*Dickens*, 163–64).

52. I owe these observations to Emily Hipchen, in her commentary on a previous version of this chapter.

53. Betty Jean Lifton, *Lost and Found*, 51–52, discusses similar behavior among some adoptees, and similar explanations by some psychiatrists.

54. This difficulty may show the continuing impact on me of the closed-record system. With a different view of Pip and Estella, Edgar Rosenberg writes, "Very likely, like Lohengrin's Elsa, he would have talked out of turn during their honeymoon." See "Putting an End to *Great Expectations*," in *Great Expectations*, ed. Edgar Rosenberg (New York: Norton, 1999), 503.

55. Hirsch, *Mother-Daughter Plot*, 47, 50.

56. Hirsch, *Mother-Daughter Plot*, 46.

CHAPTER 5

1. Bernard Semmel, *George Eliot and the Politics of National Inheritance* (New York: Oxford University Press, 1994).

2. See Behlmer, *Friends of the Family*, 272–300, on what he calls de facto adoption and its abuses. See also Martin, *Victorian Families*, 135.

3. George Eliot, *The Mill on the Floss,* ed. Carol T. Christ (New York: Norton, 1994), 90. Rosemarie Bodenheimer, *The Real Life of Mary Ann Evans: George Eliot, Her Letters and Fiction* (Ithaca, N.Y.: Cornell University Press, 1994), 32, notes that in her youth, Eliot "never had a family member who understood or shared anything about her intellectual ambition or her emotional volatility," and, of course, during her adulthood most of her relatives rejected her because of her relationship with Lewes. Semmel, *George Eliot,* 16, also discusses this issue.

4. See Gordon Haight, "George Eliot's Bastards," in *George Eliot's Originals and Contemporaries,* ed. Hugh Witemeyer (Ann Arbor: University of Michigan Press, 1992), 76–86. Bodenheimer makes the connection to *Silas* (*Real Life,* 207).

5. *The George Eliot Letters,* ed. Gordon S. Haight, 9 vols. (New Haven: Yale University Press, 1954–78), 1:94, 4:183. Further references to this edition will be included parenthetically in the text, using the abbreviation GEL.

6. George Eliot, *Middlemarch Notebooks: A Transcription,* ed. John Clark Pratt and Victor Neufeldt (Berkeley and Los Angeles: University of California Press, 1979), 56. This was probably recorded 1871–72.

7. Maine, *Ancient Law,* 26.

8. Eliot, *Middlemarch Notebooks,* 204. This was recorded in 1869.

9. Bodenheimer, *Real Life,* 188. Because Lewes had not immediately sued his wife for divorce upon discovering her infidelity, he was not allowed to do so later as it continued.

10. Bodenheimer, *Real Life,* 230.

11. George Eliot, *A Writer's Notebook, 1854–1879, and Uncollected Writings,* ed. Joseph Wiesenfarth (Charlottesville: University Press of Virginia, 1981), 23. This dysphoric adoption plot is the germ of the Tito Baldassare plot in *Romola.*

12. On the use of adoption to exemplify a nurturing relationship aware of difference, see Susan Gubar, "Empathic Identification in Anne Michaels' *Fugitive Pieces:* Masculinity and Poetry after Auschwitz," *Signs* 28, no. 2 (202): 249–76. Gubar argues that the adoptions in Michaels exemplify empathy, which recognizes difference, rather than sympathy, "which supposes affinity among people" (253).

13. Page references are taken from *Silas Marner* (London: Everyman, 1993).

14. See Howe, "Fontane's 'Ellernklipp.'"

15. This difficulty in imagining adoptees as adults still appears in recent journalism. See David W. Matta, "A Cryin' Shame," *Pittsburgh City Paper,* May 10, 1996, 1, 12–14. This article about the open-records movement, interviewing adults, is illustrated, on the newspaper's front page, with a photograph of a screaming baby, and on p. 12 with a blurred photo of a young child. It can

be argued that the legal discourse on the closed-records side also treats adoptees as children.

16. Michael Ragussis, *Figures of Conversion: "The Jewish Question" and English National Identity* (Durham: Duke University Press, 1995), 105, 189.

17. *Sybil*, 65–66, quoted by Ragussis, *Figures of Conversion*, 191.

18. Susan R. Cohen, "'A History and a Metamorphosis': Continuity and Discontinuity in *Silas Marner*," *Texas Studies in Literature and Language* 25 (1983): 416.

19. Bodenheimer, *Real Life*, 206. Sandra Gilbert, in "Life's Empty Pack: A Literary Daughteronomy," *Critical Inquiry* 11 (1985): 355–89, treats Eppie's move from her mother to Silas as an allegory for the transition from mother to father in a typical girl's life, considering fatherhood as essentially a "social construct." Some writers associate adoptive links with chance, but Gilbert claims that "*God-free* Cass . . . is only by chance (*casus*) her natural father" (363).

20. Nancy Paxton, *George Eliot and Herbert Spencer* (Princeton: Princeton University Press, 1991), 110.

21. The name of the most famous of the opiates frequently used for children in the nineteenth century was Godfrey's Cordial. Eliot's name choice for her character resonates with his own deliberate unconsciousness of his responsibilities, and perhaps also with the sense that Eppie is better off without Godfrey, as well as without Godfrey's Cordial. See Virginia Berridge and Griffith Edwards, *Opium and the People: Opiate Use in Nineteenth-Century England* (New Haven: Yale University Press, 1987), 99.

22. See Frye, *The Secular Scripture*, 101–2, 161.

23. Godfrey buys the land on which Silas lives in the process of starting a dairy, a kind of substitute for the children whose absence bothers Godfrey and Nancy so much. As Nancy's sister says, "There's always something fresh with the dairy." This involvement with natural growth produces discoveries that motivate Godfrey's decision to attempt to reclaim Eppie.

24. Paxton, *Eliot and Spencer*, 114, has commented on the rewriting of *Winter's Tale* both in Eppie's decision and in the discussion of gardening. I quote *Winter's Tale* 4.4.95–97 from the *Complete Works*, ed. David Bevington, 3d ed. (Glenview, Ill.: Scott Foresman, 1980). Eliot quotes this passage in GEL 4:364, 4:469, and elsewhere.

25. George Eliot, *Romola*, ed. Andrew Sanders (New York: Penguin, 1980), 148.

26. George Eliot, *Felix Holt*, ed. Peter Coveney (New York: Penguin, 1972), 149. Page references will be given parenthetically in the text.

27. See my *Engaging with Shakespeare*, 69–93.

28. Eve Sedgwick, *Epistemology of the Closet* (Berkeley and Los Angeles: University of California Press, 1990), 75–82, analyzes Proust's use of Racine's *Esther* in relation to parallels and contrasts between hidden Jewish and gay identity. When I was in grade school and certainly did not know Racine, Handel, Proust, or Eliot, I wrote a short story about a girl named Esther who disguises herself as a boy so she can go to Bethlehem with the Three Wise Men.

29. It has been suggested that he should have known he was Jewish because he was circumcised. However, his mother was so opposed to Judaism that she

might not have had him circumcised, and, on the other hand, nineteenth-century English Gentiles were often circumcised for health reasons. See Sutherland, *Can Jane Eyre Be Happy?* 169–76.

30. For a detailed discussion of this theme in *Deronda*, see Dever, *Death and the Mother*, 143–75.

31. George Eliot, *Daniel Deronda*, ed. Graham Handley (New York: Oxford University Press, 1988), 142. Page references will be given parenthetically in the text.

32. Though adoption was not formalized in England at the time, soon after the book was published, a defense of adoption on the Roman model assumes that it means assimilation and equates it with the naturalization of immigrants, so Sir Hugo's desires for Daniel would not have been unexpected for most readers. See Edward Augustus Freeman, "Race and Language," *Contemporary Review* 29 (1877): 711–41, excerpted in *Images of Race*, ed. Michael D. Biddiss (New York: Holmes and Meier, 1979), 214–35.

33. This critique of adults' casual attitude toward the children whose fate they determine is a subtler version of that made in "Mr. Gilfil's Love-Story," where Caterina is expected by Lord and Lady Cheverel "to be ultimately useful, perhaps, in sorting worsteds, keeping accounts, reading aloud, and otherwise supplying the place of spectacles when her ladyship's eyes should wax dim." See *Scenes of Clerical Life*, ed. Thomas A. Noble (Oxford: Clarendon Press, 1985), 104. At this point Caterina is not to be adopted; when her singing voice is discovered, "Insensibly she came to be regarded as one of the family" (111), but the attitude to her is still instrumental.

34. Ironically, there was a nineteenth-century view, articulated among others by the German anthropologist Riehl, one of whose works Eliot had earlier reviewed with praise, that Jews were "rootless": see George L. Mosse, *The Culture of Western Europe* (New York: Rand-McNally, 1971), 82–84.

35. *Adam Bede*, chap. 4.

36. Quoted in Bodenheimer, *Real Life*, 214.

37. Bodenheimer, *Real Life*, 227–30.

38. This is not true in *The Spanish Gypsy*, where Gypsy tradition is described in secular terms.

39. In his 1877 review in *Contemporary Review*, Edward Dowden related *Deronda* to the contemporary rise of nationalism; see the excerpt in *George Eliot: The Critical Heritage*, ed. David Carroll (New York: Barnes and Noble, 1971), 446. In her next book after *Deronda*, Eliot celebrated nineteenth-century revivals of national traditions; see "The Modern Hep! Hep! Hep! Hep!" in *Impressions of Theophrastus Such* (1879), ed. Nancy Henry (Iowa City: University of Iowa Press, 1994), 142–47. On changing modes of nationalism in the nineteenth century, see Benjamin Barber, *Jihad vs. McWorld* (New York: Ballantine, 1995), 159–60; and Eric Hobsbawm, *Nation and Nationalism since 1780* (Cambridge: Cambridge University Press, 1992), 101–23. On the greater biological emphasis in late-nineteenth-century racial theory, see Robert J. C. Young, *Colonial Desire: Hybridity in Theory, Culture, and Race* (London: Routledge, 1995), 118–41; and George W. Stocking Jr., *Victorian Anthropology* (New York: Free

Press, 1987), esp. 63, 116, 143. In a notebook that includes material on Jewish history relevant to *Deronda,* Eliot also records evidence of hereditary gestures found in Darwin and Galton. See William Baker, ed., *Some George Eliot Notebooks: An Edition of the Carl H. Pforzheimer Library's George Eliot Holograph Notebooks,* vol. 3, ms. 711 (Salzburg: Institut fur Anglistik und Amerikanistik, 1980), 13.

40. Haight, *George Eliot* (New York: Oxford, 1968), 469–71; Ragussis, *Figures of Conversion,* 261–63.

41. Brownstein, *Becoming a Heroine,* 208, discusses this strategy.

42. William Baker, *George Eliot and Judaism* (Salzburg: Institut fur Englische Sprache und Literatur, 1975), 64–66. Cf. Gillian Beer, *George Eliot* (Bloomington: Indiana University Press, 1986); and Ragussis, *Figures of Conversion.* Eliot's views on this were not unusual. See Stocking, *Victorian Anthropology,* 63–64, 106, 235–36. In "The Modern Hep, Hep, Hep" Eliot takes a surprisingly constructivist view of "that national education (by outward and inward circumstance) which created in the Jews a feeling of race, a sense of corporate existence, unique in its intensity" (150).

43. Dever, *Death and the Mother,* 157, shows that Mordecai "represents, more than anyone else in the novel, the potential fulfillment of [Daniel's] eroticized phantasy of maternal reunion."

44. Beer, *George Eliot,* 54.

45. Ragussis, *Figures of Conversion,* 97.

46. Ragussis, *Figures of Conversion,* 263ff.; quote is from 281.

47. Ragussis, *Figures of Conversion,* 289.

48. "Notes on the Spanish Gypsy and Tragedy," in *A George Eliot Miscellany,* ed. F. B. Pinion (Totowa, N.J.: Barnes and Noble, 1980), 126–27.

49. The significance of this essay in relation to women's conflicts in many of Eliot's works is discussed by Susan Meyer, *Imperialism at Home: Race and Victorian Women's Fiction* (Ithaca, N.Y.: Cornell University Press, 1996), 127–30.

50. Young, *Colonial Desire,* 6, writes that in the nineteenth century *hybrid* "was used to refer to a physiological phenomenon; in the twentieth century it has been reactivated to describe a cultural one." I am not using the word in the nineteenth-century sense involving a crossing between species or races.

51. Gillian Beer, *Darwin's Plots: Evolutionary Narrative in Darwin, George Eliot, and Nineteenth-Century Fiction* (London: Routledge and Kegan Paul, 1983), 201.

52. See Young, *Colonial Desire,* 17; and Hobsbawm, *Nation and Nationalism,* 33, 108.

53. David Marshall, *The Figure of Theater* (New York: Columbia, 1986), 219.

54. Beer, *George Eliot,* 109.

55. Modell, *Kinship with Strangers.*

56. Eliot's stepsons sometimes called her "Mother," but according to Bodenheimer (*Real Life,* 192) she usually signed herself "Mutter"—both a German translation and a pun—and that is how Charles and sometimes the others addressed her.

57. As the previous chapter has shown, emphasis on good adoptive fathers is common in the British fiction of Eliot's time and before. Perhaps she is more unusual in her lack of interest in critiquing adoptive mothers—the chief example would be Lady Cheverel. It is interesting to compare the dynamics of Eliot's writing about adoptive fathers with those of Anne Michaels in *Fugitive Pieces*, as discussed by Gubar, "Empathic Identification," 253. Like Michaels, Eliot is interested in showing the adoptive parent acknowledging difference, and Silas, who has suffered betrayal and expulsion from his community, experiences regeneration through adoption comparable to that discussed by Gubar (255).

58. Paxton, *Eliot and Spencer*, 110, 215. However, belief in maternal instinct may be expanded to suggest the basis for women's fitness to adopt. See Julie Berebitsky, *Like Our Very Own: Adoption and the Changing Culture of Motherhood, 1851–1950* (Lawrence: University Press of Kansas, 2000), 103–4, or for that matter Eliot's own description of "the feminine character," which I will quote shortly.

59. This theme is treated, for example, by Meyer in *Imperialism at Home*. However, I disagree with her argument that gender issues are displaced onto racial issues. As she indeed observes, there are many moments of protest against women's subordination in the novel. For more discussion of these, see Novy, *Engaging with Shakespeare*, 123–24, 130, 132.

60. See Meyer's comments in *Imperialism at Home*, 158–60, on how Daniel combines self-assertion and self-sacrifice at the end, while Fedalma's self-sacrifice allows her no self-assertion.

61. See Tess O'Toole's chapter on Eliot in her book in progress on adoption in Victorian literature, *'Native Slip from Foreign Seed': Adoption in the Nineteenth-Century British Novel*.

62. Cohen, "History and Metamorphosis."

63. See for example unsigned review, *Saturday Review*, September 16, 1876, in Carroll, *George Eliot*, 377, which asks, "what can be the design of this ostentatious separation from the universal instinct of Christendom, this subsidence into Jewish hopes and aims?"

64. Terence Cave, introduction to *Daniel Deronda*, ed. Cave (New York: Penguin, 1995), xvii–xviii; see esp. xii–xxii.

65. Meyer, *Imperialism at Home*, 191.

66. See Lifton, *Lost and Found*, 54–57. His extended sense of responsibility can also be read as a sign of his hereditary connection with the Jewish tradition of social concern (a message that I believe very few of Eliot's English readers would have received, because the dominant image of Jews was so negative).

67. See comments on biological nationalism in relation to Nazism and adoption fiction in Estrin, "Ending in the Middle," 276, 278. Yet such ideas persist, and occasionally surface, even in academic writings; see, for example, Richard J. Hernstein and Charles Murray, *The Bell Curve* (New York: Free Press, 1994), which met many refutations.

68. James Carroll's *Constantine's Sword: The Church and the Jews* (Boston: Houghton, 2001) has influenced my thinking about the depth of Christian anti-Semitism.

CHAPTER 6

1. Paton [Kittson], *Orphan Voyage*, 39.

2. Paton, *The Adopted Break Silence*.

3. Jean Paton, personal communication, 1993, 2001. His name is not given in the book. Other biographical details come from Mel Gussow, *Edward Albee: A Singular Journey* (New York: Simon and Schuster, 1999).

4. Albee didn't much like the term, but defended the style he shared with Beckett, Ionesco, and other Europeans, in "Which Theater Is the Absurd One?" *New York Times Magazine*, February 25, 1962, rpt. in *The Modern American Theater*, ed. Alvin B. Kernan (Englewood Cliffs, N.J.: Prentice-Hall, 1967), 170–75. Kernan in his introduction says that Albee "for many represents the best hope for the future of our theater" (11).

5. Melosh, *Strangers and Kin*, 2.

6. See Carol Singley, "Building a Nation, Building a Family," in *Adoption in America: Historical Perspectives*, ed. E. Wayne Carp (Ann Arbor: University of Michigan Press, 2002), 53.

7. Berebitsky, *Like Our Very Own*, 22; Carp, introduction to *Adoption in America*, 7–9.

8. Behlmer, *Friends of the Family*, chap. 6.

9. Berebitsky, *Like Our Very Own*, 128.

10. E. Wayne Carp, *Family Matters* (Cambridge: Harvard University Press, 1998), 53–54. This was the reason given by Sheldon Howard and Henry Hemenway, two vital statisticians, in their proposal.

11. Carp, *Family Matters*, 110.

12. Maxwell Anderson, *The Bad Seed: A Play in Two Acts . . . the Dramatization of William March's Novel "The Bad Seed"* (New York: Dodd, 1955).

13. See Carp, *Family Matters*, 17–19.

14. Albee, *American Dream*, 98. Subsequent page references will be given parenthetically in the text.

15. Paton, *Adopted Break Silence*, 152.

16. Jean Paton, personal communication, 1993, 2001.

17. Berebitsky, *Like Our Very Own*, 5, 4.

18. Carp, *Family Matters*, 97.

19. Typically, gay and lesbian youths feel different from their parents, in a way analogous to that of some adoptees, and both homosexuality and adoption break the link between sex and procreation. See Lifton, *Journey of Adopted Self*, 122–24, for more discussion of such commonalities.

20. See Leonard, "The Immaculate Deception," 123–24.

21. Berebitsky, *Like Our Very Own*, 130; Gussow, *Edward Albee*, 22.

22. Leonard, "The Immaculate Deception," 134–35.

23. Gussow, *Edward Albee*, 22–23.

24. Kirk, *Shared Fate*, 114–15. Kirk did important research on adoption in Canada in the 1950s and 1960s, especially with regard to the issue of the difference of the adoptive family; the first edition of his book was published in 1964.

25. Albee had left his parents at twenty, feeling their requirements were so

restrictive that they were in effect throwing him out. He never saw his father again, but renewed contact with his mother much later, after she had a heart attack.

26. Gussow, *Edward Albee,* 13.

27. Wayne Carp shows this change taking place most clearly during the 1950s: "Social workers' attitudes became more rigid and less forthcoming, while adoption agencies' policies of disclosure and cooperation gave way to secrecy and legalism" (*Family Matters,* 107). But Elizabeth Samuels, "The Idea of Adoption: An Inquiry into the History of Adult Adoptee Access to Birth Records," *Rutgers Law Review* 53, no. 2 (2001): 367–436, shows that as late as 1960, 40 percent of the states still opened birth certificates for adult adoptees, and most of these records were closed in the 1960s, 1970s, and 1980s.

28. See for example Marshall D. Schechter and Doris Bertocci, "The Meaning of the Search," in *The Psychology of Adoption,* ed. David Brodzinsky and Marshall Schechter (New York: Oxford University Press, 1990), 73; Leonard, "The Immaculate Deception," 119, 130.

29. Lifton, *Twice Born;* Florence Fisher, *The Search for Anna Fisher* (New York: Fawcett Crest, 1973).

30. See especially Arthur D. Sorosky, Annette Baran, and Reuben Pannor, *The Adoption Triangle: The Effects of the Sealed Record on Adoptees, Birth Parents, and Adoptive Parents* (New York: Anchor Press/Doubleday, 1978). Carp, *Family Matters,* 148, emphasizes the influence of these researchers.

31. *Roots* was televised in 1977; Carp, *Family Matters,* 164–65, discusses its role in promoting genealogical research nationally and in gaining understanding for adoptee searchers. One article he cites, "Everybody's Search for Roots," *Newsweek,* July 4, 1977, 25–38, a cover story, with discussion of both these aspects, is in my own file of adoption-related clippings; my own search was proceeding at the time. Adoption groups such as Florence Fisher's Adoptees' Liberty Movement Association (ALMA) often use a quote from Haley, e.g., "The truth of his origins is the right of every man," in their newsletters.

32. Open records were recommended by an English parliamentary commission. Probably this change was influenced partly by the fact that open records already existed in Scotland.

33. Wendy Wasserstein, *The Heidi Chronicles and Other Plays* (New York: Vintage, 1991). The Madonna and Child pose is not written in the script, but was used in the 1989 New York production, and emphasized by a background slide show of Madonna and Child statues and paintings. The published script gives the final image as "a slide of Heidi triumphantly holding Judy in front of a museum banner for a Georgia O'Keefe retrospective" (249), an image that emphasizes Heidi's career as well as linking her with an artist whose flower paintings are often associated with female genitals. A later play about a single woman who adopts is *Approximating Mother,* by Kathleen Tolan. This play takes a more detached approach to the adoptive mother on whom it focuses; a musician, she has not found a man she could marry without compromising too much, and at the end of the play, to amuse her child, she is making up songs about potty training. Compare also Timberlake Wertenbaker's *Break of Day,* a

British play about a group of friends in which one couple adopts and another one meets the adoptee girlfriend of their son, who is searching for birth parents.

34. Harvey Fierstein, *Torch Song Trilogy,* (New York: Samuel French, 1979).

35. In Dove's earlier version (Brownsville, Ore.: Story Line Press, 1994) he kills her; in the revised version (3d ed., Ashland, Ore.: Story Line Press, 2000), in which she has given him up because others convince her it is best for him, he is supposed to kill her as part of the rebellion, but she kills herself instead.

36. Caryl Churchill, *Top Girls* (New York: Samuel French, 1982), first produced at the Royal Court (London), 1982.

37. Thanks to Carol Schaefer for sending me the text of her play, performed off-Broadway in 2002, by e-mail, and for her comments when I gave a version of this chapter at the American Adoption Congress in 2002. References will be located in the text. The echo in the protagonist's name of Bridget, Tom Jones's birth mother, is probably just a coincidence; the name functions more here as a suggestion of Irish Catholic tradition.

38. Verrier, *The Primal Wound,* 12.

39. A very recent play, Paul Harris's *Lost and Found,* performed at the small Upstart Theater in New York City in May 2003, presents Ken, a troubled adoptee but a successful salesman, meeting Rachel, his birth mother, a successful anthropologist, and her husband, Tom. Tom is angry at the previous secrecy, and not used to the idea of sharing Rachel with another person (Ken is very similar to his dead father, still vivid in Rachel's memory). Ken says some very bitter things, but at the end they all look forward to a continuing relationship.

40. Lanford Wilson, *Redwood Curtain* (New York: Hill and Wang, 1993), premiered in Seattle, January 1992. *Redwood Curtain* was performed on television in 1993 and has been adapted into a film. There was a performance of the play as part of a Wilson festival in Cincinnati in 2001. John Olive, *Evelyn and the Polka King* (New York: Theatre Communications Group, 1992), was commissioned and first produced by Mad River Theatre Works, West Liberty, Ohio, 1991. I saw it at the City Theater in Pittsburgh in 1993. Page references to both of these plays will be included in the text. Lanford Wilson is the best-known playwright of those I discuss, apart from Albee, and he, like many American playwrights, is known for his portrayal of dysfunctional families. His parents were divorced when he was five, and he was separated from his father until he was nineteen, when he spent a year in San Diego getting to know him again—one of the few biographical details available to suggest the origins of any of these playwrights' involvement in the adoption/search experience. See *Lanford Wilson: A Casebook,* ed. Jackson R. Bryer (New York: Garland, 1994), xvii.

41. The generally favorable review of the Cincinnati production, Rick Pender, "Searching for Roots," *City Beat,* April 26–May 2, 2001, says, "Wilson's script includes some odd moments about Geri having magical powers, and those moments come across as false in this production."

42. See the discussion of gender among searchers in chapter 1.

43. I learned about this play from Josephine Lee's paper "Korean Adoptee Experience in Recent Plays by Theater Mu," presented to the Meeting of the Modern Language Association, New Orleans, 2001. Mu is an Asian-American theater, but the focus on Korean adoptees is understandable when we find that there are ten thousand Korean adoptees in Minnesota, more than in any other state except California. Shiomi is himself Japanese, and it may be partly in view of the strained history between those two countries that editions of this play emphasize the role in its creation of interviews with Korean adoptees and also of a Korean drummer and director.

44. Rick Shiomi, *Mask Dance,* in *Bold Words: A Century of Asian American Writing,* ed. Rajini Srikanth and Esther Y. Iwanaga (New Brunswick, N.J.: Rutgers University Press, 2001), 364.

45. I am grateful for receiving the text of this play by e-mail. Page references will be included in the text.

46. Anita Gates, September 21, 2001, E5. Weedman first performed this play in Seattle; by the time she played it in New York, she was known as a correspondent for Comedy Central's *The Daily Show.*

47. I have found one American play that deals with the extended family after reunion, Rachel Rubin Ladutke's *Grace Notes,* performed in April 2000 by the Gemini Theater of Pittsburgh.

48. Schechter and Bertocci, "Meaning of the Search," 66–67, summarize twelve studies of searchers between 1973 and 1987 and find that in all of them most searchers were female. Most searchers were in the twenty-five to thirty-four age range, though they extended from teenagers to seventy-year-olds.

49. See Leonard, "The Immaculate Deception," 115.

50. Edward Albee, *The Play about the Baby* (New York: Dramatists Play Service, 2002). Page references will be included in the text.

51. Kristine Thatcher, *Emma's Child* (New York: Dramatists Play Service, 1997), was first produced by the Oregon Shakespeare Festival, by which it was commissioned, in 1995. It won the 1995 Susan Smith Blackburn Award, and three awards in 1997, including one from Resolve, a national self-help organization for dealing with infertility. In recent years it has been performed in regional theaters in Seattle, Denver, Los Angeles, Reno, and elsewhere, and continues to get good reviews. Jane Anderson, *The Baby Dance* (New York: Samuel French, 1992), was originally produced by the Pasadena Playhouse, State Theatre of California. Page references for both will be included in the text. My discussion of *The Baby Dance* is based on the published script; I note a few contrasts, but many more of the lines I quote, which are among the places where the play's satire is strongest, are cut from the video.

52. The men in both would-be adoptive couples are Jewish, and their wives are Christian or Christian-raised. As I will discuss in a minute, anti-Semitism becomes an open issue in *The Baby Dance.*

53. Pertman, *Adoption Nation,* 189, 199.

54. The video was made for Showtime. Jane Anderson both wrote and directed the adaptation.

55. Leonard, "Immaculate Deception," 111.

56. See Leonard, "Immaculate Deception," 111–32, for more on the rele-

vance of *Zoo Story*, *Who's Afraid of Virginia Woolf*, and *Tiny Alice*, as well as *The American Dream*, to the experience of Albee as an adoptee.

CHAPTER 7

1. There are surprising affinities between the "lost cultures" explored by these two novelists. As Daniel Boyarin points out, "They are simultaneously seen as noble cultural ancestors of the groups that dominate them (Christian Europeans and white Americans, respectively) and denigrated as marginal and backward relics": "Europe's Indian, America's Jew: Modiano and Vizenor," in *American Indian Persistence and Resurgence*, ed. Karl Kroeber (Durham: Duke University Press, 1994), 200. In *Pigs in Heaven*, Annawake will explicitly compare Cash's desire for custody to that of the parent in the Baby M case who wanted a child with his heredity because he was a Holocaust survivor. See Barbara Kingsolver, *Pigs in Heaven* (New York: Harper and Row, 1993), 281.

2. Barbara Kingsolver, *The Bean Trees* (New York: Harper and Row, 1988), 18. Subsequent quotations from this edition will be included parenthetically in the text.

3. This novel can thus be related to what Jay Clayton calls "the remarkable series of political novels that came out in the last decade focusing on U.S. relations with Latin America and the Caribbean, and with refugees from those regions." *The Pleasures of Babel: Contemporary American Literature and Theory* (New York: Oxford, 1993), 114.

4. Kingsolver's training as a biologist and experience as a science writer shows up in passages such as these.

5. The importance of the doll to Turtle may recall the way Esther in *Bleak House* survives her motherless condition and toxic "godmother" partly by her relationship to a doll.

6. Compare Clayton's discussion of the importance of rituals, and in particular rituals of sacrifice, in contemporary North American fiction, *Pleasures of Babel*, 110–18, though Kingsolver's rituals are not as bloody as most of those he discusses.

7. Kingsolver has an interest in the classics of Greek literature, among others. In an interview, she states that she wanted to keep Taylor's vocabulary small to make the novel realistic and accessible, but also says she wants the novels to have "enough complexity to keep more educated and more sophisticated readers interested and challenged. So the references to Homer's *Odyssey* or the references to Walt Whitman are in there, and some people will get them." See Donna Perry, *Backtalk: Women Writers Speak Out* (New Brunswick, N.J.: Rutgers University Press, 1993), 153. Her use of Homer's *Odyssey* is discussed by Roberta Rubenstein in "Homeric Resonances: Longing and Belonging in Barbara Kingsolver's *Animal Dreams*," in *Homemaking: Women Writers and the Politics and Poetics of Home*, ed. Catherine Wiley and Fiona R. Barnes (New York: Garland, 1996), 2, 11, 13.

8. One of the critics who has recalled this connection is Kenneth Burke. See *Philosophy of Literary Form*, 311, where he says of Aristotelian catharsis,

"The shock value of Freudian analysis exemplified the same process in tiny 'closet dramas' of private life (the facing and burning-out of conflict)."

9. See Annette Wannamaker, "'Memory Also Makes a Chain': The Performance of Absence in Griselda Gambaro's *Antigona Furiosa*," *Journal of the Midwest Modern Language Association,* fall 2000; Athol Fugard's 1973 play *The Island,* about a performance of *Antigone* in a South African prison; and, on the Mothers of the Plaza de Mayo, Rita Arditti, *Searching for Life: The Grandmothers of the Plaza de Mayo and the Disappeared Children of Argentina* (Berkeley and Los Angeles: University of California Press, 1999).

10. Judith Butler, *Antigone's Claim: Kinship between Life and Death* (New York: Columbia University Press, 2000), 22.

11. Lou Ann's words echo a traditional Judeo-Christian way of dealing with a child's death: see for example Ben Jonson's "On My First Son": "Seven years thou wert lent to me, and I thee pay, / Exacted by thy fate, on the just day."

12. Barbara Kingsolver, interview by Lynn Karpen, *New York Times* June 27, 1993, 9.

13. William Byler, "The Destruction of American Indian Families," in *The Destruction of American Indian Families,* ed. Steven Unger (New York: Association on American Indian Affairs, 1997), 1. Kingsolver's Annawake claims that in the 1970s, "A third of all our kids were still being taken from their families and adopted into white homes" (75), but this is an exaggeration of how many were adopted, since the 25–35 percent figure includes children living in foster care or institutions. Still, there was "pressure on local welfare agencies to provide Indian children for adoption . . . in the prosperous post–World War II era," according to Robert Bensen's introduction to *Children of the Dragonfly,* ed. Bensen (Tucson: University of Arizona Press, 2001), 12. In mid-1970s Minnesota, "more than 90 per cent of non-related adoptions of Indian children [were] made by non-Indian couples" (Byler, 2), and this was apparently the norm elsewhere as well. Byler writes that when Indian children were removed from their families, they rarely had legal counsel, and the grounds were usually vague charges of "neglect" or "social deprivation" that did not respect Indian child-rearing practices (3, 2). In 1978 the Indian Child Welfare Act responded to these problems by giving tribes control over child placement.

14. In *The Bean Trees,* Lou Ann goes to a clinic while pregnant and is struck by the fact that the pamphlet about prenatal care she receives is illustrated not by a picture of a pregnant woman but by a picture of a mother and baby (29).

15. Although Kingsolver's doctor doesn't mention this, it is also common among people of Mediterranean ancestry, and occurs in about 75 percent of adults worldwide. See Robert Berkow, ed., *Merck Manual of Medical Information,* home edition (Whitehouse Station, N.J.: Merck Research Laboratories, 1997), 535.

16. Ruddick, *Maternal Thinking,* 40, defines "mother" as "a person who takes on responsibility for children's lives and for whom providing child care is a significant part of her or his working life." She uses the term "male mother" on p. 41.

17. I owe this point to Emily Hipchen, who made it in comments on an ear-

lier version of this chapter. Some adoptive mothers of infants have breast-fed, but it wouldn't be possible for one adopting a child of Turtle's age. Taylor's interest in feeding Turtle milk could have come not only from advertising, as she analyzes it—"The people look so perky in those commercials" (295)—but also from an attempt to compensate for not being able to nurse her.

18. See Perry, *Backtalk,* 165.

19. *Bean Trees* has established that Kingsolver is interested in Antigone, and Annawake has a name beginning and ending the same way and having the same number of letters, but another Cherokee calls her "Wideawake Annawake," so her name must not have four syllables.

20. See for example Byler, "Destruction of Indian Families," 3, 5.

21. Cf. Kingsolver's memories in *High Tide in Tucson: Essays from Now or Never* (New York: HarperCollins, 1995), 101: "My grandfathers on both sides lived in households that were called upon, after tragedy struck close to home, to take in orphaned children and raise them without a thought . . . one generation later that kind of semipermeable household had vanished, at least for the white middle class."

22. So many of Kingsolver's character names have resonance that I must note the echo here of the network of Florence Crittenton Maternity Homes, for unwed mothers who would give up their children, in spite of the different spelling. Kingsolver may be suggesting parallels between his confinement of the Indians and the birds and these homes' confinement and domestication of pregnant women while preparing them to give up their children. See Solinger, *Wake Up Little Susie,* and Regina Kunzel, *Fallen Women, Problem Girls: Unmarried Mothers and the Professionalization of Social Work, 1890–1945* (New Haven: Yale University Press, 1993), which use these homes' records. The name of Turtle's birth mother, Alma, also alludes to adoption history since the name chosen for Florence Fisher's pioneering search group, Adoptees Liberty Movement Association, resulted in that acronym. The organization's website, www.almasociety.org (accessed December 17, 2004), identifies *alma* as "the Spanish word for soul."

23. Gundi, who says, "When I was a girl in Germany we read a little story in school about the Hopi, and I wanted to grow up to be an Indian" (152), is Kingsolver's mockery of a familiar fascination. Now to Gundi the Navajo reservation where she buys jewelry is "people living in falling-down mud houses with television antennas and bottles stacked by the door" (155).

24. Circe Sturm, *Blood Politics: Race, Culture, and Identity in the Cherokee Nation of Oklahoma* (Berkeley and Los Angeles: University of California Press, 2002).

25. According to Sturm, *Blood Politics,* the Cherokee Nation is "remarkable for having no minimum biogenetic standard, no minimum degree of blood, for citizenship," 89: though every enrolled citizen must have a Cherokee ancestor, in 1996, 29 percent of the tribe, more than fifty thousand members, had "a Cherokee blood quantum somewhere between 1/64th and 1/2048" (88). Largely because of this openness, the Cherokees are the second largest tribe in the United States, and between 1982 and 2000 went from forty thousand to well over two hundred thousand (97). Sturm explores "five indexical markers of

Cherokee identity other than blood ancestry: phenotype, social behavior, language, religious knowledge and participation, and community residence and participation" (110). All of these can be affected by individual choice except phenotype. But one of Sturm's informants notes that "in the communities, people who are whiter feel a need to compensate, to put on a ribbon shirt or weave a basket" (115). Sturm points out that "Cherokees almost always refer to their religious and spiritual leaders as full-bloods, no matter how phenotypically mixed they may look" (126).

26. However, many communities have a Cherokee Baptist Church that uses Cherokee language and rituals, though not the stomp dance. See Sturm, *Blood Politics*, 127.

27. Sturm, Blood Politics, 208.

28. In *High Tide in Tucson,* Kingsolver recounts a trip to the Heard Museum with her five-year-old, which concludes with her satisfaction when the girl answers her question, "Who are the Native Americans?" with, "They're people who love the earth, and like to sing and dance, and make a lot of pretty stuff to use. . . . And I think they like soda pop. Those guys selling the fry bread were drinking a lot of Cokes" (157). Again the emphasis is on behavior in the present, and not on idealized purity.

29. Kingsolver's presentation of this ritual portrays a hybridity in Cherokee culture comparable to that discussed by Clayton in ethnic writers (*The Pleasures of Babel*, 125).

30. She changed only a few "factual" details from the first novel. In *Pigs in Heaven,* she places somewhat more emphasis on the persistence of Turtle's trauma. Here she never willingly lets go of Taylor, whereas she did in *The Bean Trees,* and her comfort object is a flashlight called Mary. In *The Bean Trees* she was able to bury and leave the less alarming transitional object, the doll Shirley Poppy. In *Pigs in Heaven* Turtle is described as unusually quiet, although she seemed to have gone beyond that stage in *The Bean Trees.* The reason for these changes is probably that the more Turtle's injuries are stressed, the harder it is to argue that she should be totally separated from Taylor. In *The Bean Trees* Taylor's great-grandfather was Cherokee; here it is her great-grandmother. This must be because descent is claimed in the female line. And while *Bean Trees* implies that Turtle's previous name was April, here it is Lacey, after the character on the television show *Cagney and Lacey.* The name change suggests how assimilated to American popular culture Turtle's birth mother was, and could also suggest a longing for female friendship.

31. She says she'll marry "When Gabe says he'll come to my wedding" (55), and there are other suggestions that losing her twin has turned all her emotional energies outside her family into work for the Cherokee Nation. With her productive work and the affection she shows for her family and coworkers, the novel manages to suggest that somehow she is both emotionally healthy and traumatized.

32. Several of my students, at least one of whom was lesbian, felt that this was implied, especially with lines like these about her childhood family: "All those penises! You all had me surrounded like a picket fence. . . . nothing personal against your body organs. But men are just not necessarily always the solution" (332–33). Annawake may simply be reacting against her brother's

comment, "You just need you a man, that's all," in a way that many women would regardless of sexual orientation. She has earlier said, "I oftentimes have communication problems with my heart" (312), which could include problems understanding her sexuality but need not.

33. But historical period and class are also important in determining how often this happens. See Kingsolver's own memories of permeable families previously quoted in note 21.

34. Elizabeth Bartholet, *Family Bonds: Adoption and the Politics of Parenting* (New York: Houghton Mifflin, 1993). Bartholet comments approvingly on the success of transracial adoptees who "have grown up in white families, which tend to live in either relatively white or integrated communities" (104), regards "the elimination of racial hostilities as more important than the promotion of cultural difference" (112), and says relatively little about the need for transracially adopting parents to educate themselves or their children about their children's culture. Contrast with the quote from the adoptive mother borrowed from Christine Ward Gailey, further on in this chapter.

35. Kristina Fagan, "Adoption as National Fantasy in Barbara Kingsolver's *Pigs in Heaven* and Margaret Laurence's *The Diviners*," in Novy, *Imagining Adoption*, 260. This novel is read more positively, as imagining "the kind of reconciliation that the sensitive implementation of the [ICWA] act can effect," by Pauline Turner Strong, "To Forget Their Tongue, Their Name, and Their Whole Relation: Captivity, Extra-tribal Adoption, and the Indian Child Welfare Act," in Franklin and McKinnon, *Relative Value*, 486. Far from sentimental about either "Indian blood" or adoption, Strong argues that "the reckoning of identity through 'blood quanta' . . . is at once a 'tragic absurdity' and a 'tragic necessity' for many contemporary Native Americans in the United States" (468), and that "Adoption across political and cultural borders may simultaneously be an act of violence and an act of love" (471).

36. Sturm, *Blood Politics*, 89.

37. Bertolt Brecht, *Threepenny Opera*, in *Plays*, trans. Ralph Manheim (New York: Arcade, 1993), 141.

38. Modell, *Kinship with Strangers*, 235, 238.

39. Shanley, *Making Babies*, 23. This revises "De-essentializing Family Ties: Feminist Reflections on Transracial and Open Adoption," paper presented at a meeting of American Society for Political and Legal Philosolphy, September 2, 1999, 27. I thank Iris Young for a copy.

40. Shanley, *Making Babies*, 40.

41. However, as Barbara Melosh writes, "In fact, in the last twenty years the model of family as 'proprietorship' has been strengthened with legislation and judicial decisions that make parental rights paramount, and that have diluted the old standard of 'best interest of the child'" (personal communication, January 2002).

42. Kingsolver, *High Tide in Tucson*, 154.

43. Perry, *Backtalk*, 165.

44. Clayton, *Pleasures of Babel*, 144. His adoption novels include Kaye Gibbons's *Ellen Foster*, Rosellen Brown's *Civil Wars*, Dori Sanders's *Clover*, Vicki Covington's *Gathering Home*, and Ann Tyler's *Saint Maybe*.

45. See Christine Ward Gailey, "Ideologies of Motherhood and Kinship in U.S. Adoption," in *Ideologies and Technologies of Motherhood: Race, Class, Sexuality, Nationalism,* ed. Heléna Ragoné and France Winddance Twine (New York: Routledge, 2000), 14.

46. Though skeptical about much of the cross-cultural learning advised to adoptive parents, Margaret Homans points out that her daughter's "having listened to the speech of Hunan Province during gestation and for nine months after her birth constitutes a physical inscription of culture on her body" ("Adoption and Essentialism," 264).

47. Personal communication, in a response to this chapter.

AFTERWORD

1. See, for example, Joyce Maguire Pavao, *The Family of Adoption* (Boston: Beacon, 1998); Elinor B. Rosenberg, *The Adoption Life Cycle* (New York: Free Press, 1992), David M. Brodzinsky, Marshall D. Schechter, and Robin Marantz Henig, *Being Adopted: The Lifelong Search for Self* (New York: Doubleday, 1992).

2. Margaret Laurence, *The Diviners* (1974; rpt. Chicago: University of Chicago Press, 1993).

3. See Margaret Laurence, *Dance on the Earth: A Memoir* (Toronto: McClelland and Stewart, 1989).

4. Toni Morrison, *Jazz* (New York: Alfred A. Knopf, 1992). Citations will be included parenthetically in the text.

5. Chang-Rae Lee, *A Gesture Life* (London: Granta, 1999), 356.

6. Oscar Hijuelos, *Mr. Ives' Christmas* (New York: Harper, 1995).

7. In an essay, "Road from the Isles," written a few years before the novel, and connected with it by the author in a later reprinting, Margaret Laurence discusses her own ethnic origins as a Lowland Scot, her fantasy identification with the Highlanders, and the surprising lack of personal connection that she felt at visiting the lands associated with the traumas of Highland Scottish history. Her conclusion, like Morag's, associates her identity with her own remembered Canadian past. See Margaret Laurence, *Heart of a Stranger* (1976; rpt. Toronto: Seal, 1980), 158–72.

8. See Pavao, *Family of Adoption,* 91: "Loss is a pervasive issue. We deal with it in many different ways. Some of us are pack rats and keep everything. . . . Our rooms are cluttered and piled high with things that we can't lose, because we're trying to calm our feelings about the people that we've lost. Some of us go to the other extreme and keep nothing." However, I would not claim that all adoptees behave in one or the other of these extreme ways.

9. Quoted by Gates, *Loose Canons,* 110.

10. Stuart Hall, "Ethnicity, Identity, and Difference," *Radical America* 23, no. 4 (1989): 19.

11. Gloria Anzaldúa, *Borderlands/La Frontera: The New Mestiza* (San Francisco: Aunt Lute, 1987), 79.

12. Sean O'Casey, *Juno and the Paycock,* in *Three Plays* (London: Macmillan, 1957), 71.

13. See Melosh, *Strangers and Kin,* 76–88, on procedures of religious matching.

14. Margaret Moorman, *Waiting to Forget: A Motherhood Lost and Found* (New York: Norton, 1998), 168.

Select Bibliography

Adelman, Janet. *Suffocating Mothers: Fantasies of Maternal Origin in Shakespeare's Plays: "Hamlet" to "The Tempest."* New York: Routledge, 1992.

Albee, Edward. *The American Dream and the Zoo Story.* Rpt. New York: Plume Dutton Signet, 1997.

———. *The Play about the Baby.* New York: Dramatists Play Service, 2002.

———. *Three Tall Women.* New York: Dutton, 1994.

Anderson, Jane. *The Baby Dance.* New York: Samuel French, 1992.

Anderson, Maxwell. *The Bad Seed.* New York: Dodd, 1955.

Baker, Susan. "Personating Persons: Rethinking Shakespearean Disguises." *Shakespeare Quarterly* 43 (1992): 303–16.

Bartholet, Elizabeth. *Family Bonds: Adoption and the Politics of Parenting.* New York: Houghton Mifflin, 1993.

Beer, Gillian. *George Eliot.* Bloomington: Indiana University Press, 1986.

Behlmer, George K. *Friends of the Family: The English Home and Its Guardians.* Stanford: Stanford University Press, 1998.

Berebitsky, Julie. *Like Our Very Own: Adoption and the Changing Culture of Motherhood, 1851–1950.* Lawrence: University Press of Kansas, 2000.

Bodenheimer, Rosemarie. *The Real Life of Mary Ann Evans: George Eliot, Her Letters, and Fiction.* Ithaca, N.Y.: Cornell University Press, 1994.

Boswell, John. *The Kindness of Strangers: The Abandonment of Children in Western Europe from Late Antiquity to the Renaissance.* New York: Pantheon, 1988.

Bowers, Toni. *The Politics of Motherhood: British Writing and Culture, 1680–1760.* Cambridge: Cambridge University Press, 1996.

Brodzinsky, David, and Marshall Schechter, eds. *The Psychology of Adoption.* New York: Oxford University Press, 1990.

Brontë, Charlotte. *Jane Eyre.* London: J. M. Dent, 1993.

Bullough, Geoffrey, ed. *Narrative and Dramatic Sources of Shakespeare.* Vol. 8, *Romances.* New York: Columbia University Press, 1975.

Burke, Kenneth. *The Philosophy of Literary Form: Studies in Symbolic Action.* 3d ed. Berkeley and Los Angeles: University of California Press, 1973.

Burney, Frances. *Evelina.* Ed. Kristina Straub. New York: Bedford, 1997.

Butler, Judith. *Antigone's Claim: Kinship between Life and Death.* New York: Columbia University Press, 2000.

Carp, E. Wayne. *Family Matters: Secrecy and Disclosure in the History of Adoption.* Cambridge: Harvard University Press, 1998.

———, ed. *Adoption in America: Historical Perspectives.* Ann Arbor: University of Michigan Press, 2002.

Carter, Angela. *Wise Children.* New York: Penguin, 1993.

Churchill, Caryl. *Top Girls.* New York: Samuel French, 1982.

Clayton, Jay. *The Pleasures of Babel: Contemporary American Literature and Theory.* New York: Oxford, 1993.

Collins, Stephen. "Reason, Nature, and Order: The Stepfamily in English Renaissance Thought." *Renaissance Studies* 13 (1999): 312–24.

Coveney, Peter. *The Image of Childhood.* Rev. ed. New York: Penguin, 1967.

Demand, Nancy. *Birth, Death, and Motherhood in Classical Greece.* Baltimore: Johns Hopkins University Press, 1994.

Dever, Carolyn. *Death and the Mother from Dickens to Freud: Victorian Fiction and the Anxiety of Origins.* Cambridge: Cambridge University Press, 1998.

Dickens, Charles. *Bleak House.* Ed. Norman Page. New York: Penguin, 1971.

———. *Great Expectations.* New York: Holt, Rinehart, Winston, 1948.

———. *Oliver Twist.* Ed. Kathleen Tillotson. Oxford: Clarendon Press, 1966.

Dolan, Frances. *Dangerous Familiars: Representations of Domestic Crime in England, 1550–1700.* Ithaca, N.Y.: Cornell University Press, 1994.

Dove, Rita. *The Darker Face of the Earth.* 3d. ed. Ashland, Ore.: Story Line Press, 2000.

Dubrow, Heather. *Shakespeare and Domestic Loss: Forms of Deprivation, Mourning, and Recuperation.* Cambridge: Cambridge University Press, 1999.

Eliot, George. *Daniel Deronda.* Ed. Graham Handley. New York: Oxford University Press, 1988.

———. *Felix Holt.* Ed. Peter Coveney. New York: Penguin, 1972.

———. *Letters.* Ed. Gordon S. Haight. New Haven: Yale University Press, 1954–78.

———. *Silas Marner.* London: Everyman, 1993.

Estrin, Barbara. *The Raven and the Lark: Lost Children in Literature of the English Renaissance.* Lewisburg, Pa.: Bucknell University Press, 1985.

Euripides. *Ion.* Trans. Anne Pippin Burnett. Englewood Cliffs, N.J.: Prentice-Hall, 1970.

Fielding, Henry. *Tom Jones.* Ed. John Bender and Simon Stern. New York: Oxford University Press, 1996.

Fierstein, Harvey. *Torch Song Trilogy.* New York: Samuel French, 1979.

Fildes, Valerie. *Breasts, Bottles, and Babies: A History of Infant Feeding.* Edinburgh: Edinburgh University Press, 1986.

Findlay, Alison. *Illegitimate Power: Bastards in Renaissance Literature.* Manchester: Manchester University Press, 1984.

Franklin, Sarah, and Susan McKinnon, eds. *Relative Values: Reconfiguring Kinship Studies.* Durham: Duke University Press, 2001.

Freud, Sigmund. *Complete Psychological Works.* Trans. James Strachey. London: Hogarth, 1959.

Gailey, Christine Ward. "Ideologies of Motherhood and Kinship in U.S. Adoption." In *Ideologies and Technologies of Motherhood: Race, Class, Sexuality, Nationalism,* ed. Helena Ragone and France Winddance Twine. New York: Routledge, 2000.

Golden, Mark. *Children and Childhood in Classical Athens*. Baltimore: Johns Hopkins University Press, 1990.

Gottlieb, Beatrice. *The Family in the Western World from the Black Death to the Industrial Age*. New York: Oxford University Press, 1993.

Greenfield, Susan. *Mothering Daughters: Novels and the Politics of Family Romance: Frances Burney to Jane Austen*. Detroit: Wayne State University Press, 2002.

Gussow, Mel. *Edward Albee: A Singular Journey*. New York: Simon and Schuster, 1999.

Hall, Stuart. "Ethnicity, Identity, and Difference." *Radical America* 23, no. 4 (1989): 9–20.

Hijuelos, Oscar. *Mr. Ives' Christmas*. New York: Harper, 1995.

Hirsch, Marianne. *The Mother-Daughter Plot: Narrative, Psychoanalysis, Feminism*. Bloomington: Indiana University Press, 1989.

Howe, Patricia. "Fontane's 'Ellernklipp' and the Theme of Adoption." *Modern Language Review* 79 (1984): 114–30.

Humphreys, S. C. *The Family, Women, and Death: Comparative Studies*. Ann Arbor: University of Michigan Press, 1993.

Ito, Susan, and Tina Cervin, eds. *A Ghost at Heart's Edge*. Berkeley: North Atlantic, 1999.

Kingsolver, Barbara. *The Bean Trees*. New York: Harper and Row, 1988.

———. *High Tide in Tucson: Essays from Now or Never*. New York: HarperCollins, 1995.

———. *Pigs in Heaven*. New York: Harper and Row, 1993.

Kirk, H. David. *Shared Fate: A Theory of Adoption and Mental Health*. 1964; rpt. New York: Free Press, 1974.

Krausman Ben-Amos, Ilana. *Adolescence and Youth in Early Modern England*. New Haven: Yale University Press, 1994.

Laslett, Peter, Karla Oosterveen, and Richard M. Smith, eds. *Bastardy and Its Comparative History*. Cambridge: Harvard University Press, 1980.

Laurence, Margaret. *The Diviners*. 1974; rpt. Chicago: University of Chicago Press, 1993.

Lee, Chang-Rae. *A Gesture Life*. London: Granta, 1999.

Lifton, Betty Jean. *Journey of the Adopted Self: A Quest for Wholeness*. New York: Basic, 1994.

———. *Lost and Found: The Adoption Experience*. 1979; rpt. New York: Harper and Row, 1988.

———. *Twice Born: Memoirs of an Adopted Daughter*. 1975; rpt. New York: St. Martin's, 1988.

March, William. *The Bad Seed*. New York: Dodd, 1955.

McClure, Ruth. *Coram's Children: The London Foundling Hospital in the Eighteenth Century*. New Haven: Yale University Press, 1981.

Melosh, Barbara. *Strangers and Kin: The American Way of Adoption*. Cambridge: Harvard University Press, 2002.

Meyer, Susan. *Imperialism at Home: Race and Victorian Women's Fiction*. Ithaca, N.Y.: Cornell University Press, 1996.

Miller, Nancy. *But Enough about Me: Why We Read Other People's Lives.* New York: Columbia University Press, 2002.

Modell, Judith. *Kinship with Strangers: Adoption and Interpretations of Kinship in American Culture.* Berkeley and Los Angeles: University of California Press, 1994.

Morgentaler, Goldie. *Dickens and Heredity: When Like Begets Like.* New York: St. Martin's, 2000.

Morrison, Toni. *Jazz.* New York: Alfred A. Knopf, 1992.

Neill, Michael. "'In Everything Illegitimate': Imagining the Bastard in Renaissance Drama." *Yearbook of English Studies* 23 (1993): 270–92.

Novy, Marianne, ed. *Engaging with Shakespeare: Responses of George Eliot and Other Women Novelists.* Athens: University of Georgia Press, 1994.

———. *Imagining Adoption: Essays on Literature and Culture.* Ann Arbor: University of Michigan Press, 2001.

Olive, John. *Evelyn and the Polka King.* New York: Theatre Communications Group, 1992.

Paster, Gail Kern. *The Body Embarrassed: Drama and the Disciplines of Shame in Early Modern England.* Ithaca, N.Y.: Cornell University Press, 1993.

Paton, Jean. *The Adopted Break Silence.* Philadelphia: Life History Center, 1954.

———. [Ruthena Hill Kittson, pseud.] *Orphan Voyage.* 1968; rpt. Cedaredge, Colo.: Country, 1980.

Pavao, Joyce Maguire. *The Family of Adoption.* Boston: Beacon, 1998.

Paxton, Nancy. *George Eliot and Herbert Spencer.* Princeton: Princeton University Press, 1991.

Pertman, Adam. *Adoption Nation: How the Adoption Revolution Is Transforming America.* New York: Basic, 2000.

Pinchbeck, Ivy, and Margaret Hewitt. *Children in English Society.* Vol. 1. London: Routledge and Kegan Paul, 1969.

Pomeroy, Sarah. *Families in Classical and Hellenistic Greece: Representation and Reality.* New York: Oxford University Press, 1997.

Pucci, Pietro. *Oedipus and the Fabrication of the Father.* Baltimore: Johns Hopkins University Press, 1992.

Ragussis, Michael. *Acts of Naming: The Family Plot in Fiction.* Oxford: Oxford University Press, 1988.

———. *Figures of Conversion: "The Jewish Question" and English National Identity.* Durham: Duke University Press, 1995.

Rothman, Barbara Katz. *Genetic Maps and Human Imaginations.* New York: Norton, 1998.

Ruddick, Sara. *Maternal Thinking: Towards a Politics of Peace.* Boston: Beacon, 1989.

Schaefer, Carol. "The Sacred Virgin." Typescript.

Shakespeare, William. *The Complete Works.* Ed. David Bevington. 4th ed. New York: HarperCollins, 1992.

Shanley, Mary Lyndon. *Making Babies, Making Families: What Matters Most in an Age of Reproductive Technologies, Surrogacy, Adoption, and Same-Sex and Unwed Parents.* Boston: Beacon, 2001.

Shell, Marc. *Children of the Earth: Literature, Politics, and Nationhood.* New York: Oxford University Press, 1993.

Shiomi, Rick. *Mask Dance.* In *Bold Words: A Century of Asian American Writing,* ed. Rajini Srikanth and Esther Y. Iwanaga. New Brunswick, N.J.: Rutgers University Press, 2001.

Singley, Carol. "Building a Nation, Building a Family." In *Adoption in America: Historical Perspectives,* ed. E. Wayne Carp. Ann Arbor: University of Michigan Press, 2002.

Skura, Meredith. "Interpreting Posthumus' Dream from Above and Below: Families, Psychoanalysis and Literary Critics." In *Representing Shakespeare: New Psychoanalytic Essays,* ed. Murray Schwartz and Coppelia Kahn. Baltimore: Johns Hopkins University Press, 1980.

Solinger, Rickie. *Wake Up Little Susie: Single Pregnancy and Race before Roe v. Wade.* New York: Routledge, 1992.

Sophocles. *Oedipus the King.* Trans. David Grene. In *Sophocles I: The Complete Greek Tragedies,* ed. David Grene and Richmond Lattimore. New York: Washington Square, 1957.

———. *Oedipus at Colonus.* Trans. Robert Fitzgerald. In *Sophocles I: The Complete Greek Tragedies,* ed. David Grene and Richmond Lattimore. New York: Washington Square, 1957.

Sturm, Circe. *Blood Politics: Race, Culture, and Identity in the Cherokee Nation of Oklahoma.* Berkeley and Los Angeles: University of California Press, 2002.

Thatcher, Kristine. *Emma's Child.* New York: Dramatists Play Service, 1997.

Tolan, Kathleen. *Approximating Mother.* New York: Dramatists Play Service, 1994.

Tulsa Studies in Women's Literature. "The Adoption Issue." Vol. 21, no. 2 (2002).

Unger, Steven, ed. *The Destruction of American Indian Families.* New York: Association on American Indian Affairs, 1997.

Van Boheemen, Christine. *The Novel as Family Romance: Language, Gender, and Authority from Fielding to Joyce.* Ithaca, N.Y.: Cornell University Press, 1987.

Wadia-Ellis, Susan. *The Adoption Reader: Birth Mothers, Adoptive Mothers, and Adopted Daughters Tell Their Stories.* Seattle: Seal, 1995.

Wasserstein, Wendy. *The Heidi Chronicles and Other Plays.* New York: Vintage, 1991.

Waters, Catherine. *Dickens and the Politics of the Family.* Cambridge: Cambridge University Press, 1997.

Waters, Mary. *Ethnic Options.* Berkeley and Los Angeles: University of California Press, 1990.

Weedman, Lauren. "Homecoming." Typescript.

Wegar, Katarina. *Adoption, Identity, and Kinship: The Debate over Sealed Birth Records.* New Haven: Yale University Press, 1997.

Wertenbaker, Timberlake. *Break of Day.* London: Faber and Faber, 1995.

Wilson, Lanford. *Redwood Curtain.* New York: Hill and Wang, 1993.

Zeitlin, Froma. *Playing the Other: Gender and Society in Greek Literature.* Chicago: University of Chicago Press, 1996.

Zelizer, Vivian. *Pricing the Priceless Child: The Changing Social Value of Children.* New York: Basic, 1985.

Index

Marianne Novy is Professor of English and Women's Studies at the University of Pittsburgh. She is author or editor of numerous books, including *Imagining Adoption: Essays on Literature and Culture*, *Love's Argument: Gender Relations in Shakespeare*, and *Engaging with Shakespeare: Responses of George Eliot and Other Women Novelists*.

"A breath of fresh air . . . Illuminates the tension between families, birth and adoptive, that is always there, and is always much more complex than the all-nature or all-nurture camps try to make it . . . She makes us all question our dearly held myths and icons . . . and she stretches our imagination to encompass the complexity and diversity of adoptees and adoption as it is lived."
　—Mary Anne Cohen, *Bastard Quarterly*

"Notable . . . and courageous—in its blending of the personal and the scholarly . . . a book of monumental interest."
　—Carol J. Singley, Rutgers University-Camden

"With her extraordinary combination of life-writing and literary analysis, Novy presents her reader with a new way to read old books . . . Novy places her work as a mediator between the extremes of opinions about adoption. This position enables her to question the assumptions of those too easily influenced by the literary conventions as well as to challenge those who—wishing to undo the formula altogether—believe that adoption is the answer to many world problems."
　—*Women's Studies: An Interdisciplinary Journal*

"An essential resource not just for scholars but for anyone who cares about adoption's pervasive influence in our culture."
　—*Lifewriting Annual*

"Art imitates life and vice versa in Marianne Novy's thought-provoking, evenhanded analysis of the classic plot device, from ancient Greece to the present: the abandoned child. Drawing on her own experiences as a person adopted in the 1940s and as a mother, along with her probing insight as an academic, Novy explores the evolving definitions of 'parent' throughout literature and history with sensitivity, wisdom, and fairness."
　—Sarah Saffian, author of *Ithaka:*
　　A Daughter's Memoir of Being Found

"*Reading Adoption* is one of those rare creatures in academic writing: a 'good read.'"
　—*Children's Literature Association Quarterly*